WARRIOR-KING OF SHAMBHALA:
REMEMBERING CHÖGYAM TRUNGPA

WARRIOR-KING OF SHAMBHALA

REMEMBERING CHÖGYAM TRUNGPA

by Jeremy Hayward

Foreword by Sakyong Mipham

WISDOM PUBLICATIONS • BOSTON

Wisdom Publications
199 Elm Street
Somerville MA 02144 USA
www.wisdompubs.org

Library of Congress Cataloging-in-Publication Data
Hayward, Jeremy W.
  Warrior king of Shambhala : remembering Chögyam Trungpa / by Jeremy Hayward ; foreword by Sakyong Mipham.
     p. cm.
  Includes bibliographical references and index.
  ISBN 0-86171-546-2 (pbk. : alk. paper)
  1. Hayward, Jeremy W. 2. Spiritual biography—United States. 3. Buddhists—United States—Biography. 4. Trungpa, Chogyam, 1939-1987. I. Title.
  BQ962.A38H39 2008
  294.3'923092—dc22
  [B]
                              2007036421

12 11 10 09 08
5   4   3   2   1

Cover design by Gopa & Ted2, Inc
Text designed and typeset by by Gopa & Ted2, Inc. Set in Palatino 10/15.2.

Wisdom Publications' books are printed on acid-free paper and meet the guidelines for permanence and durability of the Production Guidelines for Book Longevity of the Council on Library Resources.

Printed in the United States of America

This book was produced with environmental mindfulness. We have elected to print this title on 50% PCW recycled paper. As a result, we have saved the following resources: 73 trees, 51 million BTUs of energy, 6,434 lbs. of greenhouse gases, 26,706 gallons of water, and 3,429 lbs. of solid waste. For more information, please visit our website, www.wisdompubs.org.

This book is dedicated to
the Vidyadhara, Chögyam Trungpa Rinpoche

Over and over again, you asked us, "Please cheer up."
I want you to know
that in the end
we did.

Born in the snow land of Tibet,
You conquered the barbarians of the West.
Living in the land of technology,
You tamed the untamable beings.
Glorious guru we supplicate you, may we never
*   be separated from you.*

There being no self,
You radiated boundless compassion.
There being no other,
You worked tirelessly for all sentient beings.
Glorious guru we supplicate you, may we never
*   be separated from you.*

Seeing phenomena as dreams,
Your shrill cry awakened us.
Seeing many lumps of butter,
Your fierce heat melted us.
Glorious guru we supplicate you, may we never
*   be separated from you.*

Hearing the clickety-clack of samsara,
Your humor turned it into chimes of laughter.
Seeing the sorrow of the setting sun,
Your kind smile brought one flavor.
Glorious guru we supplicate you, may we never
*   be separated from you.*

As prairie dogs naturally pop in and out of their holes,
As children naturally chatter and play in the sunshine,
As thoughts arise and return to non-thought,
So may we follow your example in non-meditation.
Glorious guru, we supplicate you, may we never
*   be separated from you.*

May you ever continue to guide us to the sacred land
*   of Shambhala.*

Contents

Foreword

T HAS BEEN MANY YEARS since the passing of my father, the Vidyadhara Chögyam Trungpa Rinpoche. As time goes by, more and more people are realizing his incredible courage as well as his profound impact in terms of transplanting Buddhist wisdom from East to West. He was among the last of his generation to receive the complete traditional training and education from some of Tibet's greatest Buddhist teachers. Many of these teachers took extra care to transmit their wisdom to him, predicting the pivotal role he would play in the future. Later, studying at Oxford University, he delved deeply into the heart of Western culture, tradition, and intellect. It was this unique blend—Buddhist wisdom combined with a true understanding of the Western mind—that intrigued Dr. Jeremy Hayward.

The Vidyadhara went on to spend seventeen years in North America, teaching ancient Buddhist wisdom as well as the sacred courageous path of Shambhala. It was during this time that Jeremy became enthralled by his brilliance, humor, and warmth, becoming a student, and later, a friend. Over the years, Jeremy also became one of the principal supporters of my father's vision of creating enlightened society, often accompanying him on his travels.

I know Jeremy meant a lot to my father, just as he does to me. I've always found him to be an unusual mixture of intelligence, stodginess, and playfulness. For years he told me that he wanted to write this book, and I am delighted that it has finally happened. The book is unique in describing the personal journey of a student in relation to his teacher, as well as telling the story of how an incredible legacy was created.

The Sakyong, Jamgön Mipham Rinpoche

July 2007

Preface

T HIS BOOK ATTEMPTS to offer a peep-hole glimpse into the vast and inconceivable mind of a great *mahasiddha*, a being of great spiritual accomplishment, Chögyam Trungpa Rinpoche.

This project really began at Rinpoche's cremation, in 1987, when groups of us would sit around and tell stories of being with him. I thought to myself then that "somebody" should write all this down. My own effort began in 1990, but all of it was still too close and too personal—and I did not get very far. Over the years I occasionally gave talks on "The Life of Trungpa Rinpoche" or, as I would insist, my life *with* Trungpa Rinpoche—because, after all, who could speak of *the* life?

In 2004 when I was teacher in residence at Dechen Chöling, the European residential Shambhala Center, I was invited to give such a talk at a month-long program of advanced study, by its director David Schneider. After the talk, I received a supplication to write these stories down signed by all seventy participants and staff. I was aided by the fact that Fabrice Midal had already produced a very thorough objective account of Chögyam Trungpa's outer activity in North America,[1] so that did not need to be done again. Now, I felt, it was possible to write a personal account of how it was to *be* with Rinpoche without worrying about completeness or objectivity.

I thought that it would be a project that would take many years, but now was the time to begin. It turned out to be much simpler. I went on retreat and, with a small Sony tape-recorder held at my heart, I began, "I first met Rinpoche in September nineteen seventy." From that point on the memories flowed out non-stop for ten days. It was as if Rinpoche were right there with me, reminding me, encouraging me, forgiving me for my stupidity, laughing with me. I shall never forget the moment: I was sitting outside in the French countryside on a warm sunny December afternoon, and the sun was just setting behind the hillside across the beautiful valley of the Vienne River, when the story reached the point of Rinpoche taking his final breath. My tears and heartbreak, joy and sadness, were as if it were happening at that very moment.

Writing this has been just like living through those years—an extraordinary journey of ups and downs, closeness and distance, sorrow and joy, remorse and laughter. But at the same time, as has been said, "The story of your life is not, in the end, your life; it is your story." Just so, this is neither my life nor Rinpoche's life, but it is our story. I must emphasize that it is a personal view. Surely others will say, at least in places, "that wasn't how it happened," or "he was not like that *at all*." I cannot say what *really* happened, just how I saw it— or how I thought I saw it. No ordinary person can say how Rinpoche *really* was; each and every one of us ordinary students can only say how *I* saw him and the events around me. I believe that the only way to build up a picture of what it was like to go through that living dharma journey with Rinpoche would be for many of his student friends to write their own personal memories. And I sincerely hope that many more will do so.

One of the important aspects of my own journey with Rinpoche was the struggle between the logical, rational way of thinking that dominates our culture today, and my actual experience of what was happening at the moment. The skepticism and doubt of my science-trained intellect not infrequently came into conflict with a deeper, more direct perception of Rinpoche's way of manifesting. Put another way, my conceptual interpretations came into conflict with my direct experience of what was going on. I had to learn to trust that experience without giving up the genuine openness and questioning of the intellect. I was not always successful and this sometimes gave rise to holding back, misunderstanding, and even, occasionally, to panic.

In turn this colored my interpretation of what was taking place, which will be apparent as the story unfolds. Perhaps, though, it can be helpful for some readers, who find such a challenge in their own journey through life, to see my struggle between the rationality of intellect and the direct perception of the heart. Please don't give up! It is worth the effort to harmonize what we *think* is the nature of reality with our direct experience of it, while sacrificing neither the clarity of the intellect nor the intuitive knowing of the body. This harmony brings a deeper joy to life and seems to be essential on the spiritual path.

I hope, nevertheless, that I will be forgiven for any supposed inaccuracies or distortions. I have tried to be as accurate and true to the so-called facts as possible, checking against written accounts and other people's memories.

I have included a glossary defining those Tibetan and Sanskrit words, as well as important dharma terms, that I have used frequently.

May you enjoy this small contribution to the story of a very great man whose profound and vast accomplishment in bringing the true buddhadharma to the West has yet to be fully realized.

And may this bring benefit to many beings.

1970: A Stubborn Scientist Meets a Phenomenal Magician 1

 FIRST MET TRUNGPA RINPOCHE in September of 1970, at a public talk in the East-West Center on Marlborough Street in Boston. Marlborough Street is one of those older streets with rows of tall, narrow, red brick houses. As I entered one of these, I found the large living / dining room set up with cushions on the floor and filled with people, mostly young and in all manner of dress. Some were wearing fairly conventional, casual clothes (such as myself; I was wearing ordinary trousers and a sweater, probably rather dirty), and others were dressed in white pajamas with beads around their necks, orange one-piece jump suits, and other unconventional attire. I had come alone and a young man with curly red hair and freckles made room for me against one wall, opposite a row of cushions along the other wall which were obviously reserved for Rinpoche's party. On the mantle shelf there was a large statue of a seated Buddha with a *naga*, a serpent deity, rising up behind him, offering protection.

People were chatting and laughing and there was an excited, joyful atmosphere. I was fairly familiar with the spiritual seeker scene by then, having been to hear a number of "gurus" of various traditions—

yogis, Sufis, and so on—and this seemed typical, though perhaps less pretentiously "spiritual" and solemn than some.

Quite a while after the talk was scheduled to begin, the door burst open and a very large lady wearing a flowing gown, and short black hair, swept majestically into the room like a ship sailing in. She was followed by a young, attractive blonde woman, fairly tall and very obviously pregnant, and a small, limping Tibetan man. The man, of course, was Trungpa Rinpoche, dressed in casual trousers and a sports jacket. The young lady was Rinpoche's wife, Diana, who was biting on the lapel of his sports jacket, trying to make a hole in it to put a rose in. Rinpoche was quietly grinning as he walked into the room with her. Diana plunked herself down next to the lady in the flowing gown, whom I later found out was called Kesang.

Rinpoche sat down in a wicker chair with a high back, which was in some strange way an echo of the *naga*, and started speaking. His talk, full of lightness and humor, was on how to transcend ego through mindfulness meditation. At the end of the talk, I put my hand up to ask a question. At that time in my life I was angry, depressed, and nihilistic; I didn't know what I was doing with my life. I had left England because I felt cramped and claustrophobic, and my family was not a happy one. I had felt that I simply had to get out of there, so I had come to America on a two-year fellowship and just stayed on for no particular reason. I had a Ph.D. in physics and four years of research in biology, but in none of it had I found what I was really searching for. At this point I was teaching high school, and altogether it was a very unsatisfying situation.

Like many people, I misunderstood the idea of transcending ego and thought that one had to get rid of ego—that ego had to somehow be *demolished*. So when questions were invited, through gritted teeth I asked, "Rinpoche, when you get rid of ego, what happens?" Although by then I had been involved in a spiritual search for some years, this question seemed to arise quite fresh, with no expectation. At the same time, it seemed to be a reflection of my continuing deep nihilism and fear. Rinpoche gave me a sweet, gentle, youthful smile, slightly shook his head, and replied, "There's something left, don't worry." He spoke directly to me with warmth and tenderness, and he somehow caught my underlying doubt as to whether there is any true reality *at all*, beyond surface appearances. With that, I was hooked.

CHÖGYAM TRUNGPA RINPOCHE, BORN IN TIBET

Who, then, was this gentleman? Who was this person whom we later came to know by many different titles, but whom I always thought of, in my heart, as "Rinpoche"? (*Rinpoche* is a title bestowed in Tibet on highly realized teachers; it means "precious one".)

Trungpa Rinpoche was born in 1940 to a nomad family in Tibet, the Land of the Snows. He was recognized at the age of one year as the eleventh *tulku* of the Trungpa line of realized masters. *Tulku* is usually translated as "rebirth" or "reincarnation" of an enlightened being; however, this conveys a rather naïve understanding of the Buddhist view of life and death. As we will see, direct examination of the nature of mind in mindfulness meditation shows that there is no solid permanent self, but rather a composite heap of many constantly changing elements.

According to the Buddhist teachings, an enlightened being is one who has deeply realized this truth, and therefore there is no sense in which a permanent self, ego, or soul of such a being would be reborn, since it has been thoroughly realized to be illusory. However, Tibetan Buddhists assert that beings with this great depth of realization have long ago taken a vow not to dissolve altogether into vast mind-space upon death, but to take on another physical form in order to help other sentient beings. Thus, due to this vow, some aspect or energy pattern of the original being is implanted in another physical body after the death of a previous one. It is, then, in this sense that we speak of Rinpoche as the eleventh Trungpa *tulku*.

The baby Rinpoche and his mother were taken to the Surmang monastery, the traditional seat of the Trungpas in the Kham district of eastern Tibet, and there he began his training. At the age of twelve he met his own main teacher, Jamgön Kongtrül of Shechen, and at the age of fifteen was already teaching and expounding on all of the highest teachings of Tibetan Buddhism. By this time he was renowned throughout Tibet as one of the most brilliant and highly realized of his generation.

The entire culture and environment of Tibet was steeped in an unbroken tradition of over a thousand years of living teachings and practice of Buddhism. While technologically Tibet remained medieval, no religious or psychological tradition of the West comes close to the Tibetan understanding of the depths of mind and the creative process of perception. When the Chinese invaded Tibet beginning in the early '50s, attempting to annihilate this precious culture, over six thousand monasteries were destroyed, and hundreds of realized teachers were murdered along with over a million people.

Yet Buddhism remained alive and well in the hearts of the people.

One of these was Rinpoche's nephew, Karma Senge Rinpoche, who spent fifteen years traveling around Tibet and collecting all of the teachings that Rinpoche had left behind when he escaped in 1959— amounting to over six hundred pages of text. He told us that people had preserved these teachings, sometimes on small scraps of paper. Whenever the Chinese aggression rose to a dangerous level they would bury these scraps of paper, and then they would take them out again as soon as the latest wave of aggression passed.

This was the culture of devotion and bravery in which Rinpoche grew up. There was no belief in "original sin"; rather the tradition of Tibet, as in the traditions of other Buddhist cultures in places such as Japan and China, was to acknowledge the basic goodness and inherent wisdom of all people. The secular culture of Tibet was deeply influenced by the tradition of Shambhala, an ancient kingdom that likewise was based in all its societal forms on trust in people's inherent wisdom. In addition there was, in Tibet, tremendous trust in the path of buddhadharma to awaken and realize this wisdom, and deep appreciation for those who had fully accomplished such realization.

TO THE WEST

Rinpoche left Tibet in 1959, leading a large party over the most wild and rugged parts of the Himalayas during an eight-month ordeal that was characterized by extraordinary bravery and cheerfulness. Rinpoche's upbringing and escape are movingly described in his autobiography, *Born in Tibet*.[2]

After his escape, Rinpoche spent two years in India during which time he was discovered by an English social worker, Frieda Bedi, and with her co-founded a school for refugee tulkus, the Young Lama's Home School. While in India, determined to go to the West, he learned English so rapidly that he became useful as a translator for the Tibetan community. Rinpoche stayed for a few months with James George, who was at that time the Canadian High Commissioner to India and Nepal and who later became the leader of the Gurdjieff movement in Canada. At this time, Rinpoche was awarded a scholarship to study at Oxford University in England, but when he told George that he was going to England, George replied, "Rinpoche, you are too big for England; you are going to America!"

Rinpoche did, however, go to England first. From 1963 to 1967 he studied Western philosophy, comparative religion, and the arts at Oxford, and at the same time continued to improve his English. At this point Rinpoche, with his companion Akong Rinpoche, was invited to take over the leadership of a contemplative center in Scotland. They transformed it into a Buddhist center and named it the Samye-Ling Meditation Center. Of this move Rinpoche wrote, in his epilogue to *Born in Tibet*, "This was a forward step. Nevertheless, it was not entirely satisfying, for the scale of activity was small, and the people who did come to participate seemed to be slightly missing the point."

In 1968, Rinpoche spent several weeks visiting Bhutan as the guest of the queen. While there, he spent ten days in retreat in Tagtsang, the cave in which Padmasambhava, the renowned Indian scholar and master of meditation, had meditated before bringing Buddhism to Tibet in the eighth century. Revered and considered to be a second Buddha by many Tibetans, Padmasambhava was responsible for firmly establishing Buddhism in Tibet and thereby initiated the Nyingma lineage, or "old school," of Tibetan Buddhism. Soon after this, Buddhism was temporarily suppressed in Tibet until it was revived by a new wave of great practitioner-teachers in the eleventh century. One of these "new schools" was the Kagyu lineage, and it was to this lineage that Rinpoche, as a tulku of the Trungpa line, officially belonged. At the same time he was also deeply trained in the Nyingma teachings by his own main teacher, Jamgön Kongtrül of Sechen.

While meditating at Tagtsang, Rinpoche had a vision of Padmasambhava manifesting in a form symbolizing compassionate wrath, known by the name of Dorje Trollö. While in this visionary state he received the Sadhana of Mahamudra, a ritual practice *(sadhana)* involving visualization of deities. It is a very powerful sadhana of the highest level of vajrayana, and it combines the highest teachings recognized by all schools of Tibetan Buddhism. At the same time, this sadhana is an expression of what Rinpoche called "cutting through spiritual materialism," the tendency to misuse spiritual understanding and practice to build up the personal ego. "Cutting through spiritual materialism," Rinpoche realized, was the key to laying the ground so that Buddhism could be presented properly in the West, and so that the true dharma could actually be heard by Western students.[3]

FINDING SHAMBHALA

The problem of spiritual materialism, according to Rinpoche, is not merely a problem of individuals but is a symptom of the declining understanding of genuine spirituality throughout society. From very early on, Rinpoche had a deep interest in transforming society according to the principles of the enlightened society of Shambhala. Growing up in Tibet, alongside his Buddhist training Rinpoche was also immersed in the tradition of Shambhala.

This tradition is the very foundation of the social customs of Tibet with its simple teachings of dignity, bravery, and wisdom, and the

IN BHUTAN, RIDING UP TO TAGTSANG.

power to arouse one's life force through connecting with the natural energies of the world; it was passed down through the generations through the epic songs and stories of the great King Gesar. The importance of Shambhala to Rinpoche shows in the story of his escape from Tibet, when he had to go into hiding from the Chinese for a few months. During this time, he took the opportunity to write two major works: one on mahamudra, the highest teachings of the Kagyu school, the other on Shambhala. To our great loss, both these texts had to be left behind in the final phase of the escape as Rinpoche's party crossed the Brahmaputra River into India in small rowing boats, fired on by the Chinese who had finally caught up with them.

The Kingdom of Shambhala is a mythological kingdom that is said to have existed at the time of the Buddha. Its reputation is known throughout Asia and as far north as Siberia. In Tibet it is said that the first king of Shambhala visited the Buddha and asked him for teachings that he and his subjects could put into practice without becoming monastics but continuing to pursue the householder's life in the world. In response the Buddha taught the Kalachakra Tantra, the highest tantric teachings of Buddhism.

Some scholars believe that Shambhala may actually have existed on earth somewhere in the region of the southern Gobi desert, while others say that it has only mythological significance. Many Tibetan teachers say that the Kingdom of Shambhala exists as a Pure Land that is visible only to those who have sufficiently purified and awakened their own hearts and minds through the practice of meditation. And some accounts say that, though the Kingdom existed on earth for a period during the time of the Buddha, it eventually disappeared into a more subtle realm when all the subjects reached a high stage of development in their spiritual path.

The basic vision of the Kingdom of Shambhala is of an enlightened society, that is to say, one based on the belief that all beings have inherent wisdom and goodness. Shambhala is by no means a utopia—the citizens are ordinary humans with the usual human faults and virtues. But it is a society in which people are encouraged to follow the basic teaching and practice of meditation in order to reveal that wisdom in themselves and each other, and in which the structures of the society are organized according to this principle of *basic goodness*. Rinpoche did not speak of Shambhala to his students in the West at all until the mid-'70s, but there were hints of things to come along the way.

Shortly after his escape from Tibet, he had met up with his old friend and colleague, Kenchen Thrangu Rinpoche, who had also just escaped from Tibet and who is now well known and much loved among Western students of Tibetan Buddhism. Thrangu Rinpoche asked him, "What are you going to do now?" To this Rinpoche replied, "Well, I'm not staying around here long. I want to go to the West, and particularly to America. I saw in the *prasena* that I could find Shambhala there." The *prasena* is a form of divination, using a mirror, with which the diviner must possess particular ability and be specially trained. Trungpa Rinpoche was well known as a young boy in Tibet to have exceptional ability with the prasena. It was said to have been an invaluable tool as he guided hundreds of people through the uncharted mountains and valleys of the Himalayas.

During the 1968 visit to Bhutan, on his way through India, Rinpoche had re-visited his old friend James George. George reports[4] that Rinpoche told him that "although he had never been there [Shambhala] he believed in its existence and could see it in his mirror whenever he went into deep meditation." George describes witnessing Rinpoche gazing into a small hand-mirror and describing in detail the Kingdom of Shambhala. As George says, "…There was Trungpa in our study describing what he saw as if he were looking out of the window."

And in the Tagtsang retreat, immediately after writing the Sadhana of Mahamudra, Rinpoche had some intense discussions with a visitor about the principles of enlightened society. As Sherab Kohn reports:

> Early on in the three-week Tagtsang retreat, a young Australian named Lorraine, like Rinpoche in Bhutan as a guest of the queen, arrived at Tagtsang on a sightseeing visit. Finding interesting company there—notably the young Trungpa Rinpoche and two of his English students—she decided to stay for a few days. She had in her backpack a copy of Erich Fromm's book The Sane Society [which discusses how a society must be structured to support and favor the arising of sane human relations, loving communication, and meaningful action, which represent the fulfillment of human existence]. She passed this book along to Kunga Dawa (Richard Arthure), one of the English students, who read it and passed it on to Rinpoche. Rinpoche had just finished

writing the Sadhana of Mahamudra, and was already energized to the point where he was hardly sleeping. Now he positively caught fire with the ideas expressed in Fromm's book.

Even before leaving the UK for India and Bhutan, Rinpoche had been thinking about a new society. He had given a talk at Cambridge in which he spoke of Maitreya, the Buddha of the future, not as a person but as a future state of society. He spoke of lost tribal structure that had to be recovered in new form. Now, at Tagtsang, Fromm's ideas sparked his socio-political thinking anew. Intense discussions of those ideas began among the four English speakers at the retreat, which continued day after day from early evening until deep into the night.[5]

As I've said, Rinpoche did not speak of his keen interest in transforming society, or the principles of Shambhala, for many years after coming to the West. Until the mid-1970s his emphasis was on personal practice. In the early years, when he was asked about getting involved in politics—protesting against the war in Vietnam or nuclear-bomb production, for example—he would always bring us back to working with our own aggression first. Nevertheless, it became clear very soon after the Tagtsang retreat that Rinpoche's energy was not to be contained in the traditional image of a great spiritual teacher wearing robes and sitting on a throne.

PLUNGING IN COMPLETELY

After his return to Scotland, Rinpoche went through a tumultuous period that ended when he was involved in a serious car accident. While driving, he blacked out at the wheel and drove into the front of a joke shop, the kind that sells novelty magic tricks. When he awoke in hospital, he found that he was paralyzed on his left side, and he recognized the accident as a profound message and a strong warning from the phenomenal world. As he says in the Epilogue to *Born in Tibet*:

When plunging completely and genuinely into the teachings, one is not allowed to bring along one's deceptions. I realized that I could no longer attempt to preserve any privacy for myself, any special identity or legitimacy. I should not hide behind the robes of a monk, creating the impression of inscrutability which, for me, turned out to be only an obstacle. With a sense of further involving myself with the sangha, I determined to give up my monastic vows. More than ever I felt myself given over to serving the cause of Buddhism.[6]

Following this, Rinpoche took off his monk's robes, as he saw these to be the final obstacle to students being able to meet his mind directly. He also began to be open about his drinking and having girlfriends. This had been going on for some time before the accident, and, while controversial on many levels, such behavior is not regarded as a problem in Tibet for those at a high level of accomplishment. In fact, for certain types of visionaries, known as *tertons*—about whom I will have more to say later—taking a consort is regarded as necessary. However, until this point, Rinpoche had kept this aspect of his life private in deference partly to the expectations of Western students but also to the expectations of his Tibetan colleagues. Now it was no longer so.

On January 3, 1970, Rinpoche married Diana Pybus and left Scotland for America. He had to stay in Canada for some months while waiting for an entry visa to the United States and finally entered in the spring of 1970, staying first at a farmhouse in Vermont which had recently been purchased for his use by a few of his students from Scotland. This farmhouse had been named "Tail of the Tiger" (TOTT) by the students, after one of the hexagrams of the *I Ching*.

Rinpoche was already becoming well-known throughout the United States and Canada, through *Meditation in Action*,[7] his first dharma book published in America. And so in September, he was invited to Boston to talk at the East-West Center. This, then, was the person who had so completely drawn me in on our first encounter in that Boston living room in 1970.

A LIFE WITHOUT PRIVACY

As my story will not be the first to show, Rinpoche was not embarrassed to live openly. He was not a "holy man," wearing robes and preaching abstract religious doctrines that neither his students nor he lived in practice. Outwardly, he lived an ordinary life—he married and had children; he drank and fell in love; he entered into human life with an intensity of joy and sadness that I have never seen in another person and could not have imagined possible before I met him. Yet because he lived a human life alongside his students, he was able to *show* us how to wake up rather than merely talk about it.

He made it very clear that the paths of buddhadharma and Shambhala had nothing to do with rejecting human society. On the contrary, the main point was to work toward building a genuinely good society. Many of his students in the 1970s had come from the hippie and drug cultures. He had attracted a rather cynical, though intelligent, bunch of educated drop-outs. But gradually, with Rinpoche's encouragement, we went back to school, started businesses, got married, and reentered the flow of society. One young woman tells of saying to him one day, in the early years, "I would do anything to serve you. Please tell me what I can do." His reply was, "Be a solid citizen."

As well as warm and benevolent, however, Rinpoche could also become overpoweringly wrathful, berating us suddenly and unexpectedly, cutting through our arrogance and hesitation with piercing accuracy. He overflowed with stark compassion that was uncompromising with conventional niceness, often creating friction and feistiness among us that ignited a flame of great power and energy—all so that we could have the chance to leap to another level of genuine understanding. Because of his radiance of love and his fierce authenticity, he was loved intensely and passionately by thousands of students. But hero-worship was definitely not demanded and neither was it appropriate.

He did not hold himself back from involving himself in all aspects of his students' lives. He cared about how we dressed, what food we

IN THE FOOTHILLS OF THE ROCKY MOUNTAINS.

liked, and who we were dating—he even paid attention to how we ate our peas. He taught that the discovery of our true nature, unconditioned basic goodness, comes only from working with life's ordinary conditions and situations—washing clothes, eating breakfast, drinking a cup of tea, paying bills, and all the rest. Thus, Rinpoche's teachings at the beginning were surprising, even disappointing, to those of us who imagined that spirituality had to do with escaping the painful realities of ordinary life. Yet their simple down-to-earth sanity, though shocking, was tremendously appealing.

RINPOCHE'S ACCOMPLISHMENTS

Rinpoche's accomplishments during his few years in the West would have been extraordinary even for someone who had lived here a whole lifetime. Even before he died, his life had become almost legendary to many thousands of students in the Western world as well as throughout Asia. He established an international network of Buddhist centers, practicing vajrayana Buddhism strictly according to the tradition but in a completely fresh expression. He brought to earth a new path of spirituality in daily life, free of religious dogmas of any kind: the teachings of Shambhala warriorship. He established the Naropa University, now considered one of the leading institutions in the world that offers an alternative within the established academic education of our time; and he founded a school system that eventually covered all ages from preschool through university—the Alaya Preschool in Boulder, Colorado, and the Vidya School, covering first through twelfth grades, that later transmuted into the Shambhala School in Halifax, Nova Scotia. He wrote many hundreds of poems. He created thousands of powerful calligraphies in a unique style. He established a new form of theater and a psychological training program, Maitri Space Awareness, based on methods of vajrayana Buddhism. He founded a school of Japanese *kado*, the contemplative art of flower placement, and together with the Japanese *kyudo* master Kanjuro Shibata Sensei, a school of archery as a contemplative practice. His life was a true exemplification of his teachings. He showed us how to live an ordinary but magical life so that every moment, every person, and everything in it becomes sacred.

Rinpoche was tremendously concerned about the future, how the teachings would continue after him. Sometimes he would say to his students, "You are just stepping stones for future generations," or, "We are undertaking a five-hundred-year project." He put a tremendous amount of his energy into establishing organizations that could survive him to contain the teachings, and he worked closely with the administration for many years.

These organizations are today admired and wondered at by other great Tibetan teachers trying to establish Buddhism in the difficult conditions of the modern culture, which seems to thrive on the glorification of self-interest. This is a little ironic, perhaps, in that while these other great teachers have continued to propagate the traditional Tibetan Buddhist forms and styles of teachings, and have continued to wear the robes of Tibetan monasticism, Rinpoche abandoned all that in order to be able to make a direct and true relationship with his students, for which reason Rinpoche was at first scorned and dismissed by both Tibetan and other Buddhists. Yet it was Rinpoche who first created strong and firm organizations, and new forms that carry the fresh wakefulness of the dharma. Later, this was acknowledged and often emulated by other Tibetan teachers with growing communities of students in the west. Rinpoche was also during his lifetime almost unique among Tibetan teachers in showing tremendous trust in Westerners' capacity to understand the dharma and pass it on to others.

"THE MAIN POINT OF ANY SPIRITUAL PRACTICE
IS TO STEP OUT OF EGO'S CONSTANT DESIRE FOR
A HIGHER, MORE TRANSCENDENTAL VERSION
OF KNOWLEDGE, RELIGION, VIRTUE, JUDGMENT,
COMFORT, OR WHATEVER IT IS THAT THE
PARTICULAR EGO IS SEEKING."

CHÖGYAM TRUNGPA RINPOCHE,
FROM *CUTTING THROUGH SPIRITUAL MATERIALISM*

1970: 2
So What *Is* Left?

 HROUGH WHAT strange paths could such an unlikely person as myself, a thirty-year-old Englishman, trained as a scientist at Cambridge University, have come to meet Rinpoche in Boston, Massachusetts? I had been living in the Boston/Cambridge area for five years, having moved there from England in 1965. I had come to the spiritual search through a route that was not the most common then, and still is not: my search for truth had begun in science.

I had fallen in love with physics when, one April day at the age of sixteen, I sat under a blossoming apple tree in our English garden reading *The Mysterious Universe*[8] by James Jeans. Jeans was one of the physicists involved in the quantum physics revolution of the 1920s and '30s. I was most fascinated by Jeans' statement that to many physicists at that time the universe was beginning to seem more like a great mind than a great machine, the latter being the classical scientific view of the universe. Looking back, I realize that it was the possibility of *knowing what mind is* that I fell in love with then. At the time, however, I thought the object of my love was quantum physics.

This search for the truth of the universe, motivated by love, took me all the way to a doctorate. However, long before I had completed my degree, I found that few physicists were any longer interested in mind, and I myself had forgotten my original inspiration. To most modern physicists questions about the basic meaning of quantum theory were merely the speculations of metaphysics and therefore not important. What was real and interesting to them were the details of *matter:* how many different kinds of elementary particles there are, how many fundamental forces, and how they all fit together to make a "theory of everything." Matter was everything, and there was no longer room, or need, for mind as a fundamental aspect of the universe.

At the same time that I was becoming sadly disappointed in physics, a new research field was developing—molecular biology, the study of DNA, which biologists were enthusiastically claiming to be the basis of life. I was seduced by the hope of finding this basis of life, and thereby its deeper meaning. After finishing my Ph.D. in physics and apprenticing in the famous Medical Research Laboratory in Cambridge, I crossed the Atlantic to do research in Molecular Biology at MIT. However, disappointed again, I quickly found that these biologists were not really looking at life. They were breaking up living cells and examining the small, lifeless parts, and no one really knew, or knows even to this day, how to put them back together again to make living cells.

While desultorily performing experiments on the bits and pieces of cells, I had begun to read about mind—psychology, philosophy of mind, and Eastern ideas about consciousness. Realizing that consciousness, or at least what we are conscious *of,* was deeply connected with language, I intensively studied linguistics and symbolic logic. Finally I understood that the truth of consciousness was to be found only at the point where language stops. As Wittgenstein had written, "Whereof man cannot speak, thereon he must be silent."[9] But how to see this point directly, personally, beyond the words?

With a thick, black marker, I placed a single black dot in the middle of a sheet of white paper. Underneath it I wrote the word WHAT, and tacked this paper on the wall by my bed; every morning when I awoke the first thing I saw was the piece of white paper with a dot and WHAT. This stopped my mind momentarily, but that was as far as I could get on my own. Later, under the guidance of Trungpa Rinpoche, I was to discover the nature of that moment, however brief, when thought is silent.

In the 1960s and early '70s, young people in America were beginning to become fascinated by the idea of "spirituality" but had little understanding of what it was really about. In addition, a lot of ideas were highly influenced by the drug culture. In the '70s in North America, there was a tremendous influx of spiritual teachers of all kinds: yogis, Indian gurus, Maharaji, Maharishi, Sufi Sam. I began to visit the various teachers who came through Boston, and I also frequented a little bookstore in Cambridge, Massachusetts, called East-West Bookstore. I would glance through books there, buy a few, go away and read them, and come back. Some of my friends who were in the "spiritual supermarket," as Rinpoche called it, used to visit there, too. Sometimes we would meet and chat about the different paths that were being offered.

IN THE GURDJIEFF WORK

In this way, I discovered the ideas of G.I. Gurdjieff, a Russian teacher of spiritual ideas and methods of inner work.[10] Although Gurdjieff never disclosed the origins of his teaching, it was clear that, during the twenty years that he disappeared as a young man, he had visited esoteric schools of Christianity and Sufism, as well as Tibetan Buddhist monasteries. When he returned to Russia he began to teach all of these in a powerful synthesis, unique to himself, attempting to interpret the traditional teachings in the scientific concepts of the time. In this, though the scientific concepts of that time were particularly limiting, he was remarkably successful, speaking and writing in a way that cut through much of the sentimentality of Western spiritual seekers.

Studying and practicing these spiritual methods was known to his students as the Work, referring to inner work on oneself, and I joined a group practicing these methods. This involvement in the Work meant a great deal to me and some of Gurdjieff's ideas, which I will describe briefly, carried through with me during my subsequent years of study with Rinpoche.

First there is the utter and complete mechanicalness of the ordinary man and woman. Gurdjieff was completely uncompromising on this point: men and women are ordinarily machines, all asleep. Every one of us believes that "I am conscious and have free-will, and I determine the course of my own life." In fact none of this is true. From the moment we think we awaken in the morning to the moment we believe we have fallen asleep, we are simply driven mechanically by thoughts, emotions, or physical sensation that are not of our own making, but are purely the result of conditioning and physical make-up. Our normal waking lives are swept along unconsciously, just as in a dream. Later, I found this to be in complete resonance with the Buddhist view that we will inevitably repeat habitual patterns of thought and behavior if we do not wake up to them through awareness.

According to Gurdjieff, the only way to wake up to this mechanicalness, and to free ourselves from it, is by going against it. Every moment we make the choice to go against our mechanicalness, our habitual patterns of thinking, feeling, or acting, is a moment of waking up—or at least of stirring in our sleep. But such moments produce suffering in us, in this case "conscious suffering," brought about by the "voluntary labor" of going against habit. Thus "voluntary labor" and "conscious suffering" are important aspects of work on oneself.

Gurdjieff taught that, while we all believe we are a single, unitary "me," we are not. When we look more closely, we see that we do not have just one idea of "me," but many. We have different "me's" for different occasions. The different "me's" are like roles that we play—a different one for each situation—or like masks we put on to cover how we are really feeling. We slip into our roles automatically, without even realizing it. Each role has different thoughts, different feelings, different moods, and even different muscular tensions and bodily postures. The change of role is so smooth, and the roles themselves so familiar, that we don't really even notice the changes happening. We think each role is the same "me" feeling a different way. We don't notice the automatic nature of the whole process. And if we were asked to describe ourselves we would probably describe only one or another of our various roles, depending on who was asking us.

This understanding of the multiplicity of our "I's" is very helpful in understanding the Buddhist view of egolessness, which means similarly that although we believe and act in ordinary life as if we were a unified, independent, permanent "I," such an "I" does not in fact exist. Seeing the multiplicity and impermanence of our moment-by-moment "I's" can be a valuable step on the road to discovering true egolessness.

To help us wake up, Gurdjieff taught the dual practices of "self-observation" and "self-remembering." Self-observation is the continual effort to see ourselves just as we are—good, bad, or indifferent—without judgment, self-praise, or self-blame; it is to see ourselves, in a sense, as others see us. Self-remembering does not mean excessive focusing on the momentary "me," or anxious self-consciousness in the conventional sense, but is a moment of being fully present, to the moment and to one's own being in the moment, free from daydreaming, discursive thought, or fuzziness of perception. It is a direct knowing of a larger sense of self beyond the "me." During this period, as I read around in other spiritual traditions, these practices of self-observation and self-remembering seemed to me to have much in common with Buddhist mindfulness and awareness practices.

In Gurdjieff's view, our mechanicalness is driven by three main centers of energy: the intellectual or thinking center, the feeling or emotional center, and the moving or instinctive center. These three centers, in every ordinary, asleep human are completely unsynchronized with each other, even working in opposition to each other—our thoughts do not correspond to what we feel, our body resists what we desire or what we think we should do, and so on. Thus, the first stage of awakening, absolutely necessary for everyone, is to harmonize these three energy centers. Many of the practical exercises Gurdjieff gave were directed toward this aim. The purpose of self-observation, for example, was mainly to see, at any moment in active daily life, how disharmonious our three centers are.

Regarding the joining of mind and body, Gurdjieff was very clear: "Magic lies in awareness of the body," he would say. While we were never given long practices to do, such as the sitting practice of mindfulness/awareness, we did have a morning exercise known as the "collection exercise." This consisted basically in what has come to be known more widely as a "body scan," in which one brings awareness successively to the different parts of one's body, beginning with the feet and arms, moving up the torso and head, and coming to rest in the heart. This was, for me, a powerful and important daily practice.

Another potent instruction was that whenever I come to a moment of remembering myself, remembering my aim to wake up, whatever activity I am involved in at that moment, to immediately bring my attention to the inner sensation of a particular, already-decided-upon part of my body, such as the sensation of my left forearm. This has the magical effect of bringing me right into the present moment. It is especially powerful if, for example, I remember myself in the middle of a heated discussion. These ideas and practices were later to have strong parallels in Rinpoche's teaching, especially in the Shambhala teachings in which a great deal of emphasis is placed on "joining mind and body."

Gurdjieff was very far from being merely an intellectual purveyor of ideas. He had a mischievous and at times brutally sharp sense of humor with which he would cut through his students' pretentiousness and self-importance. And he would often push his students to extreme physical, emotional, and mental hardships to help them break through their mechanicalness. His emphasis was on the development of attention in ordinary life—what Buddhists would perhaps call meditation in action. One of his main methods for arousing attention was a series of highly complex exercises, the "Movements," and "Sacred Dances," both of which demanded increase of attention far above the usual. These, too, he had brought back and synthesized from his journeys East, and I was fortunate enough to have a skilled teacher of the Movements for the Work group which I joined in Boston.

The Work with the Gurdjieff group had a powerful, life-changing effect on me. I can still recall, almost forty years later, a period of a few days when the world seemed to become alive. The space around me seemed to be bright, vivid, almost luminous and filled with life. Suddenly, for those few days, I was lifted out of my habitual depression into a quiet joy and appreciation of the world around me. This was the moment when I began to realize that a different dimension to life—the inner, spiritual dimension that I had been reading about all these years—was real, actually attainable. I am forever grateful to the Gurdjieff work and to Gurdjieff himself, for giving me some little hint, as well as direct experience, of this greater perspective.

A teacher is necessary at the beginning of the path, according to Gurdjieff, although no amount of following great men would ultimately free me; in the end, only I can do it through my own efforts. Yet at this point Gurdjieff had been dead for over twenty years. He had no definite lineage to carry on his work, and his teachings had no clear history. People who had known him were leading our groups, and when they spoke they seemed to almost always refer to Gurdjieff: "Mr. Gurdjieff said this; Mr. Gurdjieff said that." I began to feel his absence: "Where is Mr. Gurdjieff?" So my search for a living teaching and teacher continued, even while I took part in the Gurdjieff group.

Knowing that the Gurdjieff work had its origins in some combination of Christianity, Sufism, and Tibetan Buddhism, many of us read a great deal about these other spiritual methods. I found myself most drawn to the Buddhist practice of mindfulness meditation and the Buddhist teachings on egolessness, and recognized these in some of the central ideas of Gurdjieff as I have described.

FINDING RINPOCHE

One day, I bought a book called *Meditation in Action*. It was a beautiful early September afternoon, warm, fresh, and sunny. I went to sit by the banks of the Charles River and started to read this book. It was quite short and very simple, and I read it all the way through, sitting there on the banks of the river that afternoon. At the end of it I had a strange feeling, something between disheartenment—a flat, washed-out feeling—and a kind of joy, a kind of excitement. I wanted to find out more about Chögyam Trungpa, the man who had written this book. I wanted to meet him.

At the back of the book it said, "If you would like to correspond with the author, his address is Samye Ling, Eskdalemuir, Scotland." Here I was, an Englishman now living across the Atlantic Ocean in Boston, and to meet this person I had to go back to Scotland! So, disappointed, I returned to the bookstore that very afternoon to look for something else. There I told a friend, "I just read this really good book by a Tibetan, but he lives in Scotland." "You mean Trungpa Rinpoche?" my friend replied, "He's giving a seminar in Boston this weekend!" The seminar was to be held at the East-West Center on Marlborough Street in Boston and, on the Thursday before the program, Rinpoche was giving a public talk there.

And so it was that my heart and mind were opened that Thursday evening in September 1970. The kind smile that accompanied Rinpoche's answer—"There's something left, don't worry"—in response to my desperate personal question, went straight to my heart. I knew then that I had found what I had been searching for all my life.

WHAT IS LEFT?

Rinpoche went on to explain that if you write on a sheet of blank, white paper and then erase the writing, you are left with the pure, brilliant white paper. The response suggested that nihilism was not the final answer to the question I had been asking ever since I sat under the apple tree as a boy of sixteen, the question, "What is the reality behind (or beyond, or within) appearance?" (I'll explore this analogy a bit more in the next chapter.)

So what *is* the "something" that is left? The absence of anything on the brilliant white paper is an analogy for *shunyata*, emptiness, the state beyond ego, beyond conceptual mind. The brilliant whiteness symbolizes what remains in shunyata. Rinpoche, in his luminous and joyful way of being, seemed to embody that "something," as well as the freedom from fixed mind, which *is* emptiness. And his kind simple answer to my question seemed to suggest that I, too, could discover this for myself in my own experience. This question—"what's left?"— was to continue with me, and gradually unfold, through the many years with Rinpoche.

As you read this story of Rinpoche, and the journey with him of one stubborn student, you may sometimes wonder why I and his other students stayed with him at all. As you will see, the voyage was increasingly intense, at times joyful, but often painful. Perhaps the simplest answer to this is that this first exchange between Rinpoche and me was an exchange of genuine love, the first time I had experienced such full and undemanding love in my life. And through all the ups and downs of life with him, that love—his for me and mine for him—continued and deepened.

Perhaps the other most important reason I, and so many others, stayed with him through thick and thin was the direct experience of the teachings and path of practice that he laid out for us—from the simple, formless "sitting" meditation of mindfulness and awareness, to the complex visualizations of deity practices, finally returning to the simplicity of formless meditation in mahamudra practice. As the years went by and I saw these teachings gradually verified in my own experience, and I saw substantial positive changes take place in myself and others in response to them—then at each step of the way my trust gradually deepened in Rinpoche's genuineness and his power to help us awaken.

WORK, SEX, AND MONEY

The topic of the weekend seminar that followed that first talk was "Work, Sex, and Money,"[11] and what Rinpoche said was very simple. He was light and cheerful and seemed to be bursting with joyful humor, and all of his talks were filled with that sense of lightness and humor. He grinned a lot, we laughed a lot, and sometimes he would just stop and burst into giggles. During the talk on money, he commented quite seriously, "Money is very…" and he put his hand into his sports jacket and slowly drew out a dollar bill, saying, "flat." Somehow we all found this to be hilarious.

At the same time, the talks were straightforward and helpful, conveying the inner meaning of work, money, and sex. He talked about the ego side of each topic as well as the way we could relate to it with sanity and a balanced state of mind. In the case of work, he spoke of the neurotic styles of trying to fill all of space with our work or of using our intelligence to escape work. On the other side he spoke very simply of relating directly to the earth, and discovering when to act practically and directly, with awareness of what we are doing and why we are doing it.

In speaking of sex, the topic was really passion and love. He said, "Like anything else in life it is largely based on the very important point of 'center or centerless.' There is a vast store of energy which is not centered, which is not ego's energy at all. It is the energy which is the primordial background, not just a blank state, but containing a tremendously powerful process of energy." So there was the theme of "what's left?" again.

These energies, he said, have the characteristics of "a fire quality of warmth, and a tendency to flow in a particular pattern…. The whole process…goes on all the time, whether through the confused filter of ego or not, like the ever-burning quality of the sun." The ego tries to accommodate and manipulate this energy, but it can never be wholly successful. If we look directly at this primordial energy of passion, acknowledging it without trying to control it with conventional attitudes, then it does not become neurotic at all. Real communication with another is then possible. He concludes, "We are getting into a very big topic, much more than sex. Every life situation has meaning behind it and a process of communication in it. In particular, sexual communication doesn't have to be only physical, but when two people are attracted to each other there is a tendency to open as far as you can."

EARLY DAYS AT TOTT—RINPOCHE MAKES THE TEACHING GESTURE.

During the talk on meditation and in the remainder of the seminar, Rinpoche made simple but profoundly challenging statements: "The ego does not want to see itself"; "Now, finally, you can stop and look"; "Look at your own mind"; and "The question is the answer." I sat there thinking to myself, "Why, in all my life, did no one ever tell me these simple things before? Simple, but so true." My teachers, my parents, even the Gurdjieff people—nobody had talked to me in the profoundly direct way that he was speaking. I had the strange feeling of an ancient wisdom reaching back for generations behind this youthful, funny person.

After the last talk of the seminar, I went out of the house and saw Rinpoche standing on the sidewalk. He was smoking a cigarette, surrounded by a circle of young people. I looked wistfully at him and he caught my eye, but I was too shy and timid to approach him and introduce myself. I just stood there on the perimeter of the circle for a while, and then finally walked away.

TO TAIL OF THE TIGER

In early December I was overjoyed to receive a flyer from TOTT advertising a seminar to be held over the Christmas period with Trungpa Rinpoche, called "The Battle of Ego." Thus it was with excited anticipation that, on Christmas Eve, I drove up along the lanes of Vermont to TOTT. It was already dark as I approached it on the long, winding country road, but at the end of the road I could see a rather small looking farmhouse. I parked the car and entered the house, coming directly into a small, funky old farmhouse dining room. There were several wooden tables in the room, with wooden benches alongside them. The first thing I noticed was a lady who looked to be in her late thirties, wearing a short red dress and red tights, dancing to music on top of one of the tables. People were laughing and clapping and there was a feeling of celebration.

As I walked in the door, I had a feeling I can only describe as "coming home." As I came in to this farmhouse dining room on Christmas Eve, I felt as if I had at last come back to my family, my first family. It wasn't the family I had known in England; it was a true family.

The farmhouse was full to bursting. The small dining room couldn't even begin to accommodate all of us, so we had our meals all over the place—the dining room, the living room, the library, the stairs, the sewing room, everywhere. There was little real furniture in the living room, so we sat on some wooden blocks. We crowded into the small attic shrine room of the farmhouse for Rinpoche's talks. The general atmosphere of the seminar was joyful and celebratory.

THE BATTLE OF EGO

Rinpoche gave a talk every afternoon based on the image of ego as a castle. The first few days were spent talking about how we build this castle of ego and the second half of the seminar was on how to attack it. His description began on virgin territory, or no man's land. This basic ground is not owned by anyone and is an analogy for the primordial intelligence that is free from all concepts of good and bad, *this* and *that*, *I* and *other*, inside and outside. At a certain point the all-pervading intelligence of this basic ground panics and realizes that it has no place to settle, no reference point, no nest. It runs around and tries to find something to hold on to. Discovering its first rock—an analogy for the first discrimination between this and that—it begins to build a castle.

The castle has walls, representing the ignorance of separation from the basic ground; guards, who judge the outside in terms of friend or foe; a central security officer, who determines what defensive or aggressive action should be taken at each moment; ministers, who label everything with concepts; and a king, consciousness imprisoned by ego. Later I was to discover that these five aspects of the castle of ego represent a traditional teaching of the five *skandhas*, or "heaps"—components of our body and mind which we lump together into one thing and identify with as a real "self," or ego.

The second part of the seminar addressed the question: How are we going to dismantle this castle? How are we going to deal with the foot soldiers, and so on all the way up to the king? In this second part, Rinpoche worked very much with questions and answers, asking the students questions like, "How would you get through the protective circle of the guards?" "How would you deal with the ministers?" People made suggestions, and he always responded very directly and in a way that personally related to the student who asked the question. He was warm and personal, humorous and slightly cutting sometimes, and always delightful.

Lord Pentland, the head of the Gurdjieff movement in America, was attending this seminar along with several other senior Gurdjieffians. I sat down next to him one evening in front of the fire, and said, "If it's all really so simple as Trungpa Rinpoche is presenting, why is the Gurdjieff work so complicated?" Lord Pentland replied, in his very upper

AT THE BATTLE OF EGO SEMINAR.

class, Scottish accent, "I think it is because *we* are so complicated." This was helpful. He went on to say that it is ego that is complicated, and therefore the teachings have to be complicated even though, ultimately, it may be simple. Later on, I was to find out that Buddhist doctrine can also be highly complicated, for the same reason—there are said to be as many different teachings as there are beings.

IS IT REALLY SO SIMPLE?

During this program, Rinpoche had private interviews with everyone. He was staying in one of the two rooms at the front of the farmhouse, and met with people in the room across the corridor from his bedroom. He sat in a wicker chair that was very similar to the one at the seminar in Boston, and the person meeting with him would sit on a cushion on the floor.

When it was my turn, I sat on the cushion and just looked up at him, feeling quietly joyful, and he looked down at me with his sweet smile. I said, "Rinpoche, is it really this simple?" He smiled and nodded, saying, "Yes," and added, "It's said that a cow cannot taste its own tongue. It is that close." In my memory of that exchange, which was my first personal meeting with Rinpoche, it is as if the air were filled with golden light. It isn't something that I saw at the time as a visual illusion or something tangible, but I always remember him in that room as if it were that way.

As I returned to Boston, I was very happy. I felt that I had found what I was looking for. I don't remember how I actually put it to myself at the time, but the feeling was that I had finally found my home and a genuine living teacher who could show me the way to discover what was truly real. And, after years with the rather solemn Gurdjieffians, I had discovered that it could be a joyful search, full of humor! What faced me in Boston, however, was an extremely bleak situation.

The previous year, utterly disheartened, I had quit research altogether and taken a position teaching physics in a public high school, thinking that perhaps I could reconnect with the physics that I had loved as a teenager and pass that on to others. As I had had no teacher training at all, this was turning out to be a rather disastrous experiment. I had been demoted and so, in my second year, I was teaching general science to ninth grade students who mostly seemed to think the whole thing was at best a joke! I had no idea where my life was heading, but it was clear that it couldn't continue in the same way.

FIRST TASTE OF MINDFULNESS AND AWARENESS

That February, Rinpoche gave a seminar at TOTT on mindfulness and awareness. The feeling of this seminar was very different from the

Christmas seminar. At Christmas, there had been a festive holiday atmosphere, while now in February the feeling seemed to reflect mid-winter in Vermont: cold and snowy, with gray skies and empty, stark trees. And the farmhouse was always chilly. The teachings, on mindfulness practice and the importance of meditation, were down to earth, simply how to relate to our wild minds. The message was very simple: sit, stop, and look. He gave detailed instructions on the mindfulness practice of bringing one's attention to the breath, particularly the out-going breath, and dissolving outward along with the breath. He also spoke of the awareness aspect of the practice—opening to the feeling of space around and within one, and to the panoramic awareness of the environment and the space of mind in which the whole thought process occurs.

The Tibetan word he was translating as "mindfulness" is *shi-ne*, in Sanskrit *shamatha*, which literally means "the development of peace," or "peaceful abiding." Rinpoche pointed out that the peace referred to here is not an anesthetic kind of peace that comes from suppressing our emotional energies. Rather, it is the natural peace that is discovered to be the very basis of our ordinary minds, which we can glimpse through the occasional gaps in our usual speedy and inattentive mental process. Here was another hint of "what's left" and of that moment when thought is silent that I had been seeking when I had pasted the word WHAT by my bedside. The point of this practice, he emphasized, is not to try to get anywhere or to attain any special state, but simply to be there directly and honestly with our own minds, no matter what intense thoughts and emotions arise.

Added to this was another message: disappointment—not expecting to get anything out of our sitting practice of meditation—and cutting through the solid wall of ego-centeredness. Rinpoche spoke frequently in those early years about disappointment and hopelessness—not expecting anything, giving up our "trip," coming down to earth, just being ordinary, having "no way out." A very significant theme throughout his teaching in the first few years was cutting through spiritual materialism, which is the tendency of ego to grasp on to even spiritual techniques and twist them around to boost an even greater ego. This attitude toward spirituality was rampant in those days and is even more rampant today, as spirituality becomes more and more popular and people are able to make a lot of money setting themselves up as "spiritual teachers."

Both Rinpoche's spoken teachings as well as the way he related to students reflected this two-fold aspect of cutting ego's expectation and ambition, at the same time showing directly a greater reality beyond ego and how we can discover it in our own experience. When it came time for my interview and Rinpoche asked me how I was, I said that I was feeling flat, gray, and depressed. I wouldn't say he smiled, but he looked at me with understanding and said, "Now something can grow."

I had heard that one of the staff, Carl Springer, was thinking of moving to Boulder to work with Rinpoche there. I mentioned this to Rinpoche, during the interview, and said that I was wondering about doing that myself. At this, he shook his head and, with a slightly disdainful look on his face, replied, "I'm not a charity organization, you know." He by no means always manifested as the kind daddy that we may seek from a spiritual teacher. When necessary, he could be cutting, not pampering the student but showing a greater friendliness that does not feed ego. This was indubitably such an occasion! I understood that I should not seek security or a solution to my livelihood problem by depending on him.

Accepting the decision sadly, I returned to Boston. Now I really had to think about what to do. It was clear to me that I needed to have some teacher training if I were to go on teaching high school. I applied and was accepted to University College, London, where they were teaching a particularly inspired and innovative method of teaching physics called "Nuffield Physics." I was not happy about moving back to London, away from Rinpoche, but I seemed to have no other choice. My planned departure became known to the people at TOTT, as I visited several more times that winter.

"I THINK YOU SHOULD COME TO TOTT"

In April, we got word that Rinpoche was making a surprise visit to TOTT on his way to Montreal to pick up his American immigration visa. He had been in America as a visitor until then, and his green card had finally been issued. By now, there were people interested in him from quite a wide area, including Boston, New York, and Montreal. Word went around that Rinpoche would be offering a surprise seminar at TOTT.

Now it was springtime, and the trees were beginning to blossom. It was warm and sunny, a lovely time of the year, and everyone seemed more cheerful. Rinpoche was also in a very cheerful mood, even though he had some painful broken ribs. We heard that he had been riding in a car in Berkeley, California, driven by a student who was questioning him about, of all things, awareness and meditation in action, when the student drove through a red light and crashed the car. The student wasn't hurt but Rinpoche suffered the broken ribs— fortunately it wasn't more serious.

At the seminar, we had the usual personal interviews. I went in to see Rinpoche, and after we chatted a bit he said, "I hear you're moving back to England. What are you going to do there?" I said, "I'm going to take a teacher training program." "Do you need more credentials?" he queried. I laughed, "Well, no, not really." A thought arose which had not occurred at all since my meeting with him in February, and I almost wondered whether he had somehow planted it in my mind at that moment. I said, "Actually, in the back of my mind somewhere, I was thinking about possibly moving up to Tail of the Tiger for a while." He smiled and nodded, replying, "I think you should come to Tail of the Tiger." I left the interview feeling jubilant and exhilarated.

So in May, at the end of the school year, I packed up all my belongings and drove up to TOTT.

1971: 3
Do I Want to Stay with This Man?

 N JUNE, Rinpoche arrived at TOTT for the summer teachings. The first seminar was about the *abhidharma*, the Buddhist teachings on the psychology of mind, and it made a particularly deep impression on many of us. These talks were later published in a small book called *Glimpses of Abhidharma*.[12] This was now the second time I heard Trungpa Rinpoche describe, in five stages, the way we create our world through the process of perception.

These teachings were profound and influenced me greatly, as someone who had grown up as a scientist and still appreciated true science and genuine investigation. I had come to both science and Buddhism through wanting to know what is true, and in fact I felt that my turn to Buddhism was simply a natural continuation of my scientific search. This view of how we perceive our world, how we create our world through perception, seemed to me to be scientific in the sense that it was a description of direct experience that could be verified through the practice of meditation. It was the result of genuine investigation into the nature of reality, in this case investigation of the mind and how it perceives the world, rather than merely investigation of the outer world.

INTRODUCING THE FIVE SKANDHAS OF EGO

In the Abhidharma seminar, Rinpoche described the moment-by-moment production of a flash of perception out of the nondual, unbounded space of awareness—the primordial ground in the Battle of Ego. Each moment of dualistic perception of an inner world and an outer world—an ego and what appears to that ego—occurs within a basic nondual ground. Rinpoche described this basic ground thus:

> The basic ground does not depend on relative situations at all. It is natural being which just is. Energies appear out of this basic ground and those energies are the source of the development of relative situations. Sparks of duality, intensity and sharpness, flashes of wisdom and knowledge—all sorts of things come out of the basic ground. So the basic ground is the source of confusion and also the source of liberation. Both liberation and confusion are that energy which happens constantly, which sparks out and then goes back to its basic nature, like clouds (as Milarepa described it) emerging from and disappearing back into the sky.[13]

Rinpoche described the process of the arising of a moment of dualistic perception within the basic nondual ground in terms of five stages known as *skandhas,* or "heaps." In turn, each skandha is itself a bundle or heap of smaller elements. This manner of using the skandhas to describe the moment-by-moment arising of confused dualistic perception is rare in the Buddhist teachings. The skandhas are more usually regarded as relatively stable elements of the person. However, I discovered later that Rinpoche's teachings, however fresh they appeared, were always based on the tradition, in this case probably on the works of Jamgön Kongtrül the Great,[14] the predecessor of his own teacher.

According to these teachings, a moment of perception develops over a very brief period, during which unconscious feelings, expectations, and conceptual interpretations occur sequentially. This progressive development culminates in a moment of conscious experience. The duration of each moment of experience has been variously estimated by Buddhists; Rinpoche put it at "something like a five-hundredth of a second."[15] The question of whether the arising of the five stages is simultaneous or sequential is, of course, rather a moot point at the level of thousandths of a second. Time as we usually know it is, in any case, a concept resulting from the crudeness of our perceptions.

As Rinpoche said, in answer to just this question:

> *Well it depends on our notion of time, of "simultaneously." We described how the first stage of ego and its extensions develop by thousandths of a second. In that way the whole thing develops by stages. But on that time scale, you could also say they happen simultaneously. So that process happens simultaneously or progressively. There is a beginning and an end, but the application of notions of time becomes crude and rugged here.*[16]

Our crude attention span, of course, is much longer than a five-hundredth of a second; it is more like a tenth of a second, which accounts for the fact that movies in which the frames move at more than sixteen per second do not seem jerky. This crude attention blurs together the successive moments of experience to give the illusion of a continuous world and a continuous sense of self. Through the practice of meditation we refine our attention span and begin to be able to catch the gaps between the moments of arising of thoughts; we catch a glimpse of the nondual space of awareness.

In this process, as Rinpoche described it progressively, the first four skandhas occur before the conscious "I" notices anything—they are pre-conscious or subliminal, in more familiar terms. The first stage occurs when those flashes of energy arising within the basic ground become self-conscious and panic. This panic or bewilderment is the fundamental basis of ignorance and confusion. It is "the source of all the relative concepts in the whole samsaric world."[17] Out of this panic a distinction between outside and inside, between that and this, is projected onto the basic nondual ground. Thus apparent duality is born within nonduality. What is experienced as "inside" (*this*), is the very beginning of a sense of self, and "outside" *(that)*, is what is experienced as different from oneself. Having made this first basic split between inside and outside, there is the second stage: a reaction of *feeling* related to the survival of the nascent sense of self. These feelings are positive, negative, or neutral, according to whether the "outside" is felt as supportive, threatening, or neutral to this developing self.

The third stage is the first recognition of a specific object. Still without naming it, we recognize a chair as a chair, something useful to sit on; we recognize a person as a person, friend or foe; and so on. Along with this bare recognition comes an impulse to action in relation to that object, based on the positive, negative, or neutral feelings of stage two. All of this is still not conscious—and this is a very important point: impulsive action may occur without any involvement of intellectual judgment or consciousness. An example of this is when we say something unkind or even hit someone in anger before we can stop ourselves—the word or action is over before we are really conscious of the impulse to do it. Another example would be running away when we come upon a ferocious animal on our path: we turn around and run before even recognizing exactly what it is, before naming it—which only comes as we are running down the path in the opposite direction!

Now the conceptual process of naming begins, the fourth stage. A chair is named as a "chair," with all of the connotations of "chairness." All of the belief systems we have—philosophical, religious, economic, scientific, political, personal, or whatever—are unconsciously applied to the developing perception at this stage. This, for example, is the point at which we might automatically form an opinion about someone which, combined with the previous feeling, becomes dislike merely because they look "foreign." The conscious "me" is still not aware of these automatically formed opinions and judgments.

Only after all of this processing comes the fifth stage, the brightness and clarity in which a thought or a sense perception is directly known to the conscious "I," the king or queen of the castle of ego. Ordinary consciousness keeps up an inner narrative or storyline that brings a narrow sense of coherence to our conscious life. Although all of these five elements, from the first primitive sense of differentiation to the final consciousness, are occurring in every moment of experience, our attention is normally so coarse that we experience them smoothed together in a continuous stream of consciousness.

The view that the ordinary dualistic consciousness keeps up the illusion of a continuous world and a continuous "I" is nicely summarized by cognitive scientist Joseph Ledoux: "We are not consciously aware of all the information our mind processes or the causes of all the behaviors we produce, or of the origin of all the feelings we experience. But the conscious self uses these as data points to construct and maintain a coherent story, our personal story, our subjective sense of self. Weaving such tales about the self and its world is a primary function of consciousness."[18] Ledoux is a not, as far as I know, a Buddhist.

Western science has discovered similar pre-conscious processes in the production of a moment of perception.[19] Science, though, has no idea of the basic nondual ground since it is based on the assumption that the "outer" side of our perceived world of duality is the ultimately real world, the "objective" world. Beyond this first arising of duality, however, the way the brain-mind-body creates the appearance of an external world has been described in great detail by the brain-mind sciences, and there is much in agreement with the Buddhist view. As Vernon Mountcastle, an elder of psychobiology, said, "Each of us believes himself to be directly within the world that surrounds him, to sense objects and events precisely, and to live in real current time. I assert that these are perceptual illusions."[20] And cognitive psychologist Richard Gregory comments, "The 'external world' is a hypothesis."[21]

This teaching of the process of perception and the primordial ground within which it arises every moment was to be a key teaching in my practice and understanding of the dharma as the years went by. In the analogy of erasing the writing on a brilliant white sheet of paper, which Rinpoche had given in our first encounter in the East-West Center in Boston, the writing would be the illusion of duality created by clinging to belief in the ego and its projections as real.

Rinpoche had given this analogy of the white paper as a relative teaching to help me overcome my nihilism. However, later I was to realize that the white paper and the writing are ultimately inseparable. A better analogy might be those writing tablets on which one can write or draw with water and a brush: the writing appears in black on the tablet, only to dissolve back into the grey background of the tablet a few minutes later. The writing only appeared to be separate from the background, but was actually inseparable from it. The brilliant white paper and the grey surface of the tablet, the "something left," symbolize the primordial, energetic space within which the five skandhas of ego and its world flash momentarily in and out of existence— emptiness and luminosity beyond duality.

Luminosity, a word we rarely hear outside of specialized contexts nowadays, essentially means "light." However, it should not be confused with outer physical light, although the inner light of the mind and outer physical light are essentially inseparable, as even some physicists would now agree;[22] in fact, we see outer objects only because of this inseparability. But *ösel*, the Tibetan word for luminosity, light, or radiance, can also be translated as "clarity." The mind, while empty of forms or concepts, is essentially luminous, clearly knowing. Through its clear transparent nature the mind illuminates or knows whatever appears to it as object. When we speak of a person being "luminous" we are referring to an inner glow, a radiance and joy that speaks to us from beyond conceptual mind.

CASUAL FRIENDLINESS WITH "RIMP THE GIMP"

Rinpoche's teachings were profound even at this early stage of his students' development. But in some ways, Rinpoche's behavior toward his students was even more striking that summer than his formal teachings. He would join in the parties seemingly with great enthusiasm, even trying to dance to the blaring music of the Rolling Stones. On one such occasion, people were sitting in a circle on the lawn outside the front door of the house and Rinpoche was with them, wearing a cowboy hat, drinking Colt 45 beer (which was his favorite drink at the time), smoking a cigarette, and playing the bongo drums—all the while wearing a huge, broad, slightly quizzical grin. It could almost be said that he was "coming down to our level," really meeting us eye to eye—speaking our language, using our colloquial, hippie, American terminology, cracking jokes, and just thoroughly enjoying the situation (or at least seeming to thoroughly enjoy it). Yet even at those times, if you looked into his eyes, there was a feeling of tremendous openness, warmth, and uncompromising firmness—and a sense of vastness that could be frightening.

People were extremely familiar with him and, being quite un-American myself, I was shocked at times. Once, as Rinpoche and I were walking down to the seminar tent together, a young lady named Gretel came up to him, put her arm around him, and said in her Southern-accented American voice, "Hiya, Rimp, haa're y'all today?" This was an example of the personal quality of the relationships that Rinpoche was having with people at that time, quite familiar and filled with humor. Some people used to refer to him as "Rimp the Gimp," referring to the limp he had because of his paralyzed left side.

People would collect in Rinpoche's bedroom at all times of the day. They would especially gather in the evenings, often just walking in without knocking. There would typically be a huge crowd sprawled around on the floor, while he sat either in a chair or on his bed. Sometimes he was unembarrassedly naked, and people would be joking, laughing, and usually drinking. It almost felt like a continual party.

Rinpoche loved to drink. At first it was beer and Scotch, but when he discovered the Japanese rice wine, saké, that became his drink. He had no embarrassment about this drinking and neither tried to hide it nor exhibited any kind of shame or hesitation about it. And even in this first year of knowing him, his drinking did not seem to me like an obstacle, or a blemish on his "spirituality." Great teachers often use unconventional means to show the way beyond egotism and conventional mind. Marpa, the great teacher and translator, brought Buddhism from India to Tibet in the eleventh century and thereby founded the Kagyu lineage, the school to which the Trungpa line of tulkus belongs. Marpa was a married farmer, and was one of many teachers of the Tibetan tradition who drank alcohol. In the Japanese Zen tradition, too, there are stories of great teachers, like master swordsman Yamaoka Tesshu, who enjoyed drinking in large quantities—shocking small minds and stirring the sleep of their students with their humor and wild antics.

At the same time, Rinpoche also made it clear that his circumstances were extraordinary, and he discouraged his students from imitating his way of drinking. In an article entitled "Alcohol as Medicine or Poison," Rinpoche wrote:

> Whether alcohol is to be a poison or a medicine depends on one's awareness while drinking. Conscious drinking—remaining aware of one's state of mind—transmutes the effect of alcohol. Here "awareness" involves a tightening up of one's system as an intelligent defense mechanism. Alcohol becomes destructive when one gives in to the joviality: letting loose permits the poisons to enter one's body.... Alcohol's creativity begins when there is a sense of dancing with its effects—when one takes the effects of drink with a sense of humor. For the conscious drinker, or for the yogi, the virtue of alcohol is that it brings one down to ordinary reality, so that one does not dissolve into meditation on nonduality.... But naturally the ordinary drinker who tries to compete with or imitate this transcendental style of drinking will turn his alcohol into poison.[23]

During all the years I was with him, I rarely, if ever, saw a situation in which his drinking impaired his ability to teach, to relate directly and penetratingly with his students, or to carry out all of his many and various activities. And when we look at all that he accomplished in the mere seventeen years that he was in North America, of which I gave only a partial listing in chapter 1, the question that sometimes arises as to whether he was an "alcoholic" (a question always from someone who didn't know him) seems to be a moot point. In my view, there was little question that he was a master *of* alcohol, rather than being mastered *by* it.

"GOTCHA!"

While Rinpoche seemed to have little concern or need for privacy, he also took delight in teasing us about ours. There was one main upstairs bathroom in the old farmhouse, shared by the twenty to thirty residents in the off-season. It was considered very uptight to lock the door of this bathroom. It was still the hippy days, when everything should be free and open and one should not show any embarrassment about bodily functions or being naked in front of people. Some of us, including myself, usually did try to lock the door when we were taking a shit—and Rinpoche could occasionally be seen outside in the corridor peering through the keyhole. At one point, comments were made to him that some people were insisting on locking the door, and he replied, looking directly at me, "I know—I saw someone's hairy legs!"

He loved to creep up behind people and shout "Boo!," poking them gently in the side, and saying "Gotcha!" with a delighted giggle when we jumped. We never heard him coming, so we would always be startled and then embarrassed by our lack of awareness—like little cats who stumble and then seem to pretend like nothing happened—while at the same time enjoying the humor and affection in his gesture.

For me, that summer was marked by simple little incidents and exchanges with Rinpoche. I was uptight and desperately wanted to chat with him and talk with him, so I would try to think of things to talk to him about. One day I met him in the corridor outside his room, and I said, "Hello, Rinpoche—I was wondering if I could talk to you sometime about how you used to bring children up in Tibet." He smiled and said, "Well, I think we used to use the stairs…" But I was just not able to relax and smile at this joke myself.

On another occasion, when we had stopped for a drink at a little café, he picked up a salt shaker and said that the English are very sticky, like a salt shaker with jam on it that stops the salt from flowing easily and gave the example of Lord Douglas-Home, at that time the British Prime Minister. I took this as a message to me that I could perhaps loosen up with him—and immediately became even more uptight!

I had a hard time even opening the door of Rinpoche's room to walk in, though I knew I was invited to do so, as was everyone. Once, I plucked up my courage and thought, "I'll go and hang out." I went to his door and listened to make sure that there was hanging out being done and, hearing voices then I knocked on the door and heard, "Come in." When I opened the door, I saw that no one was there except Rinpoche and Diana. They seemed to be involved in an intense conversation, and I didn't know what to do; I was almost frozen. So instead of politely saying, "Oh, I'm sorry, I didn't realize you were having a private conversation," or something like that, I just looked at them with wide open eyes and said, "Hanging out or not hanging out?" They both very sweetly beckoned to me and I came in and sat over in a corner, eavesdropping on their conversation. They continued on for some time, seeming to ignore my presence, until after some minutes I felt that I should go. I said, rather awkwardly, "I'll leave now, thank you," and left.

Yet he never gave up an opportunity to help me relax into being with him. One evening that summer, I drove Rinpoche back to the little rented house he and Diana were staying in, in West Barnet a few miles away from TOTT. We parked a little way from the entrance to the house and began to walk up the path, which was next to a grassy slope that became quite steep as it went along toward the house. I held out my hand for him to lean on, on his lame left side as one did, but instead of walking along the path he started veering off onto the grassy slope. I had to really hold him, very tightly, to stop him from falling and pulling both of us down the slope. I said, "Rinpoche, I didn't realize you were *that* drunk!" He replied, "Well, gotta give you something to do!" We both laughed, and then he turned around and we went into the house.

On another occasion, I drove over to Rinpoche's house to collect the garbage. It was my job at TOTT to collect the garbage and take it to the local dump, because I had a station wagon and the garbage cans could fit into the back. I was disgusted by the low level of cleanliness. TOTT was really a big mess, and I had to go all over the place to pick up everyone's garbage.

When I arrived at Rinpoche's house, he saw me and beckoned for me to come in. I sat down opposite him at the round table by the window. It was a lovely summer afternoon, and I was completely stiff. Here was my chance; I was sitting right opposite Rinpoche, just him and me. I sat looking down at the table, unable to think of a thing to say. He offered me a cup of tea.

Finally, I said to him, "Rinpoche, how do you think Tail of the Tiger is doing?" What I really had in mind was the dirt and the garbage and so on, and I was hoping he would say, "Well, I think maybe it needs a little more discipline, and a little bit more cleanliness"—something about tightening up and making it more like what I thought a contemplative center should be. But instead of that he just smiled and said, "I think it's doing fine." While that was very helpful in turning my mind from the judgmental dissatisfaction toward something more positive, still I just sat there at the table, not knowing what else to say, still caught in the discomfort of intense self-consciousness.

After a while, he said, "Is that a lawn mower?" I opened up my ears and listened, and far away in the distance I heard the sound of a summer lawn mower, a very familiar sound which I used to love when I was a child. I loved the feeling of the outdoors, and of people doing gentle gardening things on a summer afternoon. I listened, and then replied, "Yes, I think it is." Somehow that opened up the whole space between us. It was as if I were here at last, or the space were here at last. It was also a direct teaching on the freshness of panoramic awareness. I stayed just a while longer, and there seemed to be more lightness between us.

There was another effort to shake me out of my stickiness when Rinpoche was having meetings with a few students who had been with him in Scotland, so-called "meditation instructor meetings," though what went on in them was nothing like the mindfulness and awareness meditation instruction that I had heard. I was invited in to one of these meetings to be a kind of guinea pig for their investigations. Half a dozen students were sitting in a circle with Rinpoche, on chairs or on the bed. I was asked to sit on a cushion in the middle of the circle, and then they started saying things to me and asking questions. One of them took my glasses from me, and another one said, "We know what you were doing last night," and then another said, "I saw you masturbating off the porch," and all kinds of weird things like that. These remarks were meant to provoke me, of course. I would never have risked being seen masturbating off the porch or anywhere else! I couldn't figure out what was going on, but I gathered from their comments to each other that they were trying to freak me out. They didn't really succeed, and I didn't know what any of it had to do with meditation anyway. Rinpoche didn't continue this style of meeting after the summer.

LOOKING TO FALL IN LOVE

Toward the middle of the summer, a family turned up: Sue, her husband, and their two children. Sue was a strange character—and quite attractive, with short brown hair and a slim, shapely figure. She had a sadness and loneliness about her, and perhaps this was her attraction for me. She had also been in the Gurdjieff group and had trained more than I had in the "Movements," which was also a source of friendship between us. The hippie sex scene in America at that time felt very foreign to me. People would pair up almost randomly, it seemed, at parties and whenever they got a chance. I wasn't interested in one-night stands but was always looking for something deeper, seeking to "fall in love." Something in Sue made me believe I could find it with her, even though she was married. I became infatuated with her, and we started a relationship. She stayed on at TOTT with the children when her husband returned to Boulder.

I knew that Rinpoche was not happy about my being with Sue. It was clear to most people that she was highly neurotic—even more so than most of us. One evening, soon after the meeting at which they had tried to freak me out, Rinpoche asked Sue to sleep with him. I went crazy with jealousy and anger. I was writing an article at the time, so I stayed up typing and listening, trying to hear what was going on in Rinpoche's room directly above. I felt quite wild but I finally managed to go to sleep. The next day I met Rinpoche in the corridor, and he said, "How are you?" I burst out, "If you sleep with her again, I'll really freak out!" Perhaps he was already making an effort to pry Sue loose from me. He didn't sleep with her again.

RINPOCHE'S RELATIONSHIPS WITH WOMEN

It was already very obvious to me by this time that Rinpoche was sleeping with many of his women students. Indeed he made no secret of it—nor did they. Just as with his drinking, though I was at first surprised and perhaps a little shocked when I discovered this it did not in any way detract from my seeing him as the genuine teacher that I so longed for—a teacher of genuineness. So it was not this that had freaked me out in his sleeping with Sue. Rather, I think, it was the feeling that, as he so often said, he was going to leave no little secret areas of our lives, where we could run away and hide from being open and genuine ourselves.

In the "Make Love Not War" atmosphere of the times, sleeping with multiple partners was taken for granted, especially among the hippie culture from which most of Rinpoche's students came. In meeting this culture free from pretense of any kind, Rinpoche had no intention of fulfilling people's fantasies of what a holy man should look like and how such an imaginary person should behave. Rather, he had the compassion to meet everyone fully and directly, on their own ground, and in this way was able to show that we can raise ourselves up, from right where we are, to become genuine and dignified human beings. Rinpoche was completely open about sleeping with some of his woman students—either at his invitation, or at their request. While difficult to understand from a conventional point of view, the openness of it was very important in creating an atmosphere of trust. Diana, his wife, once remarked that Rinpoche was the only person she had ever met who was completely the same in private as in public.

While he was very obviously a highly passionate young man, it seemed clear to me even at that early stage that mere self-centered passion was not the motivation for his sexual involvement with women. Rinpoche seemed to love all of his students so powerfully that his love was in some ways the hardest thing to open to for many of us, almost too much to bear. A friend told me that once, after he had been away for a while, he went into a room where Rinpoche was sitting with a few friends. My friend went up to give him a hug. "I felt so much warmth and love from Rinpoche," he told me, "that I felt a physical shock and found myself closing off and pulling back. I just couldn't stand to be loved so much."

In a TV program made after Rinpoche's death, James George commented, "Rinpoche was a man overflowing with abundant life, and abundant love." And, for those of his fortunate female students who wished it, his love could manifest in the most intimate physical manner. Those who did take up his invitation almost always remembered these times as some of the most precious of their years with Rinpoche. They were felt as times of profound teaching—though rarely was there any formal dharma discussion between them—as well as times of lightness, freedom from care, and playful humor. At the same time, of course, anyone in any similarly intimate situation with Rinpoche was pushed to the edge of their little ego games, pushed to be open and genuine; and, for many of us in the West, sex provides one of the deepest entrenchments for ego.

Altogether, Rinpoche's open and joyful attitude to sex was a powerful opportunity to work with one's own preconceptions and projections about sexuality, especially for those he slept with and their partners. In the modern culture in which people in positions of power, especially religious personages, frequently confuse their own personalities with the charisma of their office, thus leading to all manner of sexual abuses, this may all seem difficult to understand or accept. However, for those who were there, Rinpoche's relationships to women seemed altogether contrary to this, based as they were on kindness, openness, and mutual respect. Thus it seemed to me at the time, and still does to this day, that his openness and delight in taking sexual consorts was another expression of his tireless and relentless manifestation of genuine dharma, genuine love. It was also an expression of his willingness to completely give up all privacy for the sake of genuineness. I should mention here that, although in English the term "consort" is usually reserved for a marriage partner (for example, Prince Consort), the term is used in vajrayana Buddhism to refer to special sexual partners whose relationship is based primarily on inner spiritual practice. Hence, Rinpoche's sexual partners were usually referred to as consorts, and this is how I will refer to them throughout the book.

I want to emphasize at this point that, from the beginning, Rinpoche included women and men equally at every level of the organization: men and women equally became teachers, meditation instructors, senior administrators and directors of major meditation centers. The only exception to this overall equal treatment was when a new all-male Board of Directors was selected in 1977 to lead the rapidly growing organization. As we shall see, this led to a quite serious imbalance of energy, which Rinpoche then made efforts to correct.

Rinpoche always taught and demonstrated that women and men were without doubt equal in their capability to understand the dharma and their potential to attain enlightenment. And all the great Tibetan teachers who visit the West also teach the equality of men and women. Nevertheless, the culture of Tibet in which Rinpoche grew up was highly male-dominated. There were a few nunneries, but the full ordination for nuns had been lost in Tibet and nuns were definitely treated as second-class. Rinpoche grew up surrounded by male tutors, servants, and companions. Thus it is another mark of his remarkable understanding and transformation that he was able so readily to include women at all levels in his world.

SHOULD I TAKE REFUGE?

During the summer, I heard that there was going to be a refuge ceremony for a few of the staff, at their request. The refuge ceremony[24] is the
first stage of entering the Buddhist path, in which one actually declares
oneself to be a follower of the Buddha. At that time I barely knew what
refuge was, but I wanted to do it too—I didn't want to be left out. The
day before this ceremony was supposed to happen, I was Rinpoche's
driver. As we drove from his house in West Barnet to TOTT, I asked,
"Rinpoche, I hear there's going to be a refuge ceremony. I don't really
know what that is, and I'm not sure whether I should do it or not. What
do you think?" Of course, I was hoping and expecting that he would
say, "Oh, yes, you should do it." Instead of that, he immediately
replied, "Better wait." The message, I understood, was that if I didn't
even know what refuge was, I had better wait until I knew and could
decide for myself.

When Rinpoche returned to TOTT later in the fall, he offered
another refuge ceremony. By now I had some understanding of the
ceremony in which we make the commitment to develop in ourselves
the wisdom and compassion of the awakened state of mind, first manifested by the Buddha himself. The path to wakefulness, which was
taught by the Buddha and subsequent generations of teachers up to
the present time, is the Dharma. And the Sangha, or community, is the
group of people who study and practice the dharma. The Sangha is
there as a mirror and, while we all have to take the journey alone, to
offer support and sustenance when we falter. In that sense, it has
always felt to me like my true family. Outwardly, then, we are taking
refuge in the Buddha, the Dharma, and the Sangha, having realized
that no refuge is to be found in our ordinary world pursuits—our
schools or clubs, philosophies or politics persuasions, families,
friends, or wealth. Inwardly, however, we are taking refuge in our
own basic nature as Buddha, in the inherent genuineness of the world
beyond concept as Dharma, and in the basic goodness and wisdom
of others as Sangha.

THE END-OF-SUMMER PARTY. JEREMY SCRUTINIZES RINPOCHE FROM BEHIND.

In this ceremony each of us was given a new name, as is traditional. In the refuge ceremony, our name is supposed to represent a quality that we can use on our own path. The name Rinpoche gave me was Lodro Rangdrol, Self-Liberated Intellect. Here, intellect refers not just to conceptual discursiveness but to the analytical aspect of mind capable of penetrating deeply into the meaning of an idea or experience and of contemplating that meaning. In retrospect the notion that the intellect, through deep penetrative analysis of its own nature, could become liberated from ego-centeredness seems to have been a key aspect to my personal journey.

DO I WANT TO STAY WITH THIS MAN?

The summer of 1971 ended with a party on the day before Rinpoche's departure. This time it was at his house in West Barnet, and it was a wild scene, as always. People were playing guitars, drinking, dancing, and shouting, and Rinpoche was sitting in a rather deep, big armchair with a very pregnant woman on his lap.

Toward the end of the evening, there was suddenly a commotion around Rinpoche and everything stopped. Someone had asked him if he could turn water into wine, to which he had replied, "Bring me a bucket of water!" He was still half lying in the armchair, alone now. He had the bucket beside the armchair on his right side, which was his good side, and he was vigorously stirring the water around in the bucket. Then he handed out glasses of water to people and ordered them to drink the water in one gulp. Of course, if you try to drink a whole glass of water in one gulp, you become slightly hyperventilated and can feel a bit intoxicated. I heard him say, "Give some to Jeremy," so I drank the glass of water I was given and, indeed, felt a little high. Suddenly he screamed, "Fuck off! Do you think I'm Jesus Christ? Get out of here!" He was in a rage. The person who had asked him about turning water into wine went up to him and tried to apologize, but Rinpoche punched him so hard in the chest that he went flying across the room. We all slunk away, our tails between our legs.

This was another turning point for me, because it was the first time I had seen Rinpoche angry in that way. The scene was shocking in its power and in the force of his anger. Clearly, he was angry at our spiritual materialism, treating him like some sort of savior; he was angry at the amazing stupidity of it. Hadn't we got it yet? After a whole summer of teachings about being ordinary and sane, we were still asking him stupid questions like that. As I drove back to TOTT, I was in a state of complete shock but very awake, and I asked myself, "Do I want to be with this man? Do I want to be in this scene?"

I did, of course, wonder at his seeming anger. Although it was familiar from the stories of Gurdjieff, it did not fit with the popular images and fantasies of gurus and other spiritual people. Yet something felt refreshing and sane in the whole event; what Rinpoche had said and done, even his wrath, struck home as simple truth. Later we were to see this wrath again and again, but I also learned that wrath can indeed be an expression not of anger but of love and compassion, penetrating the thick walls of ego as ordinary kindness often cannot. As the well-known Buddhist teacher, Tulku Thondup Rinpoche, writes,

> *Buddhas sometimes appear in the forms, sounds and actions of wrathful manifestations and expressions. These wrathful manifestations and actions come neither out of anger, attachment, and grasping at self, nor in order to harm or cause suffering to anyone. They come out of love and compassion, and they are powerful manifestations that destroy and eliminate the negative forces, the very sources of suffering.*[25]

In the midst of the wildness around him, I had seen that Rinpoche could relate to people with penetrating directness, as well as humor and kindness; he did not seem to be caught up in it all. I was captured by the intelligence, genuineness, and warmth of what was happening, and I longed even more to know that mind. So the answer to my question, as I drove back to TOTT, was a definite "Yes."

THE TRIPLESS TRIP

At the end of the summer, Rinpoche went down to New York to conduct a seminar and he asked Sue to go along in his party. She asked if I could go too, but he replied, "I think you two need some space." After the New York trip, at Rinpoche's suggestion, Sue returned to Boulder.

By the fall of 1971, TOTT was a close, intimate, and varied community. Fran Lewis and Kesang Leontov, two of the people who had originally established TOTT, were still in charge, but there was now also an executive committee including another half-dozen or so of the longer-term staff members, of whom I was one. There were a total of about twenty staff over the winter of '71–72. There were two periods of meditation a day—before breakfast and at the end of the afternoon, after work—but these were not compulsory and few people went to all of them. After breakfast we would start with the work meeting, where we would sign up for "house jobs," or *rota*—cleaning toilets, doing the dishes, splitting and gathering wood—and whatever other work needed to be done. The rest of the day would be spent at work. This tradition of work meeting and rota continues in all Shambhala practice centers still, where such work is regarded as an important part of meditation in action.

This was my first experience of living together with a group in such intimate circumstances. We shared the one main bathroom. Sometimes there could be three people in there, men and women mixed—one taking a shit, another a shower, and a third brushing his or her teeth. We worked together and practiced together. We ate together and competed for the front of the food line. I had a real scuffle once over who was head of the food line, with the same red-haired young man that I had sat next to at Rinpoche's first talk in Boston's East-West Center, whom I knew by then as Hector McClean—we still laugh about it when we meet. All this happening in one small farmhouse! In the evenings we would all crowd into a small room at the front of the house, the sewing room, which was the only warm room in the house. We all smoked like chimneys. There was a lot of passion, a lot of anger, and plenty of humor to keep us going. It was our attraction to the truth that Rinpoche showed us, and to his own manifestation of this truth, that kept us there and bound us together, and we really just lived from one visit of Rinpoche to the next.

For myself, it could sometimes be terribly lonely and bleak. I so clearly recall standing near a little bridge over the river, at the bottom of the hill. As I loaded wood onto the flat-bed of our old tractor, I looked up the hill, completely white with snow, at the bare black outline of an oak-tree, and felt so bleak, thinking, "Why oh why am I here?" Yet I never once contemplated leaving. And there were many times of warmth and camaraderie. At last, I felt that I had a society of friends who shared a similar view and purpose in their life. The warmth and humor of this group helped me, in that first year, to begin to overcome my shyness and self-hatred. And there was the sitting practice, which I usually joined at least once a day. In sitting and simply being with whatever comes up I, like everyone, went through the whole range of thoughts, emotions, and fantasies. A lot of the time I was wound up tight, depressed, or angrily critical of myself and everyone around me, but there were those occasional moments of relaxation and peace that encouraged me to go on. Overall, I deeply valued the opportunity to sit.

One day a number of us were sitting in the office, where I was working on the financial books, and we got into a discussion about how we had all come to be at TOTT. We were all in various ways drop-outs from conventional society and I said, in a derogatory tone, "I think we are all creeps. The reason we are here is just because we can't make it in ordinary society." Some of the others were furious and told me to ask Rinpoche about my "creep" theory. On Rinpoche's next visit, I told him about our discussion and my theory that we are all basically "creeps" who simply can't make it in conventional society. "Yes?" he replied, looking at me with an amused, quizzical look as if to say, "And so what?"

The quality of intelligent cynicism and a humorous disdain for the stifling culture of our parents was what had brought us all to the path. Rinpoche made use of these qualities of humor and cynicism in his efforts to help us to see and cut through our "trips," our conceptual games, whether philosophical, sociological, or religious. Most of all he turned our cynicism and humor into a sharp blade to cut through spiritual materialism. This blade of cynicism—being unwilling to accept any trips at all, our own or others—Rinpoche called "the tripless trip." It was the entry point into the understanding of the view which goes beyond all concept, the view of emptiness.

CYNICISM AND WARMTH

It may seem strange that Rinpoche would encourage his students to be cynical. The usual way this word is often used now is defined by Webster's: " a faultfinding captious critic, especially one who believes that human conduct is motivated wholly by self-interest, and having a sneering disbelief in sincerity or integrity."

This certainly characterizes the attitudes of today's world. But why would we be encouraged to be "cynical" by a person who asserted over and over again the basic goodness of all humans, who believed it is possible to have an enlightened society on this earth, and who himself showed the greatest kindness and concern for all who crossed his path? True, Rinpoche had a sharp sense of humor that often cut through the petty uptightness and self-importance of all of us. And he used to find fault with our petty narrow-mindedness, but he was certainly not a "cynic" in the sense of denying or sneering at human goodness.

Rinpoche left many clues to be followed and gems to be found hidden within his extraordinary use of words. Many times I would hear him use a familiar English word in a strange-sounding way and wonder where he got that particular meaning. I would sometimes go to the Oxford English Dictionary, which he loved, and find to my astonishment that he was using the word in exactly the way it was meant in earlier times, sometimes going as far back as its original Latin or Greek meaning. It is also astonishing, if you do take the trouble to study the history of words, how many have completely reversed their meaning in recent generations.

As an example of this, we can find out through the O.E.D. what Rinpoche intended in emphasizing the need for "positive cynicism" in a much earlier meaning of the word, that of the ancient Greek Cynics. The Cynics were followers of Diogenes, who made it his mission to expose the falsity of most conventional standards and beliefs and to call people back to a simple, natural life. For Diogenes the simple life meant not only disregard for luxury, but also disregard of conventional laws and customs when they encouraged dishonesty and ungenuineness. From this we can begin to understand that Rinpoche encouraged his students to be "cynical," not in the modern, degraded sense of the word, but in the older sense. It was a matter of not getting caught in conventional thinking and habitual behavior—not building cozy nests for ourselves whether in material luxuries, psychological systems, or spiritual trips, including not making a nest out of Buddhism or out of our connection with him.

A year later, Rinpoche added another element when he spoke on "Cynicism and Devotion," at a seminar on Padmasambhava entitled "Crazy Wisdom."[26] In this talk he proclaimed,

> it may be time to change gears, so to speak.... Having developed accurate and vajralike [diamond-like] cynicism, we could begin to realize what spirituality is. And we find that spirituality is completely ordinary.... To relate with this, we might have to change our pattern. The next step is to develop devotion and faith."

And he concludes,

> "Our seminar here happened purely by accident.... It is a very precious accident that we are able to discuss such a topic as the life of Padmasambhava. The opportunity to discuss such a topic is very rare, unique, very precious.... So the journey goes on, the accident goes on—which is that we are here.... This is the kind of romanticism, the kind of warmth I am talking about. It is worthwhile approaching the teaching in this way.

Rinpoche was to continue this theme of the importance of warmth and devotion, along with the cynicism that cuts through spiritual materialism, as he introduced the practices of vajrayana over the subsequent years. More and more, his own tremendous warmth, patience, and love toward all of us set an example, and we in turn were more and more able to begin to develop genuine devotion toward him and toward enlightened mind. Without this warmth for each other and devotion to the teacher and the teachings, he said, we would never understand the vajrayana. Vajrayana is a steep and dangerous path, as we will see later, and the bravery to jump in and continue on this path comes from trust in and love for the teacher and teachings, as well as the grounding in intelligently knowing our own mind and caring for others.[27]

1972: Gaining Confidence in Sitting Practice

4

 N THE WINTER OF 1972, we worked on a second issue of the journal *GARUDA: Tibetan Buddhism in America,* a journal devoted to the writings of Trungpa Rinpoche and also containing a few other articles. The first edition of *GARUDA* had been published in the fall of 1970, and it was to continue for seven more years until the publication of the *Vajradhatu Sun* replaced it. I was asked to be the editor of this issue, along with another very proper Englishman, David Eaton-Smith.

The theme of this issue was to be "Working with Negativity."[28] The central article by Rinpoche explains that negative emotions such as anger, passion, jealousy, and so on are not necessarily negative in themselves, but are simply pure energy which can be felt and manifested as negative or positive, depending on whether or not they are grasped on to and manipulated for ego's gain. Rinpoche throws light on one way in which ego subtly manages this grasping and manipulation, through a process he calls "negative negativity." This refers to a second layer of negativity on top of the basic energy, which can manifest as a judgmental attitude of self-righteousness: "I'm right to be angry in this way;" or self-blame: "I am really bad for feeling like this." It is this "negative negativity" that causes problems, not the basic energy itself. He had spoken in a similar way about this basic energy of communication in the "Work, Sex, and Money" seminar a year before, and those talks were included in this issue of GARUDA.

Rinpoche spoke a great deal, even in these early years, about the vajrayana principle of "working with emotions." By this he meant neither trying to suppress or deny the basic negativity, nor merely acting it out, but trying to see its very nature and thereby allowing the energy of the emotion to move from ego-centered clinging or aggression into a more open and communicative process. Rather than escaping the negativity and thereby losing the energy in a dull and temporary peacefulness, the idea is to transform its negative, ego-aspect into wisdom beyond ego.

Rinpoche had no interest whatsoever in his students developing the hushed voices and coy smiles of people pretending to be spiritual, imitating their idea of how monks or nuns or other holy people should behave. He encouraged only directness and fearlessness in our communications with each other. In his view, the role of the teacher was to blow up the pimples of his student's egos until they finally popped. He couldn't necessarily do this personally with every one of his students, but he would create the environment for this to happen. And such an environment it was! It was as if he created a hall of many mirrors in which we could see ourselves, with all our negativities and brilliance, in whatever direction we looked.

All of our passions, jealousies, doubts, competitiveness, speed, and laziness seemed to come forth in abundance around Rinpoche, and he seemed to delight in it all. He would say, "I eat my students' shit." Once when we had stopped off at a diner near TOTT for dinner, while waiting for our table we sat in a bay window with large heavy curtains and thick curtain cords hanging down. He grabbed one of the cords and with wild eyes started growling and chewing on it. He took it out of his mouth and, with a huge grin, said, "I eat anything!"

The essential point, always, was a sense of humor, which he emphasized over and over again not only in words but in his own irrepressible humor. Sense of humor was the secret key that opened the door to understanding so much of Rinpoche's life and teachings. Rinpoche had spoken beautifully about sense of humor at the Battle of Ego seminar. Humor, he said, is the way to conquer the ministers—which symbolize the solemn and self-serious concept-forming aspect of ego, the fourth skandha. He said that the word translated as "humor" is the same word as "joy" in traditional Buddhist texts, and he described it as the natural sense of irony that arises spontaneously when one sees a situation from a broader perspective. He contrasted this with the kind of humor which consists in laughing at others or continually cracking jokes.

One illustration of the place of humor in popping negativity was a small incident I experienced at TOTT. Life was, and still is, very intense for the staff of a practice center—trying to work to support the center at the same time as working on oneself through meditation practice and meditation in action. On this particular occasion, Carl Springer and I got into an argument about people leaving their dirty boots in the entrance to the dining room. We both started to heat up, until our faces were just inches apart, and we were looking each other directly in the eyes and yelling at the top of our voices. Suddenly, we both stopped, there was a moment of silence, and we both simultaneously bent double in peals of laughter. The transformation of anger through humor had produced a tremendous sense of clarity, such that I remember the details even now: Carl's face as I yelled at him, my body posture, and so on, as well as that moment of sudden openness that brought the humor.

EMPTINESS—WITHIN AND WITHOUT

Rinpoche's spring visit to TOTT was in March–April of that year, and the seminar topic was *shunyata,* emptiness.[29] This time of year in Vermont is still like mid-winter and, not surprisingly, it is said to be the highest period of the year for suicides. This year the weather was typically bleak. The snow was practically waist deep, and it seemed there was only snow, grey skies, and dark trees—very still and cold. The seminar was held in Barnet Town Hall, which was poorly heated by a huge and very noisy blow heater in the ceiling. People wrapped up in blankets and flopped around on the floor on whatever rugs or cushions they could find.

Every seminar that Rinpoche gave had a different quality. In some ways, the teachings were conveyed in the quality—the atmosphere—of the program as much as in the words themselves. The seminar on shunyata remains in my memory for its particular quality, not of emptiness itself no doubt, but perhaps a pale reflection of it. There was a feeling in this seminar of flatness, of emptiness in a slightly nihilistic sense—just nothing happening—reflected in the season and the weather.

Rinpoche began the first talk by saying, "Shunyata is…," followed by a long silence. He simply let our minds rest in that state of openness, not knowing what was coming next, not knowing what to think. It was a moment of experience beyond concept. Then, "That's it." He continued, "It seems that shunyata means not *that*, not *this*. So we shouldn't have a discussion at all. If it's not that, not this—what else? We could sit around and scrounge up something to discuss, but it seems insignificant. Totally irrelevant. The expectation to hear about shunyata is an obstacle, the shunyata principle does not lie in expectation." There was a whole new feeling, a new quality, to the way he was conveying the teachings to us.

This sense of bleakness, an almost nihilistic feeling, is often the first impression people have on hearing about shunyata. It has given rise to many misunderstandings in the transition of Buddhism to the West, especially that *shunyata* actually *is* intended nihilistically to mean a blank void in which absolutely nothing exists. As the teaching progressed, we would learn to understand shunyata in a deeper way—that, just as well as complete emptiness, it can mean complete fullness without boundaries, complete openness. And meanwhile Rinpoche's personal radiation of joy and life was itself adequate demonstration that there was more to this teaching than mere nihilistic void.

NARAYANA

During this time, a group from the nearby village of Kirby was much in evidence. By the time I had moved to TOTT in June of the previous year, this group—Narayana (Tom) and Lila Rich, Krishna (Ken) and Helen Green, and another couple—had also moved to the area, and were running an organic bakery there. There was already a buzz of excitement, because Narayana and Krishna had originally been close students of the well-known yoga teacher Satchitananda and were former leaders of his Integral Yoga Institute in Los Angeles. A surprising number of Rinpoche's students came from either Satchitananda's yoga groups, or the Gurdjieff work—opposite ends of the spectrum of offerings in the spiritual supermarket.

Rinpoche seemed to be paying particular attention to Narayana. Narayana would come into Rinpoche's bedroom, jauntily smiling as always, and if he was wearing a new tie Rinpoche would *ooh* and *ah* over it and adjust it for him. There was obviously already a very strong relationship between them. At the end of the visit, when we were expecting Rinpoche to have dinner with the community and spend the final evening with us at TOTT, he was invited over to Kirby and went there instead. Anger and jealousy popped up their little heads once again: "How malicious of them to invite him, and how unfair of him to go," these *kleshas*, these negative emotions, screamed.

These feelings were shared by all of Rinpoche's students in one way or another. What was it we longed for? There was such a sense of brilliance, warmth, and life around Rinpoche, and this in turn woke up our own feelings of being alive and well and having something worthwhile to live for. We all wanted to be part of this brave new world, not to be left out of any smallest moment of it. He saw the potential brilliance and intelligence in each of his students and demanded everything from them, more than they even knew they had—and all of this could be quite addictive. In these early years he was drawing a group around him to work with him, so he did little at this point to deter our enthusiasm for being as close to him as we could get, even elbowing others out of the way if necessary.

Rumors began to circulate that Narayana was to be "the number one student." Naturally, this gave rise to another feast of jealousy. Much later, we discovered that this was, in fact, the time when Rinpoche had asked Narayana if he would be his regent—his lineage holder, or successor—and Narayana had said yes. This was all kept quite secret, and it wasn't until four years later that anything much more was said about it.

Choosing one successor was very important to Rinpoche. In 1971 someone had asked him about Gurdjieff, and he had slapped his thigh in a very cheerful and jovial manner and said, "Gurdjieff is a very great man." He continued, "The only problem with him is that he didn't leave one successor." Whether or not this was strictly accurate, such remarks became a cause of paranoia in the community—because if there was only to be one successor, then who would it be and what would happen to the rest of us? These were childish and silly ideas, of course—feeling that we had to be *the* one, or rather *I* had to be the one. At the same time it provided us with such a clear mirror for our own feelings of specialness and one-up-manship.

In July of 1972, Narayana and Lila moved into TOTT with their baby son, their house in Kirby having disbanded. Narayana was an utterly charming person, full of humor, which was one of his truly outstanding qualities. He had a sense of openness and generosity, as well as tremendous lightness and humor. He could turn everything into an opportunity for laughter. I began to notice that he wasn't actually doing anything around the house. He didn't volunteer for house jobs or do anything very much except occasionally cooking or working on a small garden in front of the house. At one point, I commented to him about not joining in the work of the house, and he just laughed. That was about it—he wasn't embarrassed at all. Because of his tremendously attractive joyful manner, there would always be a group around him and he was already showing himself to be a leader.

Later that year and in the following spring, Rinpoche asked Narayana and me to go together to teach two of the groups in Canada in response to requests from the organizers for someone to visit. I saw then just how good a teacher Narayana was, and how he was able to magnetize people to the dharma. He seemed in some way to be beyond the rest of us in his understanding of the dharma and his ability to communicate it, and it was not surprising that he seemed to be very important to Rinpoche.

A REFRESHING INTERLUDE IN NEW YORK

I conceived the idea of going out to Boulder after Rinpoche's spring visit. It was partly because I wanted to see what was going on and spend time with him in Boulder, but it was also to see Sue. We had been writing all through the winter, and of course everyone at TOTT was aware of my obsession with her. On my way out to Boulder, I stopped off in New York because Rinpoche was visiting there. He was staying in a large, plush apartment owned by an art entrepreneur, and I stayed on the couch in the living room. When I arrived at the apartment, I was surprised when Rinpoche opened the door himself. He looked delighted to see me and said, "Oh, what are you doing here?" I replied, "I'm coming out to Boulder to visit with you." When he asked me who I was staying with in Boulder and I told him it was Sue, his face dropped. Once again, he was gently showing me that being with Sue was not advisable, but I wasn't ready to give up yet!

The time together in New York was quite delightful, and among other things we continued to work on *GARUDA*. Most of the articles were now completed, but David and I were still working together to fine-tune some of them. One afternoon, I was sitting at Rinpoche's feet going over an article which David and I had been arguing about the day before. I told Rinpoche that David and I disagreed on how to use pronouns in this article; we couldn't decide whether we should use "you" or "one," that is, whether we should write *you* do this and *you* do that, and so on, or *one* does this and *one* does that. I looked up at Rinpoche and said, "David prefers 'one,' but I like '*you.*'" "I know you do," he responded with a smile. Such warmth and closeness encouraged me to blossom beyond my shyness toward him and to trust that my love for him shone through even though I was not able to express it directly.

I accompanied Rinpoche down on the elevator one afternoon. I was supporting him, as usual, and as we walked out of the building through the front entrance he gripped my arm and said, "Jeremy Hayward, your parents must have been 200 percent!" I didn't know what he meant exactly, but I felt as if it must be a good thing. Perhaps he was suggesting that my parents must have had some kind of certainty about who they were, and that they had given me a definite, strong sense of uprightness and strength. Or maybe he was suggesting that they had huge egos, and I likewise. One never knew how to interpret such remarks...

SELF-DECEPTION AT
ROCKY MOUNTAIN DHARMA CENTER

Following that weekend in New York, I flew out to Boulder. One of the main events of my visit was a trip to Rocky Mountain Dharma Center, as it was called then. Fran, who was also visiting Boulder, called me at Sue's house and told me that a group was going to spend a few days with Rinpoche up at RMDC. RMDC (now renamed Shambhala Mountain Center) was a large, wild piece of land, purchased the year before by the group in Boulder. It was up in the Rocky Mountains about two hours' drive from Boulder. Fran said that Rinpoche had invited me to go along with him in his car, and added, "And Rinpoche says, don't bring Sue." Rinpoche was going to give a short seminar for the people living on the land, as well as those who came up from Boulder.

There were not many buildings at RMDC. The entire traveling party, including Rinpoche, stayed in one small A-frame cabin. One day, I was outside of the cabin trying to build a fire to warm us up and to boil some water on. There was a big pile of funny-shaped tree branches that had apparently been gathered the day before, so I piled them up

and made a good fire. When it was quite thoroughly blazing, someone came out of the cabin and said, "What are you doing, burning that
wood?" I told him I was just lighting a fire, to warm up. He said, "But
that was the wood Rinpoche collected for *ikebana!*" Rinpoche had studied the Sogetsu style of ikebana (also called *kado*—the Japanese contemplative art of placing flowers and branches) in England, under
Stella Coe, reaching the level of master of this school of ikebana. I was
completely mortified, and when Rinpoche came out with a grin on his
face, I said, "I'm so sorry, Rinpoche. I burned the wood you collected."
It didn't seem to matter to him at all, and he just said something like,
"Oh, that's fine." One had the feeling that it really *was* fine—that he
had let it go, on the spot. A simple lesson in letting go, yes, but letting
go is so easy to say and hard to do.

The seminar that he gave for the staff at RMDC was on self-
deception. At that time, the students living at RMDC were smoking
huge amounts of marijuana, and they even had a business that
included making and selling hash pipes. The previous December,
Rinpoche had written a letter to the staff of RMDC referring to
reports of their smoking grass, saying, "Needless to say, repetitious
display of self-indulgency toward self-deception is regarded as
extremely dangerous. There will be little chance of individuals taking
part in the wisdom of the lineage if such self-deception continues." At
this seminar, Rinpoche's basic message to the staff, and everyone else
attending from Boulder, reiterated that sentiment and emphasized
the necessity of practicing sitting meditation.

Rinpoche spoke from personal experience of psychotropics. In these
early years he experimented with many of the drugs his students had
used, particularly marijuana and LSD. He seemed to feel that marijuana had no positive qualities at all, at least on the path of meditation,
merely increasing one's confusion. He said that he found LSD interesting, not as a way to genuine spiritual experience, but as a way to
encounter "super-samsara," in other words to exaggerate our normal
minds so much that we could see their insanity as vividly as in a mirror. I did not take LSD with him (or without him) but I was told by

everyone that did so that he did not change in the slightest during these trips.

The themes of the seminar were ego—how we deceive ourselves and what it means to go beyond ego—and hopelessness, not expecting to get anything out of meditation. Meditation is not exciting, but boring and flat, Rinpoche insisted. I looked at him with a puzzled expression on my face, and asked, "Rinpoche, but what if you actually *like* sitting?" That had been my experience of sitting at TOTT: yes, sometimes it was incredibly painful, with the unruly mind filled with anger, resentment, jealousy, and endless talking, talking, talking. But at other times it felt so genuine to simply sit there and feel the space, feel the resting. I liked meditation and was beginning to discover that natural sense of peace and to long for it.

He looked at me with a smile and said, "That's okay." I experienced this as a personal exchange between us, because most of the talk had been about not expecting to enjoy meditation or to get anything out of it, and so on. It was again an encouragement to keep going with the practice. He rarely told anyone directly, "You must practice." But in simple exchanges such as this, he would show that he really did intend it for us, however boring and difficult it might be at first (and perhaps forever!).

ASPIRING TO ENTER THE BODHISATTVA PATH

I attended the first Bodhisattva vow ceremony that Rinpoche conducted in North America during my visit to Boulder. Unlike the refuge vow, which is primarily a commitment to work with one's own state of mind, the Bodhisattva vow is a commitment to work for the sake of others.[30] As Rinpoche would say, first one must clean up one's own mess, then one can help others. And, as the Dalai Lama succinctly put it, "First try not to harm others, then perhaps you can help them." In taking this vow, needless to say, we become aspiring Bodhisattvas rather than fully developed ones.

We were each given a name at the end of this ceremony, just as in the refuge ceremony. In this case the name is said to represent the quality in us by which we can help others, whereas our refuge name represents the quality we can use to help ourselves along our path. The name Rinpoche gave me was Shi-Ö, short for Shiwa Ösel, or "Peaceful Radiation." I did not make very much of this name at the time but only years later when the seeds that Rinpoche was planting in those early years were beginning to come to fruition. Then, I came to realize that, in combination with my refuge name, "Self-Liberated Intellect," the two provided a key for me to understand "what is left?," the question I had asked back at that first encounter. The word Ösel, which Rinpoche translated as "radiation" also means "luminosity." Could it be that by using the analytical/contemplative intellect to go beyond ego, with a lot of hard work and a little bit of luck, it might be possible to discover and radiate to others that peaceful luminosity, joy?

During this visit to Boulder, I was invited to attend another meditation instructor meeting—as a participant instead of a guinea pig this time. There were about six or eight people in the group, and Rinpoche was beginning to move more in the direction of actual training in meditation. He insisted even at this early stage that we should learn to introduce others to meditation, a small step toward the Bodhisattva aspiration of helping others. We sat at a round table and Rinpoche talked about *mahavipashyana*, completely opening our awareness to the space around and within us without relying on any technique, even mindfulness of breathing. He then asked us all, in turn, to practice mindfulness-awareness meditation. After each of us had done one or two minutes of meditation, he would make some comment on our practice. When it was my turn I very carefully and seriously tried to follow the breath as I had been instructed, and they all laughed when I finished. Rinpoche chuckled warmly, "Very loyal." I supposed this to be a comment on my trying to do the practice "right," perhaps rather schoolboyishly, while others were relaxing more into the sense of space that he had talked about.

After some more discussion, he said, "The mind does not need to make the journey out." That is, mind could simply rest in its own nature as openness without projecting out onto the world. He slowly turned around, looked at a picture on the wall, and quietly said, "What's that!" Everybody turned and looked, and for a moment there was just complete, open mind. He said, "That's it." For that brief instant, our minds and the space around were not separate. It was a profound meeting of the minds of teacher and students.

Toward the end of my visit to Boulder, a few of us went up to Wyoming with Rinpoche to visit a large ski lodge in Teton Village near Jackson Hole. It was owned by a student who was planning to donate it to the community. We all stayed in an A-frame again, but a much more luxurious one this time. We walked around and looked at the hotel, and we learned that Rinpoche was considering offering a program for advanced students there. That spring, Ken and Helen Green moved to this hotel, which Rinpoche had now named the "Snow Lion Inn," to open it up as a sangha-operated hotel although it was still owned by the student and had creditors hovering in the background.

At the end of this visit, Rinpoche left directly to go on a month long retreat with a couple of students. At this retreat, he told them that they had to understand he would only be around for twenty years. When we heard this, we just took it as another of his jokes, or an instigation to us to get on with it. No one, so far as I know, really believed him.

"IF YOU'RE GOING TO BITE A CHILI..."

When Rinpoche arrived at TOTT a little later in the summer, lo and behold, he brought Sue with him. She and I had been exchanging letters all winter, and everyone at TOTT knew of my affair with Sue. I don't know whether it was her idea or his for her to come with him, but he had apparently agreed to it and there she was, planning to stay for the summer. After a short while, she began to make comments like, "It's easy for *you* to live here, but I have to try to live with my husband and children back in Boulder," and so on. She had an interview with Rinpoche to ask him about her relationship with me. After the interview, she came back to our room and told me that he had said that sometimes men only have relationships with women so that they don't have to masturbate. In some way, he really got to the heart of the matter there. Obviously, he knew that Sue would report directly back to me, and I had the feeling that Rinpoche's message through Sue was an invitation to open to him about my sexual anxieties, and thus overcome a major blockage to opening to him completely.

However, instead of taking the opportunity he had presented, I went charging into his room and sat down, saying, "I want Sue to move to Tail of the Tiger." He gave in this time, saying, "All right, okay, but you must talk with the executive committee about it." He stood up to leave the room, and as we walked to the door he put his arm around my shoulder and said, "Oh, Jeremy, you're incorrigible." So, once again, I had resisted Rinpoche's obvious hint that I would do well to give up my relationship with Sue.

The previous summer, a relationship had started between two of the staff, which some of us were a little bit unsure about, perhaps even disapproving. The woman was at least ten years older than the man, who was barely out of his twenties. She was delightful, funny, and highly intelligent, but had a very dominating personality, so we were a bit afraid for the young man. Once, when a group of us were in the room with Rinpoche and the subject of this relationship came up, we said, "Why do you let this happen, Rinpoche? Why don't you do something about it?" He said, "Well, if you're going to bite a chili, you had better eat the whole thing." In the end, I realized that he was doing the same thing with Sue and me. He might make little efforts to separate us, but he wasn't going to tell me to stop or even suggest that we stop. He would just let me "eat the whole thing."

Sue returned to Boulder and then came back to TOTT with her furniture following. I moved an extra mattress into my bedroom, making a double bed for us. The door to my room didn't have a proper latch with a handle, but just a little spring latch that made a click when it opened and closed. Rinpoche would sometimes pop in spontaneously, which always cheered me up. One evening before Sue had moved to TOTT, Rinpoche had gone off somewhere for dinner and I had gone to

TEACHING IN THE SUMMER TENT AT TOTT.
JEREMY SEATED IN THE CENTER.

bed early. I could always hear him coming up the stairs when I was in my room. On this occasion, as I lay in bed in my T-shirt, almost asleep, I heard the click of the door opening. Rinpoche came striding into the room, pulled back the covers on my bed and just looked at me, saying, "Whatcha doin'?" I don't know quite what he expected to find, but it made me feel very naked. Then he turned around and walked out. In ways like this, he poked his nose into his students' business, always paying attention to how we were conducting ourselves.

Now Sue insisted on installing a proper latch to prevent "intruders." One night after that, I heard Rinpoche coming up the stairs and asking someone, "How is Jeremy?" He tugged at the door, and I felt sad to know that I had locked him out, at Sue's command. Now that Sue was finally with me and I finally had what I wanted, I wasn't so sure that I wanted it any more. I felt very uncomfortable in the room we now shared, which one person referred to as "the lady's boudoir," and it soon became clear that I was not going to be able to stay there any longer. Three cabins had recently been built on the hillside behind the house, and when one of these became available I was allowed to move into it. The executive committee was incredibly indulgent toward me all the way through this affair.

On one occasion later that summer, probably in response to my obvious comfort-seeking tendency, Rinpoche said, "I think you should go on an uncomfortable retreat this winter." I looked over the schedule of TOTT for that winter and found reasons why it would not be possible for me to go on retreat throughout the entire winter—even though I could easily have made time for it. When I told Rinpoche this, he simply shrugged and said, "Fine." This was not the first time, nor would it be the last, that I had outright ignored an instruction from Rinpoche.

He had said to me earlier in the summer, "I will want you to teach, and you should read Herbert Guenther's translation of the life of Naropa."[31] This is the spiritual biography of one of the forefathers of the Kagyu lineage who left a prestigious teaching post at the medieval Nalanda University to try to find the true meaning of the dharma beyond the words. Though I was surprised and pleased he would want me to teach, it was many years before I read the book he suggested. On both occasions I felt badly about not doing what he asked, but was just too lazy or not willing to give in. This stubborn ignoring of Rinpoche's instructions would become a continuing theme of my relationship with him and a source of difficulties in my administrative roles as well as much remorse in later years.

GIVING OUR FIRST MEDITATION INSTRUCTION

Shortly after his summer visit, Rinpoche went down to Boston to visit the recently formed group there. Boston was one of the first places to

have a group of students, and they had been practicing together for a
year or so. A few of us from TOTT went down with Rinpoche, who
was to teach a program on meditation at the beautiful country house
of an older sangha-member. When Rinpoche told some of us to give
meditation instruction to the new students, we were shocked. We had
hardly had any training, other than the few meetings with him, and
we really didn't know what to say to new people.

"What should we say?" we asked. "Just tell them what I told you"
was his refrain, one the likes of which we were to hear again and again:
"Just do what I do." Oh, that it could be so easy! So we gave the meditation instruction on mindfulness of breathing, as we had heard and
begun to practice it. The instruction seemed to go well, and we gained
a little confidence in our understanding and the possibility that we
might also be able to pass on a little to others. Right from this early
stage, Rinpoche was beginning to show tremendous trust in his Western students, and to encourage them to take on some responsibility.

Following this small leap forward, we decided to offer that fall a
public program, the first experiment of offering teachings at TOTT
without Rinpoche. Many people came from Boston and a few from
New York, and Carl and I gave talks. It worked pretty well, even
though it was something very new for us. I had a glass or two of wine
before my first talk. Carl came up to me afterward and said, "Wow,
that was a great talk!"

The following spring, when we were talking with Rinpoche about
who should give a fundraising talk at one of his seminars, he looked
at me with a smile and said, "I hear Jeremy gives good talks when he's
had a bit to drink." It seemed that he had antennae everywhere to
check out what we were up to. So I was assigned to give the fundraising talk. And Rinpoche helped in his usual playful way. While I was
rather solemnly explaining Tail of the Tiger's need for funds, everyone suddenly started chuckling, finally bursting out into laughter. I
couldn't help joining in the laughter too, although I didn't know what
was going on—my talk didn't seem at all funny to me. Then someone
indicated that I should look behind me. I was giving the talk sitting on

JEREMY FUNDRAISING, WITH A LITTLE BIT OF ASH ON THE HEAD.

the stage in front of Rinpoche's chair and when I turned, he was flick-
ing cigarette ash onto my already balding head.

THE FIRST DATHÜN IN THE WEST

In November of 1972, the first dathün was held. A dathün is a month-
long meditation retreat. It was a huge step for Rinpoche's students,
and this is how it came about: during the autumn, winter, and spring
seasons of 1971 and 1972, we had held one-day meditation sessions at
TOTT once a week. These *nyinthüns* (*nyin* is Tibetan for "day," and *thün*
means "session" of formal meditation) began as a response to our hearing that the Zen people sat for a whole day, or sometimes even a whole
weekend. At the time, we couldn't imagine doing that. We mentioned
it to Rinpoche and he said, "I think we should do it, and we'll call it a

nyinthün." This was very difficult for some of the more action-oriented people who rarely sat at all, but many of us really appreciated the nyinthüns.

By the time August came around we were feeling very ambitious, so we asked Rinpoche, "Do you think we could, sometime, have a full *week* of meditation?" He smiled and replied, "Well, I was thinking of a month, and we'll call it a *dathün* (*da* is Tibetan for "month"). This was generally how he worked with us. Instead of being critical, or imposing behaviors on us, he waited until we came to him with our own suggestion to sit for a week, and then he extended that to a month— much to our surprise and trepidation.

This dathün was a big experiment and was a mixture of incredible agony and great fun. We did it together as a community, taking turns cooking and doing the chores. We ate our meals in silence up in the little attic shrine room. Rinpoche himself created thirty separate schedules, one for each day, all of them completely unpredictable. We could have an hour of sitting and ten minutes of walking; or ten minutes of sitting and half an hour of walking; or three hours of sitting and twenty minutes of walking; or five minutes of sitting... We never knew what was going to come next. This utterly unpredictable schedule became a characteristic of dathüns for quite a few years afterward.

Some people would get up to go to the toilet every few minutes, while others would lie down on the floor of the shrine room during sitting periods and go to sleep. Sometimes people started to snore loudly and, in a fit of irritation, I would occasionally go so far as to hurl a cushion across the shrine room to wake them. Almost inevitably, someone would initiate a giggling fit during the afternoon. People cried a lot, as well. It was a strong experience and we got through it, proud of ourselves for sitting the very first dathün. The dathün showed us depths to the practice, as well as depths to our neurosis, that we could not have seen any other way. Now, thirty-five years later, dathüns are still held several times a year in every major Shambhala practice center, and it is almost miraculous to see the profound changes that even quite new students can go through during the month.

FORMING VAJRADHATU

In September, Rinpoche had gone on a six-month retreat in Charlemont, Massachusetts, in an old country house owned by a friend of the community. It was during this retreat that Rinpoche planned the umbrella organization under which all of the properties and activities associated with his work would be incorporated. He named this organization Vajradhatu, meaning "indestructible space" in Sanskrit. The many city meditation centers that had now been started by people wanting to follow the Buddhist path Rinpoche was laying out were also to come under the Vajradhatu umbrella and were named Dharmadhatus, meaning "spaces of dharma" in Sanskrit. The creation of the Vajradhatu organization came about partly as a result of the increasing competition and one-upmanship between the directors of Tail of the Tiger and of Karma Dzong in Boulder. (Karma Dzong—"the fortress of the Karma Kagyu"—was the name given to the Dharmadhatu of Boulder, as it was also the headquarters of Rinpoche's work in the U.S.) There was competition for Rinpoche's time, competition to be the most important center, and so on. So by creating Vajradhatu, with an overseeing Board of Directors, Rinpoche was trying to cut through that kind of competitiveness.

This was a theme throughout his life: there should be one unified situation so that there can be no schisms or seeds of divisiveness in the sangha.

1973:
Vajrayana Explodes on the Scene 5

 URING RINPOCHE's Christmas–New Year's visit to
TOTT, he had asked Fran and Kesang to leave their positions, and they both moved out to Boulder soon after
the New Year of 1973. They had been the pioneers who
got Tail of the Tiger started, and their strength, loyalty, and humor
had carried TOTT through the first three years. But now, that same
strength was becoming a burden because they weren't able to let go
and make room for others. There were a few other occasions over the
years, but just a very few, when Rinpoche actually asked people to
step down from their posts because they had taken on too much personal power. This is an obstacle often faced by the pioneer leaders of
a center who sometimes begin to behave as if the center is their personal property—the fierceness of their care is flavored with territoriality, and it becomes difficult for others to blossom. Now that Kesang
and Fran had left Tail of the Tiger, Carl Springer and I took on more
leadership responsibilities.

RINPOCHE'S PUSH-PULL GOES ON

During Rinpoche's visit that spring his casual friendliness and push-pull way of working with his students continued. I drove to pick him up at the Montreal airport. When we arrived back at TOTT, it was mid-evening and there was already a dance going on in the living room of the farmhouse. I just stood there, watching. After a while, Rinpoche came up to me and said, "You look as if you're observing the whole thing."

Like so many of us, I took remarks like this to be criticisms and my ego would be wounded. Fran told me once that she had mentioned to Rinpoche her tendency to always take his remarks as criticisms, and his response was complete astonishment that we could be so down on ourselves. Nevertheless it was a message to relax and not to watch myself so much, an old habitual pattern that had become even stronger during the Gurdjieff years of "self-observation."

After Rinpoche said this to me I completely plunged myself into the party. I danced wildly along with everyone else until the party was over. I had rarely ever done this before, and I found the experience of letting go of the self-conscious watcher, so to speak, to be an exhilarating one. The next day, while I was sitting alone with Rinpoche in his room, he commented, "I heard you danced a lot last night." I said to him, "Should I try to get more into dancing and partying?" He just screwed up his face and said, "No. No need to be frivolous." That was of course not why I had asked him and his answer surprised me. I was not sure whether he was indicating to me his general view about partying—which seemed unlikely—or that for myself in particular it would be frivolous to push myself into such things.

He went on to ask me whether I had heard about the ruckus with Narayana the previous evening and told me that he had been chasing a young man drunkenly around the parking lot. He added, "*That is frivolous. You should talk to him about it.*" Rinpoche had no prejudice regarding gay men, but I wondered whether in this case it was perhaps concern with Narayana's gay interests that he was referring to. And as we will see, it was precisely this aspect of Narayana's behavior that would bring serious health problems later. In any case, I found this a rather intimidating prospect and did not look for an opportunity to talk to Narayana as Rinpoche had asked.

During that spring visit, a delegation from the New York Dharma-dhatu came up to meet with Rinpoche and the executive committee of TOTT. At that time, the New Yorkers seemed to us to be quite difficult and demanding, with many rather strong and angry women in the group. They came to complain about not being treated properly by the staff of Tail of the Tiger. At one point, I spoke up in defense of TOTT in a way that I considered quite reasonable, but Rinpoche turned on me, saying with unexpected fierceness, "The trouble with you is, you always want something new." I couldn't see any connection between that and what I had been saying, or with anything that was going on there, for that matter, but he had caught my ego off-guard and I felt crushed. His remark was very much to the point as a more general view of my life. I was always getting tired of projects I was involved in and wanted to move on to something new, just as I had moved on from physics to biology years before. I often recalled this remark later on.

Around this time, Tail of the Tiger purchased property over the hill— about two miles away by road—consisting of a hundred or so acres and a house which was badly in need of renovation. This house would be reserved for Rinpoche to stay in, so as to give him a little more pri-vacy and distance from everyone. He named it Bhumipali Bhavan ("Dwelling Place of the Female Earth Protector") and we referred to it from then on as BPB. We decided to completely strip the house inside and to replace part of the roof.

One day as I was standing on a ladder inside the open roof, pulling off old tiles and boards and hurling them to the ground, I thought of Rinpoche, who was at that very moment off visiting auctions with Narayana. I wished I could be with them, but at the same time I was pleased to be part of creating a good place for Rinpoche.

The next day I received a postcard in the mail from him, written in his own handwriting, including the address. It had a picture of a sail-ing boat on a local Vermont lake, and the message read,

Hi
We are having good
time
Wish you were
here
Love,
Me
X

I was touched and warmed by this card, thinking of him writing it and mailing it, and I thought that perhaps he had picked up my longing to be with him with a whiff of jealousy toward Narayana. A few days later he came by to see how the renovation was coming along, and as I showed him around he commented, "Somehow, I imagined you in this house."

When Rinpoche was ready to leave Tail of the Tiger at the end of his spring visit, I stood at the door of his office as he left, feeling tremendous sadness to see him go. I felt close to him at that moment, and knew that I had begun to drop some barriers. As he passed me, he gave me a big hug and said, "Hold the fort." I felt that to be an expression of trust and a confirmation of our increasing closeness. With all the warmth and friendship that he as well as others at TOTT were showing me, I was beginning to *like* myself at last and to develop some confidence that I could function helpfully in the world. And, as these stories show, I was beginning to feel more confident in my place at TOTT and in my relationship to Rinpoche, so that during this visit, I found "hanging out" to be quite delightful and not such a problem. I was able to chat with him more, although we never had what I would call a "buddy" relationship.

The push-pull pattern of the way Rinpoche related to his students comes across so clearly in these incidents. There were the times where Rinpoche would be so cutting, so ferocious, that you would feel crushed; and then there were the other times where he would say something simple, like "Hold the fort," and fill you with warmth and

RINPOCHE AND JEREMY CHAT OVER BREAKFAST. *Photograph by Karen Roper.*

confidence—though of course one had better not get hung up on such comments. It was not a matter of artificial manipulation of people, but rather of allowing the natural situations of push and pull to become teaching opportunities. In this way we were kept off balance—expecting the unexpected. Some students felt manipulated and angry. Others were more willing to go along with the roller-coaster ride—seeing it as an opportunity to learn. Actually, all of us probably felt both ways at various times.

BUDDHISM AND SCIENCE AT THE FIRST SEMINARY

By the time Rinpoche arrived at TOTT for the summer, it was confirmed that there was to be a program that fall, in Teton Village at another inn in the same area as the Snow Lion Inn, the latter having been lost to the creditors. Rinpoche told me that he wanted me to teach about Buddhism and science at this "Seminary," and I was naturally delighted. As well as the honor of teaching at the Seminary, this would also be an opportunity for me to reconnect, for the very first time, with my science background. I had completely abandoned this part of my life, not giving science a moment's thought since moving to TOTT in 1971. So, in asking me to teach Buddhism and science, Rinpoche was basically asking me to begin to reconnect with my heritage.

Rinpoche insisted over and over again that people should go back and connect with their parents and with their roots. He sometimes even encouraged people who came to him to return to their Christian or Jewish heritage rather than become Buddhists. He frequently encouraged his students to go back to college, or to go into business. He didn't want us to think that we had to leave the world and become wandering yogis, or whatever we imagined, in order to be good Buddhists. So I bought a few physics and biology books and spent most of that summer recollecting those worlds of science, and contemplating how I would go about teaching Buddhism and science in the fall.

THE FIRST VAJRADHATU SEMINARY

This first Vajradhatu Seminary was held from October to mid-December 1973 at a hotel in the Jackson Hole ski lodge village of the Grand Tetons. The hotel restaurant, on the ground floor, opened directly onto the ski lift and a gorgeous view of the mountains. This was transformed into the shrine room, where practice sessions and Rinpoche's talks were held. We ate our meals on the floor above, where there was a cafeteria with little booths and scattered tables.

The structure of the Seminary was much the same as it remained for the rest of Rinpoche's life. It was about eleven weeks long and included three periods of study, one on each of the three *yanas*, interspersed with two-week periods of sitting and walking meditation. According to Rinpoche, this interweaving of practice and study was important although it had not happened for many generations in Tibet. There the more recent tradition had been for monks to study doctrine for as many as fifteen or twenty years and then for selected ones go to off into retreat to practice what they had studied. We had rented the entire hotel without the staff, so all of us also took part in rota—helping to cook, clean the public spaces of the hotel, and so on. This "three wheels" approach of study, practice, and work still continues in all Shambhala programs at all residential centers. The work aspect is as important as the other two, allowing the possibility to bring one's understanding into the ordinary activities of daily life.

The three *yanas*—*hinayana, mahayana,* and *vajrayana*—are the three major stages of a student's journey, according to the view of Tibetan Buddhism. Rinpoche likened these three stages to building a palace: first you need the firm foundation of knowing your own mind—the hinayana; next you can build the walls and roof to create the space of emptiness and compassion, within which you can invite others as your guests—the mahayana stage; finally you can arrange the space, placing flower arrangements and calligraphies, perhaps even gold-leafing the roof—this is the vajrayana phase, in which you deal with the energy of the space, rather than simply focusing on the space itself. Rinpoche himself stressed over and over again, at every Seminary that he led, the importance of beginning with the hinayana and developing an understanding of mahayana, before getting into vajrayana.

THE THREE YANAS

The fundamental teaching of the first stage, hinayana, is that of the four noble truths. This was the first teaching the Buddha gave after his awakening and is common to all genuine Buddhist schools throughout history. The four noble truths are as follows. First, the most deep level of the ordinary, confused human mind is marked by pain or dissatisfaction—deep anxiety and fear—traditionally referred to as "suffering" or *duhkha* in Sanskrit. Second, this pain is due to the grasping on to a belief in a "me" or "I," or ego as Rinpoche referred to it, that is permanent, unitary, and independent of its world. As we have seen already in the discussion of the five skandhas, this belief is simply an error. The third noble truth is that there can be an ending to this primordial fear. This is the complete understanding that ego does not exist, emptiness, joined with the realization of luminosity, joy. Finally, the fourth truth is that there is a way to this ending of suffering, namely the path of practice. These four truths rang like a gong for me, and have reverberated throughout subsequent years as I keep returning to a renewed understanding of the deep fear and its possible release into emptiness and joy.

At the hinayana stage, then, the student first begins to look at her own mind, to experience its wildness, and to realize the suffering that this wildness causes her. Taming the mind, beginning to see the solid belief in "me," and to feel beyond this the natural peace at the basis of mind is the first stage on the path. The primary practice in the hinayana stage is sitting meditation, the practice of mindfulness and awareness based on the breath. Out of this tamed mind, the meditator begins to feel a softness and openness to others. She begins to realize that others, too, suffer in the same way, and begins to feel that suffering in others more directly, and yearns to be able to help. This is the recognition of *bodhichitta*, "awakened heart," and the entry into the mahayana, the "great vehicle." The path of mahayana is characterized by increasing bodhichitta, and by dedication of one's life to working for others. At the same time, at least at the intellectual level, there is a developing understanding of *shunyata*, the doctrine that the true nature of all phenomena is utterly beyond concept. The practice of mindfulness and awareness continues, as well as other practices for strengthening and increasing bodhichitta.

Vajrayana practice brings practice directly into daily life, working with the energies of ego and beyond ego, as they arise. As Rinpoche writes, "When we speak of transcendence in the mahayana tradition, we mean transcendence of ego. In the Tantric tradition we do not speak of going beyond ego at all; it is too dualistic an attitude. Tantra is much more precise than that. It is not a question of 'getting *there*' or 'being *there*'; the Tantric tradition speaks of being *here*."[32] The vajrayana path involves a recognition of the energy—the luminosity and wisdom—within emptiness. Rinpoche explains, "The dynamic quality of energy is not expressed enough in the doctrine of shunyata…. In the vajrayana or tantric teaching the principle of energy plays a very important part."[33] The energy of luminosity and wisdom are not separate from the emptiness itself; they are another aspect of the true nature.

To put it very simply, at the hinayana stage, when a negative emotion such as anger or jealousy arises, we simply try to acknowledge it, let it go, and return to the peace of mind more basic than this anger. In the mahayana stage, we try to see the emptiness of the anger, to rest in that emptiness, and to develop a compassionate attitude to those who express anger toward us. Finally, in the vajrayana approach, we see the energy of anger, in itself, as wisdom. Of course, if we just try to leap into the vajrayana approach without practicing and understanding the previous stages, we can run into a lot of trouble. In fact, we can misuse the teachings to generate further ego and aggression, arrogance, and self-importance. It is because of this danger that Rinpoche spoke repeatedly about cutting through spiritual materialism in those early years before presenting the actual living practice of vajrayana.

THE TEACHER IN THE THREE YANAS

Our relationship to the teacher is different according to each yana. In the hinayana stage, we view the teacher as something of a higher being, a preceptor, and someone to whom we go for teachings. The preceptor is like a traditional teacher; from him or her we hear teachings and instructions, but there is not so much of a personal relationship. In the mahayana phase, the teacher is seen as a spiritual friend, one who takes our hand and leads us along the path. At this point one has grown up enough in one's understanding of suffering and its cause that one can have a slightly more eye-level relationship with the teacher. And in turn, as Rinpoche said, the teacher might get involved in every detail of one's life.

In the early years, up to this point, Rinpoche was acting toward his students as both a hinayana preceptor and a mahayana friend. Rinpoche gave the analogy of the preceptor being like a surgeon whom one goes to in an emergency to relieve one's pain. One looks up to the surgeon and trusts that he will be able to perform the necessary operation. The spiritual friend would then be the surgeon after the operation who befriends the patient and gives advice on lifestyle, diet, job, marriage, and so on—advice given, of course, from the point of view of egolessness and compassion. In vajrayana, the teacher becomes more like a master of martial arts—one must follow his instructions and commands precisely if one is to learn how to ride the energies of the world without falling off. You begin to see the teacher, guru, or vajra master as a person who is already awake and who can point out to you the nature of the world of awake, directly, beyond words and symbols. This demands increasing openness and experiential trust on the part of the student.

Devotion is an important aspect of the vajrayana path, though the word itself is a poor translation of the Tibetan word *mögü*.[34] *Mögü* is a combination of the words *möpa* and *güpa*. *Möpa*, longing, or admiration, comes from seeing the vast vision of the vajra master and longing to join that, longing to become one with the mind of the guru. *Güpa*, humbleness or absence of arrogance, suggests that to join that vision we have to be willing to give up clinging to our own petty little version of reality. In these times, when we are all supposed to be equal and no one should be considered "better" than anyone else, such longing and humbleness in front of another person can easily be disparaged as "worshipping the great man." But the fact is that, just as there are humans who have so degraded their humanness that one would never for a moment wish to emulate them but only to pity them, so there are men and women who have so clearly fulfilled all their potentiality of the best of humanness that one can only admire and wish to emulate them.

In its actual expression, the best description of devotion is perhaps simply love—not in the sense of grasping or adulation, but in the feeling of deep appreciation and opening to such a being and wanting to emulate him or her. At the same time, devotion is not blind faith or hero worship, but a recognition of the inseparability of one's own and the teacher's buddha nature. Devotion grows gradually out of one's growing trust in the personal experience of putting the teachings into practice. As Rinpoche said, "Devotees do not regard the object of their devotion as purely an object of admiration.... Any real sense of devotion or dedication comes not from comparing, but from personal experience.... Real devotion is connected with some sense of ground, relating with our own mind."

Ordinary students tend to experience the teacher in a mixture of all of these perspectives. Now, as Rinpoche prepared to introduce his students to the actual practice of vajrayana beyond merely talking about it, it was as vajra master that they would be expected to relate to him.[35]

A WILD BUNCH

We were a very undisciplined bunch at the first Seminary. We were the so-called "senior students" of the time, but we really were just the first students who had gathered around Rinpoche—intelligent hippies, drop-out intellectuals, *avant-garde* poets, and ex-druggies. There were also a few people at that first Seminary who really didn't have a very strong connection with Rinpoche at all, but who had met him just recently and received an invitation from him to attend.

There were about eighty participants at this first Seminary. Subsequent seminaries were substantially larger, with between one and two hundred participants and a large group of teachers, meditation instructors, and other staff. The first two weeks already began to show how Seminary would proceed. Generally people were delighted to be there and began the sitting period enthusiastically, but as these two weeks progressed the sitting began to taper off. The hotel next door had heard about our large, off-season program and decided to keep their bar, the "Mangy Moose," open all afternoon and evening. And indeed, there were clients there all afternoon and evening, from our hotel.

We didn't have any rules about not drinking. There were really no rules of behavior at all, and it wasn't even clear at the beginning of the Seminary just how strongly Rinpoche wanted people to sit. All the way through his life with us he was very gentle about asking people to practice. He never "laid down the law" saying, "You *must* practice!" His style was more gentle: "Please practice," "It would be very helpful if you would practice," or "If you don't practice you will never know my heart." But ultimately it was always up to the student.

The wildness and lack of seriousness were a constant irritant to my rather proper sense of how the Seminary should be going—just as the chaos at TOTT two summers ago had been such a source of irritation. On one occasion during the Seminary I went down to the hotel room that was Rinpoche's office to ask him a question. He was just putting on his coat to leave but invited me in, and after I had asked him my question he said to me, "I hear your course is going very well." For some reason I exploded, practically yelling in his face: "Yes, that's the only thing that's any good around here as far as I'm concerned!" He just smiled at me, finished putting on his coat, and left.

I went to my room and lay down on my bed and cried. How could I say that to him? How could I yell at him like that? Obviously, my course wasn't the only thing that was any good—all of the courses were good, and his was absolutely wonderful, but I was so frustrated with the chaos that was going on.

FAILING TO BE A GRAIN OF SAND

I was told that when he returned to his house just after I had exploded at him, he expressed tremendous delight, probably because I had let down my barrier of politeness with him. He exclaimed, "Oh, Jeremy was *really* angry!" He there and then sat down and wrote a poem, which was delivered to me the next day:

> *For Jeremy*
> *Failing to be a grain of sand*
> *Venom, nectar of a power maniac*
> *Trying to catch that*
> *Brings loss of this.*

Avalokiteshvara's compassion has a smile.
Buddha is said to be humble
A follower of his is joyful
Let us be a smiling grain of sand.
Maybe with cowshit on the head.

At the same time there was a tremendously good feeling among everyone. We were all genuinely delighted to be there and excited at the prospect of actually beginning the vajrayana stage of the path, though goodness knows we were hardly ready for it. Most of us knew each other pretty well by that time and it was almost like having a party every night.

INTRODUCTION TO NAROPA INSTITUTE

Earlier in the summer Marvin Casper, one of the leaders of the community in Boulder, had come along with Rinpoche to TOTT. He and Rinpoche had spent time talking about a summer program being planned for Boulder the following year. Rinpoche had invited me to sit in on these meetings as the project seemed to be up my alley, and I thought that this might be an avenue for me to become involved in a meaningful and useful way. Rinpoche gave it the name Naropa Institute, after one of the Kagyu forefathers. Naropa was a great Indian scholar in the tenth century, a dean of the renowned medieval Indian Nalanda University.

Nalanda University, the model for the Institute, began as a Buddhist monastery in the second century and developed into a university for the study of Buddhism as well as the worldly studies of the time. Scholars from India, China, and Japan, of many different persuasions,

faiths, and opinions, came to Nalanda to study and debate. In the four-
teenth century a similar center of learning was built in Tibet. At the
height of his fame as a learned scholar, Naropa left the university in a
search to find the direct experience of the meaning behind the words,
with the help of a vajrayana guru, Tilopa.[36] Thus, the story of Naropa
embodies the principle of joining intellectual knowledge with direct
experience, or intuition, in one's life. Joining intellect and intuition,
West and East, was to be the theme of the Naropa Institute.

During the Seminary there was a lot of buzz about plans for the
opening of Naropa Institute the following summer. One day I bumped
into Rinpoche as he was leaving the hotel, and he asked me how it was
going. I said that things were fine, and asked him whether I might be
able to do something with Naropa Institute. His face lit up, and he said,
"Oh, that gives me an idea. I was wondering what we were going to do
with you." Shortly after that, I heard that I was now appointed to be
one of the vice presidents of the new Institute. I felt glad that I would
now have more of a role to play in addition to just being a staff member at TOTT, though there was little sense of what a "vice president"
might actually do.

A few days later, I was invited to a meeting at Rinpoche's house, a
few miles from the Seminary, at which there was a discussion of setting
up the Nalanda Foundation. Nalanda Foundation was to be the official
non-religious, non-profit umbrella organization of which Naropa
Institute as well as, in the future, the lower schools and other educational activities would be divisions. Rinpoche had, at first, wanted to
simply add Naropa Institute into the other activities supervised by
Vajradhatu so that all would come under the same unified umbrella
with the same Board of Directors.

All through his time with us, as I've already intimated, he was very
concerned to leave behind a set-up that minimize the possibility for
schisms. In all the oaths of office taken by the various staff, all the way
from the Directors to individual meditation instructors, there was a
clause of commitment not to create schisms. However, the lawyers
advised him that it would be better to house Naropa Institute separately

under an educational organization. Thus, at this early stage the Nalanda Foundation Board of Directors was identical with the Vajradhatu Board with the addition of one, John Baker. John and Marvin Casper were the ones who, almost alone at this point, were working to give birth to Rinpoche's great vision.

THE STUDY PERIOD: HINAYANA AND MAHAYANA

During the study periods Rinpoche taught a main course every afternoon from about four o'clock until dinner time. There were also other courses: several on various Buddhist topics like "Lineage and Devotion" and "Buddhist Philosophy"; a course by Allen Ginsberg on poetry; and my course on "Buddhism and Science." I found that I wasn't comfortable making superficial comparisons between Buddhism and science, so I tried to teach the physics in such a way that students could have enough understanding of it to see the parallels with Buddhism.

In Rinpoche's course, he took a more traditional approach than he had previously, laying out the dharma in systematic, long talks with many categories. He was studying every day in preparation for his talks, basing his teachings on the *Treasury of Knowledge* by Jamgön Kongtrül the Great. He poured forth the dharma in traditional categories, but using very up-to-date language that we could connect with on a heart-to-heart level. At the time, we didn't really know what was happening; we couldn't follow a lot of it, and we were madly taking notes. It was a very, very rich time, as he systematically laid forth the dharma for, as he said, the benefit of future generations.

During the hinayana period, Rinpoche gave detailed instructions on the practices of mindfulness and awareness and described the stages a student goes through on the path. In the mahayana period, he described, also in great detail, the practices and stages of the bodhisattva path. There was always a lengthy discussion period and here, as always, Rinpoche's responses went straight to the inner meaning of the question, rather than merely answering the words.

For example, after his presentation on the practice of mindfulness, I said that I had a constant flow of music in my head that I couldn't seem to stop. Instead of giving me a technical reply, he responded, "You must be very romantic." On another occasion when I was very seriously asking him a question, his answer, seemingly quite unrelated to the question (which I no longer even remember), was, "I think a sense of humor is always very helpful." He had a knack of getting right to the heart of the matter beneath the literal question. He continued to reminded us frequently of the value of a sense of humor.

As the vajrayana section of Seminary approached, people were sitting less and less. The ten-day period of sitting immediately preceding the vajrayana study section was particularly sparse. Rinpoche took to calling around to people's bedrooms, and if they answered the phone he would gently say something like, "Shouldn't you be sitting now?" or "Why aren't you sitting?" or "Hello, I see you're not sitting." At the end of the talks he would sometimes make very strong—but still very gentle—statements that it would be helpful and beneficial if people would practice. But we did so less and less. Why? Habitual patterns; laziness; arrogance; lack of respect and longing: not giving in; too much fun in the Mangy Moose… who knows?

THE VAJRAYANA TEACHINGS BEGIN

At last, the vajrayana period of Seminary began. The vajrayana talks were based on the Nyingma way of dividing the vajrayana stage into six sub-stages. Thus Rinpoche spoke of the three "lower" tantric yanas and the three "higher." The lower yanas are not practiced separately but are all incorporated into the higher. Rinpoche spoke first on the three lower yanas.[37] This was the first introduction of the notion of deities and deity practices. I came out of the first talk on deities in the lower yanas in a state of extreme agitation, loudly proclaiming that I hadn't come here to study this stuff about deities and visualization. It didn't make any sense—what was wrong with just sitting practice? I suppose that, in some way, there was already a tremendously heightened energy happening. Some people, of course, were very excited by these teachings, and others didn't seem to be very affected by them either way. But there was definitely a sense of increasingly potent energy. For myself, I felt that I was being pushed far out of any familiar conceptual nest. I was quite ignorant of these things when I went to Seminary and this was way beyond the nice peaceful sitting practice that I had imagined.

Especially in the culture of theism from which we all came, there is an automatic tendency to think of the deities as external beings. This is never the case in Tibetan Buddhism, which is founded on nonduality, the ultimate non-separateness of oneself and others, even of oneself and God or the gods. The view of the higher yanas is the way that Rinpoche's students would be instructed to practice when it came time to actually enter into the vajrayana some months later. In the higher yanas, one visualizes oneself as a particular deity, with all its attributes: gender, color (for example deep blue or brilliant red), number of limbs (deities often have multiple arms or faces), ornaments (jeweled, or bone, necklaces and amulets), and implements (bell and dorje, or scepter). Each deity embodies a particular wisdom energy, such as peaceful brilliance, healing, enrichment, compassionate love, or the compassionate wrath that cuts through ego's games. The details of each deity embody various aspects of the wisdom of that deity and one actually identifies with the particular deity in order to arouse in one's own being the quality of energy and wisdom that the particular deity symbolizes. And, though I had little inkling of it at the time, it is through these visualization practices that one is introduced to the direct personal experience of that energy and wisdom, that is of "what's left."

AN EXPLOSION

After three talks on the lower yanas, Rinpoche gave the talk on *anuttara-yoga* tantra, which is the highest tantra of the Kagyu lineage and the other later schools.[38] The teachings of this tantra are equivalent to the three so-called higher tantras of the Nyingma tradition. Nowadays all

Tibetan teachers emphasize that there is essentially no difference between the realizations of the new and old schools, though the methods of instruction differ. So in this talk, Rinpoche was essentially introducing us to the actual vajrayana view and practice that we were soon to begin.

This talk was explosive and dramatic, as Rinpoche actually brought the energy of vajrayana into the shrine room. He was *showing* us the vajrayana, rather than merely talking *about* it. The result was the kind of chaos and ego-explosions that he had been warning us about for the previous three years.

Rinpoche had told us the day before that he was going to examine us at the beginning of this talk, and so he called on different students to give little summaries of the previous four talks. I was called on to summarize the talk on devotion and the relationship to the vajrayana guru, and others summarized the talks on the lower yanas. Altogether, this oral exam took about an hour, so we had been there quite a long time before he finally started the anuttara talk.

As Rinpoche spoke, the atmosphere gradually intensified. There was tremendous heightened energy, a powerful atmosphere of timelessness and the feeling of having nothing habitual whatsoever to hold on to. Even the quality of my perceptions seemed to change. This was in part a result of having nothing familiar to grasp on to in what Rinpoche was *saying*; his words seemed to be speaking to something in me beyond my logical mind which could make little sense of it all. At the same time, Rinpoche, in his very presence, seemed to be bringing an energy into the room that I had never felt before, a combination of *hot, brilliant,* and *cutting*. It was as if the heat and light of the sun were being focused on us through a powerful cosmic magnifying glass.

Everyone became quite aroused, reacting in various ways. Some people reacted by laughing a lot, others by shouting out, others even standing up and wandering around. I reacted with a heightened sense of irritation. I thought that I was irritated because of the way in which other people were not paying attention and were disturbing the atmosphere, not allowing us to really hear the teachings. No doubt, however, this was merely my own style of reacting to the powerful feeling of the vajrayana teachings coming through—and being hungry.

After talking for a long time, probably well over two hours, Rinpoche said, "And now we will go on to the next topic." By now it was getting really late, long past dinnertime. I put up my hand and called out: "How about doing that tomorrow, Rinpoche?" He looked up and said, "What?" Someone else said, "He said, 'how about continuing tomorrow.'" "What?" Rinpoche loudly said again. My neighbor threw his pencil down onto his notepad and shouted, in an angry tone, "Hear, hear! I second that." There was a general uproar at this point and Rinpoche pushed over his microphone stand and went storming out of the room in a black cloud.

A few people left with him, but otherwise no one got up. It was just getting to be dusk, and we sat there, silent; no one turned on the lights as it got darker. We heard him talking on the veranda outside the entrance to the shrine room, so I went out and stood in front of him. There was already snow on the ground, but I didn't bother to put on my shoes or socks. My feet were freezing and I didn't have a coat on, but I just stood in front of him with my arms by my sides and said, "I'm so sorry, Rinpoche." I was thinking to myself, "Please hit me," and I really wished at that point that he would do so. But instead of that, he put his arm around me and hugged me. "It wasn't your fault," he whispered, "I was setting up a mandala."

I did not know what he meant at the time, but I felt such warmth and kindness as he put his arm around my shoulder. Much later I realized that he probably meant that he was bringing down the blessing energy of the tantric deity, probably Chakrasamvara since this was the deity through which he had attained his own realization. When the vajra master takes on the wisdom energy of the deity, from his perspective the room becomes the palace of the deity and the students become the deity's retinue. This would explain the incredibly heightened energy and feeling of chaos on our part—we simply were not ready or sufficiently practiced to be able to fully open ourselves to that blessing energy.

WILL HE CONTINUE TO TEACH VAJRAYANA?

The talk having abruptly ended in this way, we all went back to our rooms and sat around wondering what would happen now. That evening, nothing else happened—and Rinpoche didn't appear the next day even though a talk was scheduled. We all just waited.

For three days, Rinpoche did not appear. He went on long drives, telling people that he was waiting for a sign as to whether or not to go on. We heard later that he was seriously considering, at that point, whether or not it was safe to continue presenting the genuine vajrayana teachings in America at all. We all sat very diligently for the next three days and, fortunately, he did continue. After three days we were called to reassemble. The tone was quieter now, as we had taken the three days to settle down and contemplate how deeply each of us longed to continue studying with Rinpoche. Rinpoche spoke on the three higher yanas of the Nyingma school.[39] The talks were rich and full and he did not seem to be holding back anything. The anuttara talk as well as these three final talks, even to this day, are a unique and tremendously valuable resource. Reading them thirty years later, one can still feel the experiential quality that he was communicating, beyond the scholarly information. So, Seminary ended up on a triumphant note: the genuine vajrayana dharma had been planted in North America!

The seminaries continued to happen every year, except in 1977 when Rinpoche went on a year-long retreat. For the first three years there were always a few students present, at Rinpoche's invitation, who had not studied very much and did not know Rinpoche well, and this seemed to heighten the chaos and misunderstanding of the teachings and the teacher. So, from 1976 on, Rinpoche took great care to make sure that people accepted to seminaries were thoroughly prepared beforehand with study and practice, including a dathün. Guidelines for behavior were introduced and the energy at subsequent seminaries became more contained. It was very similar to the situation at TOTT when I had asked Rinpoche what he thought about the situation there and he had replied, "I think it's fine." There, he had responded step by step to the situation by gradually introducing more forms and boundaries. When these forms and boundaries are appropriate and heart-felt, they do not suppress the energy but, by containing it, enable the intelligence within it to shine out more clearly. Each year at the end of Seminary Rinpoche would always say, "This has been the best seminary yet."

After the Seminary ended, we all went our different ways. I made my way back to TOTT and arrived there just in time for the Christmas program. I was in a state of turmoil, or, more accurately, tremendous despair. This was probably due, in part, to breaking up with Sue. She had written an angry letter to me at Seminary, accusing me among other things of causing her to have a car accident, which was hardly possible since she was in Vermont while I was in Wyoming. I arrived back at TOTT to find that she had taken up with another man. Rinpoche asked her to leave TOTT and within a few weeks she drove back to Boulder with her new boyfriend. More than this, though, my confused state of mind was an after-effect of the Seminary. It could have been all of the personal turmoil that, like everyone, I went through there; it may have been the recognition of the vastness and depth of what was before me—a feeling of smallness and tremendous doubt in the face of what I had now discovered; probably it was both. At the same time I felt deeply, beyond all of that, that something had happened that I could not yet grasp or understand; something had opened up in me that I could never turn back from.

In retrospect, it seems as if the vajrayana talks had introduced me to a whole new vision of life, like a new land, with cities and valleys, rivers and mountains, which I could just get a glimpse of through the gate, so to speak. This vision was brilliant, colorful, powerful, inviting—even seductive—yet frightening at the same time. I was beginning to realize that "awakening" could mean something more than the sense of peace conveyed in the beautiful statues of the Buddha, sitting in meditation posture with gaze down and a sweet smile, though that peacefulness is certainly the fundamental ground of awakening. It felt energetic and active, as well as potentially chaotic for the small mind of comfort and security. Rinpoche had frequently warned us of these things, but now I was beginning to *feel* them in my guts. How this vision of fresh possibilities could be incorporated into my ordinary life, I had no idea, and perhaps this was partly responsible for my state of turmoil—I was drawn to it and horrified by it at the same time.

1974–75: Big Leaps Forward 6

FEW DAYS AFTER I arrived back from Seminary, recoiling from the brilliant vajrayana energy that had been revealed there, I slipped back into a black hole of depression. One evening when the house was empty because everyone else had gone to Rinpoche's talk and I had missed the last ride, as I lay on a sofa in the sewing room I half dozed and had a vivid dream of putting my head in an oven with the gas turned on. The next day, there was a meeting of people involved in the arts that I had been asked to attend. I arrived a little early and sat for a while in the room alone with Rinpoche. As usual, he was sitting in a chair beside his desk and I was sitting at his feet. When he asked me how I was, I told him that I was terribly depressed. He responded, "The first moment I met you, I said to myself, I would like to know this gentleman through and through. And I'm glad that now I've met you half-way through. What do you think about that?"

At first, I misunderstood him to mean that he was glad to know me through and through now. It was only later, to my chagrin, that I realized he meant that he was glad to know me half-way through now, and that his question was really an invitation for me to open further and to show him the other half. It was such an invitation to let go of my barriers and tell him, "Yes, please, I want you to know me through and through." But instead, falling back into a solemn sense of trying to be genuine and confessional, I said, "Well, there is a lot of resistance." He interrupted, seeming a little irritated, "I know *that*, I just want to know what you think."

I told him that I sometimes felt that I was more genuine before I ever met him, when I was completely alone in my search. What I meant by this was that I felt that the openness of that time of searching was very valuable and I did not want to lose it and get caught up in being a True Believer. Perhaps this feeling was somewhat influenced by my shock at what I had heard in the vajrayana talks at Seminary. However, I still today feel that not clinging to being a Buddhist and to Buddhist ideas as a refuge is essential, and I have been somewhat dismayed to see people in the West becoming True Believers when they meet Buddhism, which then becomes just another form of blind faith.

Of course, this was not what he was asking and, as he continued to look at me in silence, I realized at last that he was inviting me to open up completely to him. I was fumbling with words to express my wish to open more to him, which was much more difficult for me than speaking about my shortcomings, but I hesitated and the conversation was abruptly ended at that moment as the meeting began to assemble.

A TURNING POINT

My behavior all along was so very ambivalent, and no doubt this was true of Rinpoche's students generally. While I was obviously longing to be close to him, I resisted so many overt gestures he made to invite me to step in. Why did I so resist? To step into his awful open space, stripped naked of the usual masks, and at the same time to feel his unflinching kindness and trust—it could be unbearable, like a moth flying too near to the flame. To be around someone who himself does not have the usual ego filters, who does not have a neatly predictable personality that one can get used to and learn how to respond to, was to be called to a constant state of alertness and openness. Even to know that there are people like this at all is to have one's conventional idea of what it is to be human, and how to live in the world, smashed.

And so one holds on as best one can to something safe—even if it be one's own resistance and depression.

In spite of my tremendous stubbornness, stiffness, and distrust, Rinpoche seemed to be including me more and more in the world that he was creating around him. He was taking many small steps at that time, and we didn't know how things would actually develop. He kept saying, "There's no master plan." Yet, looking back, one can see how the seeds were being sown from which the plant would grow—a plant which would have to be shaped and pruned to form the fresh, potentially awake human society that he so clearly envisioned. And it was truly the seeds of a whole society that he left behind, not just an organization of meditation centers.

The 1973 Seminary was a turning point for the sangha altogether, as well as a turning point for myself. In the spring of 1974, I went home to England to visit my parents for the first time since 1969. My family did not know what to expect; my uncle expressed it by saying, "I am glad to see you are normal. We imagined you dressed in white robes and chanting all the time." One day during my visit, my mother asked me, "So when are you going to move back to England, dear?" I knew without doubt that I was going to stay with Rinpoche now, so I replied that I was not planning to move back at all, to her obvious distress. As I stood, one morning, in the room I had occupied during my childhood and youth, I reflected on how strange, almost foreign, I had often felt as a young boy among my playmates and even my immediate family. I realized that my life had utterly changed, and that from now on it would take a direction I could not even imagine.

MISSING THE POINT—AGAIN

After the Christmas visit to Tail of the Tiger, Rinpoche was scheduled to teach some programs in Boston and New York and asked me to go along with him. Though I had been to Boston on several of his visits there, this was the first time he made a point of making sure I was there. One of my responsibilities in Boston was bringing people in for their interviews with Rinpoche. When all of the interviews were over, feeling astonished by the amount of energy Rinpoche could extend to so many people, I said, "Whew, that must have been pretty exhausting." He looked at me, puzzled, saying, "What do you mean?"

We were about to go out and I sat down on the floor near him to tie his shoes, which he was unable to do himself due to his partial paralysis. I looked up at him and asked, "Rinpoche, what would you do if all of this collapsed?" "What do you mean?" he asked again. "Well, if all the Dharmadhatus and Tail of the Tiger just closed down, what would you do?" Again, he asked me a question: "What do you think?" I answered, with a smile, "Well, maybe you would just go back and help Diana with her antique store." During that period, Diana was briefly operating an antique shop in Boulder. What I wanted to say was that I didn't think he would be upset if he didn't have a whole group of students to teach; I guess I had some sort of romantic fantasy of the wise man hiding his light in an antique store.

There was a cold silence, and I sat down on a nearby sofa. Then he said quietly, "Sometimes I wonder why you're with me." I felt crushed, and very stupid. Somehow I seemed to have missed the point of his life altogether: that if ever he would be unable to teach the dharma and work toward enlightened society, he truly would have no reason for being on this earth. I was to see, time and again as the years went by, that Rinpoche would *never* give up. Never. When we left the building, I had to go off to do an errand and Carl asked me where I was going. I told him and then added, "And I might never come back," glaring at Rinpoche as if to say, "Alright, if you wonder why I'm with you, I may just leave." Needless to say, I did come back and, when we met again later in the day, Rinpoche was as kind and cheerful as ever.

NAROPA INSTITUTE TAKES OFF

Rinpoche went on vacation in May, dropping by TOTT on his way back, spending a few quiet days at BPB. When it was time for him to return to Denver just before the first session of Naropa Institute, I arranged to fly there in the same plane. As our plane was coming in for a landing at the Denver airport, Rinpoche leaned over to me across the vacant seat between us, shook my hand, and said, "Well, if we crash, I'll see you in the *bardo*." I asked, "But how will I find you, Rinpoche?" He smiled at me and said, "Don't worry, I'll find you."

This was shocking to me! He had never said anything like that before, or given me any hint that he believed the *bardo*—the intermediate state between death and the next birth—existed in any way. He had given teachings on death back in 1971 when one of the students in Boulder died, but he always talked about death in a very pragmatic way. His main point was always that the ego dies every moment in life, so what is the big deal about death? Every moment is a discontinuity, and he called death "The Great Discontinuity." He gave us teachings on how to relate with dying people, but he had never actually given us reason to believe that the bardo was a real phenomenon, other than being a state of mind we go through in *this* life. However, we would learn a lot more later about the extent to which Tibetan Buddhists do consider the journey through these bardos as real experience that the mind goes through between death and rebirth.[40]

We landed in Boulder and were driven to Rinpoche's house, where I stayed for one night and then moved into a dorm room which I shared with another Naropa summer faculty member. A few days after my arrival, I received a welcoming gesture from a good friend—someone arrived at our door with a large and beautiful gift basket of flowers and fruit. There was a card addressed to me that said, "Welcome to Boulder," without any indication of who it was from. I asked my roommate if he had also received such a gift, and he replied that he had not. I said, "Well, this must be meant for both of us, then." It wasn't until years later that the person who had delivered the gift told me that it was Rinpoche who had sent it, and that it was, indeed, intended especially for me.

Even though Rinpoche made such gestures to help me feel at home in Boulder, I felt somewhat like a fish out of water socially. My Englishness seemed even more out of touch with the exuberance and casualness I found there. The whole social scene there was confusing and overwhelming for me, with endless parties and a kind of Wild West atmosphere. I knew that people often went up to Rinpoche's house in Four Mile Canyon, but I was still timid and old-fashioned, and never even imagined I could just go on up to his house without an invitation. As a result of this hesitation, I didn't see Rinpoche privately very much that summer. However there were occasional moments of intimacy: in the middle of July, Narayana held a birthday party for me in a small house that he was renting. Rinpoche came and gave me a small gift, and we sat and chatted for a while. When he got up to leave, he gave me a big hug and whispered in my ear, "Thank goodness you're on earth, at least." It felt so warm and loving, though I didn't understand why "at least."

THE ACTUAL PRACTICE OF VAJRAYANA

I did go up to Rinpoche's house that summer for a very memorable event: my introduction to the actual practice of vajrayana, or tantra. Back in March, at TOTT, we had heard that Rinpoche had started something he was calling a "tantra group." He was finally introducing the students in this group to vajrayana practice, giving what is conventionally known as the "pointing out transmission," or "introduction to the nature of mind," which is the essential transmission of a vajrayana guru to the student.[41] It is a direct pointing out of the nature of mind, that is mind's simplicity and universality—all appearances arise within the mind and in that sense there is nothing *other* than mind, yet mind itself is emptiness, openness beyond concept.

The small group of fifteen to twenty had already met two or three times when I joined them. We would all sit together on the outside veranda, which bordered the very edge of the canyon. The weather was usually lovely, warm but not too hot, with a gentle breeze. There was a river ten yards below in the canyon. I well remember the warm, intimate, yet powerful atmosphere, as Rinpoche sat with us and quietly talked about the vajrayana and gave us the pointing out transmission. This transmission is utterly simple, beyond words, yet it can only be given directly from a qualified vajra master to students who are properly prepared, otherwise it can be misunderstood and create further confusion.

Some months later, after giving us time to work with this pointing out experience, Rinpoche introduced this small group of students to the preliminary practices of vajrayana, the *ngöndro* practices.[42] These consist of 100,000 each of prostrations, Vajrasattva mantra, mandala offering, and one million mantras of guru yoga. Each prostration consists of extending oneself full-length on the floor from a standing position. One visualizes that one is doing this in front of the lineage of realized Kagyu masters, whose awakened mind is not separate from one's own—so one is essentially prostrating to one's own wisdom mind, and surrendering the petty mind of security, of trying to hold on to a small, cozy, familiar world.

There is no sense of "worshipping" the Kagyu teachers as external beings, but the point is to develop a deepening sense of devotion, or *mögü*—longing and humbleness—toward their realization. Without *mögü* one is simply unable to hear and understand the teachings properly. There is, naturally, a lot of resistance to this surrendering process and the practice arouses, so that one can clearly see them, a tremendous amount of coarse *kleshas*, mental defilements. In a traditional analogy, it is as if, wishing to build a palace, one first has to clear the ground of all the big rocks. These kleshas are offered up as food to that wisdom-mind embodied in the lineage. As Rinpoche once said, "We eat anything."

The mantra practice is an inner cleansing and purification, like taking an inner shower, which flushes out deeper obscurations. The point of both of these practices is to begin to clear away the obstacles to seeing

the richness and wisdom of our own Buddha nature. The third practice, the offering in the form of small piles of rice of 100,000 mandalas
to the lineage, represents an offering of our whole being, including our
whole world, to that wisdom mind. Finally one repeats one million
mantras, calling on the blessing energy of the lineage and of one's own
guru in particular.

All of us in that small tantra group began prostrations that summer.
Once again we were pioneers, just as we had been in the case of sitting
meditation. There was no precedent in the community around us, and
none in all of America. We did not at first have fully translated instructions and relied on Rinpoche to guide us through, though very soon the
translation group began to translate the liturgies for these practices—
their first major translation project. All of this was going on while at the
same time the Naropa Institute sessions were in full swing.

A ROARING SUCCESS

The summer program was organized into two five-week sessions, and
many more students enrolled than had been expected. The hope had
been that two hundred to three hundred people would come to each
session, but in fact there were eighteen hundred altogether. We had to
increase the staff and the facilities, and the organization became gradually more and more chaotic. And so Naropa Institute was a roaring
success in every way but one—the finances. At the same time, however, it brought many, many people to Rinpoche and had a profound
effect on the Buddhist community in Boulder, more than doubling the
number of members just in that one summer.

The primary teacher that summer was, of course, Rinpoche, whose
class was held in a huge converted warehouse—known as the Public
Service Building. During the first five-week session, Rinpoche taught
two courses, one on the overall Buddhist path and the other on Buddhist meditation. In this first session, Ram Dass also taught a huge class
in the Public Service Building. He and Rinpoche taught on alternate
evenings, and many people attended both classes, enjoying the contrast

TEACHING AT THE FIRST SUMMER OF NAROPA INSTITUTE.

between the blissed-out American leading sessions in group chanting of "OM" and the outrageous Tibetan Buddhist speaking of the importance of disappointment and hopelessness on the spiritual path.

In the second session, Rinpoche gave a course called "The Tantric Journey," which was later published as *Journey Without Goal.* These were very profound vajrayana teachings, disguised, as usual, in a very simple form. It was characteristic of much of Rinpoche's public teachings, even in the early years, that he would give teachings on vajrayana topics but in a way that included simple, helpful teachings for ordinary people. At the same time he would continually issue warnings about spiritual materialism.

There were many other excellent courses, by Kobun Chino Roshi, Herbert Guenther, Gregory Bateson, Allen Ginsberg, Reginald Ray, Jack Kornfield, Joan Halifax (then Joan Halifax-Grof), Jakusho Kwong

Sensei, and others, as well as many arts and dance courses, yoga, and so on. The whole thing was a tremendous feast, an utterly delightful time for all the students, and a great success altogether. People would gather in the parking lot outside the bus station before the main courses, some playing music, some dressed in Indian *dotis* and chanting, and some just standing around looking at the scene, smoking and making cynical jokes.

I taught Buddhism and science in the first session, and I planned to do something similar to what I had done at Seminary; that is, I would go through some topics in science, mostly in physics or the history of science, with reference to how this seemed to connect to Buddhism. A few books were becoming very popular that compared science with various spiritual traditions. They were filled with comparisons between the words of physicists and those of Buddhists, Taoists, and so on. I felt that this was a rather superficial approach, like comparing the forms of two trees way off on the horizon, so far away that they superficially look alike.

It is only possible to make a true comparison by going up close and examining the leaves and the structure of each of the trees; only then is it possible to know whether they are the same or different. It is similar with Buddhism and science: sure, there are similarities in what people say, but that does not mean that the actual, real meaning of these doctrines and observations is the same. It is similar with comparisons between the various religions, which were popular at that time: they may be all *saying* the same thing, more or less, but does this necessarily imply that they *mean* the same? I personally wanted to give students a good basis for thinking about these things themselves. So I spent more time going as deeply as we could into the various doctrines of science and letting their similarities with Buddhism come out naturally.

NUMBER ONE?

During the second session, there was a meeting about the first visit to North America of His Holiness the Sixteenth Karmapa, the supreme head of the Kagyu lineage. This visit was by that time only a little over a month away. Marvin Casper, John Baker, Narayana, and I were there, as well as others involved with the visit. His Holiness had been invited by Rinpoche and was to visit many of the Dharmadhatus. The meeting had to do with finances—what we were planning for His Holiness, how much it would all cost, and how it was, actually, impossible for us to afford this visit. Someone suggested that perhaps we should not invite him after all. Rinpoche expressed great displeasure with that suggestion, saying, "We do not cut off our face to save our arms."

At some point during this meeting, Rinpoche had Narayana sit by him and he made it clear that Narayana was going to be his "Number One," his closest advisor. It was one more hint of what was to come with regard to Narayana. It also caused a new wave of painful longing to arise in me, which was intensified by the difficulty I was having reconnecting with Rinpoche after the sweet times we had had at TOTT.

The day after the meeting about the visit of His Holiness Karmapa, Rinpoche came into the bus-station for his talk and stopped to greet me, as usual. I always sat by the wall with Jan, my latest girlfriend, in a place Rinpoche would pass on his way to the speaker's platform, and every time he passed me he would stop to shake my hand and smile, and ask, "How are you?" This time, I said, "Rinpoche, could I meet with you about yesterday's meeting?" This was the first time that summer that I had requested a private meeting. Rinpoche responded, "That would be delightful." So a meeting was arranged for the next afternoon.

When it was time for my interview, I sat in front of Rinpoche's desk, chain-smoking and tongue-tied. It might seem strange that, even by that time, I was still so awkward around him. Part of it was certainly my painful shyness, even at the age of thirty-four, but it also came from the powerful sense of his just genuinely being there with no pretense and nothing on his mind. This sense of awkwardness in his presence, which never fully left me, was common to all his students. Each reacted in a different way. Some, like myself, became even more shy and embarrassed than usual; others became more brash and pushy. Few people were able to act simply and normally in his presence. But because of our understanding of ego, and of ego's remarkable ability for self-deception, we realized that being in the clear mirror of his simple presence was the best way to see ourselves honestly, so the pain of these moments was like the pain of drinking a potent but bitter-tasting medicine.

Rinpoche kindly offered me an ashtray and waited. I couldn't think of anything positive to say—I just sat there stumbling over my words. I finally blurted out something about my concern that there would be one person in charge of the whole thing. Rinpoche beckoned me to bring my chair around and sit next to him on his side of the desk in a simple gesture of welcoming a friend. I moved around and sat next to him, but I still could not relax. As we ended our meeting, he said, "When I come into the talk and see you there, it always perks me up."

That evening, I was so embarrassed by the way I had handled myself in the meeting that, when I heard his car drive up to the bus station, I left my usual spot by the wall and moved over into the crowd in the middle of the hall. I watched him come in from there, and as he passed my usual spot I saw him say something to Jan before he walked on to the stage. Jan told me afterward that he had asked, "Where's Jeremy?"

When I reflect on the jealousy and hesitation that was so strong in many of us during this time, it feels so very sad. But, in retrospect, I also realize that we never gave up! Nor did Rinpoche ever give up on me, or on any of his students. Perhaps one of the most important lessons from this is that one really has no need to blame oneself or to feel guilty for one's hesitations and difficulties in connecting with the guru. These obstacles, coming from past conditioning and karma, arise from the pain of seeing oneself nakedly, letting go of pretense. Altogether, painful though it is, it is also a precious opportunity to see oneself more deeply and honestly than one's mundane world allows. But if one were to give up and leave—possibly blaming the guru, or others, for one's inability to connect—and thereby waste that precious opportunity of meeting him in this lifetime, that would be deeply disturbing.

HIS HOLINESS KARMAPA VISITS

Instead of returning to Tail of the Tiger at the end of the summer, I stayed on in the fall to take care of Naropa Institute, as Rinpoche had asked me to do back in the spring. Marty Janowitz, who was the managing director and was in charge of the staff and other practicalities for the summer, was going to go to Seminary that fall. And John Baker who, with Marvin Casper, was primarily responsible for initiating the Institute and was currently overseeing the whole thing, was going away to study. So I was to help look after our little Institute with a grand vision in their absence. And as Naropa's summer program came to an end, we began to anticipate the visit of His Holiness Karmapa to Boulder.

Since the meeting in the summer, there had been a tremendous fundraising effort that enabled us to welcome His Holiness in a style appropriate for a dharma king. But there was no way we could have known what would actually happen. Perhaps Rinpoche himself did not quite anticipate the effect that His Holiness would have. He had been rather diffident about His Holiness during the years before that, giving us the impression that he was mostly some kind of figurehead. But when His Holiness arrived at the airport in New York, Rinpoche prostrated to him right there on the tarmac, and from that moment on Rinpoche went into an energy state that we had never seen before. Everything changed.

At various times throughout Rinpoche's life, every few years or so, there would be a sudden change of direction for the sangha. The visit of His Holiness Karmapa was one of those times. Rinpoche traveled in advance of His Holiness, always one stop ahead, and poured out his energy getting the places ready for His Holiness' arrival. He would often keep everyone up all night with preparations.

Rinpoche arrived in Boulder to set up the situation there for His Holiness' arrival from Karme Chöling, the new name that His Holiness had given Tail of the Tiger, meaning "the dharma place of the Karma Kagyus." By then a large hall that had once been the home of the Freemasons had become the main shrine hall of Karma Dzong. This was newly painted and had the *prajnaparamita* mantra, "Om Gate Gate

Paragate Parasamgate Bodhi Svaha" inscribed all around the walls. Many new banners were designed for the first time for this occasion and a high throne was built for His Holiness.

I was attending to Naropa Institute business and wasn't terribly excited about the fact that His Holiness was coming, but I could see that others were, particularly Narayana. I didn't get very much involved in all of the preparations. I was staying with Jan in a small two-room apartment a mile or so away from Naropa. I was doing prostrations and the practice was arousing all my habitual strong negative emotions, as well as occasional flashes of openness and love for Rinpoche and for the lineage. But the predominant emotion was anger. I was just flailing around, pissed off and feeling separate from what was going on up the hill, at Karma Dzong. It was a strange time. When I went over to Karma Dzong to see what was going on, there was intense activity and Rinpoche was in an almost fierce state. When he saw me, his only comment was, "Have you come to help?"

His Holiness finally arrived in Boulder, with his entourage of monks blowing their *gyalings,* instruments like Tibetan oboes. Rinpoche, wearing a Tibetan outer garment, lead His Holiness into Karma Dzong carrying burning incense in the traditional way. His Holiness gave many teachings and *abhishekas*—blessings or empowerments.

An abhisheka can be simply a way for a great teacher to bring the blessings of the lineage to the participants, or an empowerment to actually practice a particular vajrayana practice. In this case the abhishekas were simply to bring blessings. It was all in Tibetan and was altogether very foreign to me; it was the first time that I had seen any other Tibetan teacher, or any other Tibetan situation at all. My contact with Tibetan Buddhism up until then had been totally through Rinpoche, with his simple naturalness, his fluent English language, and his eye-to-eye relationship with us. Now we were experiencing this other Tibetan teacher, who sat on a throne, gave teachings in Tibetan, and performed elaborate Tibetan rituals we didn't understand. We had been constantly encouraged to be cynical and suspicious of any religious "trip," including the exotic external

HIS HOLINESS THE SIXTEENTH GYALWA KARMAPA PERFORMS AN ABHISHEKA. *Photograph by Ray Ellis.*

trappings of Tibetan Buddhism, and I could not simply suspend my intelligent doubt now. I went through the motions, and I was caught up in the energy and excitement of it all, but I really didn't connect very much with His Holiness or with the events that were going on during that visit.

HIS HOLINESS THE KARMAPA PERFORMS THE BLACK CROWN CEREMONY.

However, regardless of my own reticence, His Holiness did have a profound effect on many people and indeed on the spread of genuine dharma in the West altogether. With his tremendous kindness, his warm smile and powerful radiance, he was like the sun warming, nourishing, and cheering up the world wherever he went. He was inquisitive about everything he saw. Once in Los Angeles he pointed to all the many joggers and asked, "Where are they all going?" When he was told they weren't going anywhere but were just running he broke out into astonished laughter. He loved all animals, but especially birds. He had a large cage in his room in which he kept birds of many varieties and seemed to understand and communicate with them.

Perhaps his majesty and radiant compassion were most powerfully to be felt during the Black Crown ceremony, which he performed in every city he visited. In this ritual His Holiness ceremonially holds on his head a black crown, a replica of one that was given by Yung-lo, Emperor of China, to the fifth Karmapa. The original was said to have been made from the hairs of *dakinis* (female deities who protect the teachings) after Yung-lo had had a vision of the Crown on the fifth Karmapa's head. As the Karmapa holds the crown on his head, he slowly recites the mantra of Avalokiteshvara, the bodhisattva of compassion. It is said that during those few minutes he brings to earth the transcendent form of Avalokiteshvara and radiates the bodhisattva's pure compassion. He sat on the high throne, so that all could see him and as he sat there he truly seemed like the dharma king he was said to be—that is, a perfectly enlightened being in human body. It certainly was a magnificent occasion, but at the same time I could not simply take it on faith. I, like so many of us, had come to Rinpoche in a search to find the truth beyond dogma, and I was not about to give up my intelligence just because "Rinpoche said so."

THE SIGNIFICANCE OF
HIS HOLINESS' VISIT FOR THE SANGHA

Of great significance during this first visit of His Holiness Karmapa in September of 1974 was the creation of the Vajra Guards. Rinpoche organized people to act as drivers, to perform various service functions for the Karmapa and his party, and for protection—to provide boundaries at events and to be watchful for the safety of His Holiness and his party. When the Karmapa left, the Vajra Guards requested that they be permitted to continue by serving Rinpoche in a similar way.

This was the origin of what later became the Dorje Kasung ("Invincible Command Protectors"), a separate organization whose function is to provide service and protection to the teacher and the teachings. (In Tibetan, *sung* means "protection" and *ka* means "command" or "word," i.e. the teachings.) Later the Dorje Kasung were divided into two main branches: the kusung (In Tibetan *ku* means "body") branch, whose concern was personal service to Rinpoche, the Regent, and their families; and the kasung, who were more outwardly oriented toward general service and watchfulness over the environment in which the teachings are being presented. On many occasions in the years to follow the Dorje Kasung would join with local or national security police forces especially to protect the Dalai Lama on his visits to cities such as Amsterdam and New York.

Altogether, Rinpoche showed a completely new, devotional aspect of himself. Everything he did demonstrated his tremendous sense of devotion and respect, and he treated the Karmapa with the greatest of dignity. He even bent his shoulders in the traditional Tibetan style of humbleness when he spoke to him. This was a turning point for Rinpoche's students, because *we* began to realize how to show love and respect for a great teacher and so we saw how we could *really* show our own love and respect for Rinpoche. Up until that time, we had been so casual—calling him "the Rimp" and dropping in on him whenever we felt like it. But after the first visit of His Holiness Karmapa, our way of relating to Rinpoche, as well as his teaching style, began to change. During his Naropa Institute summer courses, while he occasionally wore a suit or sports coat he also wore baggy pants with colorful suspenders and short sleeved sport shirts. But this was to be no more and that summer was the occasion for many of us to purchase our first suits. The era of casualness was over and he was more formal with his students as well as in teaching.

There was another major change in the understanding of who Rinpoche was which resulted from the Karmapa's visit. Until this time, Rinpoche had been regarded with some suspicion, even embarrassment, by many of the other Tibetan teachers. After all, he had renounced his robes, and they heard rumors of his drinking and having consorts. Furthermore, he was teaching the highest vajrayana teachings to Westerners and seemed to be trusting Westerners and treating them as only tulkus were treated in Tibet. In contrast, many of the Tibetan teachers who were coming to the West gave out the kind of practices that would be given to peasants with little education in Tibet—deity practices like the Green Tara—not understanding the power of theism in the West. Students were doing these practices with little or no understanding of what they were doing, and no grounding in basic mindfulness practice. Many of these more traditional Tibetans, hearing of Rinpoche's behavior, proclaimed that he had gone off the rails. Yet there were precedents for all Rinpoche was doing in stepping out of the mold in the Tibetan tradition.

During his visit, the Karmapa issued a proclamation that "Chokyi Gyatso, Trungpa Rinpoche, has carried out the vajra holder's discipline in the land of America, establishing his students in liberation and ripening them in the dharma. This wonderful truth is clearly manifest." Thus, Rinpoche finally connected his Western students with the Kagyu lineage and his work in America was confirmed and blessed. From being a bunch of hippie renegades, we were now included in the great family of the Kagyu tradition of Tibetan Buddhism. From this time on, we referred to Rinpoche as the Vajracharya, meaning "vajra master," in public or in formal situations, while we still continued to call him Rinpoche in private, at least for a few more years. The Karmapa's visit was a major turning point in the life of the sangha, and in Rinpoche's teaching in the West altogether.

RETURN TO TOTT AND BACK TO BOULDER

Toward the end of December, the second Seminary ended and people, including Marty Janowitz and John Baker, began to reappear in Boulder. It was time for me to return to Karme Chöling. In the summer, while I was in Boulder, Rinpoche had appointed Carl and me to the directorship of TOTT. This had happened in a rather odd way: when the Naropa Institute catalogue appeared I was inadvertently listed in it as "Director of Tail of the Tiger." Neither Carl nor I were directors at that point and the listing was simply a mistake. When Carl saw this he showed it to Rinpoche, who immediately replied, "All right, you and Jeremy will be the directors." Rinpoche would often take advantage of such seeming accidents—nothing was pure coincidence in his view.

In February, while there was a dathün going on at Karme Chöling, I completed the prostration practice in my cabin up on the hill among the maple trees. During the dathün, Rinpoche telephoned me from Boulder to say that he wanted me to move there and take on a full-time role at Naropa Institute. He explained that he needed me there because there were difficulties, particularly in the leadership. In April, there was to be a major showing of Tibetan art at the Hayden Gallery of the Massachusetts Institute of Technology, organized by Vajradhatu and MIT together, which I was supposed to help with. So I told him this and asked if I should come to Boulder after the exhibition, but to my surprise he told me to come out as soon as possible. Accordingly, soon after the dathün was over, I moved to Boulder.

ON THE THREE KAYAS

Very soon after I arrived in Boulder, Rinpoche gave a public seminar on the three *kayas* (a Sanskrit word meaning "bodies"): dharmakaya, sambhogakaya, and nirmanakaya.[43] The three kayas correspond to the three awakened aspects of our being, which can have an ordinary, mundane, and neurotic level as well as the enlightened, awakened level. Both of these aspects are always occurring in us. In an ordinary person these three levels of being manifest as the mind, speech (emotions, the communicative level), and body.

Rinpoche had spoken about the kayas briefly several times previously, but this was the first time that he spent a whole seminar on the topic. This seminar, like so many others, was atmospheric, experiential, and mind-blowing. When the three kayas are taught in the traditional way, they seem very abstract and far removed from the experience of ordinary beings such as myself—a description of the Buddha's way of being in his enlightened body, speech, and mind. However, as usual with such traditional topics, Rinpoche taught them in a way that seemed very much accessible. He showed us that the three kayas are indeed an aspect of the experience we all have, though this experience is usually veiled by our small minds and hearts. The three kayas are an important topic for understanding much of Rinpoche's teaching, and indeed much of his life itself.

The three kayas are the awakened version of mind, speech/emotion, and body. *Dharmakaya*, as the awakened state of mind, is the realm that is beyond concept altogether, beyond existence and non-existence. It is the very space of our mind, even beyond awareness or non-awareness; yet at the same time it is bright, clear, open space, with some kind of *knowingness*. It is the vast open space of mind within which all appearances arise. It is a space that is empty of all concept, at the same time that it is full—full of potential, of possibilities, of potential forms, of potential laws. Dharmakaya is another view of *shunyata*—it is empty of all concept, yet full of all possibilities.

Shunryu Suzuki Roshi, the much-loved Zen teacher, describes the dharmakaya thus:

> *I discovered that it is necessary, absolutely necessary, to believe in nothing. That is, we have to believe in something which has no form and no color—something which exists before all forms and colors appear. This is a very important point…. It is absolutely necessary to believe in nothing. But I do not mean voidness. There is something, but that something is something which is always prepared for taking some particular form, and it has some rules, or theory or truth in its activity…. This is not just theory. This is not just the teaching of Buddhism. This is the absolutely necessary understanding of our life.*

The awakened level corresponding to speech, or emotion, is known as *sambhogakaya*, or "body of enjoyment." At this level there is pure energy, which is undistorted by "me" / "I." The energy normally experienced as the unawakened or negative emotions—passion/lust, anger, ignorance, jealousy, pride—are felt from the perspective of awake mind as energies at play in the sambhogakaya, and as wisdoms of the five Buddha families, five expressions of that basic non–ego-oriented energy. The sambhogakaya is the level of feeling, at which body and mind are completely joined and in harmony. There is a sense of dance, of play, of celebration, and of natural humor at this level, a "self-existing grin," as Rinpoche called it. It is the brilliant whiteness of the paper that is left when you erase the writing, as Rinpoche had described it in our first encounter.

The body level, from the awake point of view, is known as *nirmanakaya*. It is the entire world of the five sense perceptions, which includes our own physical body as well as the environment. At this point, because there is no dwelling on "me"—on "this, here"—there is really no distinction between "this" and "that," between "my body" and the world around.

Once, when Rinpoche was ill, one of his close students was concerned about his health and asked him to take more care of it. Rinpoche said, "Why is everyone so concerned about my health?" The student replied, "Because we care about you, we care about your body." Rinpoche responded, "My body is the whole world." That is the point of view of a being who has fully accomplished the realization of the nirmanakaya. This brings with it tremendous compassion because there is no hang-up, there is no "me"; so compassion, love for our world and for others, radiates naturally. Compassion has expressed itself, at the nirmanakaya level, in all of the physical manifestations of dharma, texts, statues, and great dharma teachers.

When I returned to Boulder in March of 1975 these were the teachings I heard. Although they were so profound, Rinpoche somehow managed to touch us with them and show us a dimension to human existence that we had never heard of before. We learned that the three kayas are part of our own make-up that we can open to right now, at least in brief glimpses.

"THE KEY TO WARRIORSHIP AND THE FIRST PRINCIPLE OF
SHAMBHALA VISION IS NOT BEING AFRAID OF WHO YOU ARE.
SHAMBHALA VISION TEACHES THAT, IN THE FACE OF THE WORLD'S
PROBLEMS, WE CAN BE HEROIC AND KIND AT THE SAME TIME.
SHAMBHALA VISION IS THE OPPOSITE OF SELFISHNESS."

CHÖGYAM TRUNGPA RINPOCHE,
FROM *SHAMBHALA: THE SACRED PATH OF THE WARRIOR*

1975–76: Shambhala Vision Proclaimed 7

HEN I ARRIVED in Boulder to take up my post as Vice President of Naropa Institute, I heard that there was lot of confusion in the community about Naropa Institute. What was it for? Why did we have to do it? These questions were even being asked among the small staff of Naropa. Until that time Rinpoche's students had comprised a fairly small community of a few hundred people, scattered about the States and Canada, many of whom felt they were able to know and be known by Rinpoche quite intimately. Many of the older community members were disturbed and upset by this sudden increase in the number of students gathering around Rinpoche, afraid perhaps that this would cause them to lose access to him and the close family feeling they had with him and each other. As well, many of these first students had come to Rinpoche out of burn-out and disaffection with the dry, intellectual, irrelevant studies forced on them in high school or university, so why engage this world again? Rinpoche was quite unhappy about this attitude and gave a very sharp talk to the community expressing puzzlement that people would be asking such a question as "Why Naropa Institute?" at all.

Rinpoche had made it very clear that he did not want the Institute to be just a "New Age" sort of place, offering all kinds of different courses with no particular basis. There were many of these New-Agey centers in America already, and more were developing. He envisioned Naropa Institute as a full, complete, accredited university, unique while remaining in the academic mainstream. He often compared it to Harvard University and Oxford University and said that it would be a five-hundred-year project.

When I began to work at the Institute in the spring of 1975 there did indeed seem to be difficulties at the top, as Rinpoche had indicated when he called me at Karme Chöling in February. At the beginning of the summer, John Baker and Marty Janowitz announced their intention to step down from the administration of the Institute to go into business, leaving a big gap in the leadership there. Rinpoche decided that Carl should take Marty's position as managing Director, while I was asked to replace John Baker on the Nalanda Board. So in that sense I was the senior person from then on in the leadership of Naropa Institute. Naturally I was proud of this, although the transition had been difficult for all of us. At the same time I did not feel entirely comfortable with the style of the Institute. Coming from seven years at Cambridge University, for which I had a lot of fondness and admiration, and also being trained as a scientist, I found many of the programs somewhat too loose. Of course, it was very early days, and I did not at the time have the vision to see the important role Naropa could play in the Western educational environment as, indeed, it does now, thirty years later.

This summer program was still very well attended and full of excellent courses, but there was a certain unrest especially among some of the faculty and students who were not interested in Buddhism and wanted Naropa Institute to be more open, more New Agey. During the break between the two Naropa summer sessions, a one-and-a-half day faculty conference had been scheduled to discuss the vision of Naropa Institute and to plan the possible degree programs. At that conference, Rinpoche gave a very powerful talk at which he said, "We are the Kagyu lineage. We follow the Kagyu lineage." This was slightly shock-

RINPOCHE ENTERS FOR ANOTHER LARGE SUMMER CLASS.
Photograph by Rachel Homer.

ing to some people because he was making it very clear that we were a Buddhist institution, following in the footsteps of our Kagyu forefathers, including the great siddha Naropa himself.

After this talk there was much debate among the faculty, some of whom were surprised, even shocked to hear Rinpoche make such a strong statement of the association of Naropa Institute with the Kagyu lineage. Gregory Bateson, the anthropologist and "elder" to many people exploring new ways of seeing the world, had made a similar statement in the spring, when we asked him what his thoughts were about the view of Naropa Institute. His strong advice to us at that meeting had been: "Don't renounce your heritage. That is what you have, namely, your Buddhist heritage, your lineage connection. Don't renounce that. If you renounce that, you will be just like any other experimental college. That is your power." This question of Naropa

Institute's relation to Buddhism, especially to the Kagyu lineage of Trungpa Rinpoche, became an ongoing debate that has continued even to the present day.

RINPOCHE APPOINTS A BUTLER

During the summer, Rinpoche appointed John Perks to be his butler and head of household. He had been on the faculty of Naropa Institute in the summer of '75 and had many previous careers including running a sailing school for delinquent adolescents, and serving as a butler. He and Gregory Bateson paired up and ran a program together in the spring of 1975; Bateson enjoyed John's non-conceptual teaching style.

That summer John Perks became obsessed with the question of who was "in" and who was "out" of Rinpoche's intimate circle. There was no defined "in" or "out" as far as Rinpoche was concerned; it was simply a matter of how much you were able to relate with his world. Although we may have realized, at times, that it was mainly our own projection, this ambition to be "in" was a driving force for much of the politics and intrigue that went on around Rinpoche. It is not so different in any group of people—there is always some kind of inner circle that everyone aspires to be a part of. The difference in this case was that it affected people at the very core of their being and longing.

One night that summer, John threw a rock through a window of one of the Naropa Institute buildings and trashed out the reception area, upturning files and emptying garbage cans all over the offices. The next day he went to see Rinpoche, and to our astonishment he came out and announced that he was invited to move into Rinpoche's house and be the butler, or head of household.

TIME TO SETTLE DOWN

Toward the end of the summer, my affair with Jan being over, I got together with Karen Wells, a staff member at the Institute. In our first weeks together I felt a peacefulness and relaxation that was difficult to find in those turbulent years. Karen's account of her first meeting with Rinpoche well describes his way of penetrating through someone's personality cocoon of habitual protectiveness, reaching straight into her heart:

I was very excited about meeting him and felt quite confident in my own right. When I was finally introduced to him, I was stunned as if I had received an electric shock. The most amazing thing I felt about him was his ability to penetrate my being, thoroughly. He held out his hand to me, and when I took it, I felt the most unbelievable feeling of gentleness I had ever known. In contrast, my own energy felt painfully aggressive. Then I looked into his eyes. There was a softness and kindness exuding which I had never experienced before and, beyond that, a depth I could not fathom. I couldn't find the person beyond those eyes. The effect on me was tremendously powerful. It was as if this man could see through to my deepest core, and yet he accepted me. I felt I had been penetrated by loving but X-ray eyes—my masks unraveled in the light of his being so real. All this took a moment—just a short exchange. I didn't understand what had happened and went immediately to my own room and sat there feeling shaken. I couldn't speak to anyone. It was as if I had been in front of an uncompromising mirror that reflected every tiniest detail and hidden corner of my mind and heart. How could it be possible for someone to reflect me so clearly and yet appreciate me so completely at one glance? I guess I fell in love. I felt that my relentless search—through theater, Christianity, philosophy, psychology, parapsychology, and transcendental meditation—had ended and something thrilling, but very scary, had started. In one moment, I knew this Tibetan man—ageless and androgynous— understood the mysteries of life. I wanted to learn his wisdom and compassion. And, strangely, I trusted him completely.

The remainder of 1975 I spent settling in at the Institute and with Karen and I had little contact with Rinpoche. Early in 1976, at the conclusion of a meeting with Rinpoche, he asked me, "How's your sex life?" I told him that I was with Karen, and was wondering if we should marry. This was only a few months after we had gotten together, and it was obvious at this time that I was somewhat desperate to find a marriage partner. Strangely, he asked me, "Does she clean?" Quite taken aback, I assumed that this was a reference to Karen's house-cleaning habits and wondered why he said it. Only much later did I realize that it was most likely a reference to my *own* rather lazy cleaning habits. Ah, the many facets of self-deception!

After a bit more discussion, he said, "I think you should leave it open," mentioning another of his close students who had more open relationships and did not try to solidify them prematurely. When Karen and I met Rinpoche a little later at a garden party, he came up to us with a big grin and said that we looked very good together. It seemed I had finally found someone I could settle down with.

My relationship with Karen was not perhaps the romantic love that I had been searching for all those years, but I appreciated her deep intelligence and a strong caring bond gradually grew between us. As was the case with many couples, we brought out obstacles and neurotic patterns in each other that we each needed to face; both of us had deep historic anger and resentment that we needed to work through. As well, both of us needed a lot of space and were rather shy. Partly out of this shyness and partly because we often found the social conventions of endless parties and so on to be rather superficial, we did not work to create a circle of friends and ended up feeling somewhat isolated from the sangha generally. All in all, as partners on the spiritual path we had plenty to work on for many years and we supported each other in this. As Rinpoche stressed many times, this seems to be the key point in a dharmic relationship.

Karen continued to work at Naropa Institute in increasingly significant positions. I respected her depth and insight, and her encouragement was important to me as I took on the role of Nalanda Director with overall responsibility for the Institute. When she left the Institute three years later for the birth of our daughter Vanessa, I lost her view from inside and began to seriously lose touch with what was going on there.

At the beginning of 1976, however, Naropa was in its infancy—its pioneer stage, so to speak—and I played a large part in all the ongoing decisions that had to be made, as well as in specific areas such as program planning, personnel, fundraising, and the ongoing campaign for accreditation. This close involvement with the day-to-day operations of the Institute was challenging and enjoyable, and was to continue for a few years.

HIS HOLINESS KHYENTSE RINPOCHE

In early April of 1976, we eagerly awaited the arrival of His Holiness Dilgo Khyentse Rinpoche to the United States. Khyentse Rinpoche was undoubtedly one of the greatest Tibetan teachers of his generation. Although he was of the Nyingma lineage, he was revered by all Tibetans—the Dalai Lama himself considers Khyentse Rinpoche as one of his teachers. Some of the younger Tibetan tulkus used to refer to him as "Mister Universe" because his knowledge and understanding seemed so unlimited. Rinpoche had known and studied with Khyentse Rinpoche in Tibet and their relationship there was like father and son, although Khyentse Rinpoche now seemed to treat Rinpoche as a spiritual equal. Preparations for Khyentse Rinpoche's visit were less elaborate than for the Karmapa's; it felt like more of a family affair, more like the visit of a favorite uncle than the state visit of royalty.

I had never met Khyentse Rinpoche and, though Rinpoche had spoken about the Karmapa for many years before he visited, we had not heard much about Khyentse Rinpoche. Even so, I woke up at dawn on the morning of his arrival, just as it was getting light, with what I can best describe as an intense sense of blissful space—when I extended my awareness into the space around, it seemed as if that space itself were filled with joy. This was the most powerful experience of this kind that I had had up to that time in my life, and the strongest that I experienced for some years to come. I lay there feeling that blissful space, thinking,

HIS HOLINESS DILGO KHYENTSE RINPOCHE.

"Khyentse Rinpoche is coming today." So, in contrast to the lack of connection I had felt with the Karmapa when he arrived, I already felt a
strong connection with Khyentse Rinpoche even before his arrival.

Khyentse Rinpoche's visit was quieter than that of the Karmapa. He
gave teachings, abhishekas, and private interviews, but it all seemed

rather low-key at least as far as formalities were concerned. Nevertheless, his presence was powerful beyond majestic. Physically he was a
truly mountainous man—over six feet tall (very unusual for a Tibetan)
and of huge girth. As he sat on his chair or throne, his eyes would roam
over the audience (sometimes each eye going in a different direction)
so that one felt seen completely through and through, but with no
judgment whatsoever. One could almost touch the deep silence of his
mind. Sometimes I had the uncanny and slightly disconcerting impression of being watched by a being of an entirely different species or from
another world.

I felt the sense of non-existence in him more than ever before, very
difficult to define, but somehow seeming as if there was simply no one

KHYENTSE RINPOCHE WITH RINPOCHE AND LADY DIANA.
Photograph by George Holmes.

there. When he spoke it was in a deep rumble and sounded as if he
were just entering into the middle of an endless discourse that seemed
to come from outer space. Yet, at the same time, one felt such caring,

such deep compassion, in his presence. To be in that presence, even when he was sitting on his bed occupied with something quite other than oneself, was to feel immersed in a living space that made every ordinary thing seem precious, each moment itself quietly complete. Of my first interview with him—we went in three at a time to ask our questions—what I remember most clearly was that he was continually reading a text softly to himself.

Someone asked him, "Do you still need to study and practice?" To this he replied, "What else shall I do?"

NARAYANA IS NUMBER ONE

The evening before Rinpoche and Narayana left Boulder for New York to greet Khyentse Rinpoche, there was a cocktail party at which they were both present. It was a gathering of the usual gang, so to speak, with the familiar drinking and talking and all the rest of it. At the same time, there was an air of anticipation because we had some hint that there was going to be an important announcement and by now it was not hard to guess what it would be. Toward the end of the evening there was a call for silence and Rinpoche told us that Narayana would be his lineage holder—his "Regent." So it was finally out, and the rumors were true: Narayana, Thomas F. Rich, was the chosen "Number One." The style in which Rinpoche made this announcement was very strong and proclamatory, even fierce, as if to say, "Don't you dare question this! This is it!" After making the announcement, Rinpoche left and the party went into an uproar. A wine glass was thrown into the air and hit the ceiling, shattering glass all over the floor. People were shouting, some with delight, others with anger. Some simply passed out on the floor, drunk as skunks. It was a wild and crazy night.

In some ways it was a relief to know what we had suspected for a long time. And many of us recognized that Narayana really was the only one who at that time could step into this role. Nevertheless, probably many expectations were shattered, just like the wine glass. I heard afterward that as Rinpoche passed another of his closest students on his way out of the door, he said, "Too bad, it could have been you." It was clear that this would mean a big shift in the way Rinpoche related to students and to the organization, but quite what that shift would be remained to be seen.

The ceremonial empowerment of Narayana as the Vajra Regent took place toward the end of the summer, on August 22. It was a magnificent affair. The shrine room of Karma Dzong was completely packed. The entire sangha was excited and joyous about the occasion, although there were still, surely, jealousies and questions like "Why him?" Nevertheless, we had been expecting this for some months by now so we were ready for it. Rinpoche was dressed in elaborate robes and Narayana was wearing an evening jacket. It was splendid, and both Narayana and Rinpoche were glowing with delight. Rinpoche was proud and delighted that he was able to pass on his lineage to a born and bred New Jersey boy! The Regent was the first Westerner to be entrusted as lineage holder of a Tibetan vajra master. From this time on, Narayana had gone. He was replaced by the Vajra Regent, Ösel Tendzin, and from then on we called him "the Regent."

From the time of his empowerment, the Regent took on a major leadership role, taking some of the burden from Rinpoche, both in the administration and in teaching. In response to questions of "what shall we do," Rinpoche would tell us with increasing frequency to ask the Regent. And the Regent began to travel and teach, which up to this time only Rinpoche had done. He was a brilliant teacher. His warmth, sense of humor, skill in relating with students, and ceaseless energy attracted many people to the dharma. Thus there began to be a new crop of students in the sangha who were attracted to the Regent and always felt closer to him than to Rinpoche.

This was not a problem but, to the contrary, just what Rinpoche wanted. He placed tremendous trust in the Regent, as he did in lesser ways in all his Western students. At the same time, of course, he was not naïve about us, being only too well aware of all our hindrances, ego-trips, and potentially serious obstacles, including those of his new Regent.

RINPOCHE AND THE REGENT SHARE A JOKE. *Photograph by Blair Hansen.*

THE THREE LINEAGES

The day after the empowerment, Rinpoche began teaching the "Three Lineages" Vajra Assembly[44] to a gathering of vajrayana students. He spoke of the three ways in which the teachings are passed on to students from an enlightened mind, known as "the three lineages of transmission." The first is the mind lineage, in which the teachings are transmitted directly, mind-to-mind, from teacher to student; the second is the symbolic lineage, in which the teachings are conveyed through symbol, through the environment and the atmosphere the teacher creates around him or her; and the third is the word lineage, in which the teachings are spoken literally. These three lineages correspond to the three kayas: teachings of the mind lineage come directly from the dharmakaya, those of the symbolic lineage are manifestations of the sambhogakaya, and those of the word lineage are expressions of the nirmanakaya.

These three ways of communicating the dharma were all evident in Rinpoche's way of teaching. Clearly there was the outer, word lineage, not just in his talks but in the way he answered questions, in his jokes and puns, in his way of dealing with administrative issues, and so on. The inner, symbolic lineage came through just as clearly in everything he did—the way he moved, raised a glass, created calligraphies or ikebana, the atmosphere that he created in every situation: giving talks, sitting in teacher or staff meetings, hosting dinner parties. The symbolic lineage was also evident in his tremendous care with the way the physical environment was set up. This first became apparent during His Holiness Karmapa's first visit and became more and more explicit later. And the secret, or mind, lineage was shown especially in the many various circumstances, formal or informal, when he pointed out directly the nature of mind. An example of this was at the meditation instructors meeting I attended in Boulder in 1972 when he pointed to a picture and said, "What's that," opening our minds to the space.

CONTINUING FINANCIAL TROUBLE
OF NAROPA INSTITUTE

By mid-summer, Naropa Institute was again in serious financial trouble and a Nalanda Board meeting was called. Naropa's enrollment was down considerably that third summer, although the students who came were more serious, with fewer "spiritual shoppers," as Rinpoche termed people who run from one teacher to another gathering teachings and blessings without seriously putting any of them into practice.

This was influenced by the fact that the Institute itself had become more serious and the summer programs were more oriented toward what we wanted to offer as future degree programs—Buddhism, psychology, dance, theater, and poetry. The financial trouble seemed so serious that Carl actually suggested that we close Naropa Institute.

Rinpoche seemed very unhappy with our attitude during this discussion, almost sullen, and he remained completely unmoving and unwilling to give in to the idea of closing. After a long discussion back and forth about what we should do, he suggested we take a short break to clear our heads and think about it. After the break, the Board meeting resumed and the conclusion we reached was that we would have a big fundraising event at which Carl would tell everyone that the Institute was in danger of closing and ask them to jump in and help—a very successful tactic.

I had previously requested a short meeting with Rinpoche with the intention of asking him again whether I should ask Karen to marry me. I was told I could slip in during the meeting of Rinpoche and the Nalanda Board, so now was the time for me to ask Rinpoche my question. The timing was terrible and, of course, he wasn't in much of a mood for a personal discussion such as that, but he did say, "You seem to be good for each other." And there was, indeed, a strong karmic connection between us, coming from our mutual love for Rinpoche and the teachings he embodied, that was to carry our marriage through the unimaginable changes and upheavals of life in the pressure-cooker world that Rinpoche created.

THE WEDDING

Karen and I scheduled our wedding for August 6, Hiroshima day, which we realized a long time later to our chagrin. The evening before the wedding, we all went to a talk that Rinpoche was giving at the Institute. When it was over the director of Karma Dzong, Lynn, came up to me and said there was to be an important meeting this evening that I had to come to. Naturally I refused, saying, "I can't! I'm getting married tomorrow." But he insisted, saying that Rinpoche had specifically requested that I come to it. I was pretty pissed off—fancy calling a meeting that I had to attend on the night before my wedding! Lynn said he would drive me there and, as we approached the house where the so-called meeting was to be held, it sounded like there was some kind of party going on. Then I suddenly realized, "Oh, *no*, it's a stag party!"

The living room was completely packed with men. Rinpoche was sitting there with an empty armchair beside him which was reserved for me. John Perks, Rinpoche's butler, handed me a large tumbler-full of pure Scotch, saying, "Here, drink this." I quickly did so and everything quickly started to become a whirl. Someone pulled out the movie projector and they showed a porno movie, which we all enjoyed in a strange, drunken way. The theme song was "Happy Days are Here Again," played over and over until it forever stuck in my memory. Rinpoche was enjoying the event as much as everyone. At one point he told me to drink up, so I drank up the rest of my Scotch and he had John Perks give me another, which I also drank up and it put me completely out—I believe I fell asleep, right there in the armchair next to Rinpoche.

When the movie was over and it was time to go, Michael Kohn offered to drive me home. As I left the living room, Rinpoche said, "Don't do anything I wouldn't do!" I remember wondering, even in my intoxicated state, what it could possibly be that he wouldn't do. When I returned home, at around two in the morning, Michael and I went into the house singing at the tops of our voices. I took our large old wind-up alarm clock, put it in the kitchen sink, and peed on it, so Karen told me the next day. I imagine I would have had to go much further than this to follow Rinpoche's parting words, but I did my best!

The next day was the day of our wedding and we were invited into Rinpoche's office to meet with him before the ceremony, as was customary. David Rome, Rinpoche's secretary, poured us tumblers of saké and Rinpoche kept cheerfully telling all of us to drink up. The energy bounced back and forth from extreme tension to extreme joviality for almost two hours. After we had finally managed to empty a second glass of saké, he said, "Let's go." Was he trying to make things as difficult as possible for us, or perhaps to help us relax and enjoy the afternoon?

As we walked into the shrine hall for the ceremony, we were all quite tipsy but managed some dignity. The hall was full; it seemed as if the entire community was there. In his talk to us, Rinpoche referred to our seeking, "many situations in our ordinary life that make ourselves secure and comfortable. But in a lot of cases, we somehow constantly miss the point. Particularly we might have some notion of security in a marital situation where the security does not quite meet our expectations. Sooner or later something happens and it begins to fall apart.... In spite of this, people try to live up to faith and morality, or whatever."

He went on to say that we could approach marriage from a different angle, in which actual friendship takes place, so that friends could be permanently friends rather than just relatives. He referred to, "a lot of interesting facets of our past here—a certain sense of hesitation and a certain sense of constant shopping and uncertainties of all kinds," which brought a lot of laughter from our gathered friends who all knew us quite well, and continued, "but all those approaches have become a healthy approach at this point because these two friends decided to actually jump out into the atmosphere, so to speak." He then spoke of our particular marriage as "the marriage of Nalanda Foundation and Vajradhatu. It finally happened, it's actually taking place, which is exciting and real for ourselves as well as these two friends, that some kind of educational aspect of Nalanda and emotional aspect of Vajradhatu have somehow met together at this point, quite helplessly, there's no choice."

After Rinpoche's talk, there followed the actual ceremony, which was very simple. Karen and I made six offerings to the shrine representing the six paramitas—generosity, discipline, patience, exertion, meditation, and transcendent knowledge—the six actions of a bodhisattva which go beyond ego. We then made the vow: "Having offered these, may we attain wisdom and compassion so that we may help all sentient beings on the path of dharma."

THE DISCOVERY OF THE *ASHE*

In the fall, we began to hear rumors of amazing things happening at the Seminary, which that year was being held at the King's Gate Hotel in Land O'Lakes, Wisconsin. In November, the Regent came back from Seminary and asked the Directors to gather at Rinpoche's house, also the dwelling of the Regent and his family. There he showed us a special mark that one made on paper with a calligraphy brush and ink. He told us it was called the *Ashe* (pronounced *ah-shay*) and explained something about its meaning, though I have long forgotten what he said. He seemed energized and excited by it and showed us how to do it, which we all did. It didn't make much of an impression on me at the time except that I felt both energized by it and disturbed by a presentiment that yet another major change was about to happen in our lives.

A few weeks later we heard the full story. At the Land O'Lakes Seminary, Rinpoche began to undergo the same kind of visionary experiences by which he had received the Sadhana of Mahamudra in Bhutan in 1968. In Tibet, someone who has the natural capability to receive visions of new dharma teachings in this way is known as a *terton* (treasure finder, or revealer) and the teachings he receives are *terma*.[45] Once he is recognized as such, a *terton* has to go through a rigorous training process.

There are antecedents for this visionary finding of teachings in the Indian Buddhist tradition, for example in the great masters Nagarjuna and Asanga. The *terma* tradition was introduced into Tibet by Padmasambhava, the great *mahasiddha* (Sanskrit, meaning "one of great accomplishment") who brought Buddhism to Tibet, and from whom Rinpoche received the Sadhana of Mahamudra in his visionary experience in Tagtsang. Thereafter, the *terma* tradition became a way for a fresh perspective, and fresh teachings appropriate to the time, to enter into the stream of Tibetan Buddhist teachings and enliven the more systematic teachings passed down from teacher to student in the usual way in the formal monastic schools. During his youth in Tibet, Rinpoche was known to be a great *terton* and did indeed reveal many *terma* while still in Tibet. *Terma* are said to be revealed in accordance with needs of people at the time, and this seemed to be the time and place for the teachings of Shambhala to re-appear on earth.

In 1975, Rinpoche had mentioned to the Regent that he felt there was a *terma* coming, and he didn't know anything about it except that it was black. One night at the 1976 Seminary, after Rinpoche had given a talk on compassion, he invited a small group of people to the tiny trailer that served as his residence some distance away from the main hotel. Rinpoche suggested that he and his guests listen to music and asked them what sound might symbolize the moment of enlightenment. Among the albums that he wanted to hear was a favorite album of Japanese *koto* music (the *koto* is a plucked string instrument). At one moment, there was a particular sound, a high, slightly dissonant and piercing note. At that moment, Rinpoche said, "That's it!" The other main music that was played that evening was Handel's "Water Music," which Rinpoche played over and over throughout the night. Later, he often enjoyed having this and the koto piece played at Shambhala events.

After hours of listening to music and conversation, in the early hours of the morning before dawn, Rinpoche withdrew with one student, his cook, Max, to a corner of the kitchen where they began doing calligraphy. The three people who were present report that the energy was extremely strong, vivid, and fierce. At one point, Rinpoche executed the first Ashe stroke and he became very animated and energized, making a similar calligraphy over and over again, fiercely, as if he were slicing through the very earth itself. He also told Max to do the stroke repeatedly, urging him loudly to put more strength and energy into it. Nobody understood quite what was happening there. The session went on for about an hour, finishing after the first light of dawn.

One afternoon a few days later, when some people were gathered around in Rinpoche's study, he suddenly started to write on some note cards. He tossed each completed card over his shoulder onto a table behind him, some cards even falling down onto the floor. He acted so casually that no one realized at first that something very significant was happening. This turned out to be the first Shambhala *terma*, *The Golden Sun of the Great East*, that described the significance of the stroke of Ashe and how to execute it, as I will explain in the next chapter.

The Regent was due to arrive at Seminary soon after this. Normally, when the Regent visited the seminaries, Rinpoche would wait for him in his suite. On this occasion, however, Rinpoche went down to the front entrance and very excitedly waited for the Regent to arrive. As they walked back to the suite together, Rinpoche was overheard saying to the Regent, "I've got it!"—a reference perhaps to his remark the year before that he felt a *terma* was coming and that it was black.

At a subsequent welcoming reception for the Regent, Rinpoche began speaking in a tone such that David Rome realized he was saying something important. David quickly got some paper and pen and started writing down Rinpoche's words as fast as he could. When the Seminary was over a few days later, Rinpoche went to Karme Chöling and completed this dictation in the living room of BPB. The completed work was a commentary on the text of *The Golden Sun of the Great East*, known as the "Auto-Commentary." When Rinpoche returned from Karme Chöling to Boulder, a few of us were given type-written copies of the text and Auto-Commentary. I read them with a mixture of astonishment, excitement, and even fear—but there was also a sense of immediate recognition.

The stroke of Ashe and *The Golden Sun of the Great East* were followed within the next year by other *terma* texts. Rinpoche's discovery of these *terma* was a major turning point—perhaps *the* major turning point—of his life and teachings in the West. Together these formed the basis of an entirely new stream of teaching coming from the pre-Buddhist cultural tradition of Shambhala joined with the highest teachings of vajrayana Buddhism. When asked where these texts came from, Rinpoche said that they were dictated to him by the Rigdens, monarchs of the ancient Kingdom of Shambhala, a society in which the cultural forms and institutions were based on the Buddhist notion of egolessness and compassion and in which the citizens aspired to awakening. Shambhala was the model for a type of society that Rinpoche soon began to speak about with increasing frequency as "enlightened society."

THE WIMPS

Toward the end of the year weekend programs of pure sitting meditation were initiated, free from any Buddhist terminology. Soon these single weekends would evolve into a fresh spiritual path known as Shambhala Training, based on the newly discovered Shambhala *terma*, as well as on the foundation of sitting meditation. But they began in a humble way as "WIMPs"—"Weekend of Intensive Meditation Programs." These arose out of a meeting between Rinpoche and Werner Erhardt, founder of the extremely popular Erhardt Seminar Training, or "EST."

Many people had gone through these intense weekend programs, and although the weekends were psychologically manipulative, all came out reporting they had "got it." Got *what*, one didn't know—but somehow got "it," got the fever, got the EST flash, or whatever it may be. People were, and still are, continually searching for some kind of spiritual zap—instant enlightenment with no hard work required!—and EST was gathering hundreds of thousands of people by promising this zap. After the initial weekend there was another program to train participants to become recruiters for EST, so there was a very well organized kind of snowball effect. Other than that, however, there was not much follow-up. People were expected to somehow incorporate the "it" into their daily lives, with little deep understanding of what they were doing. It all seemed like a gigantic feast of spiritual materialism.

Rinpoche himself hadn't said very much during the meeting with Erhardt, but as soon as the meeting ended, he turned to his students who were there with him and said, sarcastically, "We can do better than *that*." Inspired by this meeting, Rinpoche instructed some of his senior students to begin to teach programs in which meditation practice was presented to people free from the coloration of Buddhism. He wanted us to talk to them without using Buddhist dogma or Buddhist language—we were simply to tell them how and why to meditate. These were the WIMP programs.

The WIMP program consisted of many long hours of sitting, with individual meditation instruction and evening talks by the director.

They obviously did not have any of the entertainment value of EST, and nobody thought they had "got it" at the end. Additionally we really didn't have much of an idea about how to present meditation without using Buddhist terms, so the talks probably had little real content. The earliest WIMP programs were not well-attended and it was felt that the name "WIMP" was not very attractive or interesting, so a number of possibilities for a new name were suggested: the word "Shambhala" was a clear winner, being a popular topic among us at the time. To that we added the word "training," somewhat inspired by the success of Erhardt Seminar Training.

Thus the "weekend of intensive meditation programs" became Shambhala Training. These programs were first conceived as a form of outreach to bring the message of sitting practice to a wider public, so they were to be run out of the information/publicity office. At first the idea was that people wishing to continue would then be introduced to Buddhism. Soon, though, it began to evolve into a separate path of practice in its own right.

THE OPENING OF DORJE DZONG

In the fall, Vajradhatu and Karma Dzong moved into a large office building in down-town Boulder, and Naropa Institute took over the space they vacated. Called Dorje Dzong (Indestructible Fortress), it was an elegant brick building, standing alone on the corner of 13th and Spruce, with a steeply sloping green tiled roof. It had been purchased in January and the renovations had taken almost the whole year to complete. Dorje Dzong would include the offices of Karma Dzong as well as Vajradhatu and Nalanda Foundation. The entire third floor was dedicated to the main Karma Dzong shrine room, large enough for over two hundred people.

On one end of the second floor was "A Suite," which contained offices for Rinpoche, the Regent, and David Rome. At a staff meeting soon after we moved, David Rome announced that the door to A Suite would be closed whenever Rinpoche was present. The only people allowed in without previous permission would be the Vajradhatu direc-tors. Being the only Director of Nalanda Foundation who was not also on the Vajradhatu Board, I did not understand why I was excluded and went to talk it over with David Rome. The next day, I got a call from David saying that Rinpoche was going to do some calligraphies that afternoon, and that he wondered if I would like to be there.

I spent awhile that afternoon sitting quietly in Rinpoche's office, just watching him as he made calligraphies and helping him to seal them in red ink with his ancient Trungpa seal. When he was finished, he invited me to sit down and we chatted for awhile. Still intensely curi-ous about the precise way in which words were used and understood by his students, he asked me about the meaning of the word "nostal-gia." I felt that he was also pointing out to me, again, one of my main characteristics-a kind of nostalgic sentimentality. As I was sitting there, he received a phone call. When the conversation ended, he said to the person on the other end, "Love you, too." This aroused me to say to Rinpoche, "You know, Rinpoche, I love you too, but I just don't know how to express it like other people." This was, I believe, the only time that I actually spoke the words "I love you" to Rinpoche. He replied, "I know you do. And you don't have to be American about it." It was really a sweet moment, reminding me that English reserve was OK in this culture of outspokenness. Needless to say, I went in and out of A Suite freely thereafter. Whenever one made a genuine gesture of open-ing to Rinpoche, as I had done in my request to David, the space around him always seemed to open up in response.

Work continued on the finishing touches to the shrine hall, super-vised closely by Rinpoche himself, right up to the second visit of His Holiness the Karmapa in January.

1977: Shambhala Vision Unfolds 8

 T THE BEGINNING of January, His Holiness Karmapa visited the United States for a second time. A mansion had been rented for him and his party of monks which we called "wedding cake house," because it looked a bit like a fancy wedding cake from the outside. It was on the top of Mapleton Hill just up the road from Rinpoche's more humble abode. His Holiness conducted many events, talks, and abhishekas, and his monks created a sand mandala of Vajrayogini. This time Carl Springer was responsible for all of the preparations for the visit and traveled from center to center ahead of His Holiness, as Rinpoche had done during the first tour. Yet even as preparations were being made for the second visit of His Holiness Karmapa, there were other things going on that seemed to have even greater significance.

THE FIRST VAJRAYOGINI ABHISHEKA

First, there was the Vajrayogini abhisheka, or empowerment, given by Rinpoche, empowering the students to actually practice the sadhana of Vajrayogini.[46] This was to be the first such abhisheka in the sangha and the first of such profundity in North America. Like all of the vajrayana practices that Rinpoche was introducing, there was no precedent; no Western students had gone before. In an abhisheka—a lengthy ritual that can take anything from an afternoon to many days—students are introduced to the practice of a particular vajrayana sadhana. Rinpoche took this abhisheka very seriously and only gave this and all subsequent abhishekas to his students who had completed the ngöndro preliminaries (the hundred thousand prostrations and so on). A few dozen students had completed the preliminaries and were eager to enter fully into the vajra world of the guru. Rinpoche was clearly delighted that we, his stubborn, wild students, had finally arrived at this point. Rinpoche manifested, yet again, an utterly different quality. Wearing the robe of the tenth Trungpa and his special abhisheka hat, made of brocade and curving above his head in a sharp peak with long flaps coming down over the ears and shoulders, he seemed ancient—a real Tibetan lama, at last!

The sadhana had been translated into English and we were able to understand, at least in an outer sense, what was going on. This was very important to Rinpoche—he wanted us to understand clearly what we were getting into, and what we were doing; nothing should be based on blind faith at any stage of our path. So although he was wearing a Tibetan robe, it felt familiar otherwise and didn't have the same foreign quality that I had felt when His Holiness first gave abhishekas in 1974. By now I understood the notion of visualization and deity practice—that one is not calling on an external being, but rather evoking one's own wisdom mind to awaken—and I had worked through a lot of resistance and doubt through the practice of the preliminaries, so my freak-out at the '73 Seminary was not repeated. Nevertheless, the occasion of the abhisheka was baffling, astonishing, and powerful. Now, though nothing seemed graspable or ordinary, I could feel the power and magic of the mandala as Rinpoche manifested the energy of Vajrayogini and poured that energy into the space we shared, inviting us to open to it.

RINPOCHE GIVES THE VAJRAYOGINI ABHISHEKA AND THE VAJRA REGENT ATTENDS. *Photograph by Paul Kloppenburg.*

A NEW BOARD OF DIRECTORS

Also, during His Holiness' visit, Rinpoche announced changes in the Board of Directors of Vajradhatu and Nalanda. The Board was now to consist of seven people: Rinpoche and the Regent as Directors of the First Class, David Rome as chairman, and Carl Springer, Ken Green, John Roper, and myself as Directors of the Second Class. Over the next couple of years three more men were added as Directors of the Second class: Ron Stubbert, Chuck Lief, and Sam Bercholz. As well as serving on the Board of Directors, some of these gentlemen also had more ordinary careers: John Roper and Chuck Lief were lawyers, and Sam Bercholz was the founder and President of Shambhala Publications, whose first publication was Rinpoche's *Meditation in Action*. (In this story, to avoid confusion, I have capitalized "Director" when referring to a Director of the Second Class, and used lower case "director" when referring to a director of a division such as Naropa Institute.)

Each of us was assigned an area of the administration which we were to oversee and act as Rinpoche's spokesmen for—my area was education. At the same time a so-called "Privy Council" was announced. This was to be the closest group of advisors to Rinpoche and consisted of Rinpoche, the Regent, David Rome, and Lodro Dorje Holm, the Loppon (Tibetan: "master") of the Practice and Study department, who also joined the Board the following year. Rinpoche described it by saying, "We will be responsible for people and for the environment." By the "environment" here, he was referring to the cultural environment or atmosphere in which the teachings and practice happened—the symbolic lineage—rather than the environment of earth. People were, of course, always Rinpoche's main concern, and it was very interesting to note that the other most important concern for him, which he and his Privy Council would take on, was the creation of an enlightened environment.

Right from the beginning I appreciated David and Lodro Dorje very much. I always had, and still feel, tremendous appreciation for David in his capacity as Rinpoche's secretary. Whenever one went to him with something, whether it was a complaint, or an idea, or whatever it was that one wanted to convey to Rinpoche, he listened carefully and made very sure that he understood what you wanted to say, without putting his own interpretation on it. One really had the feeling that the answer you got back from Rinpoche through David was as close as anyone could get to Rinpoche's true answer and not just David's version of the answer. That seems to be an extremely important quality for a secretary in that position, and David fulfilled it very, very well.

I saw him in action with Rinpoche many times. I remember one particular time when he came in to check on some details about the printing of a text, needing to confirm with Rinpoche where the calligraphy was to go and where the actual text was to go. He showed Rinpoche the text and the possible positions, and Rinpoche pointed to where he wanted everything. Then David asked Rinpoche, several times, "So you want it here, not here... so this is how it should go..." until he was completely clear about what Rinpoche wanted. That was also how he related to people when they came to him with questions for Rinpoche.

Lodro Dorje manifested a tremendous depth of insight, a brilliant intellect, and unwavering loyalty to the dharma. With Rinpoche's guidance, Lodro was responsible for setting up a system for meditation instructor training and assigning instructors to all students. This system continues to the present day, and is much admired by other Tibetan teachers. Lodro also created a wealth of study courses and materials and a teacher training program and he was deeply trusted by Rinpoche to present true dharma. At Lodro's birthday party in the early '80s, Rinpoche offered a toast to him remarking that "Lodro is pure. He has never perverted the dharma." And this purity of presentation of the dharma, without the taint of spiritual materialism, was of very great importance to Rinpoche throughout his life. Lodro was the only one among this group to whom I could talk straightforwardly and honestly as a friend, and with whom I could go deeply into dharma, which was after all why we were in this business.

THE MEANING OF *ASHE*

Meanwhile, the Shambhala vision of creating an enlightened society was beginning to unfold. I read with astonishment my typed copy of the Auto-Commentary to the *terma, The Golden Sun of the Great East*, sitting at the desk in my office. The title of the text refers to a vision of human life and society based on human goodness and the sacredness of the world. Although in its common English usage the word *sacredness* means "consecrated or made holy by association with an external deity," this was the closest English word Rinpoche could find to describe a world that is fundamentally good and meaningful in its own nature.

The inherent sacredness of the world and the vision of a society based on this is symbolized in the Shambhala teachings by the image of the *Great Eastern Sun*. *Great* refers to a vision of sacredness shared by many human societies across all cultures and ages; *Eastern* to the wakefulness of such societies—east being the direction one first looks when one wakes up; and *Sun* to the limitless and unceasing wisdom and energy available to those who follow this vision. The image of a society guided by the Great Eastern Sun is contrasted with a society of the "setting sun," a society that is dominated by materialism, absence of appreciation of sacredness, aggression, and narrow vision based on self-interest alone. Needless to say, most societies contain a mixture of these two, and it is really a question of which vision dominates.

The central theme of the text is a description of the stroke of *Ashe* and the meaning of *Ashe*. *Ashe* is the power of basic goodness to express itself in the world. Basic goodness is not merely a nice philosophy, or a sense of calm acceptance of everything, but it has a dynamic, active quality symbolized by *Ashe*. *Ashe* is said to be a raging great blade that cuts aggression—it is a razor-sharp edge of brilliant light. But it is a two-edged blade and it is held right up to one's own throat, ready to strike at the first move of aggression. And it is said to reside in the center of the human heart. Hearing and reading these teachings, I gradually began to feel enlivened and empowered by this sense of a living, brilliant, blade of basic goodness, in the center of my heart. It gradually strengthened in me the confidence to cut abruptly through my own aggression and hesitation—doubt about who I was and how I could be useful to the world.

This practice of the stroke of *Ashe* is outwardly very simple: standing or kneeling in front of white calligraphy paper, with a bowl of black ink and a calligraphy brush, you make one stroke down on the paper. But the primordial stroke is not merely a stroke of calligraphy. It is a message from awake mind of how to rend the veil that normally prevents direct experience of the sacredness of our world. The practice of *Ashe* takes us directly and immediately to mind beyond concept, while at the same time it is expressed in a thoroughly direct and physical way. Thus, by practicing the stroke we began to *feel* the reality of the Shambhala teachings at a profound level of mind *and* body; we saw the real possibility of fully joining mind and body, heaven and earth. We began to discover, for ourselves, that spiritual energy is not fundamentally

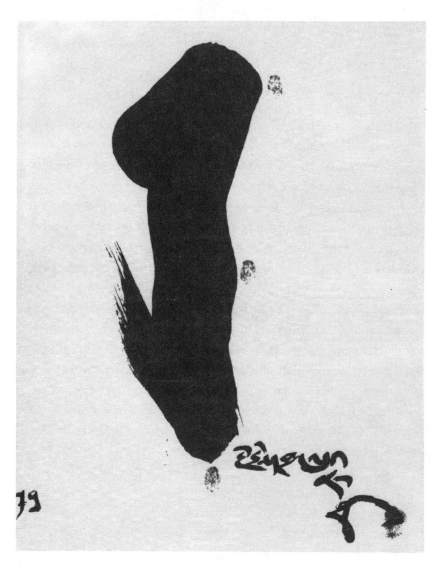

A STROKE OF ASHE, EXECUTED BY RINPOCHE.

different from physical energy. And we began to see how this might lead to being able to manifest this enlightened energy *on this earth.*

FIRST NEWS OF THE KINGDOM OF SHAMBHALA

I also read, in these texts, about the Kingdom of Shambhala for the first time. The Auto-Commentary is almost a *terma* itself, written in a very terse, symbolic language, so it was not easy to understand what this Kingdom was and how it concerned us. It soon became clear that Rinpoche saw an urgent need to bring about a change in culture and society—at least *somewhere* on this earth. He explained that in order to conquer the materialism, greed, and barbaric aggression of the modern world, it would not be enough to simply present the peaceful dharma of egolessness. It would be necessary to transform the entire fabric of society so that it could become a proper vessel for the teachings of egolessness and buddhadharma. He called this an "enlightened society," for which the Kingdom of Shambhala would be the model. He was to teach a very great deal on the principles of enlightened society in the remaining years of his life.

A chant that is repeated many times by the entire community at the end of each year, *Pacifying the Turmoil of the Mamos,*[47] refers to the darkening ages as:

> *An evil time, when relatives quarrel,*
> *When people dress sloppily in clothes of rags*
> *Eating bad cheap food,*
> *When there are family feuds and civil wars.*

All these are signs of the degeneration of the times, which had been prophesied by Padmasambhava and which, as Rinpoche foresaw so clearly, were rapidly increasing in our world. Enlightened society, Rinpoche emphasized, is not intended to suggest an idealistic society in which everyone is already enlightened, but is one in which people aspire to genuine wakefulness, in which human dignity and goodness

RINPOCHE EXECUTING A CALLIGRAPHY. *Photograph by Andrea Roth.*

are nourished; it is a society in which the cultural forms and institutions are based on trust in this fundamental goodness. Many societies, throughout the ages and across the globe, have aspired to these principles to some degree or another. But they seem now to be gradually fading in the face of the globalization of greed and opportunism. To reverse this trend was Rinpoche's intention, one to which the remaining years of his life were dedicated.

A special meeting was held in the dining room of the Kalapa Court, as Rinpoche's residence was now called. (Kalapa was the capital city of the ancient Kingdom of Shambhala). At this meeting, Rinpoche asked David Rome to explain that the Northeast region of Canada known as the maritime provinces (also, sometimes, as the Northeast Kingdom) was envisioned as the area where the future Kingdom of Shambhala would manifest on earth. This, he explained, was a place where the people still had an old-fashioned sense of basic human decency. It was not overly developed, being somewhat economically and culturally depressed, and it had an open fertile quality that could accommodate and embrace the vision of Shambhala, so it would be a mutually beneficial situation. Rinpoche added that Shambhala should be established in twenty years.

The point of establishing Shambhala vision, as a cultural basis for safeguarding the dharma of egolessness on earth, was not to find a haven for ourselves where we could retire and build another nest. It was to provide a beacon and launching pad for continuing to bring the dharma to the rest of the world. Rinpoche clearly felt the continuing degradation of human society on earth was an urgent situation and one that we had to help with. From now on, in this context, all those who had been introduced to this vision were known as subjects of the Kingdom.

At that time we took Rinpoche's time-frame literally, although subsequently it became clear that this was probably a mistake, and that when Rinpoche said "twenty years" he simply wanted us to understand that, as he said so often, "We mean business!" As Rinpoche was to repeat over and over again, "The situation is urgent, *please* help the world." If he had told us that the Kingdom would be established somewhere on earth in two hundred years, we would probably all just have stayed in our cozy domestic scenes in Boulder, leaving the project to future generations. And the vision would have passed off the earth along with Rinpoche.

At first there was tremendous confusion about this vision, but as time went by we understood that this was not intended as some kind of "take-over" or cultural imperialism. For society to really change, the momentum has to come from the general populace and its understanding of basic goodness. It has to come from joy, celebration, the ability to distinguish what is genuinely helpful to oneself and others and what is harmful, and a willingness to work on one's own state of mind. The idea was to present an option, a society based on basic goodness and caring for others, including the planet earth. This would manifest very differently from a society based on materialism. Today, we can also speak of this in terms of "sustainable societies," meaning in our case cheerful and caring societies that are socially just, inclusive, and compassionate, having clean, sustainable environments, ecologically-friendly economies, and enlightened leadership.

ELEGANCE AT THE KALAPA COURT

John Perks was now master of the household for the Kalapa Court and in this capacity he began to set up formal service. The men and women who were serving, all volunteers and Rinpoche's students, dressed in very traditional waiter and waitress outfits. At the first formal dinner, served buffet style, the invitation stipulated evening dress, which most of the men had to rent for the occasion. Altogether it felt very strange indeed. We had certainly come out of the hippie era! Most of the men now had short hair and shaved faces, and were generally dressing well, or at least in a slightly more conventional manner.

We were all very stiff and awkward at first. As David Rome was going through the buffet line, he said in a very loud voice for all to hear, "I think it will be all right if we pretend we're in a movie." There was a roar of laughter, which broke the ice, and we were able to relax a little and enjoy the scene. Although it felt to us at the time quite awkward and uptight, even edgy, it was also tremendously joyous and uplifted. The entire group energy and cheerfulness was raised up on such occasions, for guests and servers alike, and it felt as if we were celebrating the best of human existence. Guests and those serving interchanged for different occasions—sometimes one could be a guest, and at other times make the offering of serving. Either way, it was a practice of letting go, being present with genuineness. The dinner party was another step in showing us how to uplift a society—a step of formality and elegance, if we could see it that way.

Nowadays words like *decorum* and *elegance* have come to seem superficial and empty-hearted, having to do with behaving properly in public and looking fashionable. However, according to the Oxford English Dictionary, the meanings of *decorum* include "that which is proper, suitable, or seemly; fitness, propriety, congruity" and "beauty arising from fitness; orderliness." The meanings of *elegant* include "characterized by refinement, grace, or propriety," and "graceful, polite, appropriate to persons of cultivated taste." Thus we can see that both of these words have to do with fitting harmoniously into the society of humans in which we dwell. As Rinpoche wrote in *Shambhala: The Sacred Path of the Warrior,* "A Shambhala gentlewoman or gentleman is a decent person, a genuine person. He or she is very gentle to himself and others. The purpose of any protocol, or manners, or discipline that we are taught is to have concern for others."[48] This extends to recognizing and acting harmoniously with the sacredness of the natural world of which our society is an inseparable part. Whether we treat animals and trees with dignity and respect or with degradation and contempt is surely inseparable from how we relate with each other.

TUTORING RINPOCHE'S SON

In March, Rinpoche left Boulder for a nine-month retreat in Charlemont, Massachusetts, in the same old country house where he had done his retreat in 1972. There was a minimal staff consisting of Perks, who was the butler and head of household; Max King, the cook; and Max's dog. There were also usually one or two visitors. When he had first announced this retreat a year previously, he said he was going away to "see how we would do." So while he was away, we began to settle in to our new roles as Directors of the various departments. The Regent was already beginning to travel and teach a lot, but even so we had regular weekly Board meetings.

Toward the end of the summer, Perks phoned me from Rinpoche's retreat, saying that I was being asked by Rinpoche to oversee the education of Ösel Mukpo, Rinpoche's oldest son. Ösel was fifteen years old at that time, and having a very hard time in the Boulder public school. As a young boy, Ösel had not had an easy time in the year preceding his arrival in America in 1972. He was born in India in December, 1962. His mother, Lady Kunchok (as she became known to us), had accompanied Rinpoche on the escape from Tibet. On learning that she was pregnant, Rinpoche told Lady Kunchok that the child would be a boy, that he is the "emanation of a deity," and that he would grow up to be a great teacher who would "attain the glory of the happiness of beings." Ösel had been born at Bodhgaya, the site of the Buddha's enlightenment, and had lived in a refugee camp in India with his mother until he was eight years old.

When the time came for Ösel to join his father in Scotland, Rinpoche had already had the car accident that was to radically alter the course of his life and teachings. Ösel finally did arrive in Scotland just shortly before Rinpoche left Samye Ling to cross the Atlantic to America. Rinpoche had intended to send for his son as soon as he was settled in America. However, failing to understand Rinpoche's transformation after the accident from a monk to a married man wearing Western clothes, many of Rinpoche's previous British students had bitterly opposed him. These no doubt well-meaning but ignorant people held Ösel virtually prisoner and a legal battle ensued over his custody. It was two years before he was finally able to join Rinpoche and Diana in America. Lady Kunchok stayed in India until she finally visited Rinpoche and their son in America in 1986.

When I began to tutor him, Ösel could barely read English, reading almost like an average six or seven-year-old with his finger pointing at each word. In India, he had been top of his class in both reading and writing Tibetan and Hindi, but after his first traumatic year in Britain he spoke only English. Since he had subsequently received no proper training in reading and writing English, it was no wonder that he was having such a hard time in high school.

Ösel was shy with me, but charming and cheerful, with a light sense of humor. Sometimes we had a lot of fun. At one point when I was trying to teach him fractions, I tried to get him to understand what "1/4" meant, and how, when you divide the top and bottom numbers by a common multiplier, you will get a reduced fraction. For example, 20/80 equals 1/4 when you divide by 20. He was interested—really fascinated—in only one thing, which was, "Well, what's the slash for, why is there this line?" It reminded me of the (perhaps apocryphal) story of a Zen master who was asked to read a Rorschach test, in which one is asked to say what one sees in an odd-shaped ink blot—is it a rabbit, a hat, a car? The Zen master answered, "It is black mark on a piece of white paper." Ösel certainly had a very interesting mind, but it was not really interested in fractions. Nevertheless, he worked hard at his studies and he did gradually begin to read and write.

His real passions at this time were horse riding and falconry. In 1980, when Shibata Sensei, the master of kyudo (Japanese contemplative archery), came to Boulder, Ösel took up kyudo and became one of Sensei's main students. He has remained a passionate sportsman all his life; in addition to riding horses whenever he has an opportunity, he has also practiced weight-lifting for many years and enjoys golf. At the age of forty-two, he took up marathon running and competed in the prestigious Boston Marathon, finishing in the top third, a remarkable achievement. Whatever he engages in he does so with gusto and tremendous dedication. As I will describe in the Epilogue, Ösel is now holding the Buddhist and Shambhala lineages of Rinpoche and magnificently nourishing the seeds of enlightened society sowed by his father.

VISITING RINPOCHE ON RETREAT

During his retreat in Charlemont, Rinpoche let it be known that he would like each of the Directors to visit him, so I arranged to visit in November. I flew into an airport about an hour or so away from Charlemont and was met by Perks. Before going on to the retreat house, he and I stopped off in a café for a beer, and he filled me in on the retreat protocol. He told me that Rinpoche would be waiting for me in the living room and that I should go in and do three full prostrations, and then offer him a traditional silk scarf and a gift. When we arrived, I went through the proper form and Rinpoche indicated that I should sit on the seat beside him. He was quite formally dressed and was altogether fairly formal at that moment. He seemed quiet and dignified, almost as if he were on a throne. In spite of this, I immediately felt relaxed as I sat beside him and he asked me how Karen and I were and how Naropa was doing.

The next day, Rinpoche was much more informal, and every day from then on followed the same basic pattern: I would get up around 8:00 or 8:30, have some breakfast, which I usually cooked myself, and then practice Vajrayogini sadhana by myself in the shrine room. After a slow start, I had grown to love this practice and I did it a lot at home. I mentioned this to Rinpoche at the retreat and asked him if I could practice in his shrine room in the mornings before he got up, and he had readily agreed. Rinpoche had been doing a Padmasambhava sadhana during the early part of the retreat, but he wasn't using the shrine room during my visit. After that, I would go and sit at the kitchen table, which is where, in fact, we spent almost all of the retreat. Rinpoche would come down sometime between 11:00 and 12:00, always very perky. That whole week he was always lively and perky, and very relaxed. Once he came into the kitchen almost trotting, if you could say that with his lame leg, and nearly leapt across the room. There was something boiling on the stove, so he picked up the lid and made a delighted exclamation, then came back to the table with a smile and sat down.

Perks, Max, and I would have lunch, sometimes with Rinpoche join-ing us. It was usually lunchtime when he was having his breakfast, and at that time the consort visiting during that period would also be with us. But often it was only Rinpoche and me, just sitting there on adjacent sides of a corner of the table, just the two of us, not saying very much. I wasn't really, and never have been, much of a conversa-tionalist, and I couldn't think of anything to say; and Rinpoche just seemed to be responding to my energy. He told me that the visits of each of the Directors were so different that it was as if each person pro-voked a fresh movie to be rolled out for him.

I would just sit there simply enjoying the positive space of the envi-ronment and my mind that his presence evoked. All I wanted, really, was to be in that space and to let my mind expand into it. So we just sat there. I didn't feel uncomfortable or particularly uptight, as I usu-ally had in his presence before. He radiated a sense of tremendous peacefulness and simplicity, which was at the same time bright and alive and which seemed to fill the space within and without. It was similar to the simplicity I had felt long ago at Tail of the Tiger during the Battle of Ego Seminar. But I was more comfortable with myself now, with who I was, shy English Jeremy. At the Battle of Ego Seminar he didn't know me at all, so I didn't feel a need to hide anything.

Now it was more as if he had seen me so well; another way of put-ting it might be that I had seen myself so well that there wasn't so much left to hide. Now I didn't feel any need to have a conversation or to do anything to entertain him in any way, and he didn't seem to indicate that I should. We just sat there in that rich, alive space. I very clearly remember becoming aware of his breathing at one moment, as we sat at the kitchen table together, particularly noticing his out-breath. It almost seemed to me as if he were actually being mindful of the out-breath. I'm sure he wasn't doing it deliberately or intention-ally, but it was as if he were so present that it happened naturally. Lis-tening to his out-breath for that moment brought me also intensely into the present.

CONVERSATIONS

In one conversation Rinpoche asked me about the other Directors and what I thought of them. I suppose that he had this kind of conversation with everyone who visited, building up a series of vignettes about what was happening in Boulder, seeing everyone from so many different points of view. I remember saying of Carl that he seemed to feel that he could act as a spokesman for Rinpoche, as he was continually speaking on his behalf. I expected Rinpoche to be a little displeased, but instead he said, "Well, you could as well." He asked me what I thought about the Regent and I replied that he was a brilliant teacher, but much more up and down, less steady and even-handed than Rinpoche, and that he could go too far in his outrageousness. Rinpoche seemed to confirm this observation and replied, "You should talk to him."

On another occasion, as we sat at the kitchen table as usual, we discussed some of his older students who seemed to have drifted off, or become problematic. Rinpoche suddenly said, "We should form a committee to help these people back to the dharma." The idea, as far as I understood it, was that if someone strayed from the path of dharma, exhibiting excessive aggression or otherwise getting lost in doubt or worldly activities, they could be reminded of their commitment to the dharma through meetings with this committee. Rinpoche was always concerned about students who wandered off the path, and he seemed never to forget people with whom he had made a connection.

When we had been planning the Naropa Institute summer program, he asked us to contact several of his old friends from his days in England. He had particularly mentioned John Driver, who had been his friend and tutor at Oxford and whom he seemed to have tremendous respect for, as well as Alf Vial and Michael Hookham who had been among his first students in the Scotland days. Alf did teach a course at Naropa Institute, but after the session was over he told me that Rinpoche was so different now that he did not feel any connection with him or with Naropa Institute, so we never heard from him again.

Michael Hookham, who was unable to attend Naropa that summer, did keep a connection with Rinpoche and actually attended the 1980 Seminary just to check out how Rinpoche's teaching had evolved since the days in England. Now Michael is teaching and publishing independently in England, under the name Rigdzin Shikpo.

One day, Rinpoche looked through my bag, which contained the report of an arts in education program at Naropa Institute I had organized that summer and had been funded by the Rockefeller Foundation. The report included an application for a further grant for the following three years, which we did receive. When he mentioned it, I asked him what he thought about it. He said, "It's just what I was hoping for," with a delighted look on his face. Through the program we were reaching out into the academic world, in this case training school teachers through the arts and meditation and thus using what we understood to help others. This seemed to be very much the point of Naropa Institute which was clearly a project dear to his heart, even though on a day-to-day basis he was much more involved in Vajradhatu and left the Institute more to us.

A LETTER TO SHAMBHALA TRAINING

During the time of the retreat, Rinpoche heard that things were going awry in Boulder. In particular, there were reports that some of the Shambhala Training weekend programs were becoming inappropriately wild and aggressive. We heard reports that some people—including some Directors—were promoting themselves in a self-serving way and being generally arrogant, trying to mimic Rinpoche, and so on. When he heard of this, Rinpoche dictated a very sharp letter to the head of publicity who was still managing Shambhala Training.

When he had finished the letter, we left the house and went out for a drink. Rinpoche was still in an angry mood, disappointed that people were presenting Shambhala Training in such a stupid and aggressive way. I said to him, "Rinpoche, the problem is that we don't really know what to say at these weekends. We don't know how to introduce meditation without Buddhist dogma." Impatiently he growled back, "Just speak from your own experience." It was probably these incidents that inspired the series of talks he gave almost immediately after he returned from the retreat in which he showed us how to do this.

Rinpoche then started asking me to recount to him how we had met and what we had done together. He kept saying, "And what happened after that?... And what happened after that?..." It felt like he wanted to hear my side of our mutual story. When I got to the summer of '74, I just dried up and couldn't go on. I realized then how things had changed after I left Karmê Chöling, with the sense of greater distance and formality. It was only later that I realized that in some way all my friends and colleagues were probably experiencing something similar—one has a tendency to believe so often that one is the *only* one suffering!

The sense of greater distance from Rinpoche had to do with the transition from relating to Rinpoche as spiritual friend to relating to him as vajra master. As spiritual friend he is one's best friend. As vajra master, however, he is more like a martial arts master; one is an apprentice in a dance of energies that is highly dangerous because the apprentice, rather than leaping into egolessness, can so easily slip into ego-mania. In this dance, at the same time as following the teacher's instructions and trusting his wisdom, it is essential to have confidence in one's own strength and understanding, not constantly looking to the vajra master for confirmation. Soon there was to be an even greater sense of distance as we began to relate to Rinpoche as subjects toward their monarch. While at the time it felt painful and confusing, now I see it as a natural and necessary progression of our developing confidence.

CREATING THE BASIS FOR ENLIGHTENED SOCIETY

Rinpoche's main activity during much of his retreat, and particularly during the period of my visit, other than just sitting at the kitchen table, seemed to be creating societal forms for Shambhala. At one point I was moved to ask, "Rinpoche, are you still going to teach Buddhism, and give abhishekas, and so on, when you get back?" He simply nodded and said, "Yes, of course, it's my job." But clearly all of his enthusiasm and energy was going into creating the forms and the vision of Shambhala. As news of all this filtered back to Boulder and elsewhere in the sangha it was met with shock and fear by some, and with great inspiration and excitement by others.

While I was there he was also working on a manual outlining the forms of Shambhala society: *Court Vision*. *Court Vision* described the qualities and roles of the main figures of the Kingdom: the Sakyong and his upbringing as Prince; the Sakyong Wangmo, wife of the Sakyong; the Lord Chancellor, head of the Government; the Lord Chief Command Protector, head of the Dorje Kasung; Ministers (in the context of the Kingdom, the Directors of the second kind were called the Ministers, but I shall mostly continue to refer to this group as Directors from now on); subjects; and, finally, a chapter on corruption in the government.

The title *Sakyong* referred to Rinpoche and literally means "earth protector." And it was clear that Rinpoche took this role seriously, increasingly so as the years went by. At the Seminary in 1980, the faculty of a course on the Shambhala teachings met with Rinpoche to discuss the topic of Sakyong, the king of Shambhala. Rinpoche commented, "It's a tremendous burden to be Sakyong. You don't ask for it—you are commanded to do it." As far as he was concerned, he was given this command when he received the first Shambhala terma, *The Golden Sun of the Great East*. This calling of Rinpoche to take on the role of Sakyong, protector of the earth, King of Shambhala, was confirmed during the second visit of His Holiness Khyentse Rinpoche to Boulder in May of 1982, when Khyentse Rinpoche enthroned Rinpoche as the Sakyong and Lady Diana as the Sakyong Wangmo—the Lady Sakyong.

Court Vision also described ceremonial procedures and decorum for behavior in the shrine room, in the audience room of the Sakyong, and in the Court or place of residence of the Sakyong. Dress, from formal to semi-formal to informal, was described, with the occasions appropriate to each, as well as appropriate forms of address to various dignitaries in formal or informal situations. There were detailed descriptions of how to serve at a dinner party, how to offer toasts, and even how to use a knife and fork. And he wrote the "Shambhala Anthem," which was set to the Irish marching tune "Let Erin Remember."

Rinpoche was also designing a series of awards and medals for various honors, based on the English system of Lordships, Knighthoods, Orders, Medals, and Colors for dedicated service, and so on—over one hundred altogether. He said he was thinking of making one of the Directors a Knight and asked me who I thought it might be. I was perplexed as I did not really understand the purpose of these awards, and did not want to openly judge my fellow Directors.

On one amusing occasion, we were having dinner with a few guests and the meal consisted of a very classical English dish: slices of roast beef, roast potatoes, and peas. Suddenly Rinpoche asked me how we eat our peas in England. I carefully showed him how I had been taught: first you slice a bite-sized portion of meat, then of potato; you push the fork through the potato and into the meat and then pile a few peas on the fork on top of the potato. You never turn the fork over and shovel peas on as if it were a spoon—or so I was taught.

Rinpoche found this quite delightful and, to my chagrin, it later turned up in the dining section of the manual on decorum. This was to cause quite a ruckus between Lady Diana and Rinpoche a couple of years later. In the middle of a formal banquet, a fierce argument broke out between them. The argument ended in Rinpoche throwing his wine glass across the room, trying to upturn the table that was firmly held down by Lady Diana, and storming, out followed equally stormily by Lady Diana. Later I was told that the argument was about the passage in the decorum manual about how to eat peas! Lady Diana had said that this was one way English people ate peas but that it was also perfectly acceptable to turn the fork over.

It began to be clear that Rinpoche was, in a sense, designing an entire set of forms for a new society and culture, which would be based on a combination of Tibetan, Japanese, and British traditions. One of the characteristics of the coming dark ages, according to Rinpoche, is that all of the traditional forms of decent human relationships are being lost. Today simple decency or good manners are often disdained as an expression of repression and lack of freedom, and people try to do away with them and become completely casual.

All of these forms are mirrors for ego and opportunities to go beyond ego. As Rinpoche would tell us at the Kalapa Assembly a year later:

> From the point of view of Shambhala vision, egoless is slightly more direct than in buddhadharma, and could sometimes be said to be more crude. That is to say, in the buddhadharma you can always hide your lifestyle. You could have an excellent record of sitting practice but after that you still hibernate in your domestic situations or business situations or what have you. But in this case, egolessness also demands of you that there be no corners left at all for privacy—none whatsoever. There are particular Shambhalian norms associated with how to wash your dishes, how to iron your shirt, how to do your grocery shopping, how to stand and how to sit. There is a whole society being introduced, based on that particular discipline of egolessness.

The re-introduction of hierarchy, especially in a society so deeply embedded in ideals of democracy and individualism, was perhaps the most difficult form for many people to understand. However, Rinpoche made it clear that hierarchy did not mean someone at the top acting as a lid on others. Rather the further "up" the hierarchy one was, the more one should care for the welfare of others and encourage their development, like the space into which a flower can grow, warmed by the sun and moistened by the rain. He called this "natural hierarchy" and used the image of lids and flowers in a seminal talk to the community the next year. Natural hierarchy is a principle of leadership based on mutual appreciation of basic goodness and egolessness. In a natural hierarchy, higher stages of the hierarchy go along with increasing commitment to the practice of meditation and deepening realization of egolessness. This leadership style encourages communication and cooperation at and between all levels. While providing the space and warmth for people to grow, the leader is at the same time willing to say "yes" and "no" when the situation requires. All of this began to become much clearer as the Shambhala teachings unfolded over the following years.

By this time, the importance and value of form in relating to the great Buddhist teachers, such as His Holiness the Karmapa and Trungpa Rinpoche, was becoming apparent. One of the vital points to help understand this importance is the notion of the symbolic lineage, which describes the way in which the vajra master conveys the teachings environmentally, through symbols and forms, rather than literally. At every moment, Rinpoche manifested the symbolic lineage, in the way he dressed, in the way he held his water glass or lit a cigarette, or in the way he spoke the English language so precisely and clearly. Now the symbolic lineage was being manifested further in the tremendous variety of forms that he created: banners to hang on the walls, pins to be worn on the lapel, uniforms, chants, songs, awards, and orders… All of these forms are an important way that the teachings of a great siddha are passed on from generation to generation. The power of the form to convey awakened mind lies in the detail, and for this reason it is very important to keep these forms alive and to pass them on precisely.

THE JOY OF SHARING THE SPACE OF RINPOCHE'S MIND

Even with all of this activity, my main memory of that retreat is of sharing the space with Rinpoche and wanting nothing other than to be in that shared space, mixing my mind with his. And it remained very much like that for me as the years continued. The times that I felt closest to him were those times when I could just quietly be with him in his room mixing our minds in the space. There was a day a couple of years later, when I sat with him in his private living room, just the two of us and his consort. It was late afternoon and nothing much was happening with me, as usual. It was very quiet, and Rinpoche said, in a clearly pleased tone of voice, "Being with Jeremy is like being on retreat." At this his consort chuckled, "Yes, *boring*." And in a certain way it was—

nothing was happening—but this was not what I felt he meant. He was having dinner brought up to him and his consort, and he invited me to stay and join them.

Being on retreat at Charlemont with him was the first time I had really experienced the tremendous spaciousness of his mind in that way. It was such a contrast to the time, back in 1971, when I had gone around to his house to pick up the garbage and tried to chat with him, trapped in a tiny space in my own thoughts. Then he had had to open my mind to the space by asking me if I heard that sound of a lawn-mower; now it was much more natural. To have had that experience of knowing his mind filling all of space is especially important now that his physical body is no longer with us, because his mind has never moved.

The main point, of course, is not so much to know the guru's mind, but to know the true nature of one's own mind, which is not separate from that same space. The guru, being so utterly settled in that space, thereby leads the student to that point, and confidence in this was growing in me by this time. These may seem strange ideas in a culture so fixated on the materialist view that the world consists of lifeless, empty space containing nothing but material things, and that my mind is in my head and Rinpoche's was in his.

If that is the case, how could our minds "mix in space"? Sounds like rubbish! The point is that, as meditative experience suggests, the world may not be like that at all. The realization of great practitioners of mindfulness-awareness meditation is that awareness fills all of space; or to put it another way, all appearances arise within awareness, which therefore fills all of the space of those appearances. And further than this, the point is not to fixate on the guru but, because of the intensity of his genuineness, our relationship with him becomes a mirror for the relationship with our whole world. Thus as we open our awareness to our world, this is reflected in a greater openness to the mind of the guru, and vice versa.

I had been planning to spend about four days at the retreat and then go up to Boston a couple of days early, but I was having such a wonderful time that I asked Rinpoche if I could stay on for a few extra days. In the end I was there for a week. As I left, he hugged me and said, "Keep in touch."

From Charlemont I went to Boston and then over to Karme Chöling, where the Regent was giving a seminar. It was one of the first times I had seen the Regent teaching in a formal seminar situation since he had become the Regent, and it was a delightful occasion. He was teaching on devotion and his teachings were insightful and heartfelt. In the evenings, there would be joyful gatherings in BPB, where we were both staying, including a party at which the Regent had us roll up the living room carpet and dance to the theme tune of the popular movie of the time, *Saturday Night Fever*. While I was there, he told me that he had heard from Rinpoche that I had had a very good retreat time with him, and he told me to keep that up, build on it.

And indeed, I knew that it had really been a deepening of my connection to Rinpoche, and to his mind.

1978: 9
A Splendid Year of Celebrations

HE FIRST MAJOR formal Shambhala event took place at
the end of 1977, on a December morning at dawn. This
was David and Martha Rome's very elaborate wedding
ceremony, the first Shambhala wedding. It was held at
the residence of the Bercholz family up in the foothills outside Boulder.
The bride and groom were dressed in formal Japanese clothes, and all
of the forms of a full Shambhala wedding were created for that occasion. Rinpoche had been involved in every detail of the ceremony. The
preceptor and couple entered in procession to the sound of Japanese
koto music. Chants were offered to the father and mother lineages of
dralas (of which I will say more later).

In contrast to the Buddhist wedding ceremony, in which offerings
are made representing the six paramitas, in this Shambhala ceremony
the couple each executed a stroke of Ashe in front of the Shambhala
shrine and Rinpoche. The marriage oath was then taken and sealed by
the couple taking a sip of saké from the traditional square Japanese
cup. It was a truly uplifting celebration to end the year.

WALTZING FOR RINPOCHE ON HIS BIRTHDAY

The introduction of uplifted forms continued with the sangha celebration of Rinpoche's birthday in February 1978, which was held in the ballroom of the Hilton Hotel in downtown Denver. The celebration began with a trumpet fanfare and the formal entry of Rinpoche with Lady Diana, and the Regent with Lila, his wife, who now had the Shambhala title of Lady Rich. They took their seats on a stage, and everyone filed into the room, four by four in hierarchical order, to the sound of Handel's "Music for the Royal Fireworks." We walked from the entrance to the ballroom across the long open space of the dance floor, displaying our best windhorse (an important Shambhala term referring to our life-force energy) and dignity for the group on the stage. After bowing to Rinpoche and Lady Diana, we went off to our respective seats at tables that were arranged along the sides of a large dance floor. Following this procession, drinks and hors d'oeuvres were served and there was a series of formal toasts. We were then entertained by several performances, some of which were very beautiful. Then the dancing began. Rinpoche wanted us to learn the Viennese waltz as he continued to look for Western expressions of dignified festivity and uplifted windhorse.

So we had taken waltzing lessons in preparation for the birthday celebration. The dancing was initiated by the Regent and Lady Diana, who danced elegantly and were a delight to watch. However, when they had completed the opening dance we all had to get up and try it as well. That first year, there was complete chaos. Some didn't even know we were all supposed to waltz in the same direction around the dance floor. There was a sense of celebration, good cheer, and uplifted-ness, but it was also hilarious and we felt slightly ridiculous. Rinpoche stood on the dais waving his arms in the air like a traffic director, trying to get us to go faster. Most everyone plunged in to join the fun, so there were hundreds of people crowded onto the relatively small dance floor. It was quite a noble effort.

The next year we did a little better—at least we mostly went around in the same direction.

THE REGENT AND LADY DIANA OFFERING THE FIRST WALTZ.

CELEBRATING THE FIRST SHAMBHALA DAY

Continuing the sense of festivity, the first sangha-wide Shambhala Day was celebrated this year. Shambhala Day is celebrated on Losar, the traditional New Year's Day in Tibet as well as in most Asian cultures. The actual date of Shambhala Day is calculated based on a lunar calendar. It corresponds with the first stirrings of spring under the earth, and as such it is felt to be a far more appropriate time to celebrate the beginning of a new year than on January 1, in the very depths of winter. There usually is, indeed, on Shambhala Day, a sense that the depths of winter have passed, and that spring is just around the corner.

That year, the day began with a dawn gathering of about twenty or thirty people at the Bercholz residence. Rinpoche was there when we arrived, already having had a bit to drink, and was completely enlivened and delighted, radiating for the occasion. With a rich and elaborate buffet breakfast, we were served gin, which Rinpoche regarded as a special liquor since it was made from the juniper plant. The smoke from this plant is used in Tibet in a ceremony to purify and energize the environment. Rinpoche toasted the New Year. We were bemused by it all, and at some point we began to have fun. Next, we all drove down to Dorje Dzong and gathered in the shrine room, where Rinpoche gave his first Shambhala Day address to the entire community, including the children. This address became an annual event to open the Shambhala Day festivities.

Some of us were invited to go to the Kalapa Court, for an immense feast—an Indian lunch that Ken Green had organized. We were all drinking saké as well as excellent beer. After lunch, we flopped out in the living room for a while, while Rinpoche went upstairs to rest, and then returned to our respective abodes for the rest of the afternoon. These celebrations at the Court were intended to be an example of how the entire sangha was invited to celebrate on Shambhala Day.

Later, a dinner for the hundred or so subjects of Shambhala was held at the Broker Inn in Boulder. The practice of waiting for everyone to be served before saying the opening meal chant and beginning to eat was introduced for the first time. The meal consisted of lamb chops, so this was a bit of an ordeal and gave rise to a famous Shambhala riddle: "What is the difference between a Great Eastern Sun banquet and a setting-sun banquet?" Answer: "At a *setting-sun* banquet, the food is always *hot*." The throwing of the I Ching, seeking a prediction for the year ahead for the Kingdom of Shambhala, occurred for the first time that evening. This throwing of the I Ching also became an annual event, repeated at every practice center. Additionally, this was the first time that awards were given out, which likewise became one of the annual Shambhala Day rituals, at least during Rinpoche's life-time. Along with dozens of people receiving awards for their service to this new society, I received the "Warrior of the Order of the Garuda." This meant, to my utter surprise, that I had been the one whom Rinpoche had in mind when he asked me on retreat who should be a knight!

When I went up to Rinpoche to receive the award, instead of plac-ing a dot of black ink on my tongue with his Ashe brush (the new Shambhala way to seal an award or an oath) he drew an Ashe on top of my bald head, much to everyone's amusement, including mine. From then on I was known as "Sir Jeremy" within the growing circle of the people who knew about the Kingdom of Shambhala. All the other Ministers (Directors of the second class) received the simple "Order of the Garuda," which was not a knighthood, and so this meant that I was from then on considered senior among the Minis-ters. Though the title has never been widely circulated, I am still referred to in this way during formal gatherings of the subjects of the Kingdom, and occasionally at other times by people who are aware of it.

SHAMBHALA TRAINING EVOLVES

Soon after Rinpoche's return to Boulder from the retreat, he began to have a series of gatherings with thirty to forty of the people who had

JEREMY RECEIVES AN AWARD, AND AN *ASHE* ON THE HEAD.

been introduced to the Shambhala vision of creating an enlightened society on earth. We assembled for his talks in the community room in the basement of Dorje Dzong. I recall those talks with great warmth. Rinpoche gave very direct, personal talks to us there, almost like an uncle talking by the fireside. It was as if he were talking to his family, recounting what children should know.

The idea was that this group of people would be the ones who would present Shambhala Training to others. As I mentioned above, I had asked Rinpoche on retreat, "What should we say?" and no doubt, others had asked him as well. His answer in a nutshell to this question had been that we should just tell them about our own experience. In a sense, that was what he did in this series of talks—he was just telling us his own experience and thereby pointing out ours.

Rinpoche gave two talks a week during January and February. Gradually, in these talks, the terms that later became basic concepts of Shambhala Training—*basic goodness, cocoon, fearlessness, gentleness, warriorship*—were told to us very simply as ordinary human experience beyond any religious or philosophical dogma.[49] Let me say a bit about each of these terms.

The term *basic goodness* has a profound as well as a broad meaning in the Shambhala teachings: its profundity, the unconditioned aspect, is that our fundamental awareness is beyond all concepts, judgments, and discriminations, such as good and bad, accepting and rejecting, and so on. The implication is that all appearances—our perceptions of the world—are fundamentally pure before we lay our conceptual judgments on them. This unconditional aspect is equivalent, in Shambhala terms, to the basic nature that is pointed to in Buddhism by the terms emptiness and luminosity / joy. The broad aspect of basic goodness is that out of this unconditioned nature arises the possibility of humans to act decently and kindly toward one another, and to create good societies.

The *cocoon* in each one of us, equivalent to the Buddhist "ego," is all the emotional and conceptual hang-ups that cover our basic goodness and obstruct ourselves and others from seeing it. The Shambhala *warrior* is a man or woman who aspires and trains to step out of the cocoon, realize basic goodness, and help others. The term warrior does not, of course, symbolize someone who makes war on others. Rather it refers to someone who works to overcomes aggression, the fundamental cause of all war, in oneself and in the world. To do this requires bravery as well as gentleness.

During this series of talks, Rinpoche received another *terma*, *The Letter of the Black Ashe*. This text describes the four Shambhala dignities, which are qualities that exist in all humans, but are usually hidden beneath the cocoon of fear. The uncovering of the dignities describes the significant stages on the path of warriorship, equivalent to the bodhisattva path in Buddhism. These *four dignities* are: *meek*, being in touch with one's basic goodness, mindful and self-contained; *perky*, joyful and free from hesitation to help others; *outrageous*, beyond hope and fear, willing to act beyond conventional norms if necessary; and *inscrutable*, resting naturally and carefree, with humor, completely present with what is. These warriors are inscrutable because, while being fully present, they have nothing on their minds and are noncommittal (with a sense of humor), therefore there is no basis on which others can make their usual projections about what the inscrutable warrior might be thinking or how they might behave.[50]

These talks were especially oriented to the practice of teaching Shambhala Training. As such, they contain some tremendously helpful advice from Rinpoche about how to teach in general. He emphasized in particular the importance of being meek, the first dignity—genuine and grounded—and that any teaching should always be given with a meek attitude of decency and kindness. So this series of teachings came to be known as "the meek series."

The *Black Ashe* text also describes the nature of windhorse,[51] the energy or life force of all beings. When it is roused, this life-force energy is forceful and powerful like the wind, and can be ridden with dignity and confidence like riding a horse. The mentality of the setting sun steals our windhorse, thereby weakening and depressing us, catching us in the trap of doubt about our basic goodness, and ambushing us with false hopes of eternal entertainment and distraction. Therefore it is important as we go into the world as warriors to constantly raise up our windhorse, which is to re-connect with our basic goodness and confidence.

Rinpoche talked toward the end of this series about raising our windhorse, which he also referred to often by the Tibetan word *lungta* (*lung* means wind, *ta* is horse). Somebody wanted to know how to actually *do* it, how to raise windhorse, lungta (this practice may be referred to simply as "raising windhorse" or, interchangeably, as "raising our, your, one's windhorse"). So, a few days after that talk, we were invited to Rinpoche's suite to be introduced to the practice. We went one by one into his office where, with Rinpoche watching, David Rome guided us through our first taste of the formal practice of raising windhorse. This was a visualization practice which took several minutes, done in kneeling posture with hands on thighs and elbows out in the shape of a bow (though later we were to learn simpler ways of doing it).

As we awaited our turns in the hallway outside the office, it was quite amusing to watch people come out after receiving the practice; some of them had befuddled looks on their faces, and others came out with little giggles. After I had my turn, I also left feeling a mixture of befuddlement—"What happened?"—and delight that gave rise to a smile. Thus, the first transmission of rousing windhorse was part of those first director-training talks. I will not describe the details of the practice here, as it is best communicated personally in a living situation. Generally, however, when we are in a depressed state simply feeling the ground beneath us, the space all around us, and uplifting our head and shoulders and straightening our spine naturally arouses our windhorse.

That spring Carl Springer, the Director in charge of the information office and hence Shambhala Training, reported to the Board on how things were going with Shambhala Training. The participants in the Shambhala Training weekends were still largely sangha-members, even though a publicity firm had been hired to try to promote Shambhala Training to a wider audience beyond Buddhists, as was Rinpoche's intention. It was far from the major success that we had been hoping for and expecting. But, to me, there was a deeper issue: Rinpoche had said previously that one of the problems with Erhardt Seminar Training was that there was nothing for the participants to do after the one-weekend program. There was a sort of advanced EST that turned people into propagandists, or EST recruiters, but the basic training program was one weekend. Rinpoche had pointed to this as a major problem because it wasn't really a training, it was just a "zap," with a strong whiff of spiritual materialism. Although there was no zap in the Shambhala Training weekend, there was no continuing training either, unless someone immediately decided to join the Buddhist track, which was not necessarily the point.

I asked, "Well, what are they going to do after this weekend program?" At that point, in a flash, the Regent suddenly jumped in and said, "Okay, I've got it—this is what we will do. We will have five weekends: the first will be on basic goodness, the second on cocoon, the third on warrior in the world, at the fourth they will meet me, and at the fifth they will meet Rinpoche." Thus there were now five levels of Shambhala Training. The topics of levels four and five, as first taught by the Regent and Rinpoche, were awakening the heart and opening the mind to the moment of *now*. This structure made so much sense as an introduction to the path of mindfulness and awareness in everyday life, free from religious dogma, that it essentially stayed this way for many years. These five levels remain basically unchanged now, thirty years later, although other people took over teaching the fourth and fifth levels within a few years.

HOW TO LEAD: BE FLOWERS, NOT LIDS

By 1978, the worldwide sangha was growing by leaps and bounds, and the staff of Vajradhatu was growing equally to serve this sangha. Rinpoche insisted that all his students would be leaders in society at some point and frequently spoke about the enlightened style of leadership. Needless to say, as the staff grew, the "boss" mentality began to take hold. It is typical of the male "boss" mentality (not confined to people of male gender!) to feel that "I am the only one capable and responsible for making the decisions." This manifests, for example, when a meeting of people who thought they were empowered to make a decision ends with the boss saying, "Well, let me think about it," returning sometime later with "the decision."

In the case of many people in the leadership in the early years of our sangha, this would often be preceded with, "I spoke to Rinpoche and he said…" This is a very undermining form of leadership, which unfortunately goes on even to this day. One finds in leadership positions— directors of centers or whatever—just as one finds in the normal business world, people who continually disempower their staff by insisting that they alone are the ones who have to make all of the decisions. No matter how much discussion may occur, people become disheartened because they know that in the end the director is going to decide anyway.

Rinpoche gave a talk to the community, which became famous and oft-quoted as the "Lids and Flowers" talk, in which he characterized the above style of leadership as the "lid" approach. He contrasted this with the "flower" approach, in which the job of a leader is to provide the space and the warmth for people to grow. The role of the leader was to nourish and encourage, rather than to control and criticize. We all recognized, of course, the "flower" style of leadership in the way Rinpoche himself related to each of us, in the way he left us so much space to take responsibility ourselves and to make our mistakes without needing to be afraid of heavy-handed criticism. But leadership is perhaps one of the most challenging of all roles we have to play in the world. The trap of heavy-handed control (the lid) and of *laissez-faire* holding back (the flower that refuses to blossom) are hard to avoid. Looking back, it is easy to see that the latter mistake was my own obstacle.

This period saw a lot of sangha activity in the area of business. Rinpoche was encouraging people to start their own businesses at this time. It really was as if he wanted his students to begin to create a different society, by being their own bosses, so to speak, and employing other sangha people in their businesses. At the same time, he encouraged people to work for Karma Dzong, Naropa Institute, and other parts of our organization as much as possible. During 1978 and 1979 the number of staff on the Vajradhatu payroll grew tremendously, which was certainly due to the encouragement of Rinpoche. Sometimes people have the idea that working for the organization is some kind of cop-out and that we should all be out there in the "real world," working in a "normal" situation, whatever they suppose that may be. But that did not seem to be Rinpoche's view necessarily—it varied from individual to individual and from his point of view our only task was to offer buddhadharma and the path of warriorship to the world in whatever way we could, including both working for the sangha organizations and working in conventional jobs.

The whole attitude of the sangha at that time was a tremendous sense of delight and joy about the true teachings and teacher we had discovered. People were extremely exuberant and wanted to be involved, and one of the ways in which they could do this was by starting businesses. Out of this sentiment, the Ratna Society was born; its purpose was to promote the understanding among its members of the relation between good business practices, Buddhist meditation, and the bodhisattva ideal of working for the benefit of others.

The Board had continued to meet regularly, once a week, during Rinpoche's retreat at Charlemont. After Rinpoche's return from retreat, the Board meetings took on a more formal quality. The meetings were held at the dining table of the formal dining room of the Court, where we would all gather wearing three-piece suits. After we were all settled, Rinpoche would come in wearing, without fail, a cheerful grin. So, however weighed down we thought we were by the burdens of our office, Rinpoche's presence would always start us off on an uplifted note.

Rinpoche would sit at one end of the table, with the Regent on his right and David Rome on his left. During the meeting, often at a particularly tense moment, tea would be brought in with something to eat. This really made the whole situation rather awkward—we had to shuffle our papers around to make room for the tea cups and plates, wait for everything to be served, and so on—but it provided a kind of elegance as well as a break in the business and the intensity of the atmosphere. Despite having had previous study sessions with the Regent to prepare for the formal meetings, we would often plunge into a topic all over again, right there in front of Rinpoche. Sometimes we would get into very heated arguments.

Rinpoche usually just listened, occasionally saying a little to help guide our discussions, raise our gaze and show us a larger view, but almost always he left the final decisions to us. On one occasion, for example, the Board was discussing the need to find a permanent place to hold Seminary, which was still having to be moved around from one hotel to another every year or few years.

This year, again, Ken Green had to find another hotel for the following year's Seminary. A very large hotel was for sale on an island in New York state. It was a very high price for us, but a remarkably low price for such a place. It could hold Seminary as well as many other wonderful events, then and in the future. We were all enthusiastic about it, although to buy it would have demanded another tremendous fundraising campaign. After extensive discussion Rinpoche asked, "Why are they selling it?" No one seemed to have thought of this, and we never heard of the project again.

NAROPA INSTITUTE BECOMES OFFICIAL

By the summer, we had been working seriously on Naropa Institute's application to become a candidate for accreditation—the first and major step by which a college can become accredited by the regional accrediting organizations. Once candidacy is achieved, the accrediting organization has a vested interest in the Institute and guides it toward full accreditation. Receiving candidacy would mean that our courses could be listed for credit and that in some cases other colleges would accept these credits. It also meant that certain grants would now be available. In short, this was a big deal for Naropa Institute. In the case of the Institute the regional accrediting organization was the North-Central Association, and we were assigned an advisor from the NCA headquarters in Chicago. Now finally we were ready to write our extended application. I led the team who would write this report.

After the report was completed and submitted, the NCA sent a team to visit Naropa for a few days to make the decision on whether or not we would be recommended to receive candidacy for accreditation status. After the visit, we received a copy of the visiting team's report, which began, "Naropa Institute has to be seen to be believed." Naropa was, to say the least, a rather unusual college at the time, based as it was on a Buddhist foundation and an educational philosophy of "Joining Intellect and Intuition," having a Tibetan Buddhist as its President and courses on meditation integral to the degree programs. Nevertheless, the report made a positive recommendation and we were invited to visit the NCA headquarters in Chicago for a final meeting with the examining board of the NCA.

Our visit to Chicago occurred in July. We had been up late at night for days before our departure, preparing the final documentation to take with us. We went over to Rinpoche's office the day before leaving, and he suggested that each of us do an *Ashe* stroke in front of him. It was a very uplifting meeting and he was in a cheerful, encouraging mood. As we were leaving his office, he poked his head around the door with a big smile, and said, "Remember me!"

Our party of four had reserved a hotel room at the Chicago airport Hilton, where the annual accreditation conference of the NCA was being held, so that we could rest before our meeting with the examining board. The first thing we did when we found our room was to flop and rest. Shortly before it was time to go down to the meeting, we decided to raise windhorse together. There we were, then, the four of us, lined up on the floor, kneeling, with our eyes closed. Suddenly the door opened and the cleaning lady came in (she took one look at us— and closed the door again). In its own way it had a feeling between a celebration and a college exam day. Of course, we were nervous, but we were also extremely wired, extremely high. But we kept our windhorse high and rose to the occasion, answering the examiners' questions more than adequately. Then we went home and waited.

About a month later, while I was visiting Karme Chöling, I received a call to tell me that we had received the candidacy for accreditation. I immediately got on the phone to Rinpoche to tell him how well it had all gone. I added, "I think it was because we raised windhorse that we did so well." Someone who was with Rinpoche when he received my call, told me afterward that Rinpoche turned to her after he put the phone down and said, with obvious delight, "Jeremy thinks it's because they raised windhorse that they did it!" So that marked the end of this first important phase of Naropa's development.

THE FIRST MIDSUMMER'S DAY

That summer witnessed the first celebration of Midsummer's Day, which was a magnificent event organized by Ken Green and his team on a meadow just below the foothills south of Boulder. It was a beautiful location and a beautiful mid-summer's day with warm sunshine and fresh breezes. A huge white Tibetan tent on which were sewn the eight auspicious symbols, with a platform in front, had been set up for Rinpoche. There were rows of smaller tents coming down on each side to form a kind of alleyway, or processional, where people could present their offerings. Hundreds of Boulder sangha-members joined the festivities and found their places in the tents along the sides, where there was food, drink, chairs, blankets, and barbecue grills. Rinpoche arrived with Lady Diana, both on horseback. They were followed by Ösel and Gesar (Rinpoche and Diana's second son who had been recognized by Khyentse Rinpoche as the incarnation of Rinpoche's own guru, Jamgön Kongtrül, and now lives in Nova Scotia with his family), and the Regent and Lila Rich with their family. All took their seats on the main platform.

Then the parade began. The directors of Karma Dzong, the Board of Directors, the staff of Naropa Institute and Alaya pre-school, and all of the different societies that were rapidly being formed such as the Ratna Society, followed by families and children and the whole sangha, lined up four-by-four and walked up to the platform to bow to the lineage. Some performances and sports activities were conducted in front of the main tent. Rinpoche was particularly encouraging us to take up Western archery, so there was a small archery range set up behind his tent where I had my first shot at archery and thoroughly enjoyed it. For the rest of the day, people enjoyed picnics, games, and water pools for the small children. It was a fine celebration.

AN ODD BIRTHDAY PARTY

In July, I was offered a birthday party at the residence of Bill McKeever, the new director of Naropa Institute. They had set it up very nicely in their terraced back garden, with the main tables and offerings of buffet and drinks up on the top lawn. There was a table for Rinpoche, Karen, myself, and whoever else wanted to join us down on the lower terrace. Some people did come down, but they gathered on the side of the lawn as far away from Rinpoche as possible. When Rinpoche asked why we thought no one was coming to speak with him, Karen suggested, "Maybe because they're afraid." "No, it's because they are too content," he replied.

Rinpoche was not in the mood to chat that day. He had told me, in 1972 back at Tail of the Tiger, that he wanted to experience "falling in love" Western style—and now he seemed to have done it. One evening, in 1972, we were all hanging out in Rinpoche's bedroom, sprawled out on the floor around his bed. He finally announced that it was time for him to go to bed, but when everyone got up to leave he indicated that I should stay. When we were alone he said, "There was something I wanted to share with you, and that is that I'm trying to fall in love." I assumed that he was not talking about the kind of genuine love that he had for Diana, but about the infatuation, obsession, or having a crush, that often passes for "falling in love" in our culture, and that he knew I was prone to. I said, "Why would you want to do that, Rinpoche?"

He replied, "Well, just for the experience; just to find out what it's like." It seemed as if this was yet another example of his inquisitiveness into the life of this culture. I felt that he was telling me this partly as a way to include me yet further into his life and way of thinking, and also, perhaps, because he knew how much I had wanted to "fall in love." I had, in fact, fallen deeply in love with a Danish *au paire* girl during my Cambridge years. This only lasted a year, until she had to return to Denmark, and for several years after this I knew that I was looking for that love, or for her, in every other woman that I dated or slept with.

Now, he was waiting for his new love, Cynde Grieve, to arrive, with whom he had fallen in love at the Seminary earlier that year. She was to arrive by plane that day, and Rinpoche constantly looked at his watch and asked, "When is she coming?" This was basically the entire extent of our little session down at the table on the lower terrace. We finally went up to the house where some presents had been arranged on a table in the living room. Rinpoche seemed anxious to get the whole thing over with, so instead of letting me go through the gifts and open his last, he pulled his gift toward me and said, "Open this!" It was a beautiful Western archery bow. Rinpoche immediately left and the birthday party ended very soon after that.

Rinpoche's love affair with Cynde continued for many years and she later took on an important role as one of the sangyums (special consort), a role that Rinpoche created toward the end his life as a counterbalance to the all-male Board of Directors, that I will describe later. Lady Diana writes of this affair:

> During this seminary, Rinpoche had a love affair with one of the participants, Cynde Grieve. He was quite in love, which he shared with me when we talked on the phone. This relationship went beyond what I was used to, and it was a little shocking at first. However, Rinpoche was so warm and loving with me, and so open, that I couldn't hold on to my insecurities. The reference point of a conventional monogamous marriage did not apply to our relationship, which remained very strong. [52]

By this time, my own relationship with Rinpoche had slipped back from the relaxation and openness of the time at his retreat to more stiffness and sense of distance. This was quite natural given all the energy and multiple activities he was involved in, but I did long for those quiet days again!

Nevertheless, there were still some delightful intimate moments. One afternoon, I was in bed with the flu. I was watching a children's program on TV—Mr. Rogers—and I particularly remember an ad, in which the refrain was "Anything can happen and it probably will." It seemed such an apt description of life with Rinpoche. At that very moment I heard a big commotion in the living room. Rinpoche had been visiting Diana at the riding school where she taught, which was near to our house, and decided to drop by to see us. I quickly turned off the TV. He came into my bedroom and gently put his hand on my chest asking how I was. Then he delightedly went all through the house, peeking in drawers and closets, with Diana shouting at him to stop. After a short while the party left.

THE FIRST KALAPA ASSEMBLY

The first Kalapa Assembly took place in October. The Kalapa Assembly was a gathering of people who had been introduced to the full vision of the Kingdom of Shambhala. It was viewed as a sort of first statement of the planting of the Kingdom on earth. This particular year was just the beginning of the manifestation of the Kingdom of Shambhala, so we were experimenting with the new forms. There were formal dinners, and various activities such as archery and horseback riding.

Rinpoche gave talks almost every evening,[53] commenting on the terma texts, especially *The Letter of the Black Ashe*, parts of which had been read to us during the talks to Shambhala Training Directors in the previous winter. He also received another terma shortly before the Kalapa Assembly concerning the practice of arousing richness, entitled *The Letter of the Golden Key Which Fulfills Desire*.

In one of these talks, Rinpoche compared the Shambhala path with the traditional paths of Buddhism. In Shambhala terms, he said, egolessness or absence of reference point can have more spark and actually expose us more than in Buddhism, because we have to give up clutching even religious practice as a reference point for our self-centeredness. "If we are holding on to any kind of corner as a little fortress, a little capsule," he said, "we have a problem in raising windhorse.... The fruition of the warrior's path is the experience of primordial goodness or the complete unconditioned nature of basic goodness. This experience is the same as the complete realization of egolessness or the truth of nonreference point."

THE SHOCK OF HEARING OF *DRALA*

One of the most powerful and memorable events of that first Kalapa Assembly was by far, for me, the talk on "*drala*." I had been slightly bored at the two talks immediately prior to the drala talk; they had been on the dry side and covered what felt like rather familiar ground. The talks always happened very late in the evening so it was sometimes not easy to focus. Rinpoche began this talk with, "Continuing as we were talking about yesterday," and I thought, "Oh, *no*." Then he started to talk about drala. For me, the place suddenly became electric, the energy was so strong. As I looked around the room, there was so much energy that it seemed to be vibrating, shimmering as if in a heat haze. This talk was to have a powerful effect on me, although I didn't realize until some years later just how important the theme of *drala* would be.

Why was this talk so powerful and provocative? Whenever Rinpoche spoke, he evoked the atmosphere of his topic way beyond merely mouthing the words—he taught as much through the symbolic lineage as through the word lineage. In talking of drala, then, he at the same time invoked them and called them into the space. And what are drala? They are the life force of the world itself; they are the very energy of space, living patterns of energy that surround us all the time, within and without, but that we are usually too blind or coarsened to feel. In a sense they are parallel to the gods and spirits in certain other traditions, with an important proviso: like all of the space that contains them, they are not ultimately separate from our own wisdom mind. Therefore they cannot be thought of as external beings that control the world, in the way that we now interpret the gods of ancient times, or like the single god popularly conceived by followers of the major theistic traditions.

In connection with drala, Rinpoche spoke of three levels of space and presence. In this case he called these three levels the three courts, which parallel the three kayas (mentioned in chapter 6) and the three lineages (see chapter 7). The idea of "court" is a secular version of the mandala, the central figure being a secular leader rather than a deity. The three courts are essentially a way of looking at the structure of ultimate and relative reality. The ultimate court, similar to the dharmakaya, is unconditioned openness beyond concept; the inner court, parallel to the sambhogakaya, is the realm of subtle energy and luminosity—symbolized by the brilliant light of the Great Eastern Sun; the outer court is the realm of appearances and the five senses, the nirmanakaya realm. And, just as the three kayas are also inherent in the being of all ordinary people, so too are the three levels of drala.[54]

Each of these realms or levels of space, Rinpoche told us, are filled with presence—he called this presence the "inhabitants" of the realm. The inhabitant of the ultimate court is known as the primordial Rigden ("holder of awareness"). The primordial Rigden is the non-conceptual presence and awareness of our inherent awakened state, the nonreligious equivalent of the awakened mind of the Buddha. Just as with the dharmakaya, this realm and what abides in it is beyond *all* concepts, even those of existence and non-existence.

The inhabitants of the inner court, the realm of luminosity, or "intermediate plane" as Huston Smith refers to this realm in *Forgotten Truth*,[55] are known as the mother and father lineages of drala. These drala were called by Rinpoche "almost entities." They are very close to the *kami* of the Japanese Shinto tradition, and we watched a movie about this tradition during the Assembly. Rinpoche also mentioned similarities with the gods of the pre-Christian Greek, Roman, and Scandinavian traditions. The inhabitants of the outer court are, specifically, the Sakyong and Sakyong Wangmo (the King and Queen of Shambhala in the earthly realm) and more generally are master warriors—living dralas.

As well as the mother and father lineages of the inner court—which parallel the Buddhist deities, such as Vajrayogini and Chakrasamvara—there are inner dralas of human activities, such as cooking, wood-carving, musicianship, scientific investigation, and so on.

And human beings who have attained a high level of wakefulness are also said to possibly become dralas of the inner court when they leave the physical realm. Important among these ancestral dralas of the inner court are the Rigden Kings, the monarchs of the ancient kingdom of Shambhala. Sakyong Mipham Rinpoche (then Ösel Mukpo) describes the Rigdens in this way:

> The Rigdens are not some celestial entities; they represent the ultimate ruler within us all. Tibetan paintings of the kingdom of Shambhala show the Rigdens conquering the negativity of the dark age. They are often depicted sitting on thrones of diamonds, indicating unshakable possession of the awareness of basic goodness, our primordial nature, which is also known as the Great Eastern Sun. The Rigden king manifests wrathfully, but his armor is always gold, an expression of compassion. His sword represents the incisive wisdom that sees basic goodness. There are pennants on his helmet, which symbolize the courage it takes to bring windhorse—long life, good health, success, and happiness—to others. After the victory of the Rigdens, the story goes, the age of enlightenment arises. The Great Eastern Sun appears on the horizon.[56]

The great King Gesar, who unified warring tribes in Tibet and brought about a new age of peace and the spread of buddhadharma, is one example of an ancestral drala.

In Japan, too, great ancestors are sometimes revered as *kami,* or drala as we would say. As an eighteenth-century Japanese poem says:

Each of us must become a true person
Once we have become that person
We become kami
We become buddha

Connecting our own energy with the energy of the dralas raises our life force and nourishes our genuine confidence. Connecting with dralas of the mother lineage increases the quality of gentleness that comes from understanding egolessness. And connecting with the father lineage strengthens the genuine confidence that comes from fearlessly acting in the world from that gentleness.

In the phenomenal world, Rinpoche said that the dralas "ride on auspicious coincidence." Whenever something occurs in our life that shocks us, wakes us up, something that seems like a message from the phenomenal world, this could be the manifestation of dralas. This, of course, has parallels in many cultures, in which it is somehow determined such-and-such is an auspicious (or inauspicious) day to begin a project, or celebrate an important occasion such as a wedding.

It also has a parallel in Jung's description of "synchronicity" in which, having noted how often the inner state of his patients was strikingly reflected in some unpredicted outer event and often gave them some understanding of what they were going through, he extended this discovery to ordinary lives. I have experienced such moments myself. Often they are quite small incidents that could easily be brushed aside as mere coincidence, but that can make a difference to my action if I pay attention to them. But there have also been several important turning points in my life, when paying attention to a coincidence has taken my life in a new and positive direction. A clear example is the story I recounted in chapter 2, when I picked up *Meditation in Action* at a bookstore and read it in one afternoon, then mentioned to a friend that I longed to meet Rinpoche a few days before he was to give his first seminar in Boston where I lived.

Sometimes at teaching programs we ask people to tell the stories of how they first met the dharma. These stories are full of auspicious coincidence. Here is one such story: in the early '80s, a young German was at a point in his life when his relationship had ended, his job was not working out—nothing seemed to be working. He decided to spend the summer camping on a beach in Greece, a favorite haunt of European hippies at that time, and try to decide what direction to take in his life. He camped there for several weeks, but nothing seemed to be happening with him and he became even more discouraged, so he packed up his tent and drove home.

About twenty kilometers down the road, something in his mind shouted, "Stop!" He pulled the car to the side of the road wondering what to do, and that same something told him, "Go back!" Though he had no idea why he should go back, he returned to the beach, set up his tent in the same place that it was before, and went to sleep. The next morning a new camper had arrived and set up his tent right next door. They started a conversation and the newcomer gave our German friend a book—*Cutting Through Spiritual Materialism*, by Chögyam Trungpa Rinpoche. He read the book on the spot and realized that this was what he had come to Greece for. He is now a senior practitioner and member of Shambhala in Germany.

The term *drala* means literally "above the enemy," which in the case of the Shambhala tradition means "above aggression," since aggression and territoriality, the ego's reaction to space, is the fundamental enemy of the Shambhala warrior. The reason Rinpoche insisted so strongly that we relate to the dralas was to give us the strength to help others by overcoming aggression, in ourselves and in the society around us; to help, in effect, to establish an enlightened society. He emphasized repeatedly that we could not connect with the dralas without a thorough understanding of egolessness and non-aggression.

Altogether, the understanding of the presence of awake energy patterns in our world, which are not visible to ordinary perception but that we can connect with in more subtle ways, is common to most societies that are not dominated by a metaphysics, such as that of scientific materialism, that excludes such possibilities. And it is important to understand that the materialist view that dominates the modern world *is* a metaphysics. It is one *possible* theoretical construct, but is not a *necessary* consequence of the observations of science which are compatible with many other philosophies. There is, in fact, nothing in the idea of dralas that is incompatible with the actual observations of any branch of science, though their existence *is* incompatible with the standard materialist philosophy, a philosophy which is more and more coming into question even among scientists themselves. Of course, in a society such as ours in which the genuine understanding of these "almost entities" has been pushed deeply underground, what is left is often just superstition and fantasy that only goes to further the skepticism and denial nurtured by the dominant philosophy.

For many people in the Buddhist sangha, brought up by Rinpoche on the notion of "non-theism," it was a tremendous shock to be asked now to relate to "almost entities" that were very like the gods of old. This resistance to opening to the dralas continues to this day. I believe it comes in part from a deep fear of the inner realm in modern culture, coming from the historical destruction of the native pagan traditions in Europe, along with a blind faith in scientific materialism. It also arises from the misunderstanding of the notion of "non-theism" which parallels the nihilistic misunderstanding of shunyata. Non-theism does not mean that we deny all possibility of worlds and beings that are invisible to the five senses, such as the dralas and tantric deities. Non-theism is a statement of the nonduality of all appearances, that is, whatever appears to exist is not separate from our own being. Thus we do not regard the dralas or deities as being ultimately separate from us. Nevertheless on the relative level we can form a relationship to the dralas as we can with all visible beings.

INSTANTANEOUS WINDHORSE

In another talk Rinpoche introduced us to another form of raising windhorse, which he called the "instantaneous practice." This was a much quicker practice which consisted very simply of abruptly letting go of fixed mind and opening one's awareness to space. I found this suggestion, almost too simple to call it a practice, to be most helpful in lifting myself out of a depressed or negative state of fixed mind, and I realized that "raising windhorse" is in fact a very natural process that we can do often in our daily life. Since then it has become one of the key practices for me in raising my energy and cheerfulness. I also realized how important a practice it is in connecting mind and body together at the level of the heart that opens the perception of the heart through feeling and enables us to connect with the inner realm. It is raising our windhorse and connecting mind and body together in this way that enables us to open to drala in our world.

Rinpoche at times referred to windhorse as our personal drala or inner drala. Thus there are two aspects to drala—inner and outer, though as I have emphasized, this division is not fundamental. Inner drala is our own personal gentle strength and power, while outer dralas are the strength and power of the outer, phenomenal world. The equation is simple: by raising our own inner drala, we attract outer drala. It is very similar to the principle of "like attracts like"—if I think negative thoughts about others, then others will certainly reciprocate with negative thoughts about me. If I think the world is dull and gloomy, then that is the kind of world I will find, but if I think the world is bright and good then, likewise, I will find myself living in such a world.

An analogy that I have found useful for the notion of inner drala attracting outer drala is that of a tuning fork resonating with a grand piano. If you place a tuning fork on a grand piano and strike the key whose pitch matches the fork, the tuning fork starts to vibrate. It's tuning in to the larger energy of the piano and being affected and energized by it, but the note it sounds is its own. Likewise if we place our body-mind in the appropriate way, we can invite larger energies and forces in the cosmos to resonate through us and awaken our own energy and wisdom further.

A lovely story that well illustrates abruptly raising windhorse is told by Patricia Bandak (at the time), who later became one of Rinpoche's consorts. I first met Patricia when she joined the Naropa Institute staff after the 1979 Seminary and, though we had little connection for twenty years, she is now Patricia Hayward, as I will relate toward the end of this memoir.

Here is Patricia's story:

I first heard the name "Trungpa Rinpoche" in the fall of 1975, when I was twenty-four years old. I vividly remember that moment, sitting at the dinner table, when a friend told me about Rinpoche, saying, "Trungpa says that you don't have to keep running around looking for answers outside of yourself, but you just have to sit down and look at your own mind, at where the questions are coming from." At that moment, I knew I had heard the truth, really for the first time in my life. I thought, why didn't anyone ever tell me this before? It is so, so simple, so obvious. A month or so later I drove up to Karmê Chöling where Rinpoche was giving a seminar. All I remember about this seminar was that Rinpoche appeared to me as a small, golden Buddha, very peaceful and magnetizing. I was oblivious to the scene around him, just being so happy to have found this genuine situation.

I didn't meet Rinpoche personally until a few years later. I had been to Karmê Chöling many times by then, for seminars, a dathün, a two-week solitary retreat, and meditation instructor training. But I felt so certain of this path that it hadn't really occurred to me that I needed to personally meet the teacher. In 1978 I had a brief [abusive] relationship, which blew up one morning in the Dharmadhatu group house I was living in with my little son. It had been a very violent incident and I was afraid to go back to the house, and I had never experienced anything like it at all. The other people in the house had little experience with this level of aggression, and could not help me. So I flew to Boulder to ask Rinpoche what to do.

A friend in Boulder gave me a gold chain and suggested that I ask Rinpoche to tie a knot in it and make it a protection cord. So, I waited nervously outside of Rinpoche's office suite, on a very warm and sunny summer day. First David Rome brought me into his own office and reviewed the situation with me. I was forever grateful to

David for his maturity, kindness, and strength. He first talked with Rinpoche for a few minutes, and then told me to go in.

Rinpoche was sitting behind his desk, and I sat on a chair next to the desk. It was one of those experiences of atmosphere, where at the time and always in my memory there is golden space, or light, with an indescribable quality of fullness, or love. Rinpoche was very elegant, beautiful and still. He was wearing a suit and looked completely dignified. His eyes were not like other people's eyes, but were fathomless like black space. I think that most of the time we didn't say anything. But when I first came in, he said, "You have been my student for over two years. Why haven't you met me before?" It felt like a reproach for my laziness or stupidity in not seeking him out, and pointed out to me something about myself. After a while, he said, "Well, you know you have to go back." And I said, "I know, but I am afraid to go back, he is bigger than me." At that point, Rinpoche raised his already regal posture, looked very strongly at me, and forcefully crashed his two fists down onto the desk. It was a nameless, wordless transmission which I immediately "got," realizing later that it was a sort of lungta transmission, of confidence and strength. I said, "Okay, I will go back." He tied the knot in my gold chain, which I have worn ever since to this day, twenty-eight years later. I told him I was hoping to go to the Seminary the following year, 1979, and he said he would see me there.

When I returned to Washington, it was as if I had a protective aura surrounding me. Nothing was said, but within three days, the ex-lover had packed up his truck and disappeared.

THE FIRST CHILDREN'S DAY

There were many more magnificent events at this first Assembly, including another Shambhala wedding—that of Lodro Dorje and his wife Donna. And the day before the last day of Assembly our daughter, Vanessa, was born. Rinpoche visited us in the hospital and gave her the middle name Pamo, meaning "female warrior." We returned to

Boulder a few days later, inspired and radiant with the joy of all that had happened at Assembly, including the gift of a darling daughter.

Toward the end of the year Rinpoche suggested that instead of celebrating Christmas Day or Hanukkah, we would from now on celebrate the winter solstice as "Children's Day." Christmas Day is, of course, a celebration that had long ago replaced the celebration of the winter solstice, which is a more natural and fitting celebration for a nontheistic culture and one that was intended eventually to include people of all religious persuasions. Like so many of the forms that Rinpoche introduced, Children's Day was based on a Japanese celebration. Rinpoche created a special children's shrine on which the central figures on the highest level were Japanese dolls, traditionally representing the Emperor and Empress of Japan and in this case the Sakyong and Sakyong Wangmo of Shambhala, and symbolizing the majesty of being a fully awakened human. Around these, on a lower tier, were smaller toy figures of people, animals, and houses. The shrine was decorated with the usual lights and evergreen branches, and offerings of fruit and candy were placed in front.

Children's Day became, and still is, the main celebration for Shambhala families, at which presents are exchanged and the festive meal is served, although many parents with children of school age do continue to celebrate Christmas or Hanukkah (so that their children do not feel left out at school or among their non-Buddhist relatives). There is also a celebration at the main practice centers.

This begins with a ceremony of "bringing back the light," in which the preceptor lights a candle from the shrine and then passes the flame on to the candle of the next person. Everyone holds a small candle and the flame is passed on from one to another until the entire Shrine Hall is lit up. On one hand this is a reflection of the fact that the winter solstice is the shortest and darkest day of the year. At the same time, the ceremony relates to bringing the light of awakening into our society. The principle is that the light of awakening was taken from the mind of the lineage, represented by the shrine, and then passed on to us and our children. After the ceremony of bringing back the light, there are songs and performances, mainly for the children. It is a day of celebration, celebration both of children and of our joy in passing on our heritage to them.

THE BEST YEAR YET

With the advent of Children's Day the Shambhala sangha was now celebrating three important festivals: new year's or Shambhala Day; and the two solstices, Midsummer's Day and Children's Day. The latter two Rinpoche called *"nyida"* ("sun-moon") days, and suggested that eventually we would celebrate the other two nyida days, the spring and fall equinox. This now happens in the Shambhala community—the spring equinox is celebrated especially in the main practice centers as the time of planting and acknowledgement of the goodness of the garden, while the fall equinox is celebrated as the "Harvest of Peace," and a time of giving.

When we look at the variety and multiplicity of organizations, societies, clubs, associations, and businesses that were set up in this and the following few years, it becomes clear that the foundations were being laid for a fresh culture and a new society. By 1980 there was an entire school system, from preschool through high school and university; there was Ashoka Credit Union, the seed of a bank; there was the Upaya Council, to which sangha-members could take serious disputes and provided an alternative to the conventional adversarial legal system; there was the Amara Health Group, an association of health professionals out of which a medical clinic emerged; the Ratna society for business professionals; and many others. All of those societies still exist to serve the sangha. And Rinpoche was personally involved in all of these. As well he was involved in businesses of film production, investment counseling, oil exploration, and importation of gems.

The Kingdom of Shambhala was beginning to manifest in Boulder, once just a sleepy cowboy town, as well as in the Dharmadhatus around the world!

1979: 10
Deepening Practice, Shaky Leadership

 N THE MIDDLE of January, a birthday party was held for Ken Green. Toward the end of the party, Rinpoche called together the Directors for a short meeting—we all crowded into the toilet, the only private place in the house at that moment. There he told us, sternly and forcefully, that the Regent needed to have more boundaries around his behavior and that we should take care of it. Since 1976 he had manifested brilliantly as a teacher of Buddhism and in that sense was coming up to the expectations of him as Rinpoche's lineage holder. Yet he had not curbed his wild behavior, and in particular his involvement in the gay scene. It was not his gay activities as such that was the problem—Rinpoche never had a problem with that—but rather, perhaps, his recklessness. And, indeed, it was this recklessness in the end that caused his tragic and untimely death, as I will recount in the Epilogue.

That night we were called to a meeting in the Court, which the Regent joined later—someone was sent to fetch him from a party that he had gone on to after Ken's birthday celebration. While we were waiting for him, Rinpoche told us clearly that no one else could have been his Regent, and asked each of us what we thought was the source of the Regent's difficulties. I was the last to speak and said that the quality that made him the Regent—a purity that somehow was not caught in worldly things—was the same quality that was giving rise to the problems; he sometimes didn't seem to care how he behaved, I felt, and whether he was endangering himself or going against conventional norms in a harmful way. Rinpoche commented, "Your answer was the best."

He instructed us to challenge the Regent along the lines of the committee that Rinpoche had told me about in retreat, but we were not effective in getting through to the Regent and soon Rinpoche ended that part of the evening.

After we left the Court, Rinpoche continued with a smaller group to try to get through to the Regent that there was a potentially serious problem. Rinpoche himself described this incident three years later at a Shambhala Training Level Five program.

The Big No arose when I was together with my vajra regent and several other students at the Kalapa Court, my house. When the Big No came out, I had found that everybody was indulging in their world too much. I had to say No. So I crashed my arm and fist down on my coffee table, and I broke it. I put a dent in it. Then I painted a giant picture of the Big No in the entrance hall of my house: BIG NO. There was ink everywhere from that proclamation. The message was: From now onward, it's NO. Later on, I executed another calligraphy for the Regent as another special reminder of the Big No, which he has in his office. That No is that you don't give in to things that indulge your reality. There is no special reality beyond reality. That is the Big No, as opposed to regular no. You cannot destroy life. You cannot by any means, for any religious, spiritual, or metaphysical reasons, step on an ant or kill your mosquitoes— at all. That is Buddhism. That is Shambhala. You have to respect everybody. You cannot make a random judgment on that at all. That is the rule of the king of Shambhala, and that is the Big No. You

can't act on your desires alone. You have to contemplate the details
of what needs to be removed and what needs to be cultivated.[57]

The Regent clearly had a certain level of realization of emptiness and the joy that goes with this, and he was brave and forthright in expressing this understanding. But at any level of realization up to the very highest, there is always the possibility of going astray into ego-trips and misuse of the dharma and of our less-than-perfect understanding of it. We, as well as the Regent, were being warned by Rinpoche to "watch out"—as he so often told us. It was a powerful night, and a valuable lesson to us all. This split between the two aspects of the Regent's nature began to manifest increasingly and I will say more about this as the story unfolds.

THE ECLIPSE

Rinpoche's 40th birthday was celebrated on February 17. Like the previous year, there was a grand public celebration in the Hilton Hotel in downtown Denver, and later a private celebration with the Dorje Kasung that was held in the attic of an empty schoolhouse. At the end of the Dorje Kasung celebration, I told Rinpoche that the following morning at ten o'clock there was going to be an eclipse of the sun. According to Rinpoche, ten o'clock in the morning is the moment at which the physical sun best embodies the quality of the Great Eastern Sun—that the sun has completely arisen but is still fresh. So the following day there was going to be an eclipse of the Great Eastern Sun, which is, in the Shambhala teachings, an analogy for the growing dark ages. I asked Rinpoche whether we should do anything special for it, and he replied, "Good idea."

Early that morning, we all received calls to be back at the Kalapa Court by eight o'clock. There were at least twenty people there, all gathered in the living room of the Court once again. Rinpoche had prepared a big bowl full of some sort of herbal concoction, from which he had us all drink. We went into a side porch where paper and ink were set up, and each of us in turn executed a stroke of *Ashe*. Rinpoche's stroke was a three-quarter circle with an Ashe through it, representing the eclipse of the sun being conquered with the Ashe. After that, at ten o'clock, we all went outside to view the eclipse.

The next day I asked John Perks what had happened to that calligraphy, and was told it had been thrown away. I couldn't believe it! John Perks rescued it from the garbage for me, and it hung on my office wall for many years.

THE INVESTITURE OF ÖSEL AS SAWANG

On Shambhala Day 1979, there took place the investiture of Ösel, who was then still going through high school, as the *Sawang*. *Sawang* means "earth lord," and this ceremony, attended by subjects of Shambhala, represented his official recognition as the inheritor and lineage holder of the Shambhala lineage—a separate lineage from the Kagyu Buddhist lineage of which the Regent was the first holder.

This was also the occasion of the first *lhasang*—a ceremony about which Rinpoche had told us at the Kalapa Assembly in 1978, saying that it is a ceremony to invoke or bring down the dralas, to purify the space and magnetize positive energy. Powdered juniper is placed on glowing charcoal. As the smoke rises up, it is said to purify the space of outer and inner aggression and obstacles, while at the same time drala energy is attracted into the space by the rising juniper smoke.

We all hung out in Dorje Dzong, drinking saké and waiting for the ceremony to begin, while Rinpoche was making final preparations for the ceremony. I was called in to Rinpoche's office and told that I would be carrying a flag with a calligraphy of the Tibetan syllable "*SO*" on it. (A similar flag is still used in any long ceremonial lhasang.) He said that I should wave it over the lhasang smoke and call out a long drawn-out, "Soooooohh." Rinpoche made this sound again and again and asked me to repeat it. He wouldn't actually explain how to do it; he just did it and then told me to do it like that. The sound was rising and falling, similar to the sounds of loons calling their partners over

DEFEATING THE ECLIPSE OF THE GREAT EASTERN SUN.

the lake, and with a sharp, abrupt end. I couldn't get it just right, and he became impatient. Finally, he gave up and we began the ceremony.

The ceremony finally began in the early hours of the morning, with a formal parade of all the subjects of Shambhala, and the presentation by the Dorje Kasung of the colors, the flags of Shambhala and the Mukpo family that Rinpoche had designed on retreat. Then we performed the lhasang. It was powerful and intense, and I remember feeling a sort of heaviness in the atmosphere as we all circled around the big brazier in the center of the shrine room. As the juniper smoke billowed upward, I waved the "SO" banner over the cauldron, and made the appropriate sound as best I could. Then we all circumambulated the brazier chanting the Shambhala warrior's cry, "Ki Ki So So Lha Gyel Lo!" This is a traditional chant of Tibet meaning, roughly, "awake, awake, victory to the dralas." The chant was done to a primal rhythm and altogether the lhasang felt ancient, powerful, and thoroughly weird.

After this, Rinpoche always conducted lhasangs for special ceremonial occasions, such as the opening of a Seminary, and at first I would always get a tremendous headache. I finally realized that it was from the feeling of pressure I would have from the energy coming down; when I could let go into it, I would just feel the tremendous energy instead of a headache.

Rinpoche gave a talk on invigorating and strengthening our lives through the drala principle, and on great warriors of the past such as King Gesar who, he said, "Could be so gentle and at the same time heroic to help this confused world." King Gesar was the warrior king of Tibet who unified warring tribes and propagated Buddhism, and who was the progenitor of the Mukpo lineage. The Sawang then answered questions put to him by his father, like, "What is the Great Eastern Sun?" I was impressed by how confident he was, and how personal his understanding was. Most of us, in that situation, would have given answers that were very much from the book, but his were fresh.

Kneeling opposite each other, first the Sawang and then Rinpoche executed a stroke of Ashe. Following this, the Regent presented the

Sawang with ceremonial robes and sword, and read a short proclamation. Finally, Rinpoche talked about how he had brought up his son, saying that we should look into how we are going to raise our children in the future in an enlightened style of education. At the end of the evening, the Sawang knelt in front of Rinpoche who then placed a white scarf around his shoulders. Gently drawing the Sawang toward him, he gave him a long hug, whispering to him for several minutes.

The whole evening felt potent and significant. However, it did not have a noticeable effect on the sangha at large at that time, or on the activities of the Sawang, whom Rinpoche very much wanted to finish his Western studies up to attending Oxford University—from the point of view of the sangha, then, the Regent was still Rinpoche's only successor.

FEEDBACK CHANGES MY TEACHING STYLE

In February, I taught the first Level Three of Shambhala Training, which completely filled the shrine room of Dorje Dzong. There were over two hundred people, almost all of whom were sangha-members—although we had the aspiration that Shambhala Training would reach many people beyond the sangha, including people not interested in Buddhism. Since the Kalapa Assembly, everyone realized that something significant was going on with the Shambhala teachings and Rinpoche hoped that all of his vajrayana students would go through the Shambhala Training program. Shambhala and Buddhism, though different streams of teaching, are inseparable, and it was simply not advisable for students as closely involved with him as the vajrayana students to pick and choose which of his teachings they would accept and which they would reject. Also he had expressed on several recent occasions that he was concerned about not creating a "higher" neurosis, as he called it, among his vajrayana students. He did not want these students to become an elitist clique or to use the vajrayana teachings as a way to separate themselves from ordinary life. The Shambhala teachings of living bravely in the world were the way to ensure that this did not happen.

In those days I was known for my slow, boring talks, and this one lived up to my reputation. After the talk was over we had a "debrief" which included many people who had attended Rinpoche's talks back in early 1978. Everyone really laid into me with criticism, which was somewhat valid but at the same time quite harsh. I took all this to heart and returned home—feeling crushed.

The next day, I heard from David Rome that Rinpoche was going to come to my talk that evening. When it was time for the talk, I sat in my office and waited for him to arrive but, about two hours after the talk was scheduled to begin, David called to say that Rinpoche would not be coming after all. At the end of the call he added, "Oh, by the way, I thought of something else wrong with last night's talk. It had too much of the True Believer quality." Needless to say, I did not take his comment kindly at that late hour. I went directly to the shrine room and started the talk with, as usual, the help of copious note cards. After some minutes, David's comment came into my mind: "Too much of a True Believer." It was like a torrent had been let loose—I threw my notes down on the table and I just talked and talked and talked. I told jokes and stories to illustrate the teachings, people were roaring with laughter, and afterward the critics were delighted.

When I gave the last talk, on the Sunday afternoon, Rinpoche did come "incognito"—listening to the talk from the coatroom. When later I heard this and asked him what he thought of the talk, he told me that it was fine but I needed to project more, making a sweeping gesture of his hand from the center of his chest out into the space around. I wondered what he would have thought if he had listened incognito to the previous night's talk. I guessed that he would have been delighted by it!

The whole experience was really a transformation for me: I had discovered another level of confidence in teaching, more from the heart rather than just trying to reel out lists of concepts. Later I told David how much I appreciated his comment, even though it had infuriated me at the time. This is a good example of how sangha friends are able to help each other, not always relying on the guru, a sign perhaps of some maturing of the sangha.

PRACTICING VAJRAYOGINI
BRINGS MEMORIES OF CHILDHOOD

In that same month, the Board went on a group retreat for a week, during which I completed the recitation of the recommended number of Vajrayogini mantras. During those two years that I had intensively practiced the Vajrayogini sadhana, boyhood memories surfaced which had been buried for thirty or more years. I had powerful and strange moments in which I remembered long-forgotten events of my childhood—events that were clearly, somehow, related to the practice.

Once, for example, when I was in a vajrayana feast—an addition to the sadhana that is practiced in a group every month and includes eating, drinking, and singing as an expression of the sacredness of the sense perceptions—I held the cast metal dorje to my nose and smelled it.

The bell and dorje are the two main ritual objects used during a sadhana; the bell represents wisdom and the dorje skillful means. The smell of the dorje awoke a memory that had been completely lost for thirty years. When I was a young boy of about six or seven, I was out walking in our neighborhood one day when I found a piece of cast iron from an old chain-link fence that had come loose and was lying on the ground. It was shaped somewhat like a dorje. This little boy picked it up and smelled it, and couldn't stop smelling it; it produced in me an intense feeling of longing, which of course I had no explanation for. I put the iron in my pocket and kept it for a few days, taking it out to smell it from time to time. Soon, no doubt, I lost my treasure and forgot about the whole thing. As I smelled my dorje at the feast, recalling that long-forgotten memory, it seemed that the longing of the small boy had been to re-connect with that inner realm of Vajrayogini.

Again when I was six or seven, I went to a birthday party of a wealthy young girl of the neighborhood. The party was at her grandparents' house nearby, because her grandfather had a film projector. In 1947, this was a great treat, but the only thing I can remember about the film is that it had Bob Hope in it and took place on an ocean liner.

During one scene, I had a moment of realizing that *there was nothing behind the screen*. Then I looked around the room and experienced the whole room like that: that there was nothing behind it. I felt a tremendous desolation, sadness, and loneliness, feeling that life was all just like a film show. Was it, perhaps, a taste of emptiness, a longing to know what is the truth behind appearances and sadness that, even to this small boy, ordinary life seemed to be such a superficial show with nothing behind it?

These memories, and others, began to give me a strong feeling that, in some sense, I had "been here before." During these early years in the sangha, however, I was too caught up in rationality to really contemplate what that meant. I still held consciously to the scientific/nihilist view concerning past lives, and believed that, since there is no real evidence for them, we either have to trust the tradition blindly or try to understand Buddhism without such a view. I wasn't able then to put together my past feelings and memories, or to see their significance. Later I was to understand the situation very differently; after Rinpoche died I thought and studied a great deal about the possibility of some kind of continuation of awareness after death—and I will discuss this in a later chapter.

TEMPORARY EXPERIENCES OF BLISS

In May, while Rinpoche was paying his second visit to Nova Scotia, I took part in a Vajrayogini group retreat at RMDC. Rinpoche came to mind often, and sometimes I longingly wished that I could be in Nova Scotia with him. Nevertheless I greatly enjoyed the retreat and the practice. At a Board meeting including the Regent shortly after I returned to Boulder, the other Directors as well as the Regent noticed my rather quiet and spaced-out state and teased me about it—"Oh, look at him, he's been *practicing*," and similar comments. Such comments making light of practice were frequent among the Board members, and they disturbed me. On the other hand, perhaps I was just being hypersensitive…

Later, I had a meeting with Rinpoche and, though I didn't mention these comments, I asked him whether it was possible to practice too much. He replied, "Oh, don't say that, *please*." I then described to him how I had been spaced out recently, continually dropping things, for example, which I connected with too much practice. He said, impatiently, "Pay attention to your sense perceptions. How many times do I have to say that?" He seemed to be pointing out, as he frequently did, that while practice can open one to experience of greater space and energy, within and without, one has to manifest this in the world not as being "spaced out" but with even greater precision in relating with the details of one's perceptions.

During this two-year period of intensive practice of the Vajrayogini sadhana, I had some powerful experiences of joy and expansion that seemed to be related to a level of energy that was more subtle than we are usually aware of. They seemed also to have to do with a deepening of the connection between awareness and body. The strongest was accompanied by a brief vision of Vajrayogini leaping out of her picture on my shrine and entering my body. I asked Rinpoche about these experiences and after questioning me, he wrote on a slip of paper, in Tibetan and English, the words traditionally used to refer to this experience. I interpreted this to be a confirmation of the direction my experience of practice was going. Needless to say, however, it would have been inappropriate and harmful for him to express approval of this.

Such experiences are known as *nyams*, or "temporary experiences," and are well-known phenomena on the path of meditation. They are indeed pointers on the way, faint hints of the true sense of joy that is inseparable from emptiness, and in that sense a small confirmation of one's practice. At the same time they can be dangerous side-tracks: it is too easy to be caught up in them, wishing they would continue forever, or thinking that one has actually attained permanent realization. So one is always encouraged to let them go and not to seek them in one's practice. The biggest challenge is to bring the essence of those discoveries, the fundamental joy at the basis of our being, into our daily life. This gives us the genuine power to love and help others.

Finally, I went on to say that, although I wanted to care for the things and activities I was put in charge of, sometimes I just felt that I couldn't care less. He said, surprisingly, "Well, that kind of confidence is fine." At the time I did not understand this remark. I did feel that I was gaining confidence in my understanding of the practice and in my study of the dharma, as well as in my ability to convey the teachings to others, but I had asked the question in relation to taking care of my administrative areas, in which I felt no more confident than ever. Later I understood that the remark was an indication of how to transmute that "couldn't care less" attitude. Such an attitude has two sides: one is the indifference and ignorance that does not want to pay attention to problems and details, and the other is the equanimity that, while fully attentive to the situation, is not caught up in attachment to it or to any particular outcome. Rinpoche was pointing me in the direction of the latter, and away from the former.

GETTING LESS HYPER-SENSITIVE

In early summer, the Directors invited Rinpoche to a dinner party. Feeling an increasing distance from him, we sought ways to make more contact. Many new people didn't feel this distance, of course. He continued to be welcoming and open to new students and there were always, still, opportunities for a new student to step right into Rinpoche's intimate world. But he couldn't be so completely inviting and open, without boundaries, as he had been in the early 1970s, because there were now so many people and projects wanting his time. For his older students he seemed more distant on a personal level—he was becoming less and less the spiritual friend, more and more the vajra master and monarch. And as such, he expected us to "just do it," as he began frequently to say.

The dinner party was at Sam Bercholz's house, by then on Pine Street in the center of Boulder. After dinner we were sitting out on the porch of the house and Carl asked, "How are we doing, Rinpoche?" Rinpoche then proceeded to go around to every one of us, individually telling us how we were improving, which was a very subtle way of telling each of us what our primary problem was and how to transmute it. It was the same principle as his comment to me about "couldn't care less" and confidence: there are always two ways for any energy to manifest, confused or awake.

Turning to me, he said, "Sir Jeremy is getting less hypersensitive." That was really the first time I realized how hypersensitive I had always been, and how it caused me to continually react and close down at the slightest seemingly critical comment from him or others. At the same time, that hypersensitivity came from openness and sensitivity to others, so the point was to be less *hyper-* rather than less sensitive. The *hyper-* part came, of course, from fear of what others thought of me, so in saying I was becoming less hypersensitive Rinpoche was pointing to a growing strength of being settled in who I was. This was beginning to develop out of the practice but also out of being put into situations, such as being a Board member, where I was continually confronted with my hypersensitivity. All these small moments, then, were suggestions that, however painful it was, this path was a true growing process, and the pains were natural growing pains.

Shortly after this dinner, my birthday came around once again. When it came time for my birthday toast, one of the other Directors toasted me as "becoming, as Rinpoche said, less sensitive." The Regent pulled a puzzled face, whispering to Rinpoche, "What's good about being less *sensitive?*" Rinpoche promptly and loudly corrected it to "*hyper*sensitive." He gave me a present of a beautiful calligraphy of the Tibetan word *drala*, with a little poem beside it. It is an exceptional calligraphy in many ways, with an exquisite balance in the combination of the one large word, and the poem written in a smaller and different script beside it. Being such a beautiful example of Rinpoche's unique style of calligraphy, it has appeared in several collections, and now hangs in the living room of my home in Nova Scotia. The poem reads:

> *In order to join heaven and earth,*
> *May the ultimate, unchanging warrior*

Always protect you.
May you have long life, freedom from sickness, and glory.
May your primordial confidence flourish.
May the virtuous banner of the excellent windhorse
Always be uplifted.

Receiving this calligraphy was a confirmation, to me, of my growing feeling that the Shambhala teachings were my main connection with meditation practice and with Rinpoche's wisdom. It also seemed like an indication that I should look more into the meaning of drala—how I might find a genuine connection with drala in my own experience. Drala—in the sense of "almost entities" that we can connect with—reside, as I mentioned in the previous chapter, in the inner realm of luminosity / joy. Thus to connect with drala I had to investigate more deeply the experience of this realm. This was already beginning to happen through the Vajrayogini practice, but the power of drala was that it provided a way to connect with this realm in the middle of daily life activity.

SCIENCE AND BUDDHISM AT NAROPA INSTITUTE

A major conference on science and Buddhism was held at Naropa Institute during this summer of 1979. Eleanor Rosch, a sangha-member and professor of psychology at Berkeley, had received a grant from the Sloan Foundation to organize a conference entitled "Cross-cultural Perspectives in Cognitive Science." The conference was organized by Eleanor and brilliant neuroscientist Francisco Varela, both of whom were prominent and highly respected in the cognitive science world. For this reason they were able to attract many important personages from this newly blossoming field. Before the conference, the Naropa Institute contingent met with Rinpoche to seek his counsel on how we should go about the presentation of Buddhism. His advice was, predictably, to keep it very simple, and to present the *abhidharma*, the

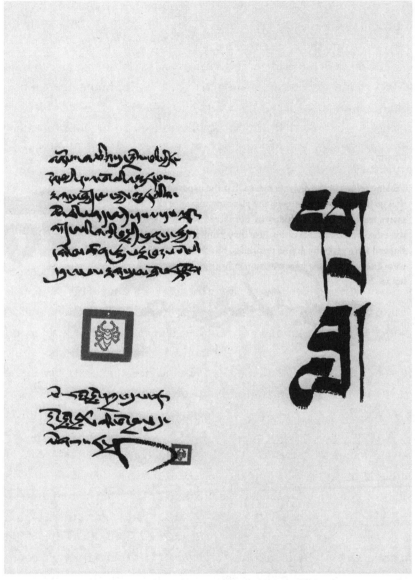

DRALA. A BIRTHDAY GIFT TO JEREMY FROM RINPOCHE.

extensive Buddhist description of the various states, components, and functions of mind. Not surprisingly, then, I was asked to offer a talk on perception and the five skandhas.

The conference was lively and controversial. Those scientists whose work had already opened them to a wider view of human perception and cognition than the narrowly dualistic/materialist view of Western science were interested in what the Buddhist contingent presented, offering fascinating contributions from their side. Particularly memorable for me were presentations by Alton Becker, an anthropologist who had spent many years in Java, especially making a study of *wayang*, the Javanese shadow theater. In a session on the nature of cause and effect, Becker spoke on beliefs concerning cause and effect in the Javanese culture.

He told a story of his own experience when one day his old mechanical typewriter, which always sat by the open window of his cabin, was stolen, and he reported the theft to the police. A few days later a policeman came to the door and told him that they had caught the thief and that he, Becker, had to go to the station with him. When he asked the reason, Becker was told that he had now to sit in the jail cell with the young thief, so that the two of them could talk until the conflict was resolved. Becker's point was that the Javanese view of cause and effect is by no means the simplistic idea of "one cause, one effect" that we have in the West. Rather, an event is a product of a complex network of multiple causes, and that in this sense Becker had to take some responsibility for helping the thief to see the problem in what he had done.

Becker told another story related to the Javanese view of causation and to the notion of auspicious coincidence that I introduced in relation to drala. One day he was being driven by a young man along a country road, which was really nothing more than a dirt track, with animals and people wandering all over it. The young man was driving rather wildly and erratically and he hit someone. The person was not seriously injured, but the young man was severely shaken. He said to Becker, "Never again will I drive on this day." Becker responded, "You mean this date of the year?" The young driver said, "No, this day."

Becker explained that the Javanese sense of time is cyclical, their calendar being an intricate combination of circular motions. So when the cycle comes around again, that day is regarded as the *same* day. In this case, that day was a bad one for the young man to drive on, and therefore he would never again drive on it. This, Becker pointed out, is an expression of the sense of the significance of coincidence and of causality being related to a much larger web of circumstances than we include in the West.

While some of the representatives from the science world were interested in the Buddhist understanding of mind and realized its value to their work, others became aggravated and cross as the conference developed. This may have been due in part to the seeming lack of scholarliness on the part of some of the Buddhist presenters, but no doubt much of it was also due to the fact that the idea of egolessness can be most irritating to intellectuals.

One occasion stands out in my memory most clearly: one of the Buddhist presenters was speaking on translation—how to unpack the text so as to show the deeper meaning as well as the literal sense of the text, and the need to keep one's ego out of the process—in the course of which he made a remark to the effect that egolessness means not putting our ego into everything. One of the visitors, a well-known philosopher of science and phenomenology, sprang up and shouted from his place in the audience, "I'll put my ego in wherever I damn well please!"—a remark perfectly illustrated at that very moment.

Eleanor and Francisco commented afterward that they felt the conference was rather a disaster. However, in 1979 cognitive science was a new endeavor and since that time the scientific study of mind and consciousness has grown exponentially. Nowadays it is the leading edge of scientific research, akin to the extraordinarily exciting period of the 1920s when quantum physics was challenging the classical worldview to its core, or the similar period of the '60s, when the role of DNA in the genetic code was revealed.

The constellation of perception, cognition, and consciousness is clearly the meeting point of Buddhism and science. Perception is the meeting point of the inner and outer, of subject and object, the first-person perspective and the third-person perspective. Buddhism, especially Tibetan Buddhism, has deeply studied and categorized the various inner states of body and mind, how they relate with each other and with the appearance of an outside world—the process of perception—as well as how they can be transformed by inner practices. This structure of mind is described in the abhidharma; the consequences of abhidharma for personal transformation are detailed in the vajrayana tantras. Cognitive science, on the other hand, like all science, begins with the objective, third-person view, the view from without. That is, cognitive scientists study the brain states of *others*, and their correlation with the subjects' reports of inner states.

Most scientists, in keeping with the mainstream philosophy of materialist reductionism, currently believe that the brain is in some way the basis for all aspects of consciousness, awareness, and our knowledge of our inner states; that is to say, all mind can be reduced to the functioning of the brain. Many scientists are deliberately seeking in the brain the neural locus, or the patterns of neural activity that correspond to the inner experience of consciousness. However, this leads to a clear difficulty: is there any relation, and if so what is it, between the activity of the brain and the corresponding conscious experience? This has become known as "the hard problem" in modern consciousness studies.

The hard problem, simply put, is this: assuming that some day it will be possible to map in detail all possible activity in the brain, and if a person reports that he is having the delightful experience of seeing a rose, what will be the relation between that person's brain scans and his delightful experience of seeing a rose? The answer is far from obvious, though many solutions have now been proposed. An excellent recent survey of the entire field of consciousness studies[58] comes to the conclusion that the solution to the hard problem is still nowhere to be found. And author Susan Blackmore concludes that consciousness itself is still nowhere to be found.

Realizing that understanding first-person experience is a crucial aspect of this hard problem, some scientists have begun to take a serious interest in the practice of meditation and the reports of meditators on the structure of mental states. In 1993, Joseph Goguen, a Shambhala sangha-member who had a distinguished career in high-level computer programming, started a journal called *Journal of Consciousness Studies: Controversies in the Arts and Sciences*. In recent years there have been several special issues dedicated to the first-person view, and issues concerning the relation between first and third-person views. Conferences now often include workshops on various aspects of "the view from within."

In particular, the Dalai Lama and Francisco Varela together initiated a series of conversations between the Dalai Lama and small groups of scientists. These were usually five or six days long, and were held at the Dalai Lama's private residence in Dharmsala, India. The Dalai Lama felt that on his visits to the West he could not take so long for relaxed conversations. I was fortunate to be invited to the first of these conversations, in 1987.[59] The number of invited scientists, on that and subsequent occasions, was usually kept to half a dozen or so, and the conversations were lively, intimate, and richly rewarding. These gatherings continued every two years after this, as the Mind and Life Institute conferences. Especially in recent years, the conversations with neuroscientists have been revelatory.[60]

Thus, from all of the subsequent developments, perhaps we can say that the infamous 1979 Naropa Institute conference on cross-cultural perspectives in cognition, or more simply put, on Buddhism and cognitive science, was perhaps not so much disastrous as definitely before its time.

A BUDDING SCHOOL SYSTEM

The previous spring, the Alaya Preschool in Boulder had become an officially licensed preschool. Alaya had been started by sangha parents a couple of years before as an informal day-care situation. The preschool was put under my supervision, as the Director of Education. However, it was very competently run by trained preschool teachers

RINPOCHE DEMONSTRATES FLOWER ARRANGING AT THE ALAYA PRESCHOOL.

and did not need much attention from me. When I asked for guidelines for how to relate to the children, Rinpoche said that the main thing was training of the teachers. They should all be encouraged to practice meditation and especially to take part in Shambhala Training. The main emphasis, then, was to nourish the basic goodness of the children, rather than treating them as untamed creatures who would get into trouble if they were not taught to behave properly—the standard approach of many modern parents and schools. This nourishing of basic goodness came not from any particular curriculum or educational philosophy, but from the training of the teachers in understanding their own and the children's basic goodness.

In September, the Vidya Elementary School opened with grades kindergarten to three, with the support of parents whose children were too old to continue at Alaya Preschool. Each year, the parents beseeched us to add another grade so that their children could continue to receive the education we offered, founded on the premise of basic goodness. When we asked Rinpoche to talk to us about the educational program at Vidya, the main thing he said was, as he had said in relation to Alaya, "Train the staff. The staff should do Shambhala Training."

Among some of the suggestions that Rinpoche made in relation to the Vidya curriculum was that the children should learn Latin and Greek so as to know the roots of their own language; that they should be told stories of the lineage figures, like Tilopa, Naropa, Marpa, and Milarepa; that they should be taught about the four Shambhala dignities (meek, perky, outrageous, and inscrutable) and the heraldic animals—the tiger, lion, garuda, and dragon—that are said to embody these dignities; that they should be told stories of great heroes of the Western world, such as King Arthur, Queen Elizabeth I of England, and Alexander the Great. His idea was to give them positive images to live up to and to give them a sense of respect for humanity, as well as inspiring them with the mythical quality of these figures. Rinpoche designed uniforms the children wore, consisting of a tie and blazer, and either a skirt or pants, similar to the uniform of a typical private school. Just as with the kasung uniforms, in addition to creating a sense of upliftedness and wakefulness, wearing uniforms cut down on the egotism of dress. There was a sense of going back to the tradition in many aspects: language, history, and keeping things clean and decent. The main emphasis was on treating the children with respect from the very beginning.

Rinpoche was much more interested in these kinds of things than in the details of the curriculum. When once I asked him if he had any suggestions for the curriculum of the Shambhala schools, he replied, "Just do it like they did to you—you turned out all right." By this I assumed he meant that, other than the special topics I already mentioned, the schools could just use a traditional curriculum, but nothing special. Vidya was increased by a grade each year until in the end, with the cooperation of the local public school system, young people were able to go all the way through from pre-school to high-school graduation. As children have gone through this schooling we have seen how much confidence and joy, as well as delight in going to school, they have when treated this way. And now, twenty-five years later we can see the fruits of this kind of upbringing in our grown children—in their confidence and ability to open to and care for others. Although the Vidya School closed some years later, it was re-born as the Shambhala School in Halifax, Nova Scotia.

THE DALAI LAMA VISITS, AND A STRANGE STORY

In October, His Holiness the Dalai Lama visited New York and a couple of other Dharmadhatus, and the Directors all went to New York to greet him. The evening before the Dalai Lama arrived we gathered in the apartment where Rinpoche was staying. He was in a subdued mood and told us a strange and rather threatening story about a Gelug-school lama who, in the nineteenth century, had vowed to destroy the dharma. We were not even allowed to mention this lama's name. This lama had, according to Rinpoche, introduced rituals and teachings which, while seeming to be legitimate, were actually anti-dharmic. Why Rinpoche told us this story, I was not sure at the time, but it resurfaced some years later on Rinpoche's second, and final, one-year retreat. It was, in fact, confirmed twenty years later when, amid some serious troubles in the Gelug sect, the Dalai Lama announced that those particular rituals were no longer to be practiced.

Rinpoche's story did not predispose us well toward the Dalai Lama and his entourage for this visit. However, we subsequently realized (as was obvious) that the Dalai Lama himself is a magnificent person, a wonderfully genuine dharma teacher, and one of the only true statesmen in the world today. And I saw the extraordinary combination of profound friendliness and brilliant intellect when I visited his residence in Dharmsala in 1987 for the Mind and Life conference that I mentioned earlier.

During Rinpoche's visit to New York, an event occurred which is a beautiful illustration of Rinpoche's use of humor to break through to the heart of his students. Madeline Bruser, a talented young concert pianist and piano teacher, was already a student of Rinpoche, though she had not yet met him. Madeline tells this story of the first time she met him:

I had offered to play for him during his stay in New York and he accepted. So, one evening, I went to his suite, where about a dozen of us were gathered. When he entered the room, I felt so relaxed in his presence that I walked right up to him and said, "Hello, I'm going to play for you tonight." And he said, "Oh! You're going to play with me!" After several minutes of silence punctuated by a few bits of conversation between him and all of us, he walked slowly over to the piano, sat down, and started slapping at the keys as though it were a big joke. I began to feel quite nervous. Then he said, "Now YOU play," and he stood up. I sat down at the piano, but he remained standing. "Aren't you going to sit down?" I asked him. And instead of sitting down, he picked up his little dog and stood next to the piano, waiting for me to begin. Since he was standing, everyone else had to stand also.

I launched into a dramatic performance of Beethoven's deeply serious "Sonata in A-flat," Opus 110. The lid of the piano was slightly raised, and soon after I started to play, Rinpoche put his dog—a very cooperative and furry lhaso apso—on the piano. Over and over, the dog slowly slid down the slanted lid as I continued to huff and puff my way through Beethoven's intense, lofty, lyrical first movement. At times, instead of putting the dog back onto the piano, Rinpoche beat time with one hand, making more of a joke out of the music. The twelve guests giggled, and I felt humiliated yet exhilarated. At one moment, I tried to challenge him by looking directly and boldly at him, but he just peered over his glasses at me and left me feeling completely powerless.

Suddenly, a minute or so into the rollicking second movement, something switched. I found myself playing with an amazing freedom and energy that I'd never known was possible. The music leapt

out of me and burst brilliantly into the room like a force of nature.
It was tremendously liberating, and I noticed that Rinpoche was
now holding his dog and listening attentively. I played with this
total abandon for about two minutes, but it was so disorienting that
I reverted back to my habitual overblown approach, and Rinpoche
gave the dog more rides down the piano lid. Thus went a twenty-
minute performance of one of the most profound pieces of music ever
written. Beethoven and I had come into contact with an enlightened
audience. The next day, I could no longer play the old way. I had
received the best piano lesson of my life from a man who never
played the instrument.

THE SECOND KALAPA ASSEMBLY

In October, the second Kalapa Assembly was held in Big Sky, Montana. There was a much bigger group this year—four hundred or so subjects of the Kingdom. Before the Assembly began, a Board meeting was called, including Rinpoche and the Regent. Some members of the Board were angry and upset with the kasung, complaining that the kasung were taking over the Assembly. These problems had been a topic of discussion a month or so previously, when the Regent and the Directors came over to my little house on Lee Hill Road for an afternoon of archery in the field just outside the house. These occasions, which happened several times that fall, were very joyful, with buffet dinners and playful banter. Besides just having fun, though, we also did talk some business. A lot of paranoia was expressed on that occasion, among some of the Directors, at the growing influence of the kasung. I didn't really understand what the problem was, since I appreciated the kasung and was never quite in tune with all the politics. Possibly it had something to do with the militaristic, almost macho style of the Dorje Kasung, which was so contrary to the relaxed and playful style of the Regent and his friends. Possibly it also had something to do with a perceived threat to the Regent's position of authority.

Rinpoche responded to the complaints about the kasung in his usual abrupt and unexpected way. In the middle of the Assembly, senior administrators and Dorje Kasung were called together late one night. We assembled in a small bedroom being used as the Assembly office. It was one of those electric occasions, when the air was vibrating like a brooding thunderstorm. Rinpoche talked about aggression and nonaggression and made us all sign a vow about loyalty and not creating schisms. We each had to sign our name, and then he personally pricked our thumbs so that we could make a thumbprint in blood on the huge piece of paper on which this proclamation was written. This did not immediately change relations between the kasung and Directors, but the injunction not to create schisms was imprinted on our memories. During the Assembly, Rinpoche gave two talks on overcoming aggression, habitual patterns, and the search for entertainment. It was clear that he was concerned about our lack of gentleness and consideration for each other, our petty in-fighting and unwillingness to cooperate together for the sake of the larger vision.

The night after these talks, the Regent stayed up late singing old '50s songs cabaret-style in the dining room with his circle of friends. Lady Diana walked through the room while this was going on and, telling the group that it was self-indulgent and disgusting, kicked over a tray. The next night, Rinpoche had Lady Diana sit up on the platform with him as he gave his talk. The talk was on Shambhala decorum and Rinpoche talked first about the Sakyong Wangmo, Lady Diana. He said, "Tonight we have decided to seat the Sakyong Wangmo on the same platform as myself. To do this at this point has significance. It is expressing that she does have wisdom and directness and goodness.... Therefore she deserves to sit on the same platform with me as a teacher of Shambhala vision."

RINPOCHE ATTEMPTS TO BRING IN FEMININE ENERGY

During this Kalapa Assembly, Rinpoche also conducted an important ceremony to bring more feminine energy into the administration.

While in the Tibetan tradition men and women are equal with respect to their innate wisdom and ability to realize the true nature of reality, in general women in Tibet, with the exception of a few powerful female teachers, did not have the same respect as men. For example, there were thousands of monks but very few nuns and no fully ordained nuns. Rinpoche never discriminated in this way with his students. As I mentioned earlier, as far as Rinpoche was concerned, both genders were equally qualified to be his students and both could practice in the same way. Women always played strong administrative and teaching roles at Karme Chöling, RMDC, the Dharmadhatus, and Naropa Institute. Only the Vajradhatu/Nalanda Board was heavily masculine, being constituted entirely of men, and Rinpoche felt the need to bring in more feminine energy.

Rinpoche had told several women over the previous year that he wanted to add them to the Board of Directors, but this had not happened. Here is an account of one of those, Lodro Sangmo, meaning "Lady of Good Intellect" (she asked that I use her refuge name rather than her Western name in quoting this letter):

> Trungpa Rinpoche was a man from another male dominated culture who had a deep appreciation of the feminine energy of the world—in art, poetry, flower arranging, and gentle communication. In his short time on this earth, it was clear to me that, of the many things he was trying to accomplish in his outrageously ambitious vision of a better world, an enlightened society, one most dear to his heart was to have a more balanced female/male culture. The first Board of Directors being all men might seem an odd solution if Rinpoche was trying to rectify this pattern. Many would agree, including the men appointed to the Board, that it displayed all the best, and the worst. Individually, they were all very decent guys, and very devoted to their teacher, however...
>
> I worked in Rinpoche's household for a few years, saw him every day and on many occasions told him about my concerns. Having a deep sense of justice, I would relay any perceived injustice or

even the slightest abuse of power—and they happened! I was not popular with these men on the Board, and I will take responsibility—I was not skillful in dealing with them. I had queried him about "When are these guys going to learn to relate with their hearts and emotions," and he responded "You're going to show them." "No I'm not," was my quick response. So you can imagine my horror when Rinpoche told me he was appointing me to the Board!

Lodro Sangmo was not, in fact, appointed to the Board, nor were any other women, and it seemed that this Ladies' Oath ceremony was intended to bring feminine energy to bear on Board activities in a different way. The ceremony at Kalapa Assembly was to be an empowerment for the wives of the Privy Council members, as well as Diana's sister, Tessa, and my wife, Karen. Rinpoche met with these women who were to take the Shambhala vow a couple of times before the ceremony to study questions that might be asked of them. At that time, he told them that they were being given this empowerment in their own right, and, if any of them were later to be divorced, they would retain their title and position. He said the empowerment was completely independent of their husbands.

The ceremony itself was elaborate with the usual procession, the formal questioning of those to be empowered by both the Sakyong and Sakyong Wangmo (Karen was asked, "What is drala?"), and the execution of the stroke of Ashe—one by one—in orange ink. During the ceremony, Rinpoche gave each of these women the title "Lady of the Court," telling them that they were to function partly as governmental representatives and partly as his family representatives and that they were to be his "eyes and ears."

This experiment did not actually accomplish what Rinpoche had intended, partially because of politics among the ladies themselves, and partially because the Ladies of the Court were given little to do beyond the formalities. Years later, shortly before he died, he empowered another group of women, the sangyums, which I will describe later.

A DEATH AND A REBUKE

Toward the end of the Assembly, we heard that a sangha-member, Bruce, had committed suicide in Boston by driving his car into the Charles River. When Rinpoche heard of this he was very, very upset and angry. He conducted a *sukhavati* ceremony, a Buddhist funeral service, in the shrine room, in which he told us that it was our responsibility to look after each other and that *we*, the sangha, were responsible for Bruce's death. He said that we should have known how he felt and that we should have cared for him. He was very definite and strong about that. He had us practice *tong-len*,[61] the practice of sending well-being and goodness to others and drawing their suffering into oneself, which is done in synchrony with the breath. Rinpoche struck the gong for each breath and insisted that we pay utmost attention to the practice.

The Assembly continued to be intense and prickly. As the Regent was leaving the Assembly, and the Directors were gathered in a circle around him to say goodbye, there was another strange moment. As he went around the circle and shook hands with each of us, he asked us to repeat after him, "All for one and one for all," the motto of Alexandre Dumas' Three Musketeers. It almost felt to me as if he was expecting some kind of battle and was asking each of us which side we would be on. Altogether, the atmosphere of this Assembly was quite edgy, not at all as celebratory as the previous year, and this seemed to reflect difficulties throughout the organization, and throughout that year.

"WHAT WE ARE DOING MAY SEEM INSIGNIFICANT, BUT THIS NOTION OF DHARMA ART WILL BE LIKE AN ATOMIC BOMB IN YOUR MIND. YOU COULD PLAY A TREMENDOUS ROLE IN DEVELOPING PEACE THROUGHOUT THE WORLD."

CHÖGYAM TRUNGPA RINPOCHE,
FROM *THE ART OF CALLIGRAPHY*

1980: 11
The Only Thing Worth Living For

B Y THE END OF 1979, it was clear to everyone that something needed to change at Naropa Institute, and that we didn't quite know what. The troubles had already begun to surface the previous January. Naropa Institute was somewhat in the doldrums: enrollments were not increasing, some courses had to be cancelled, and staff payrolls were still being missed. There were some difficulties in the leadership, and staff started coming to me to complain. As Director responsible for overseeing the Institute, I had rather neglected to spend adequate time at the Naropa offices and give Bill McKeever the assistance and support he needed during the previous year, his first as executive director of the Institute.

I had asked for a meeting to talk with Rinpoche about the situation just before he was going off to teach the 1979 Seminary. Unusually, instead of having his secretary give me an appointment to meet him in his office, Rinpoche suddenly walked into my office one day while I was sitting at my desk. We discussed briefly the difficulties with the leadership at the Institute. As he was leaving, he turned around and said, rather vehemently, "You know what to do—just do it!" Not long after that meeting, someone suggested to me that there should be a co-executive director along with Bill McKeever at Naropa Institute and proposed Reggie Ray, the head of the Buddhist Studies department. I called Rinpoche at Seminary to ask him about this, to which he responded, "Whatever you want to do." However, by December it had become clear that adding Reggie Ray to the leadership had not solved the problems. The difficulties between him and Bill had only made things worse.

Rinpoche seemed to have immense trust in his students and to see the very best possibilities in us along with our arrogance, self-doubts, and hesitations. He would put us in positions that he felt could bring out that best, such as the increasing responsibility he was giving me to look after Naropa Institute. He would push us and squeeze us and if ever anyone facing a major decision in their life asked his advice on which of the two choices they should follow, his response was, almost invariably, "I think you could do both." He was willing to take tremendous risks with his students, putting us in positions of responsibility and then leaving us to it, letting us make our own decisions and mistakes, always watching but never controlling us. And no matter what mistakes we made, he never gave up on his students.

In *Shambhala: The Sacred Path of the Warrior*, he writes of the master warrior: "He constantly challenges his students to step beyond themselves, to step out into the vast and brilliant world of reality in which he abides. The challenge he provides is not so much that he is always setting hurdles for his students or egging them on. Rather, his authentic presence is a constant challenge to them to be genuine and true." And this, indeed, captures the way Rinpoche himself related to his students.

I had been warned to pay more attention to the Institute back in the summer, at the end of July 1979. I was teaching a program to subjects of Shambhala, in the shrine room of RMDC. At the same time Rinpoche was presiding over a training encampment for the kasung in a beautiful meadow on another part of the land. Just before we were leaving RMDC at the end of that weekend, a few senior staff were called up to the encampment to see Rinpoche. Rinpoche was sitting on a log and we sat on the ground in a semi-circle around him. Rinpoche started urgently telling us that we should be taking on more responsibility because he could not do it all. He said that he couldn't be "both the head and the neck that connects it to the shoulders." It was up to us to be the neck, he said. Likewise, he compared himself to a kite flying without an adequate string to connect it with earth. He was quite forcefully pushing us to take on more responsibility, or at least to take the responsibility that had been given to us, and to do our jobs wholeheartedly and thoroughly. He kept turning to me and saying, "Do you understand?"

A week later the Board received a memorandum from Rinpoche saying that he was concerned that Ken Green was not paying proper attention to the major practice centers, which came under his supervision, and that less than 25% of the information Ken brought to the Board was accurate. He added that he saw the same problems developing at Naropa Institute. And it was true that I was neglecting Naropa. Rinpoche rarely visited the Institute and it was felt by many of the staff to be a kind of poor cousin to Vajradhatu, where Rinpoche had his office and went every day that he was in town. He was clearly expecting and trusting us to "Just do it!" But I too had my office in the Vajradhatu building, along with all the other Board members, and rarely went the few blocks down the street to visit the Institute.

The day before Rinpoche was due to leave for the 1980 Seminary in January, he gave a public talk at Naropa Institute. While we were sitting in the office before his talk, he suddenly said, "I think we need a change of leadership at Naropa Institute." Just like that. Then he turned to Chuck Lief and said, "I think your wife (Judy) would be good." There was some very small discussion, but it was clear that he had already made the decision. He turned to me and said, "We were expecting Sir Jeremy to do something, and we don't know what happened." We were all stunned, and I personally was in a state of shock. When Rinpoche left Naropa after his talk, I went down to the car with him. He gave me a big kiss on the mouth, and left. And a few months later, Judy Lief took over as sole director of Naropa Institute.

RINPOCHE MAGNETIZES A GERMAN POETRY CLUB

A few days later I also left, with Karen and Vanessa, to teach the course on Shambhala at Seminary. From 1978 on, this was a required course for all Seminary students. Still in a state of shock and remorse, I felt reluctant to be leaving Boulder while Naropa was in this tenuous state, but it felt good to be able to leave administration for a while and plunge into the study and practice environment of Seminary, which this year was to be held in the hotel Chateau Lake Louise, a beautiful spot in the Canadian Rockies.

During the 1980 Seminary we witnessed another demonstration of Rinpoche's ability to go beyond conventional norms of behavior to bring the message of dharma to people and touch them in a way they would remember—an example of his crazy wisdom power to magnetize. His horse, Drala, was stabled at the riding arena nearby, and Rinpoche decided to go riding on the open day between the hinayana and mahayana phases. He invited a party of about ten people to go with him to observe the riding. Michael Kohn, now known as Sherab, who had been posted in Europe for several years as Rinpoche's Ambassador, was the kusung (the member of the Dorje Kasung with particular responsibility for personal service to the vajra master) for the day.

Rinpoche was dressed in a brown jacket and shirt, brown jodhpurs, and shiny, brown, knee-high riding boots. His head was completely shaven. After the riding event, we went to have dinner at the large stately Banff hotel. We were in a private room with a long table set for all of us. Rinpoche seemed impatient, pushing away his food, making disparaging comments about salad, which he called "rabbit food," and clearly wanting to get on with the meal and leave. Next to our dining room, we could hear some cheerful singing and rowdiness going on. Rinpoche told Sherab to find out what was happening in this other, seemingly more interesting, dining room. Sherab returned to report that there were medieval banners hung around the room and that the people were singing German folk songs. It was a meeting of a society

RIDING DRALA AT A DORJE KASUNG ENCAMPMENT.
Photograph by Andrea Roth.

for the continuation or cultivation of medieval chivalry, in the name of a nineteenth-century German poet.

Rinpoche and the rest of us left our dining room and sat in the big reception area of the hotel, and he told us that he wanted to go to the German celebration. As it was a private gathering and we couldn't just walk in, Sherab had to figure out how to get us in. Sherab waited until someone came out to go to the washroom and offered the man some money to let Rinpoche in. Naturally, this man was insulted and refused to talk to him. Sherab then went into the room and directly asked permission for Rinpoche to go in; messages were sent back and forth between Rinpoche and the leader of the German group, and after a while we were invited in.

We were preceded by Rinpoche, looking disconcertingly military in his brown shirt, brown jodhpurs, and shiny leather boots, complete with riding stick, shaven head, and dark glasses. He pushed open the double-swing doors of the room and stood there, legs apart, surveying the room, while the rest of us stood behind him in a V-shape formation. The room had a bright, uplifted, celebratory atmosphere and people had on elaborate and strange medieval hats. There was dead silence as everyone stopped and looked at Rinpoche. Then he was invited to the lectern to speak. We all walked in procession, through the cleared aisle with the German group lining the sides, to the front of the room. Rinpoche gave a short talk on the principles of Shambhala, stressing how we believe in basic goodness. He told them that somehow we and they were colleagues and should work together. When he finished his speech they gave him a standing ovation. The leader told him some of their secret forms and songs, and then we left, feeling energized and once again blown away by Rinpoche's ability to relate so directly and daringly with people who had never met him.

THE SCORPION SEAL TERMA ARRIVES

At this seminary, Rinpoche received the last main Shambhala terma, called *The Scorpion Seal of the Golden Sun*. His first Shambhala terma,

The Golden Sun of the Great East, had been received in a very casual setting as I described in chapter 7. *The Scorpion Seal of the Golden Sun* was received in a very different atmosphere, which is beautifully evoked in this account of the occasion by Sherab Kohn, his kusung, who was the only person with him as the writing process began, though a few other people came in later. Sherab told me that, though the event took place long ago, an immediate inner sense of it arose for him from a particular detail:

I can remember Rinpoche's body wrapped in a white inner kimono and his hand placing (but failing to make stand) a piece of incense in a rice-filled incense holder. It was in the small Tenno room at Lake Louise, the last room on the right at the end of the Suite corridor, across from his bedroom. It was just before we headed down the corridor to his study and he wrote (or received) the great Scorpion Seal text. I took the incense stick out of his hand. He objected slightly, but I was very positive and firm. I stuck it up in the rice and it stayed. He was miffed slightly, maybe at my doing what it had been up to him to do, but he let it pass and lit the incense. It was a smaller matter. He was already full of the terma.

In fact now I remember he had been glowing since I had entered his bedroom at his call to get him up and dress him. He told me as soon as I entered that the text had arrived. We had been talking about it for a few days. This was at least the third time in a seventy-two-hour period that he had had me get him out of bed in the morning to write it, but it hadn't come the previous times. This time it was here. There was a great feeling that the door of sacredness had been fully opened as I wrapped his sacred, vulnerable body in the white inner kimono. The sacredness of the world was totally palpable. The whole suite seemed to be flooded with sacredness now as we walked slowly down the hall from the Tenno room. Nobody else was around. In the study I brought him hot water to drink and writing materials. I lent him my pen (which I still have; a Parker with an arrow-shaped pocket clip). I knelt on the floor in the

*corner. The whole room seemed positively flooded with white light
as he wrote.*

*He told me a number of his dreams when he woke up in the
days leading up to that terma. I remember one of them. There was
a strong wonderful scent of something like juniper mixed with
saké and honey. That scent was very pervasive and wondrous.
Padmasambhava was in the atmosphere. The air was full of bees.
Pages of wonderful texts of Padmasambhava's were exfoliating
from their abdomens and falling to the ground. The air was full
of them.*

The *Scorpion Seal* text describes a four-week retreat that is the culmination of the Shambhala warrior's path, bringing together the practices of Shambhala and ending in a week of retreat in a completely
darkened cabin. Later on, in May, while Rinpoche was on vacation in
Patzcuaro, Mexico, he wrote a practice related to the *Scorpion Seal* text
that became known as the Werma sadhana. This sadhana is a powerful vajrayana-level practice that enables the practitioner to relate
directly with the Shambhala drala lineage. It is also preparation for
entry into the *Scorpion Seal* retreat. We would begin to practice the
Werma sadhana for the first time at the 1981 Kalapa Assembly.

SHIBATA SENSEI BRINGS KYUDO TO BOULDER

That summer Kanjuro Shibata Sensei, the Japanese imperial bow-
maker and master of *kyudo*, Japanese archery, visited Boulder at Rinpoche's invitation. Shibata Sensei was the twentieth generation in a
family of bow-makers for the Emperor and masters of kyudo. Rinpoche had been wanting to bring the Japanese arts over for the Shambhala sangha for some time. Rinpoche had met Kobun Chino Sensei, an
assistant to Suzuki Roshi, in 1971, at the time he met Suzuki Roshi.
Kobun Chino Sensei, who later became a Roshi, was not only a Zen
roshi and a master calligrapher but was also a student of kyudo under
Shibata Sensei. Later Chino Roshi was to be a frequent and much-loved

RINPOCHE AND SHIBATA SENSEI WITH THEIR SONS AND HEIRS.

visiting teacher in our centers. It was Kobun Chino Roshi who first suggested that Shibata Sensei be invited to Boulder.

Sensei finally arrived in 1980. He spoke very little English, but on this first occasion he was accompanied by his son, Nobihiro-*san*, who spoke quite good English. After he first met Rinpoche, I was told, he exclaimed, "I have met my Emperor again." Sensei and Rinpoche had made a very immediate and strong connection and, when Rinpoche showed Sensei the stroke of Ashe, Sensei said, "Ashe, kyudo shot— same thing." Subsequently we, his Shambhala kyudo students, would hear this often: "Ashe, kyudo shot—same thing!" From that time on, he was to visit North America for several months every year. Finally, in 1984 he moved permanently to Boulder. In the year 2007, Sensei was awarded the rank of National Living Treasure of Japan—the highest honor accorded to anyone in that country.

He found the North American sangha more open to his approach to kyudo, "meditation style" as he called it. This he contrasted with the "sports style" that was taking over in Japan. In kyudo practice, hitting the target is not the point. Sensei would often emphasize the fact that kyudo is not a sport but is for the benefit of the mind. Any kind of competitive spirit or concern about how others were doing—or even concern for ourselves about whether we hit the target or not—is completely inappropriate in this form of kyudo.

Many people in the sangha came to take kyudo classes from Shibata Sensei. As beginners, to learn the form, we stood just six feet in front of a large target, usually made of a hay bale wrapped in a sheet. Later we did shoot at distant targets, although we would always begin a session by practicing our form in front of a close target. Over and over, we practiced the apparently simple form: taking a stance like a huge oak tree, joining heaven and earth; raising the bow; pushing the bow forward and extending the string; holding that, holding, holding, and... release! It is said that it can take ten years just to learn to release the arrow properly. The buildup of intensity and the energy arising at the release feel very much like raising windhorse.

I appreciated Sensei's combination of fierce strength and tremendous gentleness and warmth, as well as his truly disciplined attitude to his whole life. Sensei's Japanese upbringing was intensely strict and his Japanese sense of decorum was very strong, and yet within that he could be so kind, relaxed, and friendly. When he left I accompanied him to the airport with a few other people. As he walked through the departure gate, he turned around and gave us a slight wave of his hand, and left. I felt sad to see him leave and deeply touched; our connection has remained strong for over twenty-five years.

I kept up regular practice of kyudo for a few years, and then it became infrequent. However, like Rinpoche, Sensei has tremendous loyalty to all his older students. Whenever I meet one of Sensei's assistants they always tell me, "Sensei still asks about you." And whenever he comes to a practice center at which I am residing, I join in the shooting and we are so happy to see each other. I have on my office wall a beautiful and elegant calligraphy executed by Sensei when he was eighty-five years old and almost blind. In Japanese it reads: *Chi Shin Yu,* and is one of the main mottos of kyudo. It means "Listen. Offer help. Never give up!" and Sensei seems to completely embody this.

MEETING GERALD RED ELK

One afternoon in July, I was participating in the Naropa Institute science program, which was somewhat muted from the previous year, when my secretary came quietly into the classroom and whispered to me that I had to come to Dorje Dzong right away. A Dakota Sioux shaman and elder, Gerald Red Elk, wanted to see Rinpoche, but since Rinpoche was not available to meet him, I was asked to do so.

Red Elk came into my office in the late afternoon and began by saying that he believed that the Tibetans had knowledge about the Star People—their version of dralas, I presumed—that complemented the knowledge his people had of them. Together, he felt, the two peoples could help the world in the coming bad times. Red Elk's voice was very soft and low, and as he spoke, the room seemed filled with kindness and generosity and an almost magical enchantment. I felt, as we sat there, that he was pouring love out toward me, even as he spoke about almost incomprehensible things. As the sun set, the room grew dark, but I did not want to get out of my chair and turn on the light for fear of breaking the spell.

As he was leaving, Red Elk again said, "I wish I could meet the Rinpoche." I replied, "He's busy now, perhaps tomorrow." Gerald Red Elk said, "Well, I'm leaving in the morning." And that was it. He left town early the next morning, and it wasn't until four years, when Gerald Red Elk was again in Colorado to read the medicine rocks, that their paths finally crossed in a dramatic and heart-rending meeting which I describe in *Sacred World*.[62]

RINPOCHE FALLS DOWN STAIRS

In August, Rinpoche had a serious fall down the stairs. He was going up to his bedroom via the back stairs of the Court, which were only wide enough for one person. The door from the kitchen opened onto the side of the stairs at the bottom and the stairs ended right up against the wall. The kusung who was helping him up the stairs was supposed to push him or support him from behind, but instead he went in front of Rinpoche and tried to hold his hand to pull him up. Rinpoche often used to play with his kusung by almost falling down the stairs, and they would really have to strain to catch him. This time the kusung was unable to catch him and he slid down about twenty steps, head first on his back, and his head slammed into the wall at the bottom. Mitchell Levy, his physician, pinched his nipples—a painful but traditional way to bring someone out of a trance or coma. Rinpoche woke up and asked, "Why did you do that?" Mitchell said, "To bring you back, Rinpoche," to which he responded, "Well you could have done it more gently!"

Rinpoche seemed to recover fairly rapidly from the fall, and many of the sangha didn't even know about it. He always made an effort to keep his physical state very private, never wanting to spread rumors or panic among his students. At the same time, something had clearly changed in his metabolism. Prior to that, he had always kept his rooms almost icy cold; he would open the windows, even in the winter, and while other people would be shivering he would be quite cheerfully fine. But after his fall down the stairs he insisted on keeping the windows closed and being in a warm situation.

After his fall, Rinpoche began to turn the responsibility for the administration over to the Regent more and more. Administration had been a major focus of his activity from the beginning and continued to be for a while. However, very often now, when a question would come up to Rinpoche in a meeting he would say, "Ask my Regent. What does my Regent think?" He would also often say, in such a circumstance, "What does the Board think?" or "Take it to the Board." And even at the Board meetings he would leave much more of the leadership to the Regent. It was clear that this was another step of handing over responsibility to his students, especially the Regent.

At this time, the "Director of the day" system was started. David Rome's assistant, Beverley Webster, would make a week's rota for all of the Directors to take turns. The Director of the day would put all of his appointments and activities aside on that day and would be completely available to be with Rinpoche from the time he woke up until he went to bed. The purpose of this was that we needed to be present for the many informal decisions that were made during the day. The Board was trying to run the organization, and things could easily become confused when decisions that affected our areas were made informally with Rinpoche. People would come to one of us and say, "Rinpoche said we should do this," and it would be quite difficult at times, especially if people weren't completely clear about what it was that Rinpoche had said. Often people would have their own projections, or forcefully suggest something to Rinpoche to which he would agree, only to say quite the opposite to someone else. In that way we would frequently hear conflicting instructions prefaced by, "Rinpoche said..." The Director of the day system was initiated so that one of us would always be there to keep these messages and decisions clear.

Being Director of the day was both a favorite time and a most dreaded time. Rinpoche would often see the Directors as soon as he got up and was having his breakfast. We would be informed by the kusung, or by the secretary, about the scheduled activities for the day, and our job was to be available all day in any way that was helpful. Whenever I went up to this private sitting room, I would always hesitate at the door before knocking. I could feel the intensity of that space, and I experienced both reluctance and a longing to plunge in.

I'm sure that all of the Directors, with their different relationships with Rinpoche and their different personalities, had very different experiences of being Director of the day. For me, my favorite time on those days was sitting alone with Rinpoche in his upstairs sitting room, which was just off his bedroom and had a very beautiful shrine in it as well as two armchairs, a coffee table, and a couch. He spent a lot of time there; it was his personal room where he would stay when he wasn't involved in any of the formal activities which happened downstairs.

Often, we would sit there for a long time, not saying very much. Kusung would come and go, his breakfast would come and go, and I would just rest my mind in that space that was almost like a mind-to-mind transmission for me. It was on one of these days that he made the comment that I mentioned in chapter 8, that "Being with Jeremy is like being on retreat." That was when I really knew him, when I really found him—in that space. I think he recognized that that was the way for me, because when I would sometimes plan ahead and think of some conversation topic or dharma question to ask him, he would often be quite abrupt with me as if to say, "Do you need to talk?" He would eventually get dressed and go to some meeting or other, or perhaps have some interviews. If they were private, personal interviews, I usually wouldn't sit in on them. But if they were business interviews I would be present for them—that was the whole point of having a Director of the day. The Director of the day system continued until Rinpoche went on his year-long retreat in 1984.

DISCOVERING ELEGANCE IN LOS ANGELES

In September, Rinpoche traveled to Los Angeles to teach a seminar on dharma art and to organize an exhibition titled "Discovering Elegance." Rinpoche wrote of dharma art, "Dharma art refers to art that springs from a certain state of mind on the part of the artist that could be called the meditative state. It is an attitude of directness and unselfconsciousness in one's creative work. Genuine art—dharma art—is simply the activity of nonaggression."[63]

The predecessor of this festival had been an ikebana exhibition by Rinpoche at the Denver Art Museum the year before. On this occasion, Rinpoche created a series of rooms, each furnished in a combination of Oriental and modern décor. The rooms represented the education of the warrior and moved from the first nurturing received in the kitchen and home, to the study where the warrior begins scholastic and artistic training, to the Warrior room where the warrior would encounter master warriors who overcome aggression with fearlessness and compassion, to the Buddha meditation room where the warrior learns to recognize basic goodness and discover the sacredness of the world, and finally to the Tenno room, or room of the Emperor who is capable of joining heaven and earth, thereby creating universal harmony and peace.

In each room, Rinpoche, with his aides, created a large flower arrangement appropriate to the activity of that room. In addition to symbolizing the warrior's journey, the atmosphere of the rooms was designed to stop conceptual thought in the viewer and to provide a clear, crisp, awake space. Rinpoche wanted to show that simplicity and elegance need not be expensive and that, by relating to things properly as they are, people could uplift their personal space and cheer up.

Rinpoche loved flowers, trees, horses, dogs; he loved the earth and everything living on it. Sometimes, on a drive, he would simply stop by a lake and sit on a rock, silently looking out across the lake. After a while he would stand up to leave without a word. When, the following year, he was recuperating from a serious illness, he would ask to be driven to a particular tree in the foothills of the Rocky Mountains, near Boulder, and he would lie under it for considerable periods of time. His arrangements went far beyond simply placing flowers in the traditional way, but could include huge six-to-ten-foot branches, carefully selected by him.

To join him in his expeditions to find these branches, and to gather rocks and grasses to place in the arrangements, he started a group called, "The Explorers of the Richness of the Phenomenal World." He loved especially to combine a huge pine branch with chrysanthemums and this was the most important and central piece in the exhibit. The making of the Los Angeles exhibition is sensitively portrayed in the lovely short documentary, "Discovering Elegance." In it, we see a precious moment in which having made this arrangement, the centerpiece of the entire exhibit, Rinpoche bows deeply to the arrangement. At that very moment, one of the chrysanthemums slowly tips down—nature bowing back to her lover, the vajra master.

RINPOCHE STANDS BESIDE "PINE AND CHRYSANTHEMUM."
Photograph by Robert del Tredici.

Rinpoche's style of ikebana was no longer a pure Sogetsu style, the school in which he had trained in London years previously. He was interested in a style that represented the joining of heaven, earth, and man (now spoken of more accurately as "human") and one that students could master relatively easily. His style had its own unique quality, just as the Buddhism that Rinpoche was teaching us was not pure Kagyu Tibetan Buddhism but was influenced by Zen and other traditions, and adapted for Western needs. At the same time, he wanted his students to learn the forms of traditional Japanese ikebana, which they could then use to create their own forms.

In the spring of the following year, Shibata Sensei attended the Kalapa Assembly with his wife, Shibata Kiyoko Oku-san, who was a teacher of tea ceremony and ikebana. Okusan Sensei was a very dignified, gentle, and lovely lady and Rinpoche asked her to teach ikebana at the Kalapa Assembly. After the Assembly, Okusan Sensei taught workshops in Boulder in both ikebana, or *kado*, the way of flowers, and *chado*, the way of tea. And Rinpoche began giving a series of ikebana classes at the Court for the seven or eight members of a new Kalapa Ikebana Steering Committee, as well as giving a few ikebana talks for the public. Karen made a strong connection with Okusan and began to study ikebana with her, becoming the first director of the Kalapa Ikebana Society, a new school of ikebana that Rinpoche started, based on his adaptation of the Sogetsu style.

Over the next few years, Rinpoche created several dharma art exhibitions, which included his ikebana creations, powerful and dramatic yet embodying the peace and sacredness of nature. "Nature is silent," Rinpoche would say, and "free from kleshas." Thus the contemplative practice of ikebana was introduced to the Shambhala community and it has since become the most widely practiced of the Shambhala arts. At all major Shambhala centers there is someone or a group who practice kado, and ikebana arrangements are an important aspect of the environment at any major teaching program.

THE FIRST FIRE *PUJA*

While Rinpoche was in Los Angeles, the first fire offering *(puja)* was held at RMDC. The basic principle of a fire puja is that having accomplished the requisite number of repetitions of the deity mantra, students then purify and seal that practice by performing the fire puja. This version of the fire puja is known as the "amending" fire puja since the purpose is to amend any faults that one has made in the execution of the practice to that point. The participants sit around a blazing wood fire all day, practicing the Vajrayogini sadhana, and putting various offerings into the fire as symbols of burning up their obstacles. This is done for eight to ten days.

This was actually the first fire puja ever held in America, and maybe even in the entire Western world. We were a somewhat kooky bunch of about twenty-five people, ably led by the Loppon, head of the Practice and Study department, and we had to put the whole thing together from scratch. As usual, we were pioneers and didn't fully know what we were doing, but we did have the English text that the translation committee had recently completed for us. On the day we finished, the Loppon called Rinpoche in L.A. to tell him we had accomplished it and to ask him for further instructions. Rinpoche's reply was that we should just keep practicing Vajrayogini in the usual way, nothing different. David Rome, who was conveying this to the Loppon, added, "And Rinpoche said, 'Tell them that the Kingdom of Shambhala is the only thing worth living for.'"

This was quite a surprising punctuation to the fire puja, to have the vajra master tell these people who had just so enthusiastically completed a certain significant phase of the Kagyu deity practice that the Kingdom of Shambhala was, after all, the only thing worth living for. It indicated to me, again, that from his point of view his most important job now was as king of Shambhala. He had told me on retreat, in 1977, that he would continue to act as vajra master, "because that's my job," and this he did, but Shambhala was where most of his energy was going now. In receiving the Shambhala terma, he had taken on the burden to establish enlightened society on earth, and he took this very seriously. He also seemed to feel intensely, as he said more and more frequently, that the earth urgently needed such a vision.

He had, in fact, been emphasizing since 1978 that the Shambhala teachings and the vajrayana teachings were inseparable, and continued to do so throughout his life. He had become concerned that vajrayana students were creating a nest for themselves and among themselves. For example, at the Kalapa Assembly in 1978, he said, "We have to accomplish the world of buddhadharma and the world of Shambhala at once. We can't do it separately. If we try to accomplish the world of buddhadharma without Shambhala vision, then we actually promote more spiritual materialism. So we have to put both of these situations together." And in a letter, written to a student in 1981, he wrote, "I have devoted my life to the work of spreading buddhadharma and helping people. That is my vow, which can never be reversed. Equally, spreading buddhadharma is inseparable from the vision of Shambhala principles, to which I have also dedicated my life."

NOW IS WHERE IT'S AT

Rinpoche requested that there be a Director in attendance with him on his teaching trips, so the Director of the day system was extended to include his travels. I was assigned to go to Chicago with him at the beginning of December. At dinner one evening in Chicago, I mentioned to Rinpoche that I was reading a book called *Man and Time* by J.B. Priestly, a well-known poet-laureate in England. He had announced on BBC that he was investigating precognition with a team of investigators. Hundreds of people sent in their stories, and he would then send his team of investigators to examine the situation around the phenomena each had reported. In the course of this, they eliminated many obviously false or even questionable situations, but Priestley and his team were left with some stories that really seemed quite hard to question.

I asked Rinpoche what he thought of this, saying that I thought that if only one of those stories were true, it would make a very big difference to our understanding of time. I had, perhaps, hoped to initiate a conversation on psychic phenomena, precognition, and clairvoyance. All he would say was, "It's *Now!*" quite impatiently, repeating several times, "Now, it's just Now!" As usual, he was stressing the ultimate view, that there is no time at all other than *now, now, now,* and *now* again. Perhaps he also intended to suggest that any genuine knowledge of the future was to be found only in a deeper appreciation of *now.*

After the Chicago visit, we went on to Cape Breton, Nova Scotia, where Rinpoche taught a seminar on the Four Maras,[64] or illusions, which are the negative side of the four karmas. The four karmas are four enlightened actions based on going beyond ego: pacifying a situation, enriching it, magnetizing wisdom energy, and finally destroying ego's obstructions. I will describe these in more detail later. In contrast to the four karmas, the maras are actions stemming from the same fundamental energy, but based on protecting ego. The four maras are: *devaputra*, dwelling in a god-like state of pleasure and comfort; *skandha*, taking excessive pride in the self; *klesha*, getting caught in negative emotions such as passion and aggression; and *yama*, clinging to ego out of a fear of change and, ultimately, of death.

Rinpoche also presided over the first Canadian Dharmadhatu conference, which was the first statement of the formation of Vajradhatu Canada. At that conference he appointed Dr. Jim Sacamano to be the "Ambassador Plenipotentiary" to Canada and presented him with a Nyo-I, a Japanese imperial scepter, as a symbol of his authority in Rinpoche's stead, until such a time as Rinpoche arrived to take up residence in Canada.

DISCOVERING KALAPA VALLEY

The seminar was held in the Keltic Lodge, a large and elegant old hotel on the magnificent coast of Cape Breton, Nova Scotia. During this program Rinpoche conducted a lhasang at Kalapa Valley. Rinpoche had discovered the Kalapa Valley during his second visit to Nova Scotia in May 1979. The story is that he had gone for a drive one day, saying that they were "setting out to find Kalapa." In the traditional histories of the Kingdom of Shambhala, Kalapa is the name of the capital. Three cars set off around Cape Breton Island. He kept telling them to turn this way and turn that way, clearly as if he were looking for something in particular. Finally, they came to a dirt driveway and he said, "Turn here."

They came to a metal bar across the road, and couldn't see anything beyond the trees. Rinpoche said, "This is Kalapa." The party then walked into a meadow that he called Kalapa Valley, a place that he said would be of spiritual significance to the evolution of Shambhala in the future. Later the land was purchased by a group of generous sangha-members and, after being held in trust by that group for twenty years, was finally handed over to Shambhala in the year 2000. In 2002 Eva Wong, a master of Taoism and Feng Sui, the Taoist version of geomancy, visited the Valley and remarked that it was one of the energetically most powerful places she had experienced anywhere on the earth. Kalapa Valley is now an important retreat place and a sacred spot where visitors can feel the presence of the Shambhala dralas.

So, on this stormy December day, in 1980, all of the subjects of the Kingdom of Shambhala who were present at the program drove to Kalapa Valley, some distance from the Keltic Lodge. There was a blizzard that day, with a cold sleet, coming down almost horizontally—typical Nova Scotia winter weather. Nonetheless, we all arrived and trooped together into this valley, even though we didn't really get a chance to see it because of the weather. Some people managed to get a fire going in a big brazier and we performed the lhasang ceremony, the most uncomfortable lhasang I have ever experienced, yet magical and strange. It was a strange and appropriate ending to a magical year.

1981: Meeting the Dralas 12

 HE THIRD Kalapa Assembly took place in March of 1981 at Chateau Lake Louise, immediately following the Seminary that had been held there for the third consecutive year. The very moment I arrived at the Assembly—it was already fairly late in the evening—I was asked if I would be the Director of the day and was directed to the Tenno room. There I found Rinpoche with John Rockwell, a translator who had made a strong connection with Rinpoche at the Seminary. They were having a lively discussion about some Japanese calligraphy characters.

When they were finished we went up to Rinpoche's suite, where Sherab was attending as kusung. He wanted to talk to Rinpoche about some trouble he was having with the older European students (the ones in Europe), the people who had known Rinpoche before Sherab arrived there in 1978. He had cultivated a circle of newer people, and the older ones were feeling shut out. Because my sister was one of these older students—she had made strong connection with Rinpoche and the dharma when she had visited for my wedding—Sherab asked me to wait in one of the outer rooms of the suite while he talked to Rinpoche about this situation. At a certain point I heard retching sounds, and Sherab came rushing out with a tray with vomit on it, saying, "Rinpoche is throwing up." Then he went back in, and some time later he came out again and said, "Rinpoche has written a terma."

Rinpoche had said that he was having great difficulty receiving the terma because there was a lot of interference—somewhat like one radio station interfering with the reception of another. This terma was quite short, and not like the others, which were instructional practice texts. The main message of this short text was that we should build the "School of the Golden Letter, the College of Ösel, the Ashe Prince," which came to be known as the College of the Ashe Prince (a title of the Sawang). Later Rinpoche said that this should be a training school for members of the government, and he put Sherab in charge of setting it up. Some attempts were made to initiate such training later, but they did not go very far.

Rinpoche wanted all of the senior staff to gather to hear this new terma. It was already early in the morning, so everyone else had to be awakened. Some ten of us gathered around the large table in the dining room of the suite. Rinpoche remarked with impatience that he was continuing to hear the radio station, and pulled David Rome's head against his to try to get him to hear it, which of course David could not. Rinpoche then began by going around the entire table, commenting on why everyone was there. In some sense, of course, we were there by chance, just because we happened to be at Kalapa Assembly, and because we had some role: Director, physician, kusung, translator. Rinpoche made personal comments about each one of us, some quite testy and cutting, others more encouraging. About John Rockwell, he said, "He's a good friend. The Sakyong is still allowed to have friends," When he came to me, he simply said, "Sir Jeremy is a good student." Though I longed to be classed as "good friend," "good student" was good enough considering Rinpoche's current mood.

Next Rinpoche started folding pieces of paper in something like Japanese origami style, and had all of us trying to do this in the same particular way. We were sitting at his large dining room table trying to do this at two or three o'clock in the morning. We couldn't really figure out what he was trying to do at all, but he had us continue over and over again. After what seemed like a long while, he abandoned this and called for a large piece of silk, the kind used for silkscreen banners. He drew a huge black calligraphy, proclaiming the College of the Ashe Prince, on this very large piece of white silk, and then proceeded to try to make a very stiff border along the top. Normally the fabric is hemmed and then a rod is put through to hang a banner. But he called for starch, and he kept folding the cloth over, as we had been trying to do with the pieces of paper, spraying it with starch, and ironing it— now it became clear why we had been folding the paper!

He continued spraying it and folding it over and over, and ironing it, trying to make it stiff. This went on for a very long time, while we were looking on, trying to lend a hand, and drinking saké continuously. Finally at dawn, the top of the banner was just stiff enough to enable it to hang, Rinpoche seemed satisfied, and we all retired to our beds.

MORE ON DRALA

The main teaching of that Assembly was the presentation of the Werma sadhana for the first time—the practice I mentioned in the previous chapter that Rinpoche had written to enable his students to relate with the Shambhala drala lineage. The Werma sadhana was our main practice for the Assembly, and the talks as well were focused on the dralas of Shambhala. One afternoon, Rinpoche looked in on us while we were practicing. That evening, at the end of the talk, he described how he had watched us through the glass doors and noticed how uptight we were. He said, "You looked stupid and stiff." I could feel what he meant—it was as if we were anxiously praying to a mysterious external being, stiff and wanting something.

Rinpoche expressed being somewhat frustrated and he commented, "You have some relationship with the drala principle—as much as you and I have a relationship with each other—which can be transmitted and become part of you.... I feel that I could impart to you, introduce

INVITING THE DRALAS WITH A LHASANG.

to you, such wonderful ladies and gentlemen of the drala principle. They are longing to meet you. At this point, I'm afraid I have to be very bold; they're longing to meet you.... Why don't we do something so that we can actually—I don't know what you could call it. Let's actually do it!... I don't think it's that problematic at all. As far as I am concerned, I'm doing enough, as much as I can. It's like trying to introduce two friends: the dralas are there, waiting to come along and meet you.... For heaven's sake, heaven and earth, can't we just relax a little bit? And please shed a few tears. That will help a lot."[65]

It is so clear that he regarded the dralas as, relatively speaking, real entities that we can have a relation with, "as much as you and I have a relationship with each other." Of course, this was not to re-introduce theism, as his other comments to us made amply clear. Ultimately neither "you" nor "I" exists, but on the relative level of appearances we do seem to exist. On that same relative level, Rinpoche was insisting, the dralas can also be felt. By now this message was getting through to me and, considering also the calligraphy "*Drala*" that he had given me for my birthday in 1979, I began to consider seriously what it might mean to "meet the dralas."

Years later, Thrangu Rinpoche commented on the Shambhala teachings in an interview with translator Larry Mermelstein.[66] I will quote his remarks at length here, since they are helpful in understanding Rinpoche's reasons for introducing the practices of invoking drala and the forms of Shambhala:

> [Trungpa Rinpoche] told me that America in general is a very developed country, in many ways. But there was a problem because there's been so much destruction of the land, so many big roads had been built and the land has been wasted and destroyed. Also most people in America aren't from this land but come from other places originally, and are not indigenous to the land, so they don't have any particular native culture. So, although externally it was a highly developed country, the people suffer inwardly from diminished or depressed life energy, or yang, and diminished or damaged drala. He told me that because of this, because there were no native traditions, there was much damage to the customs of respect and kindness. So for one thing, people weren't happy, and for another, since it was a democracy, there was no situation where there could be mutual respect or love and kindness for people. Generally, in other societies, the people respect those higher than they, and are kind to those lower. But this kind of custom has been lost here. He said that for this reason, he had set up a system with kusung and kasung and ministers and that based on this, people's minds would benefit. Also, practices such as lhasang, the raising of dralas, wearing proper clothes instead of just anything, would heighten and strengthen the personal drala [or windhorse] of people. Trungpa Rinpoche said that he could personally see a difference now in the way people looked. Another symptom of damaged drala is being homeless, and he noticed that people in America were always moving

around and always thinking about moving: "I'm going to go to New York, and I think now I'll move to California." And as soon as they get there they think, "Maybe I'll go to Texas," but then, after that, "Maybe I'll go up to Canada." Thinking in that way comes about from damaged drala. When the drala is restored, then a person starts to feel connected to one place and decides, "I'm going to stay here, this is my home," and gains more confidence in himself or herself. So he said, therefore, that he established this kind of new order to benefit the minds of the people who were involved.

RINPOCHE'S MAGICAL GLOW

The farewell address on the last day of the Assembly, like farewells on all of such occasions, was a time of tremendous love and sadness. Rinpoche always ended such occasions by making parting remarks of appreciation: "I love you all," and, "This was a very important occasion," and the like. A considerable sized group of us were returning to Denver on the same plane as Rinpoche, and we all sat in the lounge of the Banff Airport together waiting to leave. I was sitting at another table some distance away. Again I remember that extraordinary glow, which I would often feel at times like this when it was a little bit quiet and there was not much going on. On that occasion, we were just sitting there, happy to have had a very rich Assembly, even though painful at times. It was late afternoon. I looked at Rinpoche chatting, across the way, and it was so peaceful and rich, so beautiful and warm. I felt as if I were bathing in that atmosphere, and I wanted to be just there, all my life, and forever.

Rinpoche went through the airport and onto the plane in a wheelchair—he often went to the plane in a wheelchair in those days—and I walked alongside of him. As we came up to passport control, his head was completely sunk on his chest and his eyes were closed. It really seemed as if he were asleep. Just as we stopped to show our passports to the passport control agents, Rinpoche raised his head, looked up at the passport officer and gave him a beautiful, big, beam of a smile, and the customs officer just melted. You could feel it. The officer smiled and said, "Thank you, sir," and waved us all through. Rinpoche's head immediately sank back onto his chest. It was one of those magical occasions that happened so often with Rinpoche; with just a smile, he could melt an ordinarily uptight, unpleasant, or even threatening situation.

AN ENCOUNTER WITH A ROSHI

Shortly after the Kalapa Assembly, I went out to Los Angeles to ask Taizan Maezumi Roshi if he would join a new Board of Advisors for Naropa Institute that we planned to set up as part of a fundraising effort. Maezumi Roshi had made a very strong connection with the sangha in Boulder, and in particular with myself, when he had taken over the main course on Buddhism, at Rinpoche's request, during Rinpoche's retreat in 1977. Roshi had continued to visit Boulder for several years after this and our good connection with him had continued. I was invited to lunch at Maezumi Roshi's home, and was accompanied by Steve Baker, the Vajradhatu Ambassador to L.A. We sat in Roshi's living room along with eight or ten of his students and were served sushi and lots of saké. Roshi asked me to explain again what I wanted. After I had explained the idea of the Board, the first thing he said was, "What do you *really* want, Jeremy?"

Roshi started talking to me directly, "Who does Trungpa Rinpoche think he is?" he said, "Does he think he can be a monarch just because he was kicked out of his own country?" Apparently he had heard something about the new direction we were heading in, toward the Kingdom of Shambhala. He continued to criticize Rinpoche in various ways, but I didn't take up the bait and attempt to defend or justify Rinpoche at all. Several times he turned to me and said, "What do you *really* want, Jeremy? What do you *really* want?"

I explained again that I had simply come to invite him to join Naropa Institute's Board of Advisors, to which he retorted, "But what do you *really* want?" Then he would started criticizing Rinpoche again. His continually asking that question felt like a profound teaching which I always remembered, telling me to go to the very heart of the matter and find out what I *really* wanted in the teachings and in my life. But in other ways I knew that it was just part of the bait.

Finally, he turned to his own students and said, "You see, look what good students Trungpa Rinpoche has." He and Rinpoche had, in fact, a close and good relationship. I felt that he had been trying to challenge me by seeming to insult Rinpoche, and was impressed that I did not give in. As we were leaving, he said that he would let us know about joining the Board of Advisors, and a few days later we received a letter from him declining our invitation since, as he astutely wrote, he did not want to be merely an important name on a letter head.

Some days later, when Chuck Lief was visiting my office, I told him of my visit with Maezumi Roshi and we discussed what Roshi might have intended by his highly critical judgment of Rinpoche and what he might actually think of Rinpoche's vision. After Chuck left, I sat there at my desk and, seemingly out of nowhere, I suddenly had the thought, "Could Rinpoche really be mad?" As well as his proclamation of the Kingdom of Shambhala, I was thinking about the crazy events at the recent Kalapa Assembly and the drala teachings altogether. Taken over perhaps by my old conventional and materialistic ways of thinking and feeling, I panicked and went completely cold. My mind froze at this thought that he could be crazy in the conventional sense. I was so completely in his world at this point: he was my vajra master, my guru, and my king. If he *were* insane, and if all the things he was doing were just acts of insanity, then I was lost.

Slowly, I started remembering his kindness and love, and his unsurpassed brilliance as a teacher. One by one, small thoughts entered my mind about how kind he had always been to me and to others. I realized that he had never deliberately harmed anyone, that all of his acts came from love however conventionally crazy they might seem, and that the teachings he had given had proven so true in my own experience. The frozen panic of my mind gradually melted, and a sense of warmth returned as I continued to remember his unceasing kindness.

At that point a sense of humor reappeared, and the thought occurred, "Well, if he *is* mad, then I would rather be mad, too." I never again questioned Rinpoche's basic sanity.

A SERIOUS ILLNESS BEGINS

When Rinpoche returned to Boulder after the Kalapa Assembly, he was very sick with duodenitis, an intestinal inflammation. He couldn't keep food down at all, kept a bottle of Maalox in the car, which he constantly sipped, and began to lose a tremendous amount of weight. It was that May that he wrote the *Supplication to Padmasambhava*[67] that the Shambhala community still chants every evening, calling on Padmasambhava in four of his different aspects to conquer the barbarianism of the dark ages, and to dispel and destroy all obstacles. It was very clear that he was experiencing tremendous obstacles to his work at that time.

I had to ask Rinpoche to sign a school application for Gesar, Rinpoche and Diana's second son, whose education Rinpoche had asked me to oversee, as I was doing for the Sakyong. It was Rinpoche's strong wish that Gesar attend Eton school, the most prestigious private school in England, and we were applying to send him to a preparatory school for Eton. When I entered Rinpoche's small sitting room upstairs in the Court, he was sitting there silently, completely slumped in his chair. I took the piece of paper to him, and he hardly acknowledged me at all as he signed it. He didn't look up or make any expression at all. I felt so sad and imagined I could feel the tremendous burden of responsibility that he must have.

During the period of Rinpoche's illness, I was sitting alone with him in his private living room when he received a phone call. He took the call, and spoke at some length in Tibetan. After he put the phone down, he said, "That was Tai Situ Rinpoche. He's the most like me." He was referring to one of the four young Kagyu tulkus who were the most senior after the Karmapa and were sometimes referred to as the four Kagyu princes. I said, "Do you think he will go in the same direction as you?" "What do you mean?" Rinpoche asked with some surprise.

"Well, you know, taking off your robes, drinking, and the women, and so on," I replied. He screwed up his face and said, brusquely, "I certainly hope not. *I* did what I did so that they wouldn't have to." Then he added, sadly, "It's been a very lonely journey, you know."

Rinpoche did not fully recover from this illness throughout the year. Nevertheless, he continued to be active when he could. He performed the Vajrayogini abhisheka again that year, although it had to be postponed once. During this time, he insisted on continuing to drink saké. Knowing that alcohol was a contributory cause of his physical problems, his physician asked the kusung to boil the saké before serving it to him in order to reduce or eliminate its alcohol content. When Rinpoche found out about this he was very angry, and ferociously shouted, "Stop interfering with my work!"

By this time the Regent was beginning to separate himself from Rinpoche. He had moved out of the Kalapa Court, and also moved his main office out of the suite containing Rinpoche's office and down to the other end of the corridor. He was teaching brilliantly and magnetizing many new students who were beginning to regard him as their teacher and not connecting with Rinpoche at all. But he seemed to be trying to build an independent base which, as Rinpoche said, "he is not supposed to do," until, presumably, after Rinpoche's death. It was obvious that he still had much training to go through.

And the Regent had started using marijuana and other drugs again with his circle, including some of the Directors, which Rinpoche was clearly not happy about. As I mentioned in chapter 4, years ago Rinpoche had written in a public message to the sangha that to smoke marijuana was nothing other than dangerous self-deception and to continue it would leave "little chance of individuals taking part in the wisdom of the lineage." Yet here was his own Regent taking it up again.

There was a clear disconnect with Rinpoche and many people were sent on Rinpoche's behalf to encourage the Regent to meet his guru more often. The Regent continued to take on more and more responsibility both in the administration and teaching all the way to the vajrayana level, his brilliance, energy, and humor undiminished. Yet privately, especially late at night when he was drunk, the Regent could be aggressive and cutting to fellow students, and some people were feeling very hurt by this. When I was meeting with Rinpoche that summer I mentioned this to him, wondering what we could do about it. Rinpoche replied, with a mixture of concern and disgust, "Is he *still* doing that? You should talk to him." Still Rinpoche continued to praise and encourage the Regent both publicly and privately, and would often say, "Anyone who does not respect my Regent does not respect me."

Thus, 1981 was a year of great obstacles for Rinpoche, and in a lesser way for his students as well. For a birthday gift that year, in July, Rinpoche gave me a large black pipe. As I took the pipe out of its box he said quietly, "Don't fall into the black hole"—of depression I surmised. The pipe was accompanied by a poem which Rinpoche passed to me saying, "That should be saved for the archives." The poem was signed "DD of M" (Dorje Dradul of Mukpo). Dradul was Rinpoche's Shambhala name and means "Invincible Enemy Destroyer." The poem reads:

Shining Warrior Knight

My dear sir,
All the honors and goodness in the
Kingdom are yours
All the wickedness and wretchedness
you should dispel.
Elder and leader of the ministers
in this cheerful occasion
We would like to further express
our gratitude and devotion
Cheerful Birthday
May you be saved from
The dark hole of the setting sun.

RINPOCHE MEETS THE RIGDEN DRALAS
IN SAN FRANCISCO

In September, Rinpoche went out to the San Francisco Bay Area to teach a dharma art program and to create another dharma art exhibition, "Discovering Elegance," similar to the one he had created in Los Angeles the previous year. While he was there, we heard reports that strange events were happening. In an antique store, he had seen a statue of Yung-Lo, one of the ancestral sovereigns whom he regarded as a model of a beneficent monarch, and the following day he had gone into some kind of trance.

Mitchell Levy, Rinpoche's personal physician, describes what happened in this way:

> His eyes would close and then partially open, but he was not responding to us—his mind seemed elsewhere. John Perks and I supplicated him over and over again to come back, and I tried several traditional ways to bring him back to normal consciousness. Nothing worked. The room was glowing with pure luminosity and was as if filled with his brilliance and vast mind. I had his kusung make a bowl of iced saffron water—I don't know why I thought of this. I soaked a cloth in the water and applied it to his genitals, and this brought him back for a moment. He opened his eyes and said, "You fucking son of a bitch." I replied, "I'm afraid of losing you, Rinpoche," to which he responded, "It's okay," and went back into his trance.

Later he told those who were with him that he had been visiting the Rigdens in Shambhala and had actually asked them if he could stay there, but they had told him to return to earth and continue his responsibilities as Sakyong. Altogether it seemed there was a rather bizarre situation happening in the Bay Area.

There was a big range of interpretations of all of this among the Directors, some even commenting that, "we are losing him." I person-

RINPOCHE PLACING A FLOWER FOR AN IKEBANA INSTALLATION.
Photograph by Andrea Roth.

ally did not know what to make of it and had no particular opinion, though it did not sound any more outrageous than other manifestations we had seen from Rinpoche. In retrospect, I feel that he was beginning to show more overtly his true nature as being not an ordinary human, as Khyentse Rinpoche said to us at the time of Rinpoche's cremation—or at least he was not *just* an ordinary human, though he was that as well, of course, as he himself insisted. He had made a tremendous effort at the beginning of his time in America to bring himself into our mundane view of the world, to be with us. As the years went by, and especially when he became the Sakyong, whose role is to join the ultimate openness of mind, which he called "heaven," with mundane reality, "earth," it was as if the vastness or heaven aspect came out more and more.

When he spoke of his communication with that ultimate mind, the mind of the Rigdens, he was speaking of his expansion into that vast realm, the inner realm of the dralas. One could perhaps say that he was lifting the masks that had allowed us to relate with him on the ordinary human level, when he had very much wanted us to know that we could follow in his footsteps. He had wanted us to feel that he was an ordinary human person and, as he said so often, "You could do it, too."

HIS HOLINESS THE SIXTEENTH KARMAPA
LEAVES THE EARTH

In late October, the Karmapa was flown to a hospital in Zion, Illinois, for treatment for an advanced state of stomach cancer, and Rinpoche went there to be with him. His Holiness the Karmapa had last visited the United States in 1980, and the Boulder portion of his visit occurred in June. He was thinner that time, not in good health, though he still seemed to be glowing. His kindness, laughter, and majestic radiance seemed ever more transparent. I was completely magnetized to him then, seeking extra opportunities to see him and be in his presence. Just as it was with Rinpoche, being in his brilliant presence had the magical quality of waking one up to one's own brilliance and to confidence in one's own being.

On November 5, 1981, His Holiness died. For some days before that it was clear that he was going to die, but he refused all morphine. The doctors were completely unbelieving that someone could be in such extreme pain, as they thought, and yet still remain smiling and caring for those around him. At one point during his last few days, he opened his eyes, looked around and smiled, and said, "Nothing happens." It is hard to be certain what he meant by this, but possibly he was reminding us that, according to the Tibetan view, if one retains one's fundamental awareness at the point of death, then nothing happens; there is simply no change in that awareness as one passes through the moment of death.

Rinpoche went out with the Regent and a party of about fifteen to Sikkim to attend the Karmapa's funeral, which took place on December twentieth, after the usual forty-nine-day waiting period. Speaking of His Holiness to the sangha, Rinpoche said:

> *The death of His Holiness is sad and devastating in some sense. His Holiness passed away just as the Kagyu Dharma was in the process of conquering the world. But his passing into nirvana is also a blessing. Death is regarded as similar to birth. Each time a departure or arrival of a Karmapa takes place anywhere in the world, it is a blessing in that particular land…. Certainly he cared for us and he would not die as a mark of punishment to his students or displeasure with their practice…. We do not regard His Holiness' death as an attack by unexpected obstacles. We can see it as a blessing. Never before has any realized person such as the Buddha, Jesus Christ or Mohammed set foot in the Western world.[68]*

Perhaps in this there were suggestions as to how to take Rinpoche's own death, which was not so far away as we imagined—his death, too, could be seen as a blessing; he, too, cared for us and would not die as a mark of punishment or displeasure with our practice.

1982: 13
Coemergence, Joy, and Sadness

 WAS INVITED to be the Director in residence at the Vajradhatu Seminary for 1982, which was to be held in Bedford Springs, Pennsylvania. Karen asked to be Rinpoche's
secretary for that period and Rinpoche agreed to that, so
we went up together with Vanessa. At the beginning of the Seminary,
I found myself in a constant state of bliss, which would arise whenever I thought of His Holiness.

It is said that when a great being such as the Karmapa dies, his
blessings are much more available for some period of time after he
leaves the physical body. When I thought of him, I would feel a
welling up from within of bliss, joy, love—a feeling with no name. As
well as being related to my feeling for His Holiness, it was also clearly
connected with Vajrayogini practice. It was another of the *nyams*,
"temporary experiences," that I mentioned in chapter 10, but this time
it continued for a while and pervaded my life outside of the formal
practice.

I remained in this extraordinary state for many weeks at the beginning of the Seminary. On the arrival day of Seminary, I manifested quite
unlike my usual persona of the time, greeting everyone and smiling,

and feeling utterly delighted. Contributing to this mood was the fact that I loved being in this kind of situation, with few administrative duties. It was blissful just to be with Rinpoche at the Seminary in this way—almost like being on vacation with the family.

I had many opportunities to be with Rinpoche during that time. I reported in to him every morning as soon as he awoke, sat in on the faculty meetings, and generally spent some time with him most days and many evenings. Rinpoche's health was still not particularly good during this Seminary. He cancelled many meetings, including ones involving people who had traveled great distances to Seminary especially to meet with him. Karen often found herself in the unenviable position of being in the middle—trying to serve Rinpoche while also trying to placate the many people demanding his attention. Rinpoche began to get increasingly demanding as well, saying "no" to requests more and more often. Rather than feeling sad, students often responded with anger. At this time, Rinpoche became irritated and complained to Karen that people should make their own decisions and stop relying on him so much.

His humor was nonetheless endless and unquenchable. His laughter at his own jokes was infectious even though the jokes, particularly Tibetan ones, were sometimes not at all funny in the Western style. One evening at the Seminary Rinpoche invited a small group of people to dinner in his suite. The group was rather solemn, and Rinpoche asked if anyone had a joke. When no one seemed to be able to think of one, he told one about a Tibetan peasant who placed a block of butter on the stove one night to soften it, then forgot about it and went to bed. When he awoke in the morning, the peasant went running out of the house shouting, "Someone stole my butter and peed on my floor!" Rinpoche could barely get even half-way through this joke before he was doubled over with laughter. By this time, we too were laughing heartily, but more in tune with his laughter than at the joke itself.

Rinpoche could use humor in so many different ways, to cut through people's self-seriousness as he did here, to change the energy of the situation, or simply to cheer people up. This was one of his most constant refrains: "Please, let's cheer up!" For example, the annual Vajrayogini abhisheka was held in May that year, followed as usual by a *tri*, or commentary on the practice by the vajra master. I was on duty with Rinpoche the next day, and in the afternoon we were sitting on the terrace in the back yard of the Court. During one of the long silences that often punctuated conversations between Rinpoche and myself, I turned to him and said, "That was a *won*derful *tri* you gave yesterday, Rinpoche," with a rather sugary emphasis on the word "*won*derful." He replied, "Hmm."

About an hour later, we were joined by Mitchell Levy. After chatting for a while, Rinpoche rose and walked slowly across the patio with one of us on either side of him. He stopped at a flowerbed that had a nice clump of purple begonias, opened his zipper, and pissed right into the middle of the begonias. Then, leaning a little in my direction, he said, "Jeremy, aren't they *won*derful?" with exactly the same sugary intonation.

And this story, told by Patricia (whom I described receiving instantaneous windhorse instruction the first time she went to see Rinpoche) illustrates the kind of private jokes that he used to have with friends, that could come in handy when things were getting dull:

> Rinpoche had told me that he had a secret code. The code words were "Amara Health Group." He explained that if one of us said that at any time or place, it would mean that we were thinking about sex, and that we would like to have sex now. One morning, Rinpoche and I were sitting up in bed, just having finished breakfast, when Laurie came in to take away the tray. She started asking Rinpoche a personal question, almost as if having an interview, which people are not supposed to do when in a service role. She was rather long-winded, but Rinpoche, as always, listened to her warmly. I would never dare to interrupt a personal interview of this kind, but at one point Rinpoche turned to me and said, "What do you think?" So I quietly said, "Hmm, it reminds me of the Amara Health Group situation." Rinpoche looked at me with a rather astonished expression

on his face, then smilingly said, "Um hmm." Laurie, who of course
did not know the code meaning of this, looked quite interested and
also said, "Oh, yes," and continued on. Even though she wasn't in
on the joke, the whole situation with the three of us was very warm
and kind, as if the humor opened up the space somehow. It was a
delightful meeting of minds, created by Rinpoche's playfulness.

STRANGE MOVES WITH A WINE GLASS

One evening at Seminary, Karen happened to mention to some people that, long before she met Rinpoche, she used to experiment in the paranormal with some interesting results and they wanted to try it out. They wrote the letters of the alphabet on small pieces of paper and arranged them in a circle on a coffee table. As a pointer they used a wine glass on which several people gently rested fingers. The wine glass did start moving and pointing to some letters, which seemed to be nonsense until someone thought he recognized them to be spelling some Japanese words. There happened to be a Japanese student at Seminary, so he was woken up and reluctantly joined the group. He confirmed that the words actually did make sense in Japanese and that they indicated the presence of a cook.

The next day, several of the people who had participated in this odd event told Rinpoche about it. Rather than dismissing it as nonsense, as I had anticipated, he said, "It is someone who died here and doesn't know the War is over. So you should contact him again and let him know that the War is over." We did know that, toward the end of World War II, the hotel had been used as a Japanese American internment camp. The same group tried to contact the cook the next night, but were not able to reach him then. Rinpoche said that the Japanese gentleman had found the Tenno room (an audience room furnished in a Japanese style) and liked staying there, adding that he still thought the hotel was surrounded by barbed wire. A few nights later they were able to contact him again and explain the situation, and the next day Rinpoche said he had left. Although in this case Rinpoche clearly confirmed Karen's experience with the "wine board," (as we called it) in general he discouraged people from dabbling in psychic phenomena, trying to contact unseen energies through such things as the *Ouija* board. He warned that it could be dangerous since one could connect with aggressive, destructive, or insane energies in this way.

This strange tale was remarkably confirmed when someone found a magazine about the State of Pennsylvania with a special feature on the history of the Bedford Springs Hotel. It related that, while the hotel was being used as a Japanese American internment camp, a Japanese cook had died there of a heart attack in 1944 while playing cards. No one had known of this when they did the wine board. This whole story could be taken as an indirect confirmation from Rinpoche of the way the group had found out about the cook, though my skepticism at that time was too deep to allow me to contemplate the significance of this.

A PRE-COGNITIVE DREAM?

In the middle of Seminary, I was due to fly down to Washington, D.C., in order to speak at a fundraising event. From there I was going to fly out to Boulder for the bi-annual visit of the accrediting team to Naropa Institute, for Shambhala Day, and for a Shambhala Training level that Rinpoche was to teach—one of the first programs in which he introduced the practices of Stroke and raising windhorse to people who were not yet subjects of the Kingdom of Shambhala. A few days before I was to leave for Washington, I went to the bedroom to lie down for a few minutes. Both Karen and I were quite exhausted throughout the Seminary, since we were always on call for Rinpoche and also had to be present at many other meetings.

As I lay on the bed, I had a vivid waking dream. I dreamt that I was in an airplane and the aisle was at a very steep upward angle. Everyone was struggling up the aisle, and at the top the flight attendant was waving us out an open door to her left, through which we were obviously supposed to jump. As I struggled up the aisle, I heard someone say, "We left the tail behind in Washington!" I heard a vivid, loud explosion and everything dissolved in a brilliant flash of light. I was then floating outside the plane. I was dead. The dream was so vivid and shocking, dramatic, and intense, that I woke up shaking.

At that very moment, Karen came into the room and I told her about my dream. She immediately said that she was going to tell Rinpoche. I felt silly and told her not to, but she insisted. When she came back, she said, "He says you're not to go to Washington." I was astounded. She told me that he had looked her straight in the eye and said, very firmly, "You should tell people to pay attention to these things, to pay attention to their intuition." When she asked him how one could tell the difference between a dream that was trying to tell us something, and one that was a simple projection of our own ego, he said, "It depends on the intensity."

Rinpoche's public view of such so-called "psychic" phenomena as pre-cognitive dreams and visions, hands-on healing, and so on, seemed to be to discount them and to tell people not to waste their time on such things. This goes along with the traditional Buddhist view that, while such abilities are certainly possible and can in fact develop naturally at a certain stage in one's practice, to seek them is a distraction from the main point, the realization of egolessness and shunyata. Traditionally they are known as *relative siddhis,* or powers, to contrast them with the *ultimate siddhi,* which is realization of the ultimate truth of shunyata, the true nature of reality. In Rinpoche's Sadhana of Mahamudra such psychic powers are referred to as "the supernormal powers that need not be sought."

However in private it could be a different story. He still discouraged abstract speculation as he had with me in Chicago, when I had tried to draw him into a discussion of pre-cognitive dreams. However, when one of his trusted students came to him to report a genuine, often unexpected experience, he was not disparaging at all. Often he would even encourage the student to practice and to try to develop the *siddhi* that had manifested.

For example, a young woman, one of his vajrayana students, told him that she felt and had been told that she had healing energy in her hands. He told her to train further in this, and to become a trained nurse so that she would have an avenue for expressing her healing *siddhi*. He gave her a short sadhana practice to help her nurture this natural healing energy. Another young woman told him that on three occasions, just before a close friend or relative had died, she had had a vision of each person looking as though he or she was dead. She had gone to him to seek his advice on how to stop these visions, but he encouraged her to develop this ability. Likewise, he told Karen to pay attention to these things, and to tell others to do so as well.

The morning after my dream, when I arrived for my shift, I asked, "Rinpoche, I understand from Karen that you don't think I should fly to Washington because of the dream I had yesterday?" "Yes, that's right," he replied, to which I rejoined, "Then I would be flying directly to Boulder. Should I fly with you, in order to receive your protection, or should I fly separately to make sure you are safe?" He said, "I think you should fly separately," perhaps implying that I should not depend on him for protection, or suggesting that I might think of his safety before my own. Rinpoche arrived in Boulder somewhat before me, and as soon as I arrived I went to the Court where there was a reception. I walked in the room just as Rinpoche had finished telling the story to the gathered guests. He said "Ah, here he is!" and they all laughed and cheered.

PLEASE STOP RINPOCHE'S DRINKING

I arrived in Boulder a day or two before Shambhala Day. On Shambhala Day, I was on duty as Director of the day and toward the end of the day, before the evening event for subjects of Shambhala, I had a vigorous exchange with Lady Diana about Rinpoche's drinking. Shortly before Seminary, she had requested a meeting with the Directors to discuss her concern about this. She had asked us in a very formal way—almost a command—to help her to stop or at least to slow down his drinking. The outcome of the meeting was that we all promised her to help slow down his drinking. Although I very much appreciated and felt that I understood Lady Diana's concern, and her special role as his wife, I didn't feel entirely comfortable about this discussion. I had gone along with the group at this meeting, but afterward, when I thought about it some more, I wished that I had not gone along so readily.

At the very beginning of Seminary, Rinpoche had started drinking saké as heavily as he had before his sickness. On the night of his first talk, he became really quite drunk. The next day I asked him, "Rinpoche, why do you drink so much, especially when you have been so sick?" He replied, "A sense of celebration."

Rinpoche had over the years said many things about his drinking. He had said, "Don't interfere with my work," when he discovered that people were boiling the saké during his sickness. On several occasions he said, "I have to drink to break through the resistance of my students," although it was not clear to me how he meant this. And I referred in chapter 3 to his article on drinking, in which he writes, "For the yogi, the virtue of drinking is that it brings one down to ordinary reality, so that one does not dissolve into meditation on nonduality." I saw more and more as the years went by that this was indeed what he seemed to be doing, coming down to ordinary reality for the sake of his students.

That summer, many of Rinpoche's students were becoming very anxious about the extent of his drinking. At that time Tai Situ Rinpoche, the one of the Kagyu princes about whom Rinpoche had said, "He's the most like me," visited North America. During one of his talks to the community, Situ Rinpoche planted someone in the audience to ask him to comment about Trungpa Rinpoche's drinking, because so many people had been asking him this question. He said, "First of all, you have to understand that Trungpa Rinpoche is not an ordinary person. He is a bodhisattva." He went on to say that we could not judge bodhisattvas and mahasiddhas like Trungpa Rinpoche by the standards of ordinary people. Rinpoche was recognized by the wisest of Tibetan masters— the Sixteenth Karmapa, Dilgo Khyentse Rinpoche, Kenchen Thrangu Rinpoche, and Khenpo Tsultrim Gyamtso Rinpoche—as a mahasiddha,

THE SAKYONG AND SAKYONG WANGMO.
Photograph by Hansen Holmes.

meaning "one of great accomplishment," a rare being whose realization goes far beyond that of even many renowned Tibetan teachers.

This was how I believed Rinpoche related to alcohol and, even though we felt greatly regretful and sorrowful that it was damaging his body, nevertheless was it right to vow to stop him?

Thus it was that, on that Shambhala Day, I asked Lady Diana if I could speak with her. We were in evening dress, ready for the final event of Shambhala Day, the formal Shambhala meeting. She pulled me into the smaller front sitting room and gestured for me to sit next to her on the couch. I told her that I didn't feel comfortable about the discussion with the Board concerning Rinpoche's drinking. I went on in quite a blunt way, saying that Rinpoche was a mahasiddha, and mahasiddhas have a different approach to things and pointing out that many of them did drink a lot. I concluded that I didn't feel that we were necessarily doing the right thing, trying to get him to stop drinking. During my little speech, Lady Diana held my hand in a rigid grip almost as if she were trying to control or subjugate a wild horse. We all had our different views of what was happening and, as his wife, Lady Diana was Rinpoche's protector. For this I appreciated her then, very much, as I still do.

When I returned to Seminary the magical state I had been in had altogether evaporated, leaving me in a state of some depression. As I mentioned previously, it is hard not to get caught in such *nyams* and to believe they will go on forever, and that one has reached a permanent state of bliss. One morning shortly after, I went in to see Rinpoche just after he had woken up. He was sitting up in bed, naked and smiling. Mornings were one of the best times with Rinpoche. He would seem to be much lighter than later in the day. I described to him the scene with Lady Diana and about her request to the Directors, and I told him what I had said to her in the small sitting room. When I told him that I had explained to her that he is a mahasiddha and experiences things differently, he seemed very pleased and smiled happily, saying, "Thank goodness someone understands."

COEMERGENCE

Then I told him about the joy and the feeling of freshness that I had felt in the first weeks of Seminary. I described it as being a very joyful time of opening, so much so that I sometimes even smelled delicate perfumes that were certainly not in the environment. It was almost as if I were smelling another realm. When I told him these things, he just said one word: "Coemergence." This is an expression of the vajrayana view that samsara, the confused world, and nirvana, the awake world, are not separate. They arise together—*coemerge*—in every moment of our experience, and it is purely up to us to open ourselves from confusion to awakeness at any moment. Thus he was pointing out that I should not regard the sense of opening to a bigger world that I had been experiencing as separate from my experience of the ordinary world, or as anything out of the ordinary for that matter.

As I knelt on the floor by his bed, I felt so deeply grateful to him—he was the one who had shown me coemergence, through his constant example and through his teachings. But this was mixed with remorse about how I felt I had failed to live up to his expectations. With that mixed feeling of devotion and regret welling up in me, I tried to rise to my feet, wanting yet hesitating to say, "I love you Rinpoche." But my leg had gone to sleep. Returning to earth with a bump, I half fell onto the bed, clown-like, quickly mumbled, "I appreciate you very much, Rinpoche," and stumbled out of the room.

A few days later the vajrayana exam for the faculty of Seminary occurred. This exam was always administered by Rinpoche in preparation for the faculty to give the exam to the students. On this occasion, Rinpoche was suggesting topics as a basis for everyone to create threefold logics—a simple system for contemplating a subject by dividing it into its *ground* or basis, *path* or cause, and *fruition* or result. An example might be the threefold logic for meditation practice: *ground*, glimpsing basic goodness; *path*, through the practice of meditation; *fruition*, faith in the practice develops. Or: *ground*, to go beyond fear; *path*, we practice mindfulness; *fruition*, and develop fearlessness.

In the faculty exam, everyone would work on a threefold logic of, for example, "samaya," the mutual commitment between a vajra master and student, or "mahamudra," the final stage of realization of the vajrayana path. Rinpoche would ask, "What is the ground?" and various suggestions would be made, which Rinpoche would comment on, finally giving his own suggestion. Then, we would respond in a similar way to "What is the path?" and "What is the fruition?" Quite frequently the answer "guru" was proposed, which Rinpoche declined each time commenting after a while, "The guru seems to be quite popular today." When the question, "What is the ground of coemergence?" came along, I did write down "guru" but didn't say it aloud because of Rinpoche's comment. After everyone had given their responses, Rinpoche turned to me with a smile and said, "I think the ground of coemergence is the guru."

A TRANSMISSION ON SADNESS

One morning at Seminary, while I was on duty with Rinpoche in his bedroom, David Rome came in and reminded him that he was due to go down to New York in a few days to teach Level Five of Shambhala Training, which only he had done up to that time. David suggested that, since Rinpoche's health still seemed to be uncertain, perhaps he should take someone with him who could take his place if he wasn't able to teach some or all of the Level Five. Rinpoche said he thought that was a good idea, then turned to me and said, "What about Jeremy?" So I accompanied him to New York.

As might be expected, when he woke up on Friday, the day of the first talk, Rinpoche decided that I should give the talk, even though I was sure he was not sick. During the day, Carl brought me transcripts of the previous three or four Level Five courses that Rinpoche had taught. Knowing I was to give Talk One, I went through all of his transcripts for that talk and made notes from them on cards. I basically included everything that he had said in every previous Level Five, Talk One.

Just before I was due to give the talk, I went in to see Rinpoche and asked him if I could go through my notes with him. I thought that I could hardly have missed anything, since my notes covered not only one but *all* of his Level Five programs. So, although very nervous, nevertheless I felt quite satisfied with my preparation. After I finished reviewing my notes, there was a pause, and then he said, "I think something is missing. Sadness." It felt very clear that this was more than just a statement about something that should go in the talk, but was almost like a transmission. He was pointing me to the genuine heart of sadness, and bringing me, once again, more in touch with that—the real, non-conceptual experience of being human.

As Rinpoche writes in *Shambhala: The Sacred Path of the Warrior*:

> *Experiencing the upliftedness of the world is a joyous situation, but it also brings sadness. It is like falling in love. When you are in love, being with your lover is both delightful and very painful. You feel both joy and sorrow. That is not a problem; in fact, it is wonderful. It is the ideal human emotion. The warrior who experiences wind-horse feels the joy and sorrow of love in everything he does. He feels hot and cold, sweet and sour, simultaneously. Whether things go well or things go badly, whether there is success or failure, he feels sad and delighted at once.*[69]

Nowadays, sadness is always associated with depression, so much so that people seem to have difficulty distinguishing between the two. But of course they can be very different indeed. The root of the word *sad* is the same as that of the word *satisfaction*, and earlier meanings of the word reflect this sense of fullness, according to the O.E.D. Sadness is the feeling of deep tenderness and aloneness, of the kind that can come with a feeling of fullness—for example after having a delightful and warm dinner with close friends. In his Shambhala teachings especially, Rinpoche over and over emphasized the warrior's aloneness.

He writes:

> *Although the warrior's life is dedicated to helping others, he realizes that he will never be able to completely share his experience with others. The fullness of his experience is his own, and he must live with his own truth. Yet he is more and more in love with the world. That combination of love affair and loneliness is what enables the warrior to constantly reach out to help others. By renouncing his private world, the warrior discovers a greater universe and a fuller*

and fuller broken heart. This is not something to feel bad about; it is a cause for rejoicing.[70]

THE URGENCY OF THE SITUATION

As well as New York, Rinpoche visited Boston during the Seminary. There he gave a public talk called "Creating an Enlightened Society,"[71] organized by Shambhala Training. More and more in these years Rinpoche was encouraging us to think of building enlightened society, helping the world, caring for the earth. We could probably quite safely say that by this time he regarded this as the purpose and goal of his life, namely, to bring the message of enlightened society to the world. The idea of enlightened society was not meant to be an idealistic utopia, but rather a society in which the basic goodness of all humans was recognized and nourished. We can see from these excerpts from the talk just how serious he was, how urgent he felt the situation to be:

> *Ladies and gentlemen, please try to think beyond your home, beyond your burning fire at the fireplace, and beyond sending your children to school. Please, please, please try to think bigger... please try to think bigger. We could try to help this world. I'm very very very serious. Please... think bigger. If you don't do it, nobody will do it. So it is your turn to help this world. That doesn't mean to say that every one of you has to become President of the United States, or mayor of such and such a city. But you can do it on your own, work with your relatives, friends, and people around you. Please think that you are not off duty, and don't just relax. Please don't just relax. We need your help a lot. The whole world needs a lot of help.*

KHYENTSE RINPOCHE'S SECOND VISIT

In May, His Holiness Dilgo Khyentse Rinpoche made his second visit to Boulder. The main event of that visit was the enthronement of Rin-

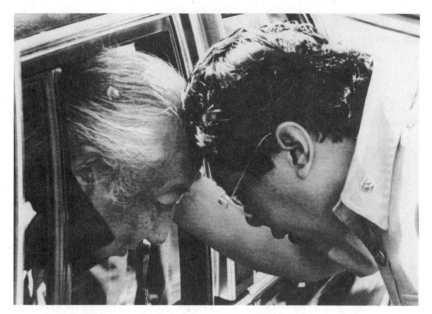

BIDDING FAREWELL TO KHYENTSE RINPOCHE. *Photograph by Andrea Roth.*

poche as the Sakyong, and of Lady Diana as the Sakyong Wangmo—the Lady Sakyong. This ceremony, known as "The Blazing Jewel of Sovereignty," was the same ceremony that was traditionally performed in Tibet for the enthronement of kings. It was first performed by Padmasambhava for Trisong Detsen, the first Buddhist king of Tibet who had invited Padmasambhava to Tibet. His Holiness Khyentse Rinpoche had performed precisely the same ceremony to enthrone the King of Bhutan. It was also at this time that Khyentse Rinpoche formally recognized Rinpoche's Shambhala texts as *terma*. Rinpoche told Khyentse Rinpoche of his vision regarding establishing Shambhala in Nova Scotia and gave him copies of all of the *terma*. Khyentse Rinpoche requested Rinpoche to give him the *lung*, or reading empowerment to study the *terma*, and took them with him back to his home monastery in Bhutan, placing them in the special cupboard in which he kept his own *terma*.

Another memorable moment for me during this visit was an audience with the staff of Naropa Institute, which was still struggling with low enrollments, cancelled classes, and missed payrolls. One of the staff told Khyentse Rinpoche this and asked for advice. Khyentse Rinpoche's response was, "If you let the roots go deep enough, the tree will blossom abundantly." And indeed now, twenty-five years later, Naropa University is bursting with students, three campuses in Boulder, an extension program in California, and programs abroad in Nepal, Bali, and elsewhere. I often remember this advice when someone expresses concern that their center is not getting enough students, or not expanding fast enough: "Let the roots go deep enough."

Khyentse Rinpoche's visit was again characterized for me by a sense of huge space with no one there. There seemed to be nothing there at all except profound but precise insight and such love and compassion that one's own sense of self was overwhelmed like ice melting in the mid-day sun.

"WE DIDN'T COME TO HEAR JEREMY HAYWARD!"

In June, Rinpoche was due to give a Level Five in Boulder. When I came back from work on the Friday evening of this Level Five, David called to tell me that Rinpoche was not feeling well and wanted me to give the first talk of the program. He said that it was possible that Rinpoche would not be well for the whole weekend, and that I may have to give more talks, perhaps sharing them with David. It was fortunate that I had already given the first talk of Level Five once, and was somewhat prepared. I gave the Friday night talk to a packed shrine room at Dorje Dzong.

Lo and behold, Rinpoche was still not feeling well on Saturday *or* on Sunday so I gave the second and final talks and presented the certificates and pins that mark the culmination of the first stage of Shambhala Training. I'm sure this was really a tremendous disappointment for many of the participants! One angry participant was heard to proclaim afterward, "I didn't come here to hear Jeremy Hayward." Increasingly now, though, Rinpoche was pushing his students in this way, basically implying, "You have to carry on—don't expect me to keep doing it."

That summer, Rinpoche told the Board that he wanted to move Shambhala Training out of the publicity office. After some discussion it seemed clear that it had by now developed into an education pro- gram and had not really belonged in the publicity office for a long time. So it was transferred to my department.

Along with the increasing trust that was clearly being shown in myself and others in these ways by Rinpoche, he seemed to be taking on a more and more impersonal, or beyond personal, quality. He seemed to be creating more distance, and at the same time emanating a kind of majestic quality that made it harder and harder to approach him at a personal level. He was deliberately showing us, in various ways, that we had to stand on our own feet. We couldn't rely on him forever, or, in fact, any more, in the way we had in the past. When he gave public talks to beginners, he was still charming; he continued to welcome beginners and was very sweet to them. In relation to his "older" students, however, he was creating a tremendous space and in some sense pushing us away, or cutting the umbilical cord, you could say. In these days he began to repeat often, "You people ask too many questions."

SADNESS AND LONGING AGAIN

Toward the end of August, feeling this distance, and perhaps also my inadequacy to fulfill his aspirations, I wrote the following poem and sent it to Rinpoche at the Court:

> *Monkeys run and squeak,*
> *Hummingbirds hover and hum,*
> *Bees and crickets hop and chatter,*
> *The mountain does not move.*
> *Dear Sir, I bow in limitless gratitude.*

Clouds blacken and thunder,
Earth quakes and erupts,
People panic and get upset,
The sun always shines.
Dear Sir, I bow in limitless gratitude.
Budgets get very red,
Hearts are very black,
Atmosphere is very grey,
The blue sky always remains clear and profound.
Dear Sir, I bow in limitless gratitude,

People scatter in all directions,
Projects succeed and fail,
Students express complicated doubts,
The guru has never given up.
Dear Sir, I bow in limitless gratitude.

Dear Sir, this student is not a good student
—a poor administrator, lazy, hesitating, not carrying out
   your commands
—a poor practitioner, not trusting, not following the guru's
   instructions, short on ordinary human kindness
Altogether not deserving the great richness you have poured
   on me.
Dear Sir, to see your smile is ultimate joy and sadness.

There is no greater joy, no greater sweetness, no greater beauty
   than the vision of your smile,
There is no greater sadness, no greater longing than the memory
   of your smile.
There is no way in heaven or earth to repay you adequately.
Dear Sir, I bow in limitless gratitude.

When I first met you at TOTT I said, "Is it really as simple
  as this?"
You smiled and said, "Yes."
The room was filled with joy.
Dear Sir, you have never changed from that moment.

Please forgive my inadequacy and doubts,
Please continue to be patient as I go up and down, up and down,
  up and down.
Please continue to be as you have always been.
The joy and goodness you give is unmeasurable, how is such
  generosity possible?
May I discover one-billion-billionth of such generosity,
So that I may carry out your command.
Dear Sir, I bow in limitless gratitude.
May I never be separated from your purity, your clarity, your
  brilliance, and your immovability.

THE BOARD JOCK CLUB

Toward the middle of the summer of 1982, David Rome and his family left Boulder to move to New York where he was to take up a senior position in his family publishing firm. He was sorely missed in Boulder. Though Beverley Webster carried on well the job of Rinpoche's secretary, David's insight and directness was missed. At the end of a program a few months later, when all the Directors were gathered in Rinpoche's office, and were sitting around the room with very little being said, Rinpoche suddenly said, in a quiet, sad tone, "I miss David. I miss his sense of humor."

As well, the sense of decorum at Board meetings degenerated rapidly. All the members of the Board were unquestionably loyal and dedicated to their tasks, but there was very little genuine communication going on at the meetings, and they had become chaotic and painful. The old collegial spirit of just a few years ago, when we had taken a retreat together and shot archery in the field behind my little cabin, had largely dissipated. The previous year Rinpoche had added to the Board, the two *Dapöns* or heads of the Dorje Kasung, Marty Janowitz and James Gimian (who now headed the two main branches of the Dorje Kasung— the kusung and kasung branches), along with Rinpoche's doctor, Mitchell Levy. I was told many years later that Rinpoche had told these gentlemen, when he added them, that the Board was very "stuck" and that their role was to "break up the Board." If that is true, then they did a very good job. We sorely missed the calm and sane guidance of David Rome.

To me the environment among the Board members seemed similar to a college locker-room mentality, which I was only too familiar with from my days at an all-boys school and in the rowing club at college. I felt this atmosphere prevented the possibility of our touching deeper heart topics. Individually people were very different, but it seemed that the group atmosphere was conducive to this mocking mentality. The feminine element was entirely lacking, no doubt about that. I would have been glad to leave the Board at this point.

However, back at the Kalapa Assembly of 1978 I had asked Rinpoche if I could go and find a job. My family was having a very hard time financially due to missed payrolls, and Karen having to leave work altogether after the birth of our daughter, Vanessa. Rinpoche's reply to my request had been a definite *no*—and I never thought of leaving again.

INVITATION TO WRITE A BOOK

So I was delighted when an opportunity to broaden my activities came along in the form of an invitation to write a book. It happened this way:

During the fall of 1982, Carolyn Gimian, Rinpoche's editor, had talked to Rinpoche about the possibility of publishing his Shambhala teachings in a book. Rinpoche gave his approval, but said that he wanted a book written by a student to be published before his. Probably he was envisioning this as a sort of publicity-type book, including various testimonials from people who had been through Shambhala

Training. TM (Transcendental Meditation) and EST had books like this, where people would describe their experiences and talk about how wonderful and exciting it all was. This could then be followed by Rinpoche's book on the actual teachings upon which that was all based. There was some discussion about the student's-eye book being written by one of Rinpoche's students who was a journalist by profession, but in the end I was asked to write the book. I began to write the book on an extended visit to Europe at Christmas, but I did not feel enough confidence in my understanding of the Shambhala teachings, and it transmuted into a book on science and spirituality: *Perceiving Ordinary Magic.*[72] It was not until ten years later that I finally wrote the book on Shambhala, *Sacred World.*[73]

By now, while of course still appreciating all that I had been given through the practice and understanding of Buddhism, I was beginning to feel more and more identified with the Shambhala way of expressing the essential truth of human nature. The Shambhala teachings are no different from the essence of Buddhism, but they are less encumbered by the historical and cultural adornments of Tibetan Buddhism. Indeed, Rinpoche's way of expressing Buddhism was also largely free from such trappings, but the Shambhala teachings felt like a fresh expression of the essence of spirituality in terms that spoke directly to my heart.

In addition the Shambhala teachings had the powerful emphasis on direct action in the world, and joining with the energies of the world—the dralas—to create a good society. Contributing to this vision was beginning to seem to me the most urgent need, more so perhaps than individual spiritual accomplishment. At the same time, the Shambhala teachings without the complement of the Buddhist view of mind could be misunderstood to be very lightweight—"Buddhism Lite" as some misinformed people called it.

A HARD NUT BEGINS TO CRACK

Later that summer, the first Advanced Training Session for Vajrayogini students was held at RMDC. It was a tremendously joyful occasion.

Rinpoche seemed to be glowing with delight, embodying the soft-ness and openness of the feminine principle. At the end of events such as these, especially the seminaries and Kalapa Assemblies when we were all together with Rinpoche as a vajrayana sangha, he would always give a very moving farewell address. He would often begin his address with, "Not much more to say, really." Then he would almost always say what a wonderful event it had been, how hard we had all worked and how proud he was of us, that the lineage was proud, and how sad it was that we were all going in our different ways now but that we would be together again. He would end up with, "I love you all."

As he left the tent or the room, there was always such a feeling of richness, love, and sadness at another ending. We had been in the mag-ical world he opened up for us for however long it was—two weeks, or two days, or three months—and now he was leaving us. We were always in that magical world, as he would always insist, but it was so much harder to see its brilliance and realness without his presence. So to see his physical body leave the room always touched the heart deeply. At the end of this ATS, I was asked to thank Rinpoche for the teachings. I read a poem that I had written for the occasion, which again expressed the deepening sense of sadness, longing, and love.

In November, there was a Naropa Institute faculty meeting at Norlha House, the residence of Directors Chuck Lief, Ron Stubbert, and their families. This meeting had a warm, open, contemplative feeling, like many of the meetings that I sat in on with Rinpoche, par-ticularly with the faculty of the Institute or one of the lower schools, Alaya or Vidya. We would sit in a group in front of him, and he would say a little and then invite comments, questions, and discussion. When someone would comment, he would simply nod and say, "Mmhm, mmhm." Gradually the conversation would become more quiet; peo-ple would offer quiet observations, and he would continue to respond, "Mmhm, mmhm." One could feel his mind and heart extending out, binding the room. There was a sense of contemplation in the room as we talked, as well as warmth and love. Sometimes he would answer questions, and sometimes there was humor, but always there was a sense of really being there.

I rode back from the meeting in Rinpoche's Mercedes. I was sitting in the front seat, and in the back seat were Rinpoche and the Sawang; between them was Rinpoche's consort. On the twenty-minute drive back, I started to cry. I felt an incredible softening and breaking up of something inside of myself; I felt such sadness and longing toward Rinpoche, and felt my unrequited and unrequitable love for him so intensely. I tried to scrunch down in the front seat so that Rinpoche wouldn't see that I was crying. As we approached the Court, Rinpoche said, "Take Jeremy home." The house that I lived in by then was only two or three houses down from the Court. "No, no," I said, "I can walk." He repeated, "Take him home." So the Mercedes drove up into the driveway of our house. I was no longer crying as I turned around to say goodnight but there were still tears on my face. Rinpoche said, "I love you so much." Unable to respond, simply, "I love you too, Rinpoche," I turned to the Sawang and made some comments to him about his studies. It was no doubt an indirect, if feeble, attempt to demonstrate my love. I left the car, went into the house, and wept again, filled with longing and sad joy.

Many times, especially in vajrayana situations, Rinpoche had talked about the unrequited love for the guru, of devotion as unrequited love. This is precisely how it felt—constantly unrequited, constantly wanting more. It was really an expression of sadness and longing, but it was hard to have enough distance to realize that at the time. I think that the common experience in the senior sangha, at least at that time, was this sadness and longing because Rinpoche was distancing himself from us more and more. It was as if, as his time on earth grew closer to ending, he pulled back more and more, dissolved more and more into the space of vast mind—and so we felt more distant from him.

Later, while speaking with a friend about this sense of sadness, she told me of an exchange she had had with Thrangu Rinpoche when he was visiting the 1980 Seminary. Rinpoche was away for a few days, as he often used to leave Seminary to do a teaching program at one of the centers. My friend went to greet Thrangu Rinpoche who has a very cheerful demeanor, a big smile, and a hearty laugh. He asked her how she was and she replied, "Oh, I'm feeling sad today." When Thrangu Rinpoche asked her why, she said, "Because Rinpoche is away and I miss him so much." Thrangu Rinpoche laughed heartily and said, "But the sadness *is* Rinpoche." He meant, of course, that the sadness is the wisdom mind of Rinpoche, which is not separate from our own wisdom mind. In longing for Rinpoche we are longing, in that sense, to know our own wisdom. The sadness at being separate from the best part of ourselves comes along with the joy of knowing that that best part is true and genuine.

I believe Rinpoche knew my love for him more than I was able to realize it, or profess it to him, when he was alive. Perhaps it was because he understood my love for him that he never gave up on me, in spite of my incredible stubbornness. That love grew only deeper and deeper as the years went by, and I have perhaps only really been able to see it and accept it years after his death. That love of which I write is not the romantic kind of "falling in love," nor the sentimental "love" often expressed in superficial religiosity. It is really not different from the delight and peace that comes with relinquishing the grip of ego. When we touch this joy, however briefly or partially it may be, it naturally expands into a sense of warmth for others, and a feeling of inseparability with others, which is genuine love.

So it was that 1982 became the year in which the hard crust of armor around stiff old Jeremy's heart finally began to crack open, and my ability to love began to peek through like a tender shoot in springtime.

1983: How to Speak Properly 14

N THE FALL OF 1982, the Regent had announced at a Board meeting that Sherab was to attend Rinpoche as kusung at the 1983 Seminary, and wanted someone to come out and hold his seat as Rinpoche's ambassador in Europe during that period. I was asked to go out and live in Marburg, Germany, which was then the center of Vajradhatu Europe, for part of the time that Sherab would be at Seminary. My time there was to begin with a week-long seminar between Christmas and the New Year.

As a way of beginning to gather material for the book on Shambhala, I decided that the topic of this seminar would be an overview of the Shambhala teachings—the first presentation of the Shambhala teachings to occur in Europe. So, in January, Karen and I went out to Marburg with our daughter Vanessa, who was then four years old. We found that Sherab had gathered a lively and enthusiastic group of young students around him and as I traveled to Dharmadhatus in several different countries, I was interested to see the variety of ways in which people of different cultures were taking to the dharma.

While in Marburg, I took the opportunity to write a short draft of the Shambhala book based on the talks I gave at the Christmas seminar in which I had included some explanations of science and spirituality. A common response from a few people I asked to read that first draft was that the science part was the best. And so the Shambhala book morphed into a book called *Perceiving Ordinary Magic: On Science and Spirituality*.[74] Ten years later, I was ready to write my Shambhala book, which was published as *Sacred World*,[75] long after Rinpoche's book, *Shambhala: The Sacred Path of the Warrior*, had already been on the bookshelves.

RINPOCHE BECOMES AN AUTHOR

In April, Rinpoche himself began to write a new book. He rather proudly made it clear that he had authored this book himself, in contrast to the terma texts to which he disclaimed authorship having instead, he said, simply written down what he heard. The book, called *The Memoirs of Sir Nyima Zangpo*,[76] was the account of an aging secretary to the Sakyong who had been in the Sakyong's service for many, many years. The story took place in an imaginary, or visionary, Kingdom of Shambhala. The book began during an evening of spontaneous poetry, which Rinpoche frequently enjoyed, often asking students to write poems as well. On this particular occasion he was spending an evening at the Regent's house, which was now a separate residence a few blocks away from the Court in Boulder. Rinpoche would describe a scene, periodically pausing to add short poems that were spoken spontaneously by himself and the others present. This then became the first chapter of the book.

Rinpoche continued to work on the *Memoirs* in May, when he went on a one-month retreat with the Regent at Fasnacloich, a large country house belonging to the parents of a sangha-member. Various people visited him on this retreat, including Carolyn Gimian, his editor, who worked with him on the book from then on. *The Memoirs* is a unique evocation of what the Court and life of the Sakyong might be like in this visualized Kingdom of Shambhala, full of insights, instructions, humor, and accounts of extraordinary events.

A READING OF THE MEMOIRS AT FASNACLOICH, WITH CAROLYN GIMIAN AND THE REGENT. *Photograph by James Gimian.*

In it, there are descriptions of cabinet meetings and meetings with foreign dignitaries, which are hilariously funny and at the same time very insightful. There are descriptions of a vegetarian diet, which he called the "nyida diet," the "sun and moon diet," writing: "From the sun, we take yellow, which includes green, and from the moon, white. We do not need the aggression of red. We *can* keep our diets truly nyida." There are also colorful and exuberant descriptions of the marriage of the Sawang to a beautiful Tibetan princess, and of a battle with ego-maniacs in which, as weapons, the Shambhala warriors use guns that shoot anesthetic darts instead of bullets, so as not to kill. The *Memoirs* gave us great insight into the mind of Rinpoche.

While on retreat at Fasnacloich, Rinpoche saw many ghosts, sometimes rooms-full. He reported to his staff what they were doing—in one room, he said, they were having dinner, in another some kind of sexual orgy. He tried to get the others to see the ghosts, but they could not. One of these ghosts was Charles McVeigh, who was an ancestor of the family that then owned Fasnacloich, and had had a distinguished career as a diplomat. Rinpoche told us that Charles McVeigh was particularly attracted to him and in fact he followed Rinpoche when he returned to Boulder. Rinpoche kept a picture of Charles McVeigh in his private living room and told us that he had given Mr. McVeigh refuge and bodhisattva vows. Sometimes, when others were with him in the living room, he would say "Charles McVeigh is here." And occasionally people would report a definite change in the atmosphere then. One normally very down-to-earth person said that she actually saw an indentation on the sofa when he announced Charles' presence, that she was certain she had not seen previously.

A NEW PHASE OF TEACHING—ON SPEECH

At the same time, on retreat, Rinpoche began to create elocution exercises that were to be spoken in Oxonian English. Carolyn became Rinpoche's model American student in learning to speak English properly. On his way to this retreat he had stopped off at the Philadelphia Dharmadhatu, and it was there that the first elocution exercise was written. This first one was called, "How to Speak the English Language Properly, and How Not to Speak Americanism." It is said that this was inspired by comments suggesting that Rinpoche's accent was becoming slightly American. For several months before the retreat he had asked people wherever he went, "Do you think my accent is becoming American?" When he had asked me, and I answered in the affirmative, he was not happy!

When Rinpoche returned to Boulder after this retreat, a new phase of his teaching began—the teaching in speech. We received formal, printed invitations for a soirée at the Court, evening dress required. The evening started in a dignified way, with ordinary conversation, Japanese *hors d'oeuvres,* and saké. Poetry was read, especially Rinpoche's poetry, and also some by the Regent. Then Rinpoche uttered the phrase that from then on ushered in the beginning of the next phase of such evenings: "I think we should have a reading of the *Memoirs*." Rinpoche selected a chapter which Carolyn then read in her best Oxonian. This was all completely new and somewhat astonishing to us— not only the elocution itself but the content of the *Memoirs*.

ELOCUTION LESSONS

When Carolyn had completed her reading of a chapter or two, Rinpoche said, "I think we should do some elocution." Accordingly, some of the elocution exercises that he had written at Fasnacloich were brought out, and the lesson began. After someone was selected as the guinea pig, first Rinpoche then Carolyn would read the exercise. Finally the selected person would have to read the exercise, being corrected along the way by Rinpoche, in the same rather unhelpful repetitive process that I had experienced trying to pronounce "soooooh" at the Sawang's empowerment. Certain sounds, such as the final *-tl* in "monumental," were very difficult for most Americans to pronounce. (Most would say "monumen*tal*.") Rinpoche would ask Carolyn to help correct the guinea pig, and at one point he asked me to do it. Although my accent is not Oxonian, it is much closer to Oxonian than the American accent is and it was easy for me to do a reasonably acceptable job. Hence, from then on Carolyn and I became the elocution co-trainers with Rinpoche.

We learned that there are three stages to elocution practice: first one tries to speak Oxonian, which feels awkward and forced; then one relaxes into that; finally, one returns to one's natural language, with a renewed sense of precision and heart to one's native speech. The point was not, of course, to make us all into proper little English men or women, but to lead us all to greater awareness of the speech process. It was a practice of learning to listen to our own speech, to feel the words, and to say what we mean to say properly and precisely.

I asked him once why he had chosen Oxonian, in particular, as a vehicle for teaching elocution—apart from the fact, of course, that this was the style of English that he himself had learned—and his response

296 / WARRIOR-KING OF SHAMBHALA

was, "It is the purest form of English going all the way back to medieval English." I had no idea at the time whether this was true or, if it was, how he knew it. But the pure nature of Oxonian was later confirmed by an English student, who happened to be a linguist by profession. Rinpoche added that because of this there is a mind-transmission aspect to Oxonian; that is, I surmised, that there is some understanding of how to live a dignified human life, perhaps of the nature of medieval chivalry, handed down with the language. Rinpoche's command of the profundity and layers of meaning in the English language never ceased to astonish.

THE QUALITIES GAME OF UTTER BOREDOM—
AND SURPRISING BLISS

The last event of that evening soirée was the "Qualities Game," which was another new experience for us. This was derived from a common party game, though with a twist: Rinpoche would choose a subject of the game, and he would write down the name of this subject on a card and turn the card face downward on the table in front of him. The entire group would have to figure out the subject by asking him questions in a certain form: "If this person were a geographical formation (or a national meal, or an article of clothing, etc.), what kind of a geographical formation (or national meal, or article of clothing, etc.), would he or she be?" The answer is supposed to be the geographical formation, etc., which is closest in *quality* to the chosen person.

After each question there would be a long pause, and then he would come up with something—a mountain, or a lake, whatever it was. We were also allowed three direct questions, to which the answer would be a simple *yes* or *no*. These had to be very specific and carefully put, such as, "Is this being a male?" and so on, or an actual attempt at the answer. This game could go on for hours. Even if someone guessed the answer, it didn't make any difference, as Rinpoche would often still insist on continuing.

One of the standard direct questions is normally, "Is this person alive or dead?" In other words, is this person someone like Queen Victoria, who is now dead, or the Sawang, who is now alive? That would be the usual way of asking this question, so that the players are able to narrow it down to a historical figure or a presently living figure. However, there are other beings who don't fit into any conventional categories of being "alive" or "dead," such as the Rigden, who was often the subject of the game. (The Rigdens, ancient monarchs of the Kingdom of Shambhala, are said to have existed on earth long ago and to continue to exist now in the inner drala, or sambhogakaya, realm.) We quickly found that it was no good to ask this question in the usual simple way, even for people one would have thought were obviously "dead," such as His Holiness the Karmapa. The question had to be formulated in a way that would elicit the kind of answer we were looking for: "Is this person inhabiting a human physical body, on this earth, at this moment of time?"

This sequence—reading of *The Memoirs,* elocution, and the Qualities Game—began to become the standard event of any reception at the Court. Toward the seeming end of such receptions, Rinpoche would almost always make the dreaded statement, "We should have a reading," and we all knew we were in for a few hours of incredible tedium. On one such occasion, having gone through the usual sequence, we played the Qualities Game over and over again. The evening dragged on and on. We were all continually drinking saké and getting sleepy, drunk, and mentally exhausted. Nevertheless, Rinpoche insisted on continuing to play. He was at one end of the living room, as usual, and everyone was sitting in a long oval around the room. Hoping I could get a little bit of a nap, I leaned my head against the wall, inconspicuously I thought, so that it was hidden from Rinpoche's view by Karen. But the very moment I closed my eyes, I heard, "Jeremy isn't asking a question."

Thus the night wore on. At various times we all got up, went to the bathroom, or went outside on the little side porch off the living room to take a breath. People were going out to the porch and asking the kusung, "Can't you get him to bed?" But nothing would get him to bed, and there we were, stuck with him, playing this endless Qualities Game. Was this heaven or hell, or some intermediate state? Finally, when it was well past dawn and fully light—it was about eight o'clock in the morning—Rinpoche wished us a cheery "goodnight" and went to bed.

As I left the court, still in my evening dress, not so drunk but completely exhausted and slightly dizzy, the morning servers and housekeepers were just arriving, bright and cheery and looking curiously at us strange folks who were just leaving. We walked back to our house, fortunately just down the road, and flopped on the bed without even getting undressed. When I woke up only a little while later, I had a feeling of extraordinary bliss. It was a little bit like the bliss with which I had awoken at dawn years before when Khyentse Rinpoche was coming, but in some sense this was more of an earthy bliss, and more intense. I could feel my body vibrating with a sense of joy. I realized that we had been receiving a transmission that night—a transmission of what, I couldn't say, but a transmission nonetheless of some kind of wisdom energy.

SPEECH—THE GATEWAY TO THE INNER REALM

I began to really appreciate these evenings after that. Although they continued to be physically and psychologically agonizingly boring, I also felt them as very profound teachings. Rinpoche had previously described the speech center as being the main location of ego, and it was interesting to me that speech was in some sense the last of the three centers—body, speech, and mind—that he worked with. When he first arrived in America and was first working with us as students, he worked mainly with mind—the sitting practice of meditation, how we work with thoughts and emotions. Later on, in the 1976–79 period, he worked with body—how we dress, how we organize our household, how we conduct ourselves socially, in business. During this period we were all beginning to get our hair cut, wear decent clothes, and dress elegantly, and generally to uplift our appearance, environment, and behavior to others. As the Kalapa Assemblies unfolded, we were made aware of forms of service, how to create the environment in a Shambhala household, all these forms of uplifted living. That was our body training.

The final area he worked with, then, was the area of speech. This also connected, from my perspective, with the way in which he was leading us further into the inner realm of luminosity, the sambhogakaya realm. In a sense, it almost felt as if he were beginning to dwell more and more in that realm himself at that time. His body was still alive, on earth, so there was still a vehicle for his nirmanakaya manifestation; but his energy, it seemed to me, was much more at the sambhogakaya level.

Sambhogakaya corresponds to speech—the *quality*, or *energy* level, of our being. This, in my view, was the secret point of the elocution exercises. That was also the point, as I understood it, of the Qualities Game. Rinpoche was leading us into feeling the *qualities* of things—the red*ness* of red, the mountain *quality* of someone, the Indian-curry-like *quality* of another person.

It is precisely through feeling the energy of these qualities, he told us, that we can connect with the energies of the inner realm, and through which we would find the dralas. The dralas are to be found in the qualities of things—the redness of red, the wetness of water, the solidness of earth, etc. This then is what he was doing, as far as I understood; unendurably irritating though it could be, he was leading us and instructing us in a very profound teaching.

BETTER MAKE A MOVE

That summer, the Board of Directors received a memorandum from Rinpoche, saying that he was not happy about the pace at which we were organizing the move to Nova Scotia. His vision was to begin to work seriously toward creating Shambhala in Nova Scotia, and this required the transfer of the capital and center of our worldwide operation to Halifax. The memorandum stated further that perhaps we thought there was going to be some magic on his part that would suddenly bring about Shambhala but, he emphatically made very clear to us, that wasn't going to happen. He pointed out that it was up to us—we had to do it manually, so to speak. The memorandum ended by calling for a meeting of the Board to discuss this, along with other senior officers of the organization and members of the Court.

The meeting was held in the dining room of the Court, which for this purpose had been transformed into a Tenno room—a Japanese imperial-style audience room. We were seated on Japanese straw tatami mats, men on one side of the room, women on the other. The Dapöns—heads of the kasung and kusung—sat at the end, facing Rinpoche. All of this was very much in accord with the description of the Court of the Sakyong in *The Golden Sun of the Great East,* and also in accord with the traditional way we were seated at Kalapa Assemblies. There was a Shambhala shrine set up for the occasion.

Rinpoche was sitting cross-legged on a tatami mat that was placed in front of the shrine. He was holding a Nyo-i, the Japanese imperial scepter, and wearing Japanese imperial robes, including a strange kind of black cap with a large black wire-mesh plume curling back, apparently the Japanese imperial headdress. The cap kept slipping back on his head, which was completely shaven during this period. This could have been slightly comic had the mood in the room been one in which anyone felt like laughing. We were served tea as usual.

He was impatient, forceful, and intense. He talked about some problems with the relations between the Cabinet and the organization, but the main point he wanted to discuss was why we weren't doing it— why weren't we organizing the move to Halifax? He invited discussion, and concluded by saying that he wanted one of the Ministers (Directors) to move up to Halifax very soon and that we should have a separate meeting to decide who would go.

A few days later there was a meeting with Rinpoche of his Privy Council. I and the Dapöns, James Gimian and Marty Janowitz, had been added to this Council back in the winter, standing in for David

Rome. The topic of who might go to Halifax was discussed. We went through the Ministers, one by one, finding reasons why each of them would not be able to go. In the end it all pointed to me. I made a rather lame excuse about still being needed by the Vidya School in Boulder, to which Rinpoche commented, "Oh that's too simple, you are not needed for that." This was true and I had no adequate response, and so I acquiesced in the decision that I would be the first to move to Nova Scotia with my family.

From then on my thoughts and activities were intensely directed toward this move—we had to get visas, arrange for our household furniture to move there, and find a place to live and a way to make a living, since the salary I was receiving from Vajradhatu and Nalanda would by no means be enough to cover our life in Nova Scotia. In the end it was decided that, to save money, my family would take up residence in the fairly large and stately (though run-down) house that had recently been purchased in Halifax for the future Kalapa Court, in preparation for when Rinpoche would move up there.

RINPOCHE VISITS JAPAN

In October, Rinpoche, the Sawang, and a group of about ninety students visited Japan. I did not go along, though I heard many strange and wonderful stories of the trip. Many days, Rinpoche spent much of the time in his room, apparently sleeping. He said later that he had been meeting the local dralas and inviting them to join us in the Kingdom of Shambhala. He was, nevertheless able to pay homage to many of the places of importance to his work: Zen and Shingon Buddhist shrines and temples, and the imperial palace. An especially important visit was to the Ise shrine near Kyoto. Ise is the main shrine of the Shinto tradition, the pre-Buddhist tradition of Japan and the source of the *kami* lore, which Rinpoche had often likened to the *drala* principle.

There are three courtyards to the Ise shrine complex, nested one within the other, and normally the general public is allowed only into the outermost court. Within this there is an inner court to which only the priests of the temple and other special guests or dignitaries are allowed. Shinto being the family tradition of Kanjuro Shibata Sensei's family, Sensei was able to arrange for Rinpoche and the Sawang to enter the inner shrine, a rare and great honor for guests from outside Japan.

Within the inner shrine is the innermost court where Amaterasu Omi Kami resides. Amaterasu Omi Kami is the sun goddess and progenitor of Japan. She is said to reside in a mirror in the innermost court of the shrine complex, in a small temple room to which only the Emperor has access. This mirror was said by Rinpoche to be a symbol of the cosmic mirror, an important image within the Shambhala teachings, essentially another teaching on the dharmakaya. According to this teaching, from the boundless space of the cosmic mirror (dharmakaya), which neither exists nor does not exist, all appearances arise like reflections in a mirror.

As master of kyudo to the Emperor, it was the role of each generation of Shibatas, on special occasions, to perform a major purification ceremony known as the Shihoberai, at the Ise shrine. This ceremony is very ritualistic and, as are all Japanese rituals, has to be performed extremely precisely. On this occasion, as always, Shibata Sensei was to have performed this ceremony at the Ise shrine in front of the assembled *kami*, as well as the human keepers of the shrine and guests. However, Sensei had badly cut his finger while making a bow just days before the ceremony, and was unable to shoot. So, he asked the Sawang to perform the shihoberai in his place. The Sawang had begun the practice of kyudo during Sensei's first visit to Boulder in 1980. He had become Sensei's star pupil, and a close bond had grown between them. The Sawang did a fabulous job, we heard, and Sensei was delighted. As the Sawang writes in his book, *Ruling Your World*,[77] "Sensei was so happy that afterward he took me out to lunch at his favorite noodle shop."

PEACEFUL ISE FEELING

I had the extraordinary good fortune to visit Ise myself a few years later, when I was invited to present a paper at a conference on "Nature,

Man, and Life" for the Kyoto Zen Institute. Ise itself is a large park area with various smaller shrines, as well as the main shrine. The paths wind through huge Japanese pine trees and alongside a broad, shallow river of crystal-clear water, flowing gently on a bed of pebbles. At the main shrine, I did not go inside the inner court but stood at the gate looking in. Through the next gate, I could just see the small innermost court that contained the temple of Amaterasu Omi Kami.

There was a thin white curtain covering the doorless opening to the court. We stood there for a long time. Innumerable Japanese tourists kept stepping in front of me to take photographs, seeming not to actually be looking at the shrine at all. They simply arrived, quickly took photographs of themselves standing in front of the main entrance, and just as quickly left. In between these interruptions, there were few other visitors and I continued to gaze at the innermost shrine. Sometimes the white curtain would gently lift up as if in greeting, though the air seemed quite still. I felt a sense of living silence, white darkness, movement-in-stillness, calling, peace; what to call this singular feeling? I remember it simply as the "Ise feeling."

Rinpoche asked Sensei to invite Amaterasu Omi Kami to join in and help Shambhala, and requested Sensei to direct the design and building of a small Shinto shrine at RMDC. The shrine was completed, only after Rinpoche's death, a few hundred yards up a winding path on the hill behind the encampment meadow. When it was finished there was an elaborate consecration and opening ceremony, for which Sensei invited a senior Shinto priest from Ise. The priest, or one of his deputies, has returned every subsequent year to celebrate and refresh the shrine. After a few years, the priest declared "Amaterasu Omi Kami is here."

Some years later, on a visit to RMDC, I walked up to visit the shrine for the first time. As I walked up the path, I first came upon a small Japanese-style roofed fountain, at which I ritually cleansed my hands, then passed through a *torii* gate (the traditional orange gate found at Shinto temples) and walked on up a path that climbed through a narrow and extraordinarily lush little valley formed by a mountain stream. As I climbed the path, a strange, yet vaguely familiar feeling came to me. I walked on, asking myself, "What is this feeling? I know I have felt it before, but where?" Suddenly it came to me—it was the Ise feeling. Visiting Amaterasu's shrine, as I have done whenever I am at RMDC since that time, is an intense, joyful-sad opportunity to meet the mind of Rinpoche.

This year, particularly the period of the teaching on speech, was for me a step further in understanding how to open to luminosity and the sacred perception of our world—through the perception of the heart that comes from deeply joining body and mind. By "perception of the heart" I mean an actual shift of the center of awareness from the brain to the heart. When we join our awareness with our body in that profound way—and this is what the teaching on speech is about—and open our eyes or ears, rather than merely seeing or hearing with our usual conceptual categories, our feeling reaches out into the world and joins with our perception of sight or sound, opening up a fresh perspective. In a sense, we can realize our oneness with that sight or sound and thus have a deeper insight into its qualities beyond categories.

1984: Going Beyond 15

984 BEGAN with Rinpoche's goodbye talk to the community before departing to Seminary, which was once again going to be held in the Bedford Springs Hotel in Pennsylvania. It was bitterly cold weather, minus twenty degrees. Rinpoche would not be returning to Boulder after Seminary, but planned to go directly into retreat at Mill Village, Nova Scotia. In this goodbye talk he spoke of emptiness, and the atmosphere felt immensely desolate. When he finished the talk I had such a sense of solitude, almost of being abandoned, as if our father were leaving us on our own. When he invited questions, the Regent stood up—which was extremely rare for him by that time—and asked, "Sir, how do we live in this emptiness?" Rinpoche replied, "With a smile. Like the Cheshire cat." *Alice in Wonderland*'s Cheshire cat used to disappear leaving only his smile, and this felt like a hint to us of what was to come.

I was not scheduled to attend the Seminary or the Kalapa Assembly that would happen immediately after Seminary, again at Bedford Springs. However, I received a call to tell me that Rinpoche was insisting that I come out to the Seminary to assist with elocution. Rinpoche did, indeed, conduct elocution at the end of every talk. After one such lesson, following a talk on mantra (Sanskrit for spell or incantation) in which he described mantra as "mind protection," he commented:

> *Because Buddhism is nontheistic, it has the possibility of mixing together cultural phenomena with spiritual understanding. Of course we don't want to make a trip out of it, but nonetheless, it is true in every case.... Speech, as we have just discovered, is mind protection. It is also a cultural situation, a cultural phenomenon. When you speak properly, then it has power and reality and magic to communicate to your attorney, your taxi driver, your shopkeeper and so forth. So it is very important to have awareness of speech.*[78]

I couldn't stay all the way through the vajrayana part of Seminary, because the accreditation team would be making their biennial Naropa Institute visit during that time. But Rinpoche insisted that I come back after that in order to continue to help with elocution at the Kalapa Assembly which immediately followed Seminary.

The talks at the vajrayana part of the Seminary had been extremely short in terms of content, categories, and so on, although the atmosphere was, as usual, a powerful teaching in itself. The same was true of the Kalapa Assembly. It was a very rich time. Rinpoche said at the beginning of the Assembly that he was going to work mostly on speech, and in fact the talks consisted largely of elocution training. There was a gradual reversal of day and night, because Rinpoche would begin his talks later and later each evening until the final talk, originally scheduled to begin at 8:00 p.m., actually ended closer to 8:00 a.m. the following morning. All the schedules had to be adjusted accordingly as the days went by, and gradually our sense of time became fluid.

This in itself was a potent teaching in going beyond our normal reference points. To end the final session of every Assembly, Rinpoche had performed a vow ceremony—a commitment to the vision of Shambhala. To the sound of *gagaku*, old Japanese instrumental music, every participant went up to him to seal the vow by receiving a dot of black ink on the tongue with one of the brushes Rinpoche used for executing the stroke of Ashe. This year, the vow ceremony ended at 10 a.m., said by Rinpoche to be the "hour of the Great Eastern Sun." Although people were exhausted, the atmosphere was filled with love, longing, and lungta.

LEAVING FOR NOVA SCOTIA WITH A WARNING

Shortly before Rinpoche left for Seminary and retreat, there had been a Board meeting at which we were all asked to give reports on our areas. I said that I was preparing to leave for Nova Scotia and explained how the education area was going to be handled after I left. Rinpoche told me that I was being very naïve, and then he turned to the whole group and said that this applied to everyone. He said that there would be family, economic, and domestic problems of all kinds in moving to Nova Scotia, and that we had created comfortable nests for ourselves in Boulder. It was a warning to all of us that we would not find it easy to make the move—in particular, at that moment, myself.

In July, with this warning ringing in my mind, we packed up all of our belongings, put some of them in storage and were ready to drive to Nova Scotia. But our departure from Boulder turned out not to be as simple as we planned. Rinpoche used to tell us that the Kagyu lineage was known as the "mishap lineage," and mishaps always provide excellent opportunities to learn. But we could certainly have done without any at this time.

First, a few days before we were due to leave, the main seal on our Volvo broke under the strain of the U-Haul we had packed many of our belongings in. We had to unload it all into a storage shed to be brought later and wait several days for the seal to be fixed. Then, just as we were ready to leave again, some officers from the U.S. Narcotics Bureau arrived to seize the house we were living in that was owned by a wealthy sangha friend, Fleet Maull. They put up notices on all the windows announcing that the house had been "arrested." They searched through all of Fleet's rooms and told us that we should not remove any of our belongings from the house. We received a subpoena to be witnesses before the Grand Jury in St. Louis, Missouri, and had to wait another week or so in Boulder until the court date. Within a few months Fleet would be arrested and, eventually, jailed for many years in a maximum-security prison. Fleet was jailed on the charge of heading a large drug-trafficking enterprise. Fleet himself, while admitting that he dealt drugs, vehemently denies that he was a kingpin.[79]

The story did have an extraordinary outcome. While I was visiting Rinpoche in his retreat in Mill Village in 1985, I told him that Fleet had been arrested, and that everyone was very worried for his welfare. Rinpoche responded, "He'll be fine." And this is how it turned out, thanks to Fleet's courage, devotion to the dharma, and compassion. Fleet, who had been very much the party playboy, was completely transformed. He cleaned out a janitor's closet in the prison in which to finish his prostrations, then he went on to finish *ngöndro* altogether and Thrangu Rinpoche visited the jail to give him the Vajrayogini abhisheka.

While in jail Fleet studied for a Ph.D. in sociology and began to take care of other inmates who were dying from AIDS, and from this he started the Prison Hospice Network. When it came time for him to be transferred to a minimum-security jail in compensation for good conduct, he requested to stay where he was, so that he could continue to care for the dying. Since his release, Fleet has continued to carry on his extraordinary work for the benefit of others. Fleet's story has always been for me an extraordinary example of the power of dharma to carry us through the most difficult life situation, where another person might easily have succumbed to depression or, as so often happens, have turned into a lifelong criminal himself.

Finally we drove away, about three weeks later than we had planned. I was glad to be leaving Boulder. It was a command from Rinpoche, and from that point of view we had no alternative, but I also felt happy to be leaving the in-grown politics and narrow social life of Boulder, and especially to be leaving the Board. I was beginning to find it increasingly difficult to relate to the Regent and his buddies among the

other Directors, perhaps partly due to my rather serious Englishness—
as Winston Churchill has said, "The Americans and the English are
two peoples separated by a common language"—and partly to the
cliquishness that I was feeling among them, exacerbated by a then new
and popular drug Ecstasy. One evening, just before we were to leave
for Nova Scotia, the phone rang in our house and when I answered
one of the other Directors said, "Jeremy, I have a message from the
Regent: 'Drugs, sex, and rock 'n' roll.'"—and I heard peals of laughter
in the background.

I was the only one of the Directors holding the rank of the Order of
Warrior, or "knight," and Rinpoche regularly dropped hints to me that
I could try to live up to that. Back in 1979, for example, the Directors
were called to the Court to play *Diplomacy* with Rinpoche—a popular
game at that time, requiring skill in negotiations and strategy. After
several hours of playing with us—probably in more ways than one—
Rinpoche called an abrupt halt to the game. As we left, I hugged him
and said, "Thank you, that was a lot of fun," to which he replied, "You
were the best." And in '83, while Karen had been assisting Rinpoche
with a dharma art exhibition, he had suddenly turned to her and said,
"Why doesn't Jeremy be more English!" I was slightly shocked when
she told me this; I had been trying to be as American as the rest of the
guys! On hearing what Rinpoche had said, I realized how ungenuine
this was.

He used to tell us that we were chosen to be Board members not so
much for our individual qualities, but for the chemistry we made
together. And he had told Karen, "Jeremy keeps the other Ministers
[Directors] sane." So perhaps even if it was uncomfortable both for
myself and the others, the reticent, somewhat self-serious, intellectual
Englishman provided a useful contrast to the general flavor of the
group—well characterized by a quote from the cult movie of the time,
Buckaroo Bonzai: "Laugh while you can, monkey boy." I do want to
emphasize, however, that this was a group phenomenon; individually
the Directors were quite different, warm, witty, intelligent, and loyal to
Rinpoche's vision.

FIRST NEWS FROM MILL VILLAGE

So, finally arriving in Nova Scotia felt like the beginning of a fresh new era. And, indeed, I have always felt more at home in Nova Scotia than anywhere else I have lived, including my youth in England. We arrived to take up residence in the Kalapa Court the day after Rinpoche had left retreat to preside at the annual encampment for the Dorje Kasung at RMDC.

It was during this encampment that he finally met with Gerald Red Elk, whom I had met four years before, as I described in chapter 11. We met Rinpoche at the airport on his return from encampment and, when someone mentioned having heard of his momentous meeting with Red Elk, Rinpoche looked up at me and said, sadly, "Yes, and I understand I could have met him four years ago." I realized then, regretfully, that I should have made more effort to arrange for Rinpoche to see him that night. "I wanted to meet a Tibetan lama," Red Elk had said after their meeting, "because we understand the heart of what they are. We call anybody in that state of mind a 'common man of the earth' because they live the laws of the earth, they understand, and we [he and Rinpoche] could communicate without talking."

Gerald Red Elk became ill with cancer shortly after his meeting with Rinpoche and died a few months later. When Roger La Borde, Red Elk's adopted nephew and apprentice who had accompanied him at the meeting with Rinpoche, went to visit Red Elk in his hospital room just before he died, the first thing Red Elk said was, "How's Rinpoche?"

As soon as we arrived we began to hear news from Rinpoche's retreat in Mill Village. This was about two hours drive from Halifax and people were constantly going back and forth, to take supplies or to ferry staff who were joining or leaving the retreat. Generally, we heard that Rinpoche was in fine fettle, hosting visitors and preparing elaborate and sometimes strange meals for them, playing elaborate practical jokes, and taking daily outings. We also heard that Rinpoche had been telling Mitchell for some time that he was expecting another *terma* and that this one was to be on the martial arts. When finally

QUIET DELIGHT AT THE DORJE KASUNG ENCAMPMENT.
Photograph by Andrea Roth.

Mitchell had asked him why the *terma* was not appearing, Rinpoche said that he had learnt from the Rigden that his students were not ready. Such a *terma* never manifested.

Within two or three weeks of our arrival, the International Sangha Conference was held in Halifax, attended by about 175 members of the sangha. One of the major reasons for the conference was to give sangha-members a chance to visit Nova Scotia, now widely known to be the place to which the center of the mandala was being moved. There were three days of panels on various aspects of social action: Livelihood, Politics and Society, Health, Relationships, Education, and Culture and the Arts. Rinpoche himself had requested that this occasion be a forum to discuss action in the world, so the first large-scale conference the sangha held on this topic was in Nova Scotia, precisely the place which Rinpoche had chosen as fertile ground for mutually beneficial interaction between Shambhala and the local culture.

At the end of the Conference, Rinpoche visited from his retreat for two days. After the formal banquet on the last evening, which included waltzing late into the night, Rinpoche expressed delight at being able to hold such an event together in Nova Scotia, and being able to bring along our family and friends. The next day, he gave the closing address to a mixed audience in which non-sangha friends were invited. He spoke of his vision for establishing the buddhadharma in Nova Scotia, and about our responsibility as a sangha to work harder in our practice and livelihood and not to take for granted the auspiciousness of our lives.

RINPOCHE ASKS TO HOLD SEMINARY AT RMDC

The Board of Directors met during the time of the International Conference, when many of the Vajradhatu staff were in Nova Scotia. Ken Green informed us that Rinpoche wanted the next Seminary to be at RMDC. He reported that, in Rinpoche's view, the tremendous effort and expense we were putting into renting hotels every year, as well as the energy of the dharma that was brought down as blessings in those hotels, should go to benefit RMDC. While presenting this to the Board, Ken also expressed the view that he didn't think we could do it, and the Board agreed that Ken should present to Rinpoche our common view that this presented too many difficulties, involving such huge costs of money and labor.

When Rinpoche heard about this he was very angry. He commented at a Standing Committee meeting later, "My ministers are like vultures," referring perhaps to the fact that the income from seminaries and other programs he taught was a major resource in paying the huge payroll of Vajradhatu, which included the salaries of most of the Directors. He also expressed impatience that none of the other Directors had yet made any effort to move to Nova Scotia. Three years later, after Rinpoche's death, all the Board and Privy Council members did move there for a while, but eventually half of them moved back to the States.

Needless to say, Rinpoche insisted that Seminary be held at RMDC. And Ken almost miraculously pulled it together, with the help of another extraordinary effort on the part of the sangha. A major donor came forward to fund the project; hundreds of tent platforms were built as well as two new bathroom facilities. So, in fact, Seminary was held at RMDC the following summer, with over two hundred participants. We all realized what a huge positive change this made to RMDC and to Seminary. Now we did not have to try to convert hotels and bring the dharma and drala energy to them. Our own place, RMDC, which was already soaked in and tamed by all the dharma teachings and practice that had already happened there, was transformed from a small camp facility to a major program and conference center.

MEETING WITH THE STANDING COMMITTEE

Rinpoche visited Halifax frequently to meet with the Standing Committee—a group of people Rinpoche had appointed to look after the Canadian situation, to stand in for the Board, headed by Dr. James Sacamano, Rinpoche's Ambassador to Canada. He requested that each of them prepare a report on the situation of Nova Scotia in their particular areas, especially politics, economics, finances, education, and the arts.

During the early fall, Rinpoche had several discussions with members of the Standing Committee about how to proceed with the project of cultivating enlightened society in Nova Scotia. On one such occasion, in September, Rinpoche was asked whether we should be considering joining one of the political parties of Nova Scotia and try to influence things positively in that way. Rinpoche responded that it should be through education, not through political influence, that we should contribute to the culture and society of Nova Scotia. It was clear from similar comments on many occasions that it was not to be through conventional politics, nor through trying to propagate traditional buddhadharma, but at least at first through the arts, the schools, and the Shambhala teachings—in other words through the activities of Nalanda Foundation—that we would be able to attract people to join in his great vision of creating an enlightened society once again on earth. This was, perhaps, in part why he asked me to be the first Minister to move up there.

As Rinpoche was leaving the Court after this meeting, I stood outside with him for a moment. I looked down at him (it's so strange to visualize looking down at Rinpoche, but of course he was much shorter than myself) and said, "That was so helpful, sir." He looked up at me with a big but slightly sad smile and, with a touch of bravado, said, "I never give up." He added, "Come and visit me soon—and bring a notepad and pen."

This was the second time he had told me to come and visit him in Mill Village: at the closing reception of the Kalapa Assembly earlier in the year I told him that I was preparing to move to Nova Scotia with my family and asked him, "How should I *be* there?" His response: "Come and see me as soon as you get there." And his request, this time, for me to bring something to take notes with was very unusual— in fact the first time he had ever requested such a thing of me. Still, I did not make any arrangements to visit him. It was, I suppose, the same old hesitation that I had always had about speaking with him, magnified many-fold by the tremendous uncertainty about this project we were beginning to set in motion in Nova Scotia which still seemed so vague and fantastic. How could it possibly come about, and what could be my part in it? There seemed to be few normal reference points for my life any more, and I did not feel that Rinpoche was likely to provide any.

A MOMENTOUS VISIT TO PRINCE EDWARD ISLAND

Shortly after this Standing Committee meeting, I received a phone call from Walter Fordam, who had replaced John Perks as master of Rinpoche's household and was then with him in his retreat at Mill Village. Rinpoche was planning a visit to Prince Edward Island and invited Karen and me to come with him. This trip would be the first occasion on which I spent any time with Rinpoche since arriving in Nova Scotia. We went in separate cars to Pictou, where we embarked on the ferry to Prince Edward Island. In Rinpoche's car with him were his companion, Shari Vogler, and Walter. In our car were myself and Karen, with another sangha couple, Jim and Ellen Green, who lived in the nearby town of Chester. We drove straight to the hotel when we arrived. PEI was very deserted and, since it was the last weekend of the tourist season that the hotel would be open, there were hardly any guests.

The main outing of the trip was the visit to the Canadian Agricultural Department Research Station. Rinpoche had instructed Jim Green to call and tell them that Lord Mukpo, a Prince of Tibet, would like to visit. This title was not so outrageous or inappropriate as it might seem. In Tibet, as well as being the Abbot of the Surmang group of monasteries, Rinpoche was the civil governor of the Surmang region. These regions in Tibet were, at that time, quite autonomous, rather akin to the principalities of medieval Europe or of India before the British invasion. We went, then, as the Prince of Tibet and his party. Rinpoche was dressed for the visit in his Geeves and Hawkes–tailored Admiral's uniform. We were hoping that no one at the Research Station would remember that Tibet was surrounded by mountains with no ocean within hundreds of miles, but Rinpoche couldn't seem to care less. Walter and Shari were also wearing military uniforms and the remainder of the party was in civvies. The staff seemed genuinely honored, welcoming Rinpoche and graciously showing him and his party around their facility.

The most astonishing moment of all was a meeting between Rinpoche, the Federal Minister of Agriculture, and the Director of the research station. We all sat around a long conference table listening to a serious and fascinating conversation between the three in which Rinpoche, Lord Mukpo, asked penetrating questions about the region's economy and agriculture, exports and imports, sources of electrical power, breeds of dairy animals, crop rotation, and more. The Director of the research station and his staff saw that here was someone who really wanted to understand how the Province worked, and a lively discussion ensued.

It was suggested that Lord Mukpo might like to visit their experimental dairy facility. While we were there, we passed someone pushing a wheelbarrow containing grain. Rinpoche scooped up a handful of the grain and inspected it closely as he let it fall slowly back into the wheelbarrow. He told the Director that they should be careful not to put too many wheatberries in the feed, since these could expand in the cow's stomach and cause digestive problems. The man holding the wheelbarrow put it down and excitedly said that he had been trying to tell people this for years. In another incident, a young calf had recently been separated from its mother. They were at opposite ends of the barn and were crying to each other. Rinpoche looked sad, saying to us, "This shouldn't happen. We won't do it that way."

As we were leaving, we were shown a photograph album of previous royal visits. We were told, "We have had many members of royalty here: the Queen, Prince Charles, Prince Andrew; but we have never had a royal visitor from Asia." They took Rinpoche's photo to put in the album. As we drove away the Director and all the employees of the facility lined the driveway, waving and smiling, some with damp eyes.

Rinpoche was quite delighted with the day's excursion and with the people he had met, as well as the ease with which he had gained their respect. Walter Fordham comments, in his journal, "His royal bearing was impeccable. We who had the opportunity to witness Rinpoche in action today learned that the magnetism that drew Buddhist students to him is no less powerful when applied to ordinary people who have no inclination to hear Dharma."[80] At dinner that evening he chatted amiably with our young waitress and invited her to his suite to join us for a glass of saké. After chatting for a while, Rinpoche asked her if she would like to take off her shoes, which she did. He then asked to see the soles of her feet and gently tickled them for a short while, after which he told her the story of the Mukpo family. She seemed charmed by the whole affair and, after some more light conversation, she left quite cheerfully.

On the ferry returning to Nova Scotia, I went out onto the deck where Rinpoche was sitting alone on a bench. I felt that he was giving me the opportunity to sit with him and talk about how he would like me to manifest there but I pretended not to notice him and went to lean against the rail. Soon Shari came out and sat next to him and the opportunity had passed. I realized then, though dimly, that it was now *I* who was keeping distance between us. Though I had thoroughly enjoyed the trip, I had continued to feel awkward and unconnected with Rinpoche and his activity.

GETTING INTENSE AT MILL VILLAGE

The atmosphere both in Halifax and Mill Village was now becoming more and more intense. The Halifax sangha was gallant and tireless in supporting the retreat. The sangha was still very small, only forty or fifty people at that time, and they did all of the driving of guests down to Mill Village and back. Additionally, any supplies that were needed in the retreat, that couldn't be found in the nearby town of Bridgewater, were driven down by the sangha. Essentially all of the support for the retreat came from the Halifax sangha, two hours drive away, particularly from the few kasung in that sangha. Of course, they considered it an honor and a gift to be able to serve Rinpoche in that way, but at the same time it was putting a great deal of stress on them.

I, for one, was beginning to experience huge anxiety attacks such as I had never experienced before nor have since, which continued the entire fall. There were probably many reasons contributing to this. There was the cultural shock of moving to Canada. We were residing in the Court, which was not a home at all but a constant thoroughfare for all manner of sangha, and so we were unable really to settle in. We had been asked by Rinpoche to care for Gesar during that year, which was a handful in itself. After less than a year, he had been taken out of the Eton prep school. Much of his life so far he had, he told us, "bounced from school to school." Now, at thirteen years old, we had managed to get him into the private school in Halifax and had to make sure he got there, did his homework, and so on—which was not an easy task. He was tremendously insightful and could be extraordinarily kind and considerate, or penetratingly mean, skillfully getting to our sorest spots.

And I did not know what I should be doing there for the Kingdom; at the same time neither Karen nor I were able to look for other work because our permanent visas did not come through until the next summer. When I had asked Rinpoche what I could do in Nova Scotia, back in 1983 at the Privy Council meeting at which I first volunteered to move up there, he replied, "You could be a consultant to Dalhousie University." Even at the time this seemed a little far-fetched, but Rinpoche was never one to go for less than the best. I had attempted to get my immigration visa through my educational work with Naropa Institute and the schools, but that did not seem to be workable, so in the end I had applied and been admitted as a Buddhist minister of religion. This was also legitimate, as I was qualified and authorized as such, but I did not feel comfortable in this role or in engaging the Nova Scotia community as a minister of religion. So I felt quite stuck for something useful to do. And beyond all these personal things, my anxiety was due in part to my increasing uncertainty about how to continue communicating with Rinpoche and working to fulfill his glorious but outrageous vision of engaging the Nova Scotians with a manifestation of enlightened society.

CAN WE GO BEYOND CONVENTIONAL SANITY?

In October, Rinpoche came up to Halifax several times from Mill Village to stay at the Kalapa Court for a few days. Like all the rooms in the Court, his bedroom was unrenovated, with peeling paint and creaky old floorboards. My daughter, Vanessa, who was then six, tells me that one of these visits affords her most clear memory of Rinpoche. She writes, "He was lying in his bed and a bunch of people were standing around. I climbed up onto the bed and he tickled my feet. He and I were both giggling and I remember it as a warm and precious moment."

On one of his visits, Rinpoche stayed in his room for a week, with the blinds drawn, allowing no one into the room except, from time to time, the kusung. At one point, a small group of us entered the room and stood around his bed—whether we just finally decided to go in, or whether he had indicated that he wanted us, I don't remember. He was slightly propped up on the pillows, with his eyes partially open. At one moment he said, "Your Holiness, Your Holiness," in a tone of love and veneration. It seemed as if he were seeing the Karmapa, and I sensed a deeply peaceful, glowing feeling in the room. Then he said, in a soft, gentle tone, "Soooo beautiful, sooooo beautiful." We started singing the Shambhala Anthem. It was the best thing we could think to do. The atmosphere in the room was so sweet, and intense, and sad at the same time. After singing the Anthem we left the room. Shortly thereafter Rinpoche dressed and returned to Mill Village.

At the end of October, I returned one evening from a trip and was told that Rinpoche was having dinner with a group in a local Greek restaurant, called Old Man Morias, to which I was invited. Arriving there, I saw an empty chair next to him to which he kept turning as if to say something, and I was told that the chair was for Vajrayogini. Needless to say, we could see no one and nothing sitting in the chair.

After dinner we returned to the Court where Marty Janowitz explained that Vajrayogini had appeared to Rinpoche, in person, and that she was present right now and pretty much all the time. Rinpoche then described what Vajrayogini was wearing, including her perfume. He was in a very intense, but not very talkative, dark mood. We were all utterly befuddled, although we were familiar with his ability to see beings that we could not, for example Charles McVeigh at Fasnacloich in 1983. We did not know at the time that such clear, vivid visions of a practice deity are known to happen in the tradition to those of very high realization, but they are very rare. Rinpoche had commented once to a group of Vajrayogini practitioners, jokingly we thought at the time, "You had better watch out, because Vajrayogini might actually appear to you in person, then you might really freak out."

In a poem, entitled "Meetings with Remarkable People"[81] and written as early as December 1977, Rinpoche makes very clear his own view, and experience, of the reality of these beings. First he describes three beings, one of whom is clearly identifiable as Ekajati, protectress of the tantras. She is wearing a tigerskin skirt, "a giant smile but one tooth," and "turquoise hair but elegant gaze from her single eye." The second is a lovely maiden riding a white lion. And the third is recognizable as Rahula, also a protector of the dharma, with "a most gaping mouth opening in his stomach, with somewhat polite gaze; he possessed nine heads, all of them expressing certain expressions."

Rinpoche concludes the poem with the lines:

> *Can you imagine seeing such people and receiving and talking*
> *   to them?*
> *Ordinarily, if you told such stories to anybody, they would think*
> *   you were a nut case;*
> *But, in this case, I have to insist that I am not a nut case:*
> *I witnessed these extraordinary three friends in the flesh.*
> *Surprisingly they all spoke English;*
> *They had no problem in communicating in the midst of American*
> *   surroundings.*

I am perfectly certain they are capable of turning off the light
　　or turning on the television.
What do you say about this whole thing?
Don't you think meeting such sweet friends is worthwhile
　　and rewarding?
Moreover, they promise me that they will protect me all along.
Don't you think they are sweet?
And I believe them, that they can protect me.
I would say meeting them is meeting with remarkable men
　　and women:
Let us believe that such things do exist.

After Rinpoche had introduced Vajrayogini, there was an intense and somewhat anxious conversation in an effort to understand, and a few questions were asked. I asked what this implied for the establishing of the Kingdom of Shambhala, to which he replied, "The Kingdom of Shambhala is *already* established," in a tone that implied the unspoken final words: "you idiot." This reminded me of a time at the first Kalapa Assembly in 1978, when Rinpoche held a small cocktail party for the Directors. As I stood next to him at one moment, I said, "Sometimes I'm not quite sure whether I am directing a small Buddhist religious organization, or helping to run a kingdom." He drew himself up and said in a tone of dignity and finality, "*I* never have that problem."

All the people in the room were practitioners of the Vajrayogini sadhana. Some of us in the room had completed the requirements to receive the abhisheka for the next practice, the practice of the Chakrasamvara sadhana, and there were a hundred or so others in the sangha who were ready for this abhisheka. In Tibet, the specialty of the Surmang monastery, of which all the Trungpas including Rinpoche had been the abbots, was the teachings and practices associated with the Chakrasamvara deity. The monastery was famous for the ritual dances based on this deity that were performed there once a year and Rinpoche had become skilled in these dances before he left Tibet. We were told by Khyentse Rinpoche that Rinpoche attained his awakening through his complete accomplishment of the practice of Chakrasamvara, that is through becoming one with and embodying completely the wisdom energy of that deity.

We were all looking forward to receiving this abhisheka, for which some of us had been waiting for over four years. So someone naturally asked Rinpoche, "Does this mean you will be giving the Chakrasamvara abhisheka soon?" To this, Rinpoche replied, "This *is* the Chakrasamvara abhisheka, I *am* Chakrasamvara." This was a perfectly reasonable comment in view of his connection with that deity. But, the moment he said that, I felt completely washed through with a cold panic. The atmosphere in the room was just so intense and all that was being said and shown to us was simply beyond anything I could grasp conceptually. I started to lose any sense of reference or normal reality. The only thing I knew, and kept repeating to myself, was not to leave the room. I literally held on to the bottom of my chair and the panic slowly passed. It was one of many times during this retreat period in which Rinpoche pushed us way beyond anything we could grasp with our conventional ideas of how the world works.

A short while later, on November 10, Rinpoche conducted a Vajrayogini abhisheka for a small group, at Mill Village. A day or so after the abhisheka, Rinpoche suddenly arrived at the Court early in the morning. We quickly dressed and went downstairs to find Rinpoche sitting alone in the living room. Karen and I sat with Rinpoche, the only ones there for a while.

He seemed to be partially in another realm, with little concern for our level of reality, to the extent that he momentarily picked up a glass paperweight on the table beside him as if it were a drinking glass. A tear started trickling down Rinpoche's cheek, and he said, "Where have all my students gone?" I replied, "We are here, sir, Karen and I, and we love you very much." It was clearly not what he was talking about. At another point he said, "They're all hungry ghosts." Was he referring to all of *us* or to beings in that other realm, I wondered? Mitchell came in after a while, and Rinpoche decided to leave. As he was leaving he asked Mitchell, "What was that line?" and told him to fetch a copy of the sadhana. Rinpoche then indicated the line to me, which referred to "transcending madness, manifesting as [the deity]." And the following line was, "With devotion to the guru and compassion for others." This helped me to realize that he probably understood what we were going through in our concern for him.

Rinpoche was going to go back to Mill Village unaccompanied other than by his driver. Mitchell supplicated me quite strongly to go with him, saying that he wanted somebody to accompany Rinpoche whom he felt comfortable with. I somewhat reluctantly climbed into the car with Rinpoche (and presumably Vajrayogini) and drove down to the retreat for the afternoon. This was my first visit to Mill Village. When we arrived I accompanied Rinpoche into the living room. While we sat there, he said, "Let's talk about Vajrayogini." My mind was blank at that point; I felt as if I no longer knew the person sitting next to me. I lamely repeated a technical question the driver of Rinpoche's car had asked on the way down, and Rinpoche gave me exactly the same answer he had given then. I could think of nothing more to say and that was it. The visit was very short. The kusung who had been at the retreat attending Rinpoche was driving back to Halifax, and I returned with him.

REVERSING THE CALL OF THE DAKINIS

The Regent had attended the abhisheka and was staying at the Court after visiting Mill Village. He was asked by Rinpoche to call Lama Ugyen Shenpen, in Boulder, to have him put through a request to Khyentse Rinpoche. Rinpoche was saying that the dakinis, female protectors of the dharma, were calling him to their realm, telling him that his students were too stuck and that he should leave them now. He needed help to reverse this call and wanted to put through an urgent request to Khyentse Rinpoche to perform a practice for him known, in fact, as "Reversing the Call of the Dakinis." This Khyentse Rinpoche did. I learned much later that it is believed in Tibet that visions of a deity as vivid as Rinpoche's of Vajrayogini portend the imminent death of the one who is having them.

While the Regent was at the Court, he told me that Rinpoche had said that the Regent and I should communicate more and that I needed to be watched because I could become an "unguided missile," by which he implied that I might start to make decisions on my own, without reference to the Regent or the Board. As the only minister, thus far, to move to Halifax, my task was to relay back to the Board, and especially to the Regent, what was going on there. However, the Regent and I were just not able to communicate by that time. He seemed to be unwilling to relate to me as an old friend, on a human heart-to-heart level. And I had distanced myself from him and his circle as I had become increasingly critical of behavior that seemed wild and arrogant.

Earlier in the fall, on a visit to Boulder to attend a Board meeting, I had asked for a private meeting with the Regent to express my concerns. Throughout the meeting he kept us laughing sometimes uproariously over our earlier, closer, days together. He seemed to deliberately start up the laughter again whenever I tried to speak more seriously of my concerns. Though I enjoyed the meeting and felt that the Regent was trying to recall for both of us the feeling of more friendly times together in the past, I left feeling disturbed that I had again been unable to communicate with him in a more genuine way.

It is no doubt true, nevertheless, that the Regent and I should have made an effort at least to discuss business more often at this point. And likewise myself and the other Board members should have communicated—that was our job. However, the absence of proper communication was mutual. The entire Board seemed to be absorbed in trying to hold on to the little nests that we had built for ourselves. In our own different ways, we had somehow gotten stuck in our little worlds and, thus, the entire fresh world vision that Rinpoche was trying to bring about was also stuck. Perhaps that was why the Rigdens never sent the *terma* that they had promised in the summer, and that was why the dakinis were calling Rinpoche. Nevertheless, he wasn't ready to leave just yet; as he said, "I never give up!"

BECOMING AN UNGUIDED MISSILE

Meanwhile, the Standing Committee was continuing to meet, and they also seemed to me to be very stuck. Whenever we met, there seemed to be continual discussion about what we were supposed to be doing and whether we were doing it. I was in the awkward position of having to chair the Standing Committee—awkward because I had little idea of the history of the group and what they had actually been doing—since back in September, when Jim Sacamano told me that he wanted to step back completely from his involvement in the administration to take more time for his medical work.

One dark November evening, there was a meeting in the living room of the Court. I sat in the winged-back chair which Rinpoche and the Regent would sit in when they visited, which perhaps gave me too much of a sense of authority. At this meeting, discussion came once again to that question, "What is the Standing Committee, and what should we be doing?" I felt that there was too much of a heavy sense of the concept of "Standing Committee," so I said that we should dissolve the whole *idea* of the Standing Committee, meaning to simply suggest that we should let go of the heavy concept "Standing Committee," which seemed to be burdening people. I thought that this might help us to carry on as a group of individuals each trying to do his or her assigned task, even though these seemed so vague.

However, my remark was interpreted as meaning that we should altogether disband the Standing Committee. People jumped on this idea with relief and shouts of delight: "Oh, that's a great idea! Let's have a toast to that!" I didn't have any wine in the house, so someone went off to buy some and then we toasted the end of the Standing Committee. At one point, someone did say, "Do you have the authority to do this?" which of course I did not. I was by then in a state of shock, just taking a passive role, unable to do anything but watch in astonishment what was happening. I was quite stunned by the response and I knew that something was not right, but I let it go on.

That night I dreamt that I was standing in a line with Rinpoche, and he hooked his leg around mine, tripping me so that I fell on the floor. I woke up with a terrible feeling of having done something very wrong. I remembered the Buddha's words that the sangha cannot be conquered from without, but can only be destroyed by worms within itself. I felt that, on that particular occasion, I had been one of those worms. I went to the shrine room and sat there alone for a long while, horrified at what this particular little worm had done.

1985: 16
Gone Altogether Beyond and Back

HE STAFF of the retreat at Mill Village was limited to one or two kusung, an attaché—a kasung post similar to what the Director of the day had been—and the cook. The only person who was on staff throughout the entire year was a quite new student, Joanne Carmine, whom we knew simply as *Machen*, Tibetan for "cook." I was admiring of Machen's sang-froid and her stamina. A short, tough young lady, she saw everything and was very helpful as continuity for those of us who were coming and going. She didn't seem to be phased by anything, although sometimes she did get into some kind of funk and would retire to her bed for a day or so, and she occasionally went away for vacation breaks. To be on staff demanded all one's energy, devotion, and openness to go beyond any expectations about what was real and what was not. The attaché position had been shared between Mitchell Levy, James Gimian, and Marty Janowitz, who were by now exhausted and needed a break. So they wanted a few others to take over from them from time to time. Accordingly, Mitchell came to me at the Court in January and asked me if I would take a turn at being the attaché, which I did for two two-week periods.

In describing the events that took place while I was in attendance at Mill Village, I want to make it clear that a retreat of this kind is usually done alone, or in the case of senior teachers such as Rinpoche possibly with one attendant. And in such retreats, especially at the highly advanced level that Rinpoche was manifesting, it is quite common to go far beyond the bounds of what would conventionally be regarded as sanity. In some ways, this is the whole point of such retreats for ordinary practitioners, to let one's conventional mind go as far as it will go, and thus to tune in to the deeper levels of wisdom that are usually obscured by that conventional mind. In Rinpoche's case, his wisdom was never obscured, but it seemed that he was using this retreat time to carry out activities on another plane of being. The fact that this retreat was taking place in Nova Scotia seemed significant in this regard. One might surmise that he was perhaps working with the local deities of Nova Scotia, to secure their aid in his work, as he had said he worked with the kami of Japan when he was visiting there the previous year.

So for Rinpoche to open up this retreat to people such as myself was an act of tremendous generosity and the sense of strangeness and confusion that I felt in being there was unquestionably largely my own projection. I can only tell what I saw and how I interpreted that from my own limited perspective and I do not want to suggest in any way that an ordinary, unrealized person such as myself could possibly have understood what was going on from Rinpoche's point of view.

I was, perhaps, fortunate in that I had been prepared through the previous months for the unconventional nature of life at the retreat. However, for people just dropping in for a few days, it could be more difficult. Our view of "sanity" in the West tends to be constrained by the scientific materialist approach of modern behavioral psychology and biologically-based psychiatry. Any attempts to acknowledge a spiritual dimension to unconventional behavior is usually dismissed as denial, mystical rubbish, or insanity. Of course this orthodoxy is very recent in origin, and limited to scientific materialist societies, but it is nevertheless predominant in our culture. It seemed to me that this was the conceptual trap that some of us, including myself, could so easily be caught in, in trying to understand what was going on with our limited logic of "normality."

In her autobiography, *Dragon Thunder*,[82] Rinpoche's wife Diana tells us that she had once asked Khyentse Rinpoche, "Why, when you had these descriptions of how far out vajrayana experience was, the great teachers like himself were so kind and ordinary." Khyentse Rinpoche had replied, "It's that way on the outside, but if you could see into my mind, it might look completely crazy to you." The term "crazy wisdom," which has been rather misunderstood in the West, is a translation of the Tibetan term *yeshe cholwa*, literally "wisdom run wild." It is quite the opposite of just being mad or acting in an outrageous fashion deliberately to insult people. As Rinpoche wrote:

> *Wisdom comes first and craziness comes afterward, so "wisdom crazy" is more accurate.... Crazy wisdom is the basic norm or the basic logic of sanity. It is a transparent view that cuts through the conventional norms or conventional emotionalism. It is the notion of relating properly with the world. It is knowing how much heat is needed to boil water to make a cup of tea, or how much pressure you should apply to educate your students. That level of craziness is very wise.... In other words crazy wisdom does not occur unless there is a basic understanding of things, a knowledge of how things function as they are. There has to be trust in the normal functioning of karmic cause and effect. Having been highly and completely trained, then there is enormous room for crazy wisdom. According to that logic, wisdom does not exactly go crazy; but on top of the basic logic or basic norm, craziness as higher sanity, higher power, or higher magic, can exist.[83]*

There are many precedents for such transformations from a well-behaved monk to someone who appeared outwardly to be crazy. When he was a young man in Tibet, one of Rinpoche's main teachers was the "crazy saint," Khenpo Gangshar. Reginald Ray describes Khenpo Gangshar in this way:

As a young monk, the Khenpo was renowned for his scholarly train-
ing and rigorous, indeed faultless, observance of the vinaya [monas-
tic rules]. At one point, however, he became extremely sick, was
given up for dead, and finally passed away. His corpse was laid out
in a small room. Some time later, he suddenly and most dramatically
revived, leaping up and throwing open the shutters of the tiny cell
where he had been put.

From the time of his awakening, Khenpo Gangshar had an aura
about him that frightened everyone, his disciples and detractors
included, and he did things that by conventional standards seemed
immoral. From that moment on, he seemed to have become an
entirely different person. He took a female consort, renounced his
vows and behaved in bizarre fashion. He was said to be able to tell
people's inner thought immediately by just looking at them. The
question was whether one found anything profound or valuable in
what the Khenpo said and did. Many people were deeply devoted to
the Khenpo and found his words and actions expressions of enlight-
enment; they found his attainment self-evident and became disci-
ples and devotees. Others did not like him and did not want to be
around him; they were troubled and embarrassed at this strange
behavior, were uncomfortable in his presence, and criticized and
avoided him. Trungpa Rinpoche, as far as I can see, presents much
the same configuration.[84]

THE FORTRESS OF NO CONCEPT

When I first arrived at Mill Village, I went straight up to Rinpoche's
bedroom to say hello, with Jim Gimian who was just about to go off
duty as attaché. Rinpoche was sitting up in bed. We knelt on the floor
and Gimian introduced me: "Here is Sir Jeremy who will be your
attaché for the next two weeks." My first book *Perceiving Ordinary
Magic* (the one that had started as the student's view of Shambhala and
ended as a book on science and spirituality) had just been published
and I had received some advanced copies in the mail. I presented a

copy to Rinpoche. He looked at it smiling and said, "Oh, how exciting," in a straightforward manner.

So while much of the time he seemed to be partially withdrawing his
presence from the physical realm—barely seeming to care what was
going on with the people around him—when he chose he could relate
directly with us on our limited mundane level. Patricia tells a story
showing some facets of what it was like to be with him on retreat during this period:

> I had heard that some people had been given "Shambhala names."
> (Many years later I found out that this was how the names of the
> Ladies to and of the Court were referred to.) When I was visiting
> Mill Village in November I asked Rinpoche, "What is my Sham-
> bhala name?" to which he responded, "Ask your father." I asked
> him what he meant but could get nothing further from him as he
> repeated, "Ask your father." I went home for Christmas and at that
> time I did ask my father what my name was. He replied "Patricia."
> I asked him whether I had any other names, why I had been given
> that name, and so on, but discovered nothing to solve this mystery.
>
> I visited Rinpoche on retreat again in January. When I arrived, I
> went to his bedroom to say hello. He was lying in bed, and he told
> me to pull up a chair beside him, which I did. Then he said, "Now
> is the time," and he took his stick and started beating it on his bed-
> side table. The table was cluttered with glasses, bottles, and so on,
> so the effect was unsettling. I didn't understand what was going
> on, so I just bowed as he continued to strike the table again and
> again. Later that evening, he told the kusung to bring him his cal-
> ligraphy brush and a shikishi—a Japanese calligraphy board, about
> 10 inches square and covered in gold leaf. He wrote on it a name in
> Tibetan, signed and sealed it and gave it to me. He told me it said
> "Jomo" in Tibetan, and instructed me to ask one of the translators
> what it meant and also to find out the equivalent in Chinese—some
> time previously he had told me that he and I had known each other
> "in the middle kingdom." That evening he also asked the kusung to

bring out all of his precious seals and carefully showed each one to
me, as if to say, "Now you are a member of the Court."

When I got home to Halifax I called one of our translators to find
out what "Jomo" meant. He told me it meant something like "Prin-
cess Consort" and another translator told me later that a simpler, or
more conventional, translation would be "Noble Lady." One day
many years later I was talking to a friend in Shambhala who was a
scholar of medieval chivalry. He said, "Yes, of course, Patricia means
Noble Lady." Although I had always known the derivation of my
name, I had never heard it expressed in exactly those words, and so
at that moment the whole story fell into place.

Rinpoche did not sleep very much, sometimes going for days on end without. When he was up and active, it was really a time of no concept. If I got caught in thinking that it was *such-and-such* a time, therefore we should eat, or therefore I should sleep—if I pulled back and refused to try to open to the vaster realm in which Rinpoche was operating—then I would be trapped in tiredness, fear, and doubt. Then it was a horrible, extremely painful situation. If I just opened my eyes and went into his world as far as I could, it could still be extremely exhausting, but rich and extraordinary. The retreat itself was actually called "Lötrel Dzong," which means "Fortress Free from Concept." *Lötrel*, "free from concept," is a term relating to the highest experience of Dzogchen, the final stage of the Buddhist path. And that is how it was: he pushed us beyond any concept, beyond day and night, beyond this world and another world, beyond our ideas of sanity or insanity. When Mitchell visited the retreat after I had been there for a few days, the first thing he said when he looked at me was, "Ah, retreat eyes." I knew immediately what he meant; I felt as if my eyes themselves expressed no reference point—as well as great tiredness, no doubt—no reference point, just being there without any expectation about what was normal or what might come next: *lötrel*.

Rinpoche would often decide to go for drives, any time of day or night, and he often wanted to see the "Secretariat" of Shambhala, presumably meaning to him the future seat of the government of Shambhala—again indicating to me that he was working on establishing Shambhala at a much larger level than ours. This had been happening for some time before I arrived. It was explained to me that the Secretariat was to be found at a certain spot, an open space on the main street in Bridgewater, the closest town of any size, about a half-hour drive from Mill Village. Whenever Rinpoche wanted to visit the Secretariat we would drive up to Bridgewater, drive slowly past this open space and say, "There is the Secretariat, sir." He would look at the space, sometimes asking us to stop for a few minutes, and then we would drive back to Mill Village. This seemed to satisfy him, although one never knew whether he was just going along with our pretense or whether he was somehow seeing something.

On one of these occasions it was 2 or 3 A.M., and it was very, very cold and icy outside. We were always lacking in sleep because Rinpoche would stay up for several days and nights at a stretch and, there being so few of us, we had to stay up with him, though we tried to do it in shifts. I went on this particular drive with just Rinpoche and the driver, while Machen and the kusung stayed to catch some sleep. Irritated and fed up I walked down the pathway to the car on this freezing cold February night, with the special Nova Scotian freezing rain coming at us horizontally. As I opened the car door for Rinpoche, he looked up at me with a wry smile and said, "If people would like to cheer up, they should go camping." This remark did, surprisingly, cheer me up. I responded, "To know reality, sir?" to which he replied with a definite "Yes!"

When we returned and walked in through the front door, I tripped on the threshold and went crashing down flat on my face, breaking my glasses. As I picked myself up, Rinpoche asked, "Where is everybody?" It was by now about 4:00 A.M. I said, "They're asleep, sir." He became enraged. He went around the kitchen banging on pots with a stick, shouting, "Why doesn't anybody want to wake UP!" Was he speaking of waking up in the ultimate sense? One could never be sure, but that's how it felt to me. As he raged around I felt, or perhaps projected, his tremendous frustration and disappointment at his students, so stuck in our little domestic comfort worlds.

Once, when Rinpoche had finally gone to bed and seemed to be about to fall asleep having just closed his eyes, he suddenly sat up and gestured for me to help him turn around and sit on the edge of the bed. Waving his swagger stick, he shouted, "Stop interfering with my work." Then he told me, "It's the green lady." He gestured that he wanted to go downstairs and sit in the living room. I sat in the living room with him while he had others search for the green lady. This went on for some time until he asked me, impatiently, "Have they found her yet?" "The problem is that we can't see the green lady ourselves, sir," I replied. He turned on me with a ferocious look and almost shouted at me, "That's the whole fucking problem!" Again, it seemed that he was expressing frustration that I seemed unable or unwilling to open my mind to the vaster dimensions of reality that, as he had often taught, pervade our conventional world. There were several times during the retreat when he spoke sharply like this to me, and each time it was a little shock, as if I were asleep and he had thrown cold water in my face to wake me up. It helped me to let go and open, just a little further, to the larger view of relative reality that he had so compassionately been trying to show us for so long.

HUMOR OF NO CONCEPT

As well as being constantly unsettling, Rinpoche's manifestation was perhaps his most powerful teaching. Often, it could be a source of amusement and delight, that he seemed to share. On one such occasion as I was helping him to bed, he had just lain down and closed his eyes which was always a relief because it meant that we too could get some rest. Then he quietly said, "Water. Water… head." I said, "You want water on your head, sir?" to which he replied, "Yes." I didn't know how to manage this. I fetched a bowl of water and a towel, got him half sitting up propped up against his pillow, put a towel on his chest and on the sheet, and proceeded to ladle water onto his head with a cup. I don't recall feeling there was anything strange about his request—a mark, perhaps, of the general strangeness of the times!

After a while he mused, "Doesn't seem to be working." At that moment Mitchell, who was staying over for a few days, came in and asked, "What on earth are you doing?" I replied that Rinpoche had said "water head." Mitchell, who was more familiar by that time with circumstances like this, asked Rinpoche, "Do you want a drink of water, sir?" and Rinpoche whispered, "Yes." So I got him a glass of water, and it seemed to do the trick. Rinpoche drank the water with a smile on his face, and I couldn't help wondering whether he had known what I was going through all along.

Another humorous occasion began when Rinpoche didn't want dinner to be served, and we couldn't figure out what was wrong. Finally, he said, "We're waiting for Shantarakshita." I presumed that he was referring to the great Shantarakshita, one of the great scholars who had brought Buddhism to Tibet in the ninth century, who of course had been dead for a thousand years. We sat in the kitchen, saying to each other, "What are we going to do? He's waiting for Shantarakshita to come to dinner." Then I remembered that I had seen a small announcement in the newspaper quite recently that Shantarakshita had died, though I did not know to whom the article referred—obviously not to that great scholar. In any case, I went back to Rinpoche and said, "I'm sorry to say, sir, that we just heard that Shantarakshita is dead." Rinpoche seemed to find that quite funny. He chuckled and said, "Okay," and dinner was served.

Andy Karr came as a visiting kusung. He had been in Europe for several years and rarely had the opportunity to see Rinpoche these days, so he was quite eager to be there. The rest of us had been there for a while and we had "retreat eyes," as Mitchell would say, or retreat mind—somewhat slow but very present. I was sitting at the kitchen table one day, where we spent most of our time, and Andy came running in, excited about something that was going on with Rinpoche in the sitting room. I said, "Andy, do you think you could just slow down a little bit, and not be quite so excited about the whole thing?" Tears came into Andy's eyes as he said, "Jeremy, you don't realize how much this means to me. I so rarely see Rinpoche and it is so precious for me to be here."

I was reminded how precious it was indeed to be at the retreat—exhausting and irritating, but so precious.

TRAVELING TO BHUTAN AND OXFORD

During this time, in his vaster world, Rinpoche was "traveling." In fact, or course, he never left the retreat environment, except to drive to the nearby town of Bridgewater or to visit the home of Jim and Ellen Green (the couple who had accompanied us to Prince Edward Island). He wanted to visit Khyentse Rinpoche, who he thought was in Bhutan, and then return to India via Siliguri, a customs border town. When he was traveling, Machen was, in his view, the innkeeper at Siliguri, and we would always stop off at the inn in Siliguri and have a meal. Rinpoche would graciously thank her for her hospitality and offer her money for payment, which she would graciously accept. Then we would move on.

Whether it was because I was there, I did not know, but he stopped visiting Bhutan for some period of time and visited London instead. He started asking for port and for a particular British drink which I didn't know how to make, and he wanted to travel to Oxford. One afternoon while Rinpoche was sleeping, I told the kusung, Michael Scott, that I was going to take a nap but to call me immediately if Rinpoche woke up. Rinpoche did wake up, quite soon after, but Michael did not call me. Instead, he helped Rinpoche to dress and go downstairs, and they were all set to go to Oxford when Rinpoche said, "Where is Uncle Jeremy? We can't go without Uncle Jeremy. Where is he?" Rinpoche referred to me as "Uncle Jeremy" during the retreat, perhaps because I held some responsibility for the education of his sons. Once when I was in his bedroom, he somewhat contemplatively mused, "Uncle Jeremy, who takes care of my sons."

Michael still did not wake me up, and I could never understand why he did not; when I asked him later he said, "Oh, I thought you needed to sleep." When Michael replied to Rinpoche that I was asleep, Rinpoche was furious, according to Michael's later report. He sneered, "All he ever does is eat, drink, and sleep." And right there he had captured in a nut-shell my neurosis of indulgence in comfort. Michael said, "Well, he's very tired, sir." Then Rinpoche turned on Michael, saying, "If you people want to eat shit, you eat shit."

Hearing this later, I felt again his frustration as on the night he had gone around shouting, "Why don't people want to wake up?" I felt he was trying to show us the sacredness of this world, and the luminosity that is reflected in that sacredness. Meanwhile we were still groveling in the "slime and muck of the dark age," as it is described in the Sadhana of Mahamudra, stuck in our petty conventional version of reality.

VISITING THE LOCAL RESTAURANT

Whenever Rinpoche wanted to go out to a restaurant for dinner, we took him to "Chez Vert" (the Green Home). Chez Vert was the local restaurant of the retreat world, which in the mundane world was the Chester home of Jim and Ellen Green, about an hour from Mill Village. They were tremendously open and generous in hosting Rinpoche whenever he turned up.

One evening, when we had finished dinner at Chez Vert and sat chatting for a while, I knew that Rinpoche's new companion was arriving and would be waiting for him at the Kalapa Camp (which is how we usually referred to Lötrel Dzong, the retreat house). I suppose all my English politeness came forth, and I felt we should get back to Kalapa Camp; I also felt that we should not "overstay our welcome" at the Greens', and it was already late at night or early in the morning. Rinpoche wasn't showing any signs of leaving. Several times I insisted, "Don't you think we should be getting back, sir?"

He finally agreed and we drove back to Mill Village, but when we arrived he almost refused to go into the house. He went in through the back door, which led directly into the kitchen, sat down at the kitchen table, and refused to go any further. After some time passed, during which I was puzzling about what the problem was, he turned to me and said, "It was your fucking English logic that got us here. Now get us out!" Such a clear mirror, such a powerful teaching that I have always remembered: your fucking English logic; your English uptightness and properness. It reminded me of the time, which by then seemed so long ago, when we had been sitting together in a bar and he had picked up a salt shaker and explained to me that "the English are like a sticky salt shaker." Again it seemed to me that he had dropped all masks on retreat and was showing, nakedly and now more fiercely, his crazy wisdom manifestation—and destroying what needed to be destroyed.

Apparently, the reason he wanted a break from the house was that a few weeks before I had arrived in January he had been going through an intense battle, so he said, with forces of the anti-dharmic Gelug lama whom he had told us about just before the Dalai Lama's visit in 1979. These were, he said, trying to prevent the establishment of Shambhala. At one point he had seen a dorje on his bedroom shrine and asked how it got there. He was told that someone had sent it as a gift. He became furious and told them it was sent by those people and should be buried. On another occasion, a thangka appeared on his shrine. When he asked where that came from, he was again told it was sent as a gift. He said the person depicted in the thangka was the malicious Gelug lama himself, and had it burned. Perhaps, also, the green lady whom he had told to "stop interfering with my work" was an emissary of that same lama.

Not wanting to disturb the Greens any more, I suggested to Rinpoche that we could drive to the Court in Halifax. He seemed to assent, so I called Karen (it was by now about 4 A.M.) and told her to get his bed ready. We climbed back into the car, Rinpoche in the back seat and myself in the front next to the kusung/driver. We were just about to drive away when Mitchell came running out. We opened the car windows and he said, "Where are you going?" "We are going to the Court," I replied. Mitchell turned to ask Rinpoche, "Do you want to go to the Court, sir?" "No," Rinpoche responded and added, prodding me in the shoulder, "it was this *idiot's* idea." "Would you like to go back to Chez Vert?" Mitchell asked. And so, to the Greens' we returned, where we all stayed for several days, along with the new companion and the kusung, Jerry Granelli.

The Greens' attitude the whole time was generous and accommodating, and they seemed to be thoroughly enjoying it. Rinpoche slept, got up and came downstairs, and ate meals, and in some ways it was one of the most normal, light-hearted, and enjoyable periods of my visit. One day, while Rinpoche was lying in bed, Jerry made a sculpture out of all the furniture he could find. It was a huge mound of furniture at the end of Rinpoche's bed, so big that we could hardly get into the room to see it. Rinpoche was laughing with great glee, something that rarely happened in that period when he seemed so embattled, perhaps with the anti-dharmic forces or perhaps just with the thickness and stupidity of his older students. His laughter was a great relief, and a delight to see.

Rinpoche would often ask when certain people were coming, as if he were expecting them. He would frequently ask, "Where is my Regent? When is he coming?" Once I called the Regent urging him to visit Rinpoche, but he declined. Another was someone he called "Red Diamond." Red Diamond was his name for Karen Laven, who was one of his favorite consorts and later became the first sangyum, a special level of consort about whom I will say more shortly. He used to get on the phone to Red Diamond at any time of day or night. She very gallantly slept with the phone right next to her ear so that she would be able to answer immediately if he called. One day, during our extended stay at Chez Vert, I asked Rinpoche why he called Karen by the name "Red Diamond," which would suggest Vajrayogini. When I asked this question Rinpoche was right there with me, and he responded, "Well, it's like patterns of electricity, similar patterns." He had often told us to "look for the patterns," a similar pointing out as the qualities game—how to see the larger picture beyond the outer facade of a person or event.

BEING IN THE SPACE OF HIS MIND

When Rinpoche was awake, then, we were constantly stretched to go beyond our comfort level, both physical and mental, and there was little time to rest our minds. When he was asleep, it was a different story. Then, my mind could rest in a brilliant space that was extremely peaceful—and not simply by contrast with the waking activity. It was like being with his mind, just as it had been like to sit with him in his private living room at the Kalapa Court, only much more intense than that. The whole atmosphere of the house seemed to be filled with luminous warmth and peaceful radiation. At those moments, it felt as if one could almost touch his mind.

The most vivid demonstration of this for me was one afternoon when Rinpoche was asleep and kusung Michael Scott decided to take the opportunity to go grocery shopping in Bridgewater. I thought it would be nice to get a break and go to a "normal" world for a while, so I said I would go along. As we were driving away, I started to have an awful feeling in the pit of my abdomen, wretched and empty. We had barely reached the end of the long driveway from the house and were about to turn onto the main road when I realized I felt absolutely horrible. It was like being torn away from the very best of the best, from something I loved, from something I wanted so much to be with. It was as if my whole insides were being ripped open. There was still time to say to Michael, "Stop! Let me out. I want to go back." But to my rational mind this seemed silly, so I just stuck with it.

We drove on to Bridgewater and did the grocery shopping. I steamed with frustration while Michael wandered around the store looking for little toys for his children in Halifax. All the while I could feel that terrible longing to be at the Lötrel Dzong. I can feel, even now, the sense upon returning that the house was filled with golden light, just as Rinpoche's room had been that first time I met him in 1970.

In contemplating the period of being at Lötrel Dzong, I felt that, for those who were on staff for an extended period rather than just being guests for a few days, such periods were a kind of rite of passage. It was the greatest challenge we were to face in our years with Rinpoche. It seemed like a test—but a test of what? Perhaps a test of our trust in our own sanity and confidence to open ourselves completely, to perceive with the heart as well as the intellect the vaster perspective of reality that Rinpoche had always dwelt in, and had been trying so hard all these years to help us to see. Perhaps also a trust in his sanity, far beyond the so-called sanity of our petty conventional culture. He opened the door wide for us on that retreat, but there was a big sign over the entrance:

WARNING: RISK OF LOSING CONVENTIONAL MIND.

TIME TO LEAVE MILL VILLAGE

The day finally came when Rinpoche was to leave the retreat. He said later that, from his point of view, he had to completely reassemble his body—re-inhabit, I suppose, what was left of his body. At that time Jim Gimian, Marty Janowitz, and Mitchell Levy, the three main attachés and stalwart protectors, who were by now known as the "Three Musketeers," returned to the retreat in order to help Rinpoche leave. They were not really sure, right up to the day before he left, whether Rinpoche would be able to come down to earth, so to speak. But he did; he actually reappeared in our mundane world, seeming quite his old self, if such a phrase could apply to him. And in doing so he orchestrated a mysterious disappearance that turned out to be an April Fool's joke on a magnificent scale for the entire sangha.

The party was due to come to Halifax to stay overnight at the Court before departure. Patricia, who was to be Rinpoche's companion for the night, arrived and we waited. And waited. Rinpoche did not arrive. We called Mill Village and received no answer. Finally Patricia went upstairs to sleep alone in Rinpoche's bed and, puzzled and disappointed, the rest of us went to bed as well.

The next day, the entire Halifax sangha waited for Rinpoche to arrive at the Halifax airport in order to catch his flight to Boston on the way to Boulder. We waited. The flight was called for boarding and he had not arrived. We still waited. His habit in days gone by had been to wait until the very last moment before getting on the plane. He loved to push things to the edge and make everyone extremely nervous and, in fact, he did sometimes miss his plane because of this. But this time he never appeared. Again we called Mill Village with again no reply. He seemed to have altogether disappeared.

We all returned to Halifax and waited to see what would happen. No one answered the phone in Mill Village all day. They seemed to have left. The sangha in Boulder, too, heard nothing that day. We had no idea what had happened. Everyone in Nova Scotia was very disappointed that we had not been able to see him off at the airport, after the profound and intense year we had had with him so near to us.

He was due to arrive in Boulder the following day, which was April first, and we might have been warned by this! At about 8:45, in Boulder, the Vajra Regent Ösel Tendzin peered out of the window of the shrine room, where Rinpoche was supposed to arrive, and then addressed the packed shrine room: "We don't know where he is!"

Shortly before his expected arrival time in Boulder, Machen turned up at the Kalapa Court in Halifax, driving the Mercedes. I called Dorje Dzong in Boulder to let them know that Machen had reappeared. I got through to Dorje Dzong and I could hear the buzz of the waiting crowd. It had been announced that Rinpoche had not been seen leaving Nova Scotia, and that the plane he was supposed to catch from Boston to Denver had been cancelled. Carolyn Gimian answered the phone, and we were exploring the possibilities of what might have happened, when she suddenly shouted, "Here he is! He has arrived!" And there he was, exactly on schedule.

Marchen told us that she had driven the party down to Yarmouth, on the southern tip of Nova Scotia, to a small airport where the plane to Boston would stop to pick up or drop off passengers. There they had caught the plane and stayed the night in Boston. They had asked her to lie low until they were safely in Boulder. In past years Rinpoche had customarily played some kind of major practical joke on some poor sangha group or other; this time it seemed to be the entire worldwide sangha who was fooled. Perhaps it was a sign that his old good spirits were still alive and well!

MOVING AHEAD AGAIN

During the next few months of 1985 we heard news from Boulder that Rinpoche seemed almost youthful, showing energetic interest in everything and, as Bill McKeever told me on the phone, "He's just like he was in the early '70s." So there was fresh energy and forward motion once again in the sangha, what one could almost call "hope"—hope that things would return to a relatively normal state, with Rinpoche teaching and leading us for many years to come.

Many new clubs and organizations were formed, and everything seemed to be blossoming again like the trees in spring. Rinpoche created the position of *sangyum*, which literally means "secret mother, or consort" in Tibetan and is normally used to refer to the wife of a lama. In this case it referred to consorts with whom he had a particularly strong heart and mind connection and whom he trusted to oversee aspects of the organization. Karen Laven, "Red Diamond," was appointed sangyum, along with Cynde Grieve, with whom he had fallen in love in 1978, and five others. These ladies each went through a special empowerment ceremony with Rinpoche and he called the sangyums "my eyes and ears," just as he had referred to the Ladies of the Court. However, this time he gave each of them some aspect of the organization to look after: Karen Laven was assigned to Naropa Institute, another to Shambhala Training, and so on.

I felt, and I think many did, that it was a brilliant way for him to bring feminine energy into the organization, energy that was desperately needed. Many important aspects of the organization were lead by women—Naropa Institute and Karme Chöling, for example, both had female directors—and women had taken on senior teaching and meditation instruction roles. But the overall governing body, the Board of Directors, was still all male, and, as I have mentioned, like a jock club at times, or a teenage street gang. He couldn't just have added

CALLIGRAPHING NAMES FOR THE BODHISATTVA VOWS
AT SEMINARY. *Photograph by Susan Dreier.*

one or two female Board members to that group—they would simply
have manifested their own masculine energy, or been undermined and
pushed aside. He had to bring in the feminine energy in a different
way. He told the sangyums that they were part of his family, that their
position was above that of the administration and that they could fire
anyone, even the Regent, if they felt it necessary. At last a way to bring
the feminine element into administration had been found.

When the sangyums asked Rinpoche what they should study in order to carry out their functions he advised them to learn and study two of the *terma* texts of Shambhala and, according to Fabrice Midal,[85] "learn to have good elocution, practice ikebana, not look on his work as a burden, maintain a royal attitude, avoid being frivolous, resist being Americanized, and have the generosity to govern and manifest a sense of dignity." These, then, were the qualities that Rinpoche sought in those who would lead Shambhala, his ministers, governors, and statesmen and women.

AN UNGUIDED MISSILE CONFIRMED

In June, I went to RMDC for the Kalapa Assembly, which was held immediately before the Seminary, and was hence the first program to be held in the new facilities. Rinpoche gave a few talks, this time emphasizing not so much the Shambhala teachings, *per se*, but rather the importance of actually bringing about the Kingdom. "*You* have to do it," he insisted urgently. In his most provocative talk, he announced that the Kingdom would be established in five years. Again, it was a mistake to take the statement literally, but at the least it seemed as if he was provoking us to get on with it and at the same time not expect it to be easy.

During the Kalapa Assembly, there was the first meeting of the Board of Directors with Rinpoche since the retreat. Since it was occurring at Kalapa Assembly, it was held in a very formal style. We met in a large tent that was open on three sides. It was an open meeting, so there were a number of visitors, including the various officers and staff of Vajra-dhatu/Nalanda. Each Minister was to give a short report on his area, and I reported some of the things that had happened in Halifax in the past year. I felt pretty good about what we had accomplished, considering the intensity of serving the retreat at the same time, but I was still somewhat ashamed about my role in the disbanding of the Standing Committee. At the end of my presentation, Rinpoche asked grumpily, "Did you report all this to the Board?" Of course it was obvious he knew that I did not, and I replied, "Well, sir, I am reporting it now." He said, tersely, "Well, you should have communicated with the Board more," a reference, I supposed, to my having confirmed his concern that I was becoming an unguided missile!

I stayed on for a few days at the beginning of Seminary, supposedly as Director in attendance, although I saw Rinpoche only once. Rinpoche was clearly delighted to be at Seminary, on our own land. His talks, though brief, were full of humor and joy. He could often be seen touring the central area, dropping in unexpectedly on the newly constructed kitchen, dining area, and offices. He always had a cheerful smile, at least in public, "just like the old days." The theme of the introductory talk, and in a sense of the whole Seminary, was, "Be real in your own existence…. Every moment of being awake you communicate with sights, and sounds, and feelings such as the temperature while you are taking a shower. Just be in contact with reality as much as you can."

NOT SO DIFFERENT BEHIND THE SCENES

I went to up to Prajna, the former retreat cabin which had been converted into a house for Rinpoche, and we had a short discussion of education business. After that, Rinpoche invited me stay. I sat down on the sofa, close to Rinpoche, who sat in his usual armchair. One of the sangyum came in, and sat down beside me on the sofa. We sat there for a while, played desultorily with Rinpoche's huge dog, Ganesh, a Tibetan mastiff. The sangyum told a joke or two, and I was strongly reminded of being with him at Mill Village. Mitchell came in to announce that Rinpoche's dinner was ready. Dinner customarily was preceded by taking down the flags outside Prajna, so we went out onto the porch as the sun was setting, and watched as the flags came down.

I left with a mixed feeling of gladness and sadness in my heart; although it was wonderful to have him "back," at the same time he still seemed so far, far away. It was clear that behind the scenes, with his old students, he was not manifesting so differently from how he

HELPING IN THE SEMINARY KITCHEN.
Photograph by Susan Dreier.

had been at Mill Village. I had heard, too, that during the reception for him at the Court, immediately after his arrival in Boulder, he had suddenly exclaimed in a loud and sarcastic tone, "You all think you're *permanent!*" In the front line, so to speak, he was very charming and kind to new students, but behind the scenes it was very much like a Mill Village situation, with a lot of fierce impatience toward the older students.

Although he himself seemed to be dissolving further and further into the inner realm, at the same time, he was very much trying to stay in his physical body which by now was weak and probably, at times, extremely painful to inhabit. He seemed to be doing this entirely for the sake of his students and to see the Kingdom of Shambhala established. He did not seem to care, for himself, whether he was on earth or not.

Years later, I was told a story by one of the Regent's close associates and secretary: Once back in the '70s when the Regent had been with Rinpoche, he had started crying. When Rinpoche asked him why he was crying, the Regent said, "I thought of you dying, and how it would be for me if you were to die." Rinpoche replied, "As far as I'm concerned, it has already happened." There seems little question that Rinpoche was not personally attached to staying in his physical body, but that he was really working to stay on earth for our sake.

When Rinpoche had been on retreat in 1972, he told the two students who were with him, "You have to understand—I will only be around for twenty years." At that time, although he was somewhat lame from the car accident, he seemed in very good health, sprightly and energetic. We didn't take this comment seriously at all, just forgetting all about it. But by this time, in 1985, it meant that he was not expecting to be around much beyond 1990, five years away. He had already had the severe sickness in 1981, so it was, perhaps, somewhat of an effort on his part to stay in his body.

For ordinary people such as ourselves, of course, the notion of "staying in our body" makes no sense at all; we have no control over it whatsoever. However, a tulku has supposedly chosen to be born into a particular body to carry out a particular job. And according to Khyentse Rinpoche and other Tibetan masters, Chögyam Trungpa Rinpoche was not an ordinary person, but a *mahasiddha* who came to this earth knowing what he was going to do. (Literally, *mahasiddha* means a "being of great accomplishment" and this title is used to refer only to vajrayana masters of the very highest attainment.) Presumably, then, Rinpoche had a degree of control over the relation between his body and his awareness that ordinary people do not have. At least that is what Rinpoche seemed to imply, and how it seemed to me.

In the final chapter I will discuss the question of the relation between body and awareness. Suffice it to say here that the view that there may be *some* degree of separability between body and *some* aspect of mind is common to Tibetan Buddhism as well as to many other cultures that are not based on the nihilism of scientific materialism. This should not be confused, of course, with the theistic idea of eternal personal continuity as a "soul."

RINPOCHE LEADS THE FOUR-KARMAS FIRE PUJA

In October, the first "four-karmas fire puja" in North America, perhaps the first in the Western world altogether, took place at Amaculo, a Girl Scout camp that adjoined RMDC. We eventually purchased the property so that now it is a valuable addition to RMDC. The amending fire puja (a different ceremony) was the one I had attended the first time it was held in 1980, and it had been performed several times since. In the amending puja, one is developing the karma, or enlightened action, of pacifying obstacles. In the four-karmas puja, one practices all four karmas: pacifying, enriching, magnetizing, and destroying.

The four karmas are four types of action of a person in a state of wakefulness.[86] The first karma is pacifying, resting in an impartial state of mind that creates a peaceful environment. The karma of enriching is that within that state of peace, things can naturally begin to grow; there is a sense of increasing wealth. Rinpoche draws the analogy of a tree that stands constantly still, day and night, until it finally grows and produces fruit. The third karma, magnetizing, is drawing everything into a situation. As Rinpoche says, "We retain the dignity, but we don't make any move outward. All the life situations begin to come to us." However, there is a danger that we might fall asleep in the gentle compassion of the previous three, turning it into "idiot compassion," that is, compassion based on satisfying one's own ego more than genuinely benefiting the other. Therefore the karma of destroying what needs to be destroyed is important. As Rinpoche demonstrated many times in his life, the aggression of a situation cannot always be subdued peacefully but has to be cut abruptly, or destroyed, with compassionate wrath.

Each of the four karmas is associated with a color that expresses the energy of that particular karma: pacifying is pure, bright white, enriching is brilliant, golden yellow, magnetizing is warm, inviting red, and destroying is the blue-black of a thunder cloud. Over the years, one could almost see, or feel, these colors in the space around Rinpoche in the varying circumstances of his presence in our midst.

The two fire pujas are necessary prerequisites for taking the Chakrasamvara abhisheka, and it was already planned that Rinpoche would give the first Chakrasamvara abhisheka the following spring. Because the fire puja in October would be the first four-karmas fire puja for our vajrayana sangha, Rinpoche intended to lead it. Immediately prior to this, he was to conduct the Vajrayogini abhisheka.

I was planning to fly to Boulder to attend the fire puja. I had attended every Vajrayogini abhisheka since the first one in January of 1977—seven or eight altogether—and, although they were in many ways wonderful, they could also be tiring. By that time I felt that I had had enough, and I arranged my flight so that I would be flying out to Boulder on the day of the abhisheka, thereby planning to miss it. Unbeknown to all of us, it was to be the last Vajrayogini abhisheka that Rinpoche would conduct in North America.

However, having begun the Vajrayogini abhisheka, which normally takes just one day, Rinpoche decided not to finish it but to wait until the following day. So I arrived in Boulder to discover that I would be attending the abhisheka after all! When I took my place on the side of the throne with the other Directors, Rinpoche turned and, looking directly at me, gave me a very welcoming, kind smile. I had the thought that perhaps he had postponed the abhisheka so that I could be there, but no doubt it was just another auspicious coincidence.

The four-karmas fire puja was scheduled to occur a few days after the abhisheka, and, as this was the first such puja, it was all very new for the whole sangha. I spent the time shopping for appropriately colored clothes—white, yellow, red, and black—with Sherab, my host in Boulder who had by then returned from duty in Europe. We went up to RMDC and the fire puja began. Unlike future four-karmas fire pujas, the practices were done at the appropriate time of the day for the respective karmas. That is, the pacifying practice happened in the morning; enriching in the early afternoon; the magnetizing practice was late afternoon/early evening; and the destroying practice began at midnight. Each of the karmas took two days.

The fire puja took place in the dining room of Amaculo, which was converted into a shrine room. We rigged up a fireplace in the center of the room, with a chimney going out of the window. Rinpoche stayed in the infirmary building, which had more comfortable rooms; his staff created a dining room, sitting room, bathroom, and bedroom there. We all stayed in cabins or dorms. Rinpoche would come down to the shrine (dining) room at the appropriate time, in the appropriate colored clothing. He always took the vajra master place at the fire, although he did not attend every session of each practice. He did not attend the two days of "destroying" practice, but instead did the practice in the fireplace of the living room in the infirmary.

The vajra master has to move around and face in different directions according to the karma that is being practiced and I recall vividly one occasion when Rinpoche was oriented to be more or less facing in my direction. At one point I became very much absorbed in the practice. My eyes closed for a while, and when they opened Rinpoche was staring straight at me. I was in a state of mind in which a lot of my subconscious barriers were down. Our eyes met directly. There was less hiding or pulling back on my part as there normally was when he looked directly at me, but instead a sense of quiet joy. It was a short but precious moment of meeting mind-to-mind.

One evening, I was invited up to the infirmary to have dinner with Rinpoche. When I arrived I was told that Rinpoche was not feeling well, so we had dinner without him and I went back to my dorm room. The next day I was told that, when he heard that I had been the guest the previous night, he said, "Oh, I wanted to see Jeremy," and told his staff to invite me again for that night. Accordingly, I went up again that night, and this time he was there.

We sat by the fire before dinner, and he said, sounding pleased, "I hear you have been doing some wood-carving." He was referring to my working during the previous few weeks on the carving of the intricate leaf design above the shrine in the new shrine room we were building in Halifax. I worked on this carving, silently, side-by-side with a skilled carpenter and wood-carver. He would simply show me what to do if I ran into problems, but very few words were exchanged. I had loved doing this work and went to Dorje Dzong every afternoon for many weeks. So to his query, I replied, "Yes, sir. It is like an apprenticeship. I just follow him without the need for words. It is the first time I had a teacher like that." I was thinking, of course, of a teacher in the worldly sense, not of Rinpoche, so much of whose teaching was beyond words. It was a sweet little conversation. We then sat down to dinner, after which I left.

HIS LAST HELLO TO EUROPE

At the end of December 1985, in spite of being seriously unwell, Rinpoche made a triumphant visit to Europe. This was only the second teaching tour Rinpoche had made in Europe since leaving England in 1969; the previous one had been in 1981, when he was barely recovered from serious illness. Most of the work of gathering students in Europe had been initiated by Sherab, and a few dozen had traveled to North America to attend Rinpoche's seminaries. The Regent, however, had made many visits to Europe and had gathered a large following there. So the dharma students in Europe were eagerly anticipating this visit of the father of it all.

Sangha-members gathered first in Marburg, on December 23, for the first Vajrayogini abhisheka on the continent. They came not just from all over Europe, but from North America as well. The abhisheka, which the Sawang attended, includes a section in which the vajra master empowers some of his students also as vajra master. Rinpoche took all aspects of these ceremonies very seriously; they were not merely empty rituals for him. Until this occasion, none of his students taking the abhisheka, with the single exception of his Regent, had received this vajra master empowerment. However, this time, he called the

Sawang up to his throne to be empowered as vajra master, and thereby as Rinpoche's second lineage holder in the Kagyu lineage.

Rinpoche went on to give public seminars in Marburg, Amsterdam, and London. He also visited his old college town of Oxford, where he had first learned "how to speak the English language properly," as his first elocution exercise was called. The talks at all the seminars were on basic meditation and were reported as "brief and profound." Again, as at the Seminary in the summer, Rinpoche emphasized the theme of simplicity and naturalness, of dropping any form of preconception. At the first talk in London, he expressed his gratitude at being back there: "paying homage so to speak," he said.

A report of his visit in the *Vajradhatu Sun* concludes, "The Vidya-dhara left the shores of Europe, much to the sadness of his students there, but not without promising to return soon. There was a sense that this tour had truly established his seat there. After years of laying the ground, the European sangha was able to welcome and host the Vidya-dhara, and to provide an environment in which the dharma could truly be heard and practiced."[87]

Thus the year that had begun so strangely at the Fortress of No-Concept ended on a note of victory.

1986–87: Final Goodbyes 17

 N JANUARY, on his way back from Europe, Rinpoche stopped off in Halifax for the opening of the new Halifax headquarters, Dorje Dzong. The new shrine room was ready just in time—we were putting the finishing touches to it, under the Regent's indefatigably cheerful guidance, a few hours before the opening. The event was attended by over five hundred people, far more than the room could hold; fortunately a closed- circuit TV had been placed downstairs.

Sangha came from New York, Boston, Boulder, Montreal, and Halifax, and the majority of the guests were local Haligonians—sangha and friends of the sangha. The guests included the Archbishop of Halifax, the mayor, and other prominent local dignitaries. I introduced the evening by giving a fifteen-minute history of Buddhism from the time of the Buddha to the present day, manifested in Rinpoche. He gave a very short, simple, and beautiful talk in which he emphasized over and over that "Buddhism is based on the natural state of being as we are.... Thank you very much for being so natural, so intrinsic. I very much appreciate your natural state of being with things as they are."[88] Even the archbishop smiled and nodded his appreciation. Naturalness, genuineness, was to be the theme of these last nine months of Rinpoche's active life.

FINAL WORDS ON THE INSEPARABILITY
OF SHAMBHALA AND BUDDHISM

In February of 1986, at Karme Chöling, the Vidyadhara gave his last public seminar, "Realizing Enlightened Society," in which he spoke about the inseparability of Buddhism and Shambhala.[89] He began, "We are definitely turning the wheel sunwards. And it is my greatest privilege to announce the inseparability of the Shambhala approach and the buddhadharma." In these talks he spoke very little—the transcripts of all three talks occupy only about a page and a half. He spoke very slowly and sometimes seemed to fall asleep between words. Viewing the videotapes later, it is obvious that he was dying, though we were unable to acknowledge it at the time. Yet he spoke with such purity, such uncluttered words, the purest of the pure. He said, over and over again, "Be genuine, please be genuine." His message was that Buddhism and Shambhala are inseparable yet not identical. Shambhala is the container of Buddhism, he said, giving the analogy of Shambhala as a vase and Buddhism the water it contains. He also said that Shambhala is what makes it possible to know and relate with Buddhism, like the sun and space, or the trees and animals on a mountain.

All this was a reminder of his assertion years previously that a culture different from the modern culture of self-interest would be necessary if the buddhadharma were to survive. Altogether, it perhaps makes most sense to say, as his son and heir would later proclaim, that the teachings Rinpoche brought to the West, and that thousands around the world now practice, are not purely traditional Tibetan Buddhism. But nor are they Japanese Buddhism, American Buddhism, nor English, French, German, Polish, or Greek Buddhism; they are Shambhala Buddhism.

There was a banner with a large calligraphy of an Ashe behind his head. One of the newer students pointed to the banner and asked, "What's that thing behind you?" He replied, "One." She asked again,

RINPOCHE IS ATTENTIVE TO THE QUESTIONER, AS ALWAYS.
Photograph by Marvin Moore.

in a rather scathing tone, "One *what?*" He said with love and certainty, in a quiet, contemplative tone: "One with *every*thing." And there was still the occasional touch of humor. In the final talk he said that "leading life may be putting together some kind of dichotomy, but it's workable." He was referring to the dichotomy of Buddhism as background and Shambhala as foreground, Buddhism as space and Shambhala as the embellishment of space. When a student asked, "What is the dichotomy you mentioned?" Rinpoche replied, "Cheerful but... strange," and his crooked smile was the perfect embodiment of cheerful but strange.

PASSING NAROPA INSTITUTE OVER TO OTHERS

This year, 1986, Naropa Institute was applying for full accreditation, having by now spent eight years in the candidacy process. As a step toward establishing the accreditation, the NCA had advised the Institute that it would be necessary to appoint a Board of Trustees for the Institute, which would have direct authority over its governance. For accreditation purposes it had to be transparently clear that Nalanda Foundation, the non-profit educational organization of which the Institute was a division, did not have the identical Board of Directors as Vajradhatu. Accordingly, an independent Board of Trustees was set up including people who were not associated with Vajradhatu at all, some of whom were not even Buddhists. The formation of this Board took place under the guidance of Lucien Wulsin, a gentleman who had a lot of experience as the Chairman of various Boards, in particular the Denver University Board of Trustees.

On April fifth, there was a ceremony in which Rinpoche officially empowered the newly formed Board of Trustees of Naropa Institute. At this ceremony, Rinpoche was, again, very short on words. His mouth was obviously extremely dry, and he kept making sucking motions as if trying to moisten it; he was apparently drinking cider instead of saké. He said, over and over, "We are passing Naropa Institute to other, passing to *other*." To me, the occasion was disturbing, not only because of the state of Rinpoche's health, but because I knew that this had not been his original intention in initiating Naropa Institute. He had wanted to have one umbrella organization, with one Board of Directors for everything, including both Vajradhatu and Naropa Institute. And he had viewed the Institute as an expression of the Kagyu Lineage, as he had said at the faculty meeting in 1975, while being open to all traditions just as Nalanda University had been.

However, such a unity could not be accomplished because of the need for accreditation, which was also important to Rinpoche. Under the wise guidance of Lucien Wulsin, who chaired the Board of Trustees for the next eight years, the Institute flourished in a way that it certainly could not have done if it had remained within the confines of the Buddhist organization. So, in this sense, transferring it to "other" was necessary to accomplish Rinpoche's vision of the Institute as a significant contributor to Western education.

On May 23 of 1986, Naropa Institute did receive full accreditation. This was a huge step for the Institute. Now, some twenty years later, the Institute has appropriately been renamed Naropa University. The NCA itself acknowledges Naropa University as one of its finest experiments, and it is widely regarded as an excellent model of an institute of higher education that offers an alternative to the often-irrelevant academic studies of conventional colleges worldwide. The University is now flourishing, with three separate campuses spread around the town of Boulder which accommodate over one thousand degree students. Its programs include a full four-year Bachelors and Masters degrees, and a variety of new programs too numerous to name here. Thus is being fulfilled another of Rinpoche's dearly cherished wishes in his relentless quest for means to transform our society.

THE CHAKRASAMVARA ABHISHEKA

The day following the ceremony of empowering the Trustees, Rinpoche at last gave the Chakrasamvara abhisheka, to about three hundred students. These students had completed the required number of recitations of the Vajrayogini sadhana and had been ready for this abhisheka for some years by now. Chakrasamvara is the deity whose sadhana is practiced after that of Vajrayogini in the Kagyu tradition. In this practice one arouses the skillful means of being able to apply the four karmas. In contrast, the sadhana of Vajrayogini is intended to arouse in one's being the space of wisdom. Vajrayogini is a female deity, and Chakrasamvara male, and in this sadhana the two are in union—the union of wisdom and skillful means. According to Khyentse Rinpoche, it was through his practice of the Chakrasamvara deity, a specialty of the Surmang monastery and the Trungpas, that Rinpoche had achieved his profound awakening.

One of the most senior lamas of the Kagyu lineage, Tenga Rinpoche, came to Boulder to help prepare for the abhisheka. This included creating a sand mandala—a complex symmetrical design made by carefully spreading colored sands onto a three-foot square flat surface. The sand mandala is a geometric representation of the palace of the deity and its inhabitants. At the time of this visit, Tenga Rinpoche told us that Rinpoche should now be known by the title *Vidyadhara*, meaning "holder of knowledge," a title that is very rarely bestowed during someone's lifetime and then only upon masters of the very highest realization. This is how he was referred to from then on, and is to this day.

As the Directors, Dapöns, and others waited with the Regent for the abhisheka to begin, the Regent recounted a meeting he had just had with Rinpoche. Rinpoche had warned him about what was to come in the next few years, in particular the move to Nova Scotia, saying, "We could lose *everything*." Rinpoche had made a sweeping gesture with his hand, repeating over and over, "swept away, swept away." The Regent also told us that Rinpoche had said repeatedly to him, "You are the only one," meaning the only one who could keep things going after his death. The Regent appeared to expect us to take this literally although Rinpoche had said something similar to both Lady Diana and the Sawang.

Once when I had been talking to him about his son, Gesar, he had said, "He could take over if the Regent doesn't work out." I had asked in some surprise, "Do you expect that the Regent won't work out, Rinpoche?" To which he had replied, "Not necessarily, but one shouldn't put all one's eggs in one basket." Thus, as he did throughout his life, Rinpoche continued to plant many seeds so that at least one might become full-grown.

During the abhisheka the atmosphere was profound and powerful—powerfully magical, powerfully irritating, just as had been the first Chakrasamvara abhisheka, in the living room of Kalapa Court in Halifax on the night Rinpoche had introduced Vajrayogini in person. It was also deeply disturbing because Rinpoche was clearly not well and, in fact, spent the several days following the abhisheka in the hospital. I believe it was finally beginning to dawn on us that he was very seriously ill and may not live much longer. A few weeks after the abhisheka, the Seminary began at RMDC, and Rinpoche was by then well enough to preside.

Leaving the tent with kusung at RMDC, Seminary 1986.

ANOTHER PAINFUL BOARD MEETING

There was a Board meeting in Boulder during Seminary and the Loppon left RMDC to come down to Boulder for this meeting. When Rinpoche, still at Seminary, asked where the Loppon was and was told that he had gone to a meeting in Boulder, Rinpoche said, "You people have too many meetings." One of his frequent comments in those days was, "You people talk too much." At the Karme Chöling seminar in February he had remarked, "Stop conversing more than necessary and simplify your life as much as you can." He himself had become very short on words; two of his favorite responses to the many questions still coming at him were "DRM" and "CCL," abbreviations for "Doesn't Really Matter," and "Couldn't Care Less."

By this time the finances of Vajradhatu were very bad, and the question of the huge expense of the staff, including the Directors, was raised. The discussion went around and around. It was obvious that the overall salary cost had to be cut, so people would either have to be dropped off the payroll, or everyone would have to take a fairly hefty salary cut. No one had any suggestions about what we could do and it became a stalemate. Finally, I said, "All right, I will go off salary." The Regent responded, "Good." And that was it—I was off salary. The only other person who responded at all was Ken Green, who was sitting next to me and turned to me in some astonishment and concern, saying, "Can you really do that?" Everyone else just accepted it without comment, and we went on with the next business. I was in a state of shock—I had just wiped out our family income.

After the meeting we walked out into the afternoon sun and Marty came to me with a check for two thousand dollars, signed by "Chögyam Trungpa." The check was drawn on Rinpoche's personal account. Marty said, "I want to give this to you," to which I responded, "No, I couldn't possibly accept money from Rinpoche." But Marty replied, "Rinpoche wants me to. He gave me the check as I was about to leave for the meeting and said, 'No one should be harmed.'" So I took the check, and that was what we lived on for a while, until Karen's real estate business started to take off and I began to take on part-time editing work for Shambhala Publications.

FINAL GOODBYES TO BOULDER

I returned to Halifax after this event and, within a week or so, we heard that Rinpoche had left Seminary before it was finished and gone down to Boulder. As Rinpoche was leaving Seminary, the Loppon went up to the car and asked him, "Is there anything I should tell them?" Rinpoche replied, "You can tell them they could be grateful." Having left before the end of Seminary, he had not yet given the vajrayana transmission, so the Regent, who was still in Boulder, quickly went up to the Seminary and gave the transmission.

Rinpoche wanted to go to Halifax immediately. The old Kalapa Court that I and my family had lived in had been sold and people pleaded with him, "But there is nowhere for you to stay in Halifax." Rinpoche replied, "I will live in the Regent's house. He can move out." The Regent had acquired a very large, almost mansion-like house on one of the most up-scale streets in Halifax. The house was extensively renovated, every room being individually designed for the family member who would be occupying it, with the Regent's excellent aesthetic sense. He was quite occupied with this project during the spring, putting a tremendous amount of energy and money into it and had moved into it with his family earlier in the summer.

Now there was upheaval in Halifax. The Regent's staff had perhaps two weeks to move him and his family temporarily into the house of a student. Others had to prepare for the arrival of Rinpoche at what would now become the new Kalapa Court. Rinpoche, we heard, was very impatient while in Boulder, constantly looking at his watch and saying, "When are we going? When are we going?" He also spent those last few days driving around Boulder and visiting some of the places that had been important to him during his years in Boulder, including the various houses he had lived in, and the tree in the foothills that he had often lain under when he was ill in 1981.

"IT SEEMS TO BE HAPPENING FASTER THAN WE THOUGHT"

On September 9, Rinpoche finally flew to Halifax. A reception had been prepared for him at the house the Regent had renovated that was now the Kalapa Court. As many sangha-members as possible were crowded into the living room. A chair was placed in the center of the room for Rinpoche, opposite the entrance. He was tired and weak, and almost had to be carried in. When he sat in his familiar wingback chair he looked tiny and shrunken down. He asked Jim Sacamano to bring him the Nyo-i that he had given to Jim in Cape Breton in 1980 when appointing him Ambassador Plenipotentiary to Canada. Now he had Jim formally present it back to him, announcing, "I am here."

We went up to him as usual, in a reception line—one by one, or couple by couple—and knelt in front of him. He spoke individually with everyone, which must have been a tremendous effort in his weak state. As I knelt there, he took my hand and said, "It seems to be happening faster than we thought." I didn't realize what he meant and thought he was referring to his move to Halifax, so I chuckled and said, "Yes, we noticed, sir." To my utter chagrin, I realized just a month later that he had been referring to his own death.

Most of us, even at this point, were blind to the seriousness of his illness and to the obvious truth that he was dying. When Lady Kunchok, the Sawang's mother, came to RMDC that summer to visit Rinpoche for the first time since they parted in India, her first words were, "He's dying." But few of us were able to acknowledge this. This was in part because Rinpoche had instructed Mitchell to keep very quiet about his illness, even to the Board of Directors.

In retrospect it felt as if, in leaving Seminary early and pushing his staff to get him to Nova Scotia quickly, he was anticipating his death and was squeezing out the last ounce of his life force to make sure that he died there, in the place that was, to him, the Kingdom of Shambhala. I believe that by doing this, he made it very clear to everyone that, as he so often said, "We mean business!" If he had not died in Nova Scotia, it is quite probable that the entire project, to contribute to and nourish enlightened society in Nova Scotia, could have faded away. At that time there were at most eighty sangha-members in Nova Scotia. Within a year or two after his death several hundred had moved there from all over the United States and Canada. This growth continued for some years after that, and now the Shambhala sangha in Nova Scotia is the largest in the world.

After the reception, most of the sangha left and a small group of us remained behind with Rinpoche in the living room. There was a discussion about gardening, during which he said, emphatically, "We should be self-sufficient. We should create large produce gardens, as we will have to feed many refugees." He also remarked that "my Regent should take up gardening."

WITH THE SAWANG AND THE SAWANG'S MOTHER, LADY KUNCHOK.
Photograph by Diana Church.

The Regent was arriving from out of town that afternoon and so had not come to the reception. It was arranged that he and Rinpoche would meet in the lobby of the Nova Scotian Hotel. We all went down there and waited until the Regent arrived, just a short time later. He and Rinpoche sat next to each other, barely speaking. The Regent kept turning to his companions and talking with them, while Rinpoche sat rather stony faced. It was quite an uncomfortable meeting. A sangha family had moved out of their house so that the Regent and his family could live there until another residence was bought for him a year later. Under his leadership, we tried to do "business as usual."

THE GREAT HEART PAUSES

For the next three weeks Rinpoche was quite active—visiting a photographer to have his formal portrait taken in full military uniform; visiting the Clipper Caye restaurant, also in full dress; going to the office that had been set up for him at the new Vajradhatu headquarters; going to the airport to welcome one of his sangyums.

Also during this time, in a small private ceremony at which only Marty Janowitz and the Regent were present, he re-empowered the Regent as his successor. Marty recalls that Rinpoche drove to the house in which the Regent was staying, dressed in nothing but his Japanese *ukata* (dressing gown) in his urgency to get there, to command the Regent to come to the Court forthwith for the ceremony. Thus he made a final effort to encourage the Regent to take his seat completely and thoroughly.

At the same time, Rinpoche was warning others, particularly Lady Diana and David Rome, that they should watch out for the Regent and try to contain his "misbehavior," as Rinpoche called it. This was how Rinpoche had always related to the Regent, as to a lesser extent he did with all his close students: encouraging him, empowering him, pushing him to extend his wisdom further, and at the same time setting up boundaries in his environment through the people close to him and trusted by Rinpoche. To the end of his life, he never gave up on the

Regent, loving him as his son and at the same time trying to curb his less wholesome behavior.

On September 28, he simply stopped breathing. A few minutes later he suffered a cardiac arrest and was rushed to the hospital ICU where Mitchell, being an intensive care specialist, was allowed to take over the supervision of his treatment. The doctors and staff of the Halifax Infirmary were very cooperative and so impressed by Mitchell's competence that he was later offered a senior position there. Mitchell basically saved Rinpoche's life, at least for the time being.

I visited him in the intensive care unit and stood by his bed. The doctors had put long gloves on his hands and tied them down to the sides of the bed, because he had been trying to pull out the IV tubes. I recalled what he had said to Mitchell in the Chicago hospital at the time of His Holiness the Karmapa's final illness: "Don't let them do anything like that to me." Of course, it was unquestionably Mitchell's absolute duty, as Rinpoche's personal physician, to make sure that everything possible was done to save his life. Nevertheless, I couldn't help wondering whether Rinpoche himself felt that it was time to go. As I stood there by the bed, I pleaded with him, "Come back, Rinpoche. We love you; we need you."

Rinpoche was in an extremely critical state for a week or so. Suddenly, his condition worsened, and he had to be put on a respirator. He came very close to death on that day, and we gathered in the waiting room outside of the ICU. There was an eclipse of the sun that very afternoon, and the room began to become dim as the sunlight faded. Just after the eclipse had passed, Mitchell declared that Rinpoche was now out of danger and was recovering, and within a few days he was taken back to the Kalapa Court. At the time of Rinpoche's critical illness, several of the major tulkus, including Kalu Rinpoche, practiced "Reversing the call of the dakinis." This was the same practice which, through the Regent, Rinpoche had urgently requested Khyentse Rinpoche to do during the Mill Village retreat. Kalu Rinpoche, who was then eighty-two years old, is reported to have practiced this continuously for forty-eight hours during this period.[90]

During the period that Rinpoche was in intensive care, many of the great Kagyu Rinpoches visited him and spoke to the sangha in Halifax. In his talk to the sangha, Thrangu Rinpoche said:

> *Trungpa Rinpoche's health is not like an ordinary situation…. For someone like Rinpoche, whether he is in good health or he is in ill health, whatever situation benefits beings the most, he will take that approach…. Trungpa Rinpoche's activity in the world is as though he has been specially sent to this new world, this new continent, to start the buddhadharma…. It is very important for all of us to carry on the activities of Rinpoche, so that the dharma will progress and flourish and not diminish, not only during our lifetime, but even during the lifetime of our sons and daughters, and perhaps during the lifetime of their children. It will be a situation that we can hand down to future generations.*[91]

Rinpoche returned to the Court unable to speak. He was able to make sounds that could seem like words, with great effort on his part. But he wasn't really able to speak, to dress himself, to do his toiletry, or to eat without help. There was a nurse in attendance, as well as several kusung, twenty-four hours a day. Mitchell also tried to schedule at least one of Rinpoche's close students to be there with him each day. I went there a few times during those next six months. Once I read to him a poem in which the poet, one of his students, extolled his wondrous qualities as a guru and our terrible qualities as his students. Rinpoche nodded vigorously as I read it. He clearly understood what was going on around him—that was very obvious—but he wasn't able to communicate very well back to us. After a year or so talking very little and telling us we talked too much, he simply ceased talking at all; yet he was still very much present.

In the first couple of months after the cardiac arrest, he seemed to be improving, or at least that's what we were told. A speech therapist in the sangha visited to give him elocution lessons, which he did try to do. On one occasion, I received a phone call saying that Rinpoche was going to visit Dorje Dzong, so I dashed over there. It was a half-hour drive from where I now lived, but he was still there when I arrived, just getting ready to leave. Mitchell, who was pushing his wheelchair, stopped the chair in front of me and said, "This is Sir Jeremy, sir." Rinpoche made a huge effort to speak, but it came out as an anguished roar. Was he trying to express anger, or was this simply a greeting? He was clearly making a tremendous effort to communicate something. This was characteristic of this period: he was making tremendous efforts to regain the use of his body.

SLOWLY LEAVING US

Rinpoche's condition started to slowly deteriorate. Once during those months, I sat with him in the living room of the Court, along with his nurse. Rinpoche's eyes were open and he was looking around, and it was clear to me that he knew what was going on. I just wanted to sit there in silence, as I had done so often in his private sitting room in Kalapa Court in the years gone by, just to sit there and feel his presence. For whatever reason, however, the nurse wanted to chat with me; perhaps she thought I was uncomfortable and needed cheering up. The ache in my heart, the longing to just be with him in silence, was like the longing I had had that time I left Mill Village to go shopping instead of just staying in the house. I wanted to explain to her that I would like to be quiet with Rinpoche, and not to talk, but I just went along with the situation, not wishing to be rude to this kind nurse who was very good with Rinpoche.

On Shambhala Day 1987, we tried to have a festive lunch at the Court, as usual, but it was clear by now that Rinpoche was not recovering and that, in fact, his condition had worsened. Toward the end of March, I was down in New York giving a seminar at the New York Dharma-dhatu when we got a phone call saying that Rinpoche had started bleeding severely in the stomach, and that he had been re-admitted to the intensive care unit in the hospital. I went back to Halifax, and was fortunate to be admitted to his room without question. He was sitting up in bed with an oxygen mask on. I just stood there for a while, looking at him, and then returned home to wait.

TAKING HIS LAST BREATH

On April fourth, a very curious phenomenon happened in Halifax, a phenomenon that had never been recorded previously and was never seen again. On that day, huge ice floes, almost like miniature icebergs, came into St. Margaret's Bay and the Halifax Harbor, actually blocking the harbor to shipping. That afternoon, we received a call saying that Rinpoche was in very critical condition and that we should go to him immediately. We left Vanessa at the home of a school friend, and went to the hospital. Rinpoche had been moved out of intensive care into a private room. We stood or sat around his bed, a small quiet group including Lady Diana, the Sawang, Gesar, and the Regent. We stayed there for a long time.

We listened to his breathing: long, strong out-breaths... then a long, long gap... you could hardly see him breathing in... then another long, strong out-breath. I was reminded of the time when I sat with him at the kitchen table in Charlemont. It was the same: I could feel his out-breath, and it felt like he was completely there, mindful of his breath. We stayed by his bedside, listening to him breathing and watching the little blip on the electrocardiogram. It was so long between his breaths that we never knew whether he was going to breathe out again. He opened his eyes and looked slowly round the room, looking at everyone there one by one. It seemed as if he were seeing everyone in the room, and we spontaneously, softly, sang the Shambhala Anthem. When we had finished, he looked up to the ceiling and smiled, a gentle, peaceful smile, and closed his eyes again. There was a longer silence; there was no further out-breath.

Finally, Mitchell announced, "It's over."

And Lady Diana whispered, "He's dead."

SAMADHI

After Rinpoche ceased breathing, most of us left the hospital immediately. The Dapöns and Mitchell cared for the body according to the traditional ways. Seed syllables of the protectors of Chakrasamvara were placed on specific places on his body. The body was immediately brought to the Court, where a throne was constructed in the center of the living room. Rinpoche's body was placed on the throne in seated position, wearing robes. There were curtains drawn around; sometimes people pulled the curtains back to take a peek, to see his face. For days after, students from all over the world flocked to Halifax and sat in the living room of the Court, practicing in hour-long shifts. The windows were wide open, and it was a bitterly cold April—alternating freezing rain and snow—so it was freezing cold in the room.

Marty, who was caring for the body as the most senior kusung, reported that the chest area of the body remained quite warm—warm enough for Marty to feel his freezing cold hands warming up as he adjusted Rinpoche's robes. Several others, including Lady Diana and Mitchell, verified this. This was a sign that Rinpoche was remaining in *samadhi* (meditative absorption), his mind resting in its natural state, the wisdom of bliss-emptiness. According to the Tibetan understanding, after the outer signs of life have ceased, the consciousness goes through gradual stages of dissolving into itself. At the end of this, for all of us, there is a moment when the mind does come to rest in its own state. For ordinary people, this moment is very brief and goes unrecognized. For people who have achieved some recognition of this natural state during their lifetime, they may recognize that moment after death and rest in it for a while.

This state of samadhi continued for five days. For those five days we practiced in his presence, and we could almost imagine that he was still there. Many old friends had arrived from around the world. It felt at times almost like one of the celebrations from the old days. Lama Ganga, a Tibetan lama who had cared for His Holiness the Karmapa's body, flew from California to invite Rinpoche to leave his body, and to

finally leave his students. Lama Ganga was helpful and caring in helping to prepare Rinpoche's body after the samadhi.

After the heat had dissipated in the heart area, the body was placed
in a casket appropriate for transportation by plane and driven to the
airport. Again, all the students lined up outside the Court, under
gloomy grey skies in the bitter cold rain, and the body left. This was
perhaps the saddest day of all. Now he had finally left his body, and his
body was finally leaving Halifax, and the truth struck home, on that
dismal April morning as the hearse drove slowly away from the Court,
that we would never see him again.

At Karme Chöling, the body was preserved in the traditional way:
seated as if on a chair within the box, it was packed tightly with salts
that were changed regularly. The salts were saved and placed in small
glass vials for distribution to the sangha, to place on their home
shrines. Some people have joked, "Haven't they heard of deep-freeze?"
But the point was to carry out the final rites strictly according to tradition, as he had requested in his will. The box containing the body and
its salts was placed on a throne in the center of the shrine room at
Karme Chöling, where it remained until the time of the cremation.

KHYENTSE RINPOCHE CONDUCTS THE CREMATION

The cremation was set for seven weeks from Rinpoche's death. Also
following tradition this would take place in a *purkhang*, a large cham-
ber to contain the body, under which was a huge wood fire—which
had been constructed in a meadow up the hill behind Karme Chöling.
The first members of the family, followed by Directors and their
spouses, followed the body as it was ceremoniously carried up the hill
to the purkhang. The sun was not quite out yet—it came out later—and
it was foggy and drizzling; even the weather seemed to be joining in
our sorrow.

We were led by a bagpiper, playing a dirge composed especially
for the occasion. A series of thrones had been set up on one side of
the purkhang for Khyentse Rinpoche, who was to preside over the

THE CREMATION PROCESSION, MAY 26, 1987. *Photograph by Ray Ellis.*

cremation, and the many other Kagyu and Nyingma Rinpoches who attended. On the opposite side of the purkhang was a tent for Lady Diana and family, the Regent, the Sawang, the Directors, and other staff. Four different fire pujas were practiced, one on each side of the purkhang—we practiced Vajrayogini fire offering. The hillside was covered with over a thousand students, some of whom had never actually met Rinpoche. The fire was lit, according to tradition, by a monk who had never met him. As the fire progressed, eagles appeared in the sky and circled directly above the purkhang, and a rainbow halo appeared around the sun. The body was finally about to be burned: the body that had been the locus of his mind; the body that had been the way that we had been able to contact his mind. That dear body was finally gone.

His Holiness Khyentse Rinpoche stayed in North America for several weeks, giving most wonderful and powerful vajrayana teachings, first at Karme Chöling immediately following the cremation, then in

Boulder, and finally in Halifax. It felt very much that Khyentse Rinpoche was looking after us, caring for us like a grandfather. He told people a little later that he and Rinpoche "had a very special relationship; things that I cannot finish, he will finish, and things that he cannot finish, I will finish." He closed his last talk at Karme Chöling with these words:

> Trungpa Rinpoche was not an ordinary person. He is a being who came to this earth knowing what he was going to do, how to handle beings according to their capacity. He was born in Tibet, but he spent most of his life in the West to plant the seed of his vision to create a new society. To further this vision, Trungpa Rinpoche gave many teachings in the past, and the most precious thing is to take to heart all these teachings and put them into practice. In order to create a new society which shines forth the light of great peace, it's important that each one of us develop this vision from within. The moment we can create this among us, then it will be so easy to manifest it throughout the world.[92]

After the talk was over, we all stood to sing the Shambhala Anthem, and when we had finished, instead of getting up to leave, Khyentse just remained sitting there on his throne. We stood there looking at him, and he looked back at us, for a very long time. After some considerable while, his translator, Tulku Pema, touched Khyentse Rinpoche's arm to indicate that it was time to go, but he simply brushed Tulku Pema's hand aside and remained sitting there, simply radiating compassion.

The genuine sadness in the tent was immense, and his love for us and ours for him and for Rinpoche was palpable and unforgettable.

"JOY FOR YOU.

NONETHELESS, POWERFUL HAUNTING
CLOUD SHOULD HOVER IN YOUR HOUSEHOLD
AND ON YOUR HEAD:

THE DORJE DRADUL AS MISTY CLOUDS
OR BRILLIANT SUN.

I WILL BE WITH YOU UNTIL YOU ESTABLISH
YOUR KINGDOM."

CHÖGYAM TRUNGPA RINPOCHE,
FROM "DEATH OR LIFE"

The Joy Continues 18

 N THE DAYS following Rinpoche's death, I had a strange mixture of emotions. There was, of course, deep sorrow, knowing that I would never again see his smiling face in the physical realm—or his angry face for that matter, which would have done just as well. There was also the knowledge that I would never have a chance to fulfill all of his commands, at least in a way that he could see, on the earth. I wasn't dwelling on these things, particularly, but I just felt a tremendous sense of sadness.

At the same time, there was also a mixture of relief and extraordinary joy. It is said that when a great teacher dies, his mind is actually more accessible to students who are open. This had happened during those weeks at the 1982 Seminary, shortly after the Karmapa died. Even though I had not known the Karmapa well, only having made a connection with him during his last visit the year before, I had nevertheless felt that touch of his blessings and the connection with his mind. In this case, it was much more strong and powerful, needless to say. In some ways it felt as if the veil obscuring Rinpoche had finally dropped —the veil of his persona, of his physical appearance—and I could finally just feel his mind, directly.

I had in some ways felt this in my first interview at Tail of the Tiger in 1970; sitting in his private quarters at the Court; at Mill Village, when he was asleep; and even finally at the Court on Young Avenue, when he was not able to talk, but was very much present. These were the quiet, silent times, when it was possible to just sit there and feel his being. Now that being had expanded tremendously and was so much more available. So there was also a sense of joy, humor, bliss. I sometimes wondered if it was "all right" to feel this way—but at the same time I could see that of course it clearly was.

Then there was the sense of relief. Perhaps it was that his wrath was not going to be seen in the physical realm again—along with the sadness, of course, that the smile and the love would not be felt in that way again. Perhaps the relief also came from the feeling that now it might be possible to settle into what he had taught, and try to practice it and realize it. For all of those years, he had constantly driven us, and every few years there would be a major change of direction, which was always unexpected and disturbing to our slumber. We felt his drive, his impetus to fulfill what needed to be fulfilled in his life, to do what needed to be done.

It often felt to me as if we had to wear spiritual or psychological running shoes to keep up with him and with the changes of direction that he continually created. There was tremendous pressure, and, as I mentioned before, I think we were getting very resistant and less able to follow his lead any more. So when he left, it was as if now, at last, we could do it. He had told us many times in his life, "I have given you all you need; now just do it." But it was as if we didn't have an opportunity to do it when he was alive because he would then ask us to do something else, and something else, and something else...

WHAT OF RINPOCHE'S DEATH?

And there remained, for me, the most important question of how, or what, to think of him now? Should I think, in keeping with the common pseudo-scientific nihilist style of today, "Well, that's that, he is no more.

Oh yes, sure, he continues to 'live' in his books and videos and in our memories, but otherwise he's gone, finished!" Or should I believe, in the theistic eternalist style, that he, himself, that person that we remembered and that we knew so intimately, is somehow still around in some "heaven"— perhaps even still with a limp? Or is there another possibility. In some ways this question mirrored the very question that I had asked Rinpoche at our very first encounter: "Rinpoche, what's left?"

This question arose intensely for me out of a continuing feeling of meeting Rinpoche's mind after his death. I hesitated at first to include the following accounts of my subsequent continuing journey with Rinpoche since they may seem beyond reasonable belief to some and might perhaps be felt to discredit the whole story. With the encouragement of kind readers of the draft, I decided to include them for two reasons: first, they represent a very important part of my journey with Rinpoche and I feel a responsibility to tell the complete story; and second, I feel that there are probably many people who feel a deep living connection with Rinpoche, or other great teachers who have passed on, but are afraid to acknowledge this even to themselves due to the prevailing skepticism and nihilism of our culture.

Soon after the cremation, at the beginning of the summer, I designed and taught a new program for people who had completed the Shambhala Training Graduate Program. We decided to call this program "Warrior Assembly." It was set to happen at RMDC in early July, about five weeks after the cremation. I stayed at the Mason House, a small house at the side of the property, and the program took place in the main tent that was a fifteen-minute walk or five-minute drive away.

Every day as I sat at the window preparing a talk, I felt Rinpoche's presence so very strongly. I always used to wait for some kind of sign before going down to the tent to start a talk or a session of stroke practice; it could be something quite simple like a bird landing on the fence just outside my window. One day, as I was sitting there waiting for such a sign, the horse that normally grazed in the meadow at the end of the garden came up to the fence and stared in the window, looking directly at me with wide-open eyes. I thought "Ah, that's him." At that very moment, the horse turned around, stuck his tail over the fence and produced a huge pile of shit. I laughed aloud and thought, "That's *really* him!"

Was it just wishful thinking? Perhaps, but many such coincidences occurred to myself and others, some powerful and having a significant effect on someone's life, others simply humorous—as, for example, the time when I was walking with Pat in the terminal at Toronto Airport, on the way to Colorado for the consecration of a huge *stupa*, reliquary memorial, for Chögyam Trungpa Rinpoche, The Great Stupa of Dharmakaya. (One hundred and eight feet high, this magnificent monument has shrine rooms on three floors and is filled with beautiful frescos and two huge statues of the Buddha together with many smaller statues of gurus, deities, and protectors. It had taken eleven years and several million dollars to complete, entirely through donations and volunteer work by the sangha.) As we walked along a corridor, a little lost and wondering which way to go for our connecting flight, we suddenly came upon an open door, with a chair blocking the corridor, on which was perched a huge sign with an arrow pointing through the door and the words "CTR this way." Could all these small and larger incidents be just wishful thinking, I wondered? They were coincidences, of course, but were they nothing more than *mere* coincidence, or were they somehow auspicious or meaningful?

OTHERS BEGIN TO HEAR FROM THE RIGDEN DRALAS

There were other events that impressed me so deeply that I had to contemplate very seriously about how to think of Rinpoche now. In order to relate these, we first need to go back to 1986.

In March of that year we had heard that Paul Jones (a pseudonym), who was a longtime student of Rinpoche and was fully trained in the vision and teachings of Shambhala, had been writing visionary "messages" which he felt were coming from the Shambhala dralas. When Rinpoche was asked about this he said that they should be treated as ordinary, that is without seeking confirmation or having high expectations about them. Rinpoche added that others would also experience this.

In April of that year, Paul and his wife came to Halifax and stayed at the Kalapa Court, where we were still in residence. Paul told us that he had received a message saying that we should look for a certain crystal rock under a tree, near the "split." He figured out that the place to look for this might be Cape Split, some three hours' drive from Halifax. So he invited us and some other friends, with Vanessa and their young son, to take a trip to look for the rock on a cold and slightly rainy afternoon.

After searching for an hour in the cold drizzle we were lost, somewhat frustrated, and losing heart in the adventure, and the children were starting to complain loudly, when we came to a meeting of several paths. Then Paul recalled that the message had said the children would show the way. We asked Vanessa and her friend which way to go, telling them to choose whatever direction they liked, and they went running off down one of the paths. At that moment the sun came out, and very shortly after that we arrived at the edge of the cliff. Looking around the bay, to our left we saw a huge rock, about fifty feet high, off the end of the cliff and standing out from the water. It was clear that a piece of the cliff had fallen away, leaving this massive piece of cliff standing alone—where stones and pine debris fall into a heap, as the message had said. We were to look for a crystal rock under a tree: there was a lone tree standing on top of the cliff close to the rock and when we went close up to examine the rock, there were streaks of mica (not technically a "crystal," but nonetheless sparkling and crystal-like) running through it.

It seemed that we had found the rock, and a truly magnificent and unusual rock it was. Rinpoche had spoken of certain geographical landmarks, as well as our pins and uniforms, as being potential "landing pads" for the dralas, rather as certain special trees or rock formations are considered dwelling places of the kami by the Japanese. It seemed that the rock was to fulfill a function such as this. And we had found it only when trusting in the invitation of the dralas and following their leads in the message.

In July of the same year, 1986, while doing a retreat at Gampo Abbey, to practice the Vajrayogini sadhana, Karen also began to hear unsolicited messages, signed by the Rigdens. When I went up to the Abbey to join Karen she showed me the messages. I did not really have a strong opinion about them, being at that time still cautious about "psychic phenomena," as I had been about the "wine board" at Bedford Springs four years previously. So, while I did not scoff at the messages, I really didn't know how to take them. However, I had to admit that they were written in a beautiful verse form, quite unlike anything I ever seen Karen write, with humor and with wonderful images.

For a few years, Karen continued to write these "messages from the Rigdens" privately, mentioning it to no one, not even myself. She later described this as a training process. She herself felt a lot of confusion and doubt about whether these messages came merely from her own wishful thinking. But gradually as she went on with the training she began to feel some confidence that she could distinguish between those that were merely ego-based and those that came from a bigger mind. And so too, nearly three years later, after Rinpoche's death and during the time of tremendous turmoil around the behavior of the Regent, Karen began to receive messages that contained advice on how the Board of Directors should relate with the Regent. The advice seemed to be very much in keeping with what Rinpoche might have advised— and if we had followed this advice it is possible that it could have helped us to avoid a disastrous schism.

MESSAGES FROM "CT"

These messages were signed "Chakrasamvara Tooth." All the Directors had been given one of Rinpoche's "tooth relics," relics of his teeth found in the ashes after the cremation, and I had placed mine on our home shrine in a small reliquary. We speculated, then, whether "Chakrasmvara's Tooth" might refer to Rinpoche. Soon after that Karen's messages began to be signed "CT," which was how Rinpoche had signed personal notes and postcards to his friends. A few years later, as I was finally beginning to write *Sacred World*, the student's view of the Shambhala teachings, I asked Karen if she would ask CT for help on the project. Thus began a magical summer.

Each evening, I would ask a question related to the next topic of the book, and Karen (CT?) would write an answer, again in poetic form that I had never before (nor have since) seen from Karen. The next morning I would write the next chapter of the book, incorporating into the text what Karen written. It was inspiring and tremendously helpful to me in what felt like a daunting task. The writing of CT gave practical exercises for the reader on experiencing the cocoon, working with fear, mindfulness in action, first thought and letting go; there were further instructions on dralas and exercises to connect with the elemental dralas of earth, water, fire, and air; and a verse about the practice of raising windhorse.

During this period, CT instructed Karen to tell a few people about these events and invite them to form a group to work together under his guidance. Some, but not all, who were invited decided to join in. The group lasted about a year, and one of the main things that CT tried to impress on us during this time was that we could all hear him as much as Karen could. When Karen once asked him, "Why me?" his response was, "Because you are willing to listen." When we asked her *how* she listened, she told us, "By raising windhorse and tuning in, like tuning in to a radio station."

CT tried in several ways to help others in the group to "hear" him. In particular, he instructed us to experiment with the "wine board." We did this in pairs, and the result of this experiment was that when some, but not all, of us paired with Karen, the wine glass would clearly spell out various comments or instructions. In this intentional group situation a very definite practice environment was created which seemed to offer an important protection against connecting with other, unwanted and possibly malicious, entities, as Rinpoche had warned in regard to the Ouija board.

This process of relating with CT in a similar way started again in 1998, after Karen and I were divorced. We had been together for twenty-three years by then, throughout the unceasing turmoil of being in Rinpoche's world, the joy of bringing up our daughter Vanessa, and the chaos that happened after his death. During this time, we helped each other on the path—a role that is, I believe, the most important one for partners in the dharma. When we finally parted, in 1998, it was in the mutual understanding that our karma together as a married couple had run its course. This seemed to be the way that Rinpoche advised couples who felt stuck and wanted to separate—sometimes he would suggest that they stay together and at other times that it seemed fine to separate. The difference seemed to lie in whether there was still some karma that needed to be worked out between them, some mutual kleshas that still needed to be seen through and dissolved.

The experience with CT started again with Pat whose story of first meeting Rinpoche I quote in chapter 10. I had known Pat at a distance since she worked at Naropa Institute back in 1979. Our families had moved together to Nova Scotia in 1984, but she had moved to Ojai, California, in 1989 with the Regent. In the 1990s, she was living in Washington DC, where she became the Director of the Shambhala Training program and invited me there to teach several times. In December of 1998, she invited me for a teaching visit during which we enjoyed each other's company in a simple friendly way. Shortly after my visit, Pat wrote to tell me of a series of striking dreams that she had had, morning and evening, for several days in a row. Pat describes the dreams thus:

> In each dream, Rinpoche and I were together, with Jeremy nearby, in an atmosphere of pure love. Finally, on the third day, I "got it"— it was so clear that I sat straight up in bed. It was as if the dreams were each removing a veil, or barrier, that was obstructing my seeing Jeremy clearly, and seeing what we were to each other. It was as if I had finally "found" him.

Reading Pat's letter, something woke up in me as well. It was as if the dreams were telling us that we could find in each other a profound love that neither of us had before experienced in a partner. And this is how it has been.

I visited Washington again in April of 1999 when we were able to spend several days together. On the last night of my visit, I told Pat about listening for CT in the way the group had been instructed many years previously. She agreed to try it with me and we did manage to communicate quite clearly with CT. I left Canada six weeks later to take up an appointment as *acharya* (senior teacher) in residence at Dechen Chöling, the European practice center in France. Pat visited me in Dechen Chöling several times over the next months, and I visited Washington, and we again practiced communicating with CT on many evenings during these visits. We decided to marry the following spring, with the encouragement and blessings of CT, and Pat joined me in France. We have continued this practice over the years and through it we have received profound and pragmatic guidance for our spiritual path, our relationship, and our actions in the world— guidance that we simply could not have given to ourselves, at least in our mundane state of mind.

The guidance we received in this way has been sometimes overflowing with love and encouragement and sometimes painfully scathing, at times pragmatic and at other times far beyond ordinary logic yet profoundly meaningful—all characteristics that we knew so well in Rinpoche. At first we felt the atmosphere and sense of Rinpoche's palpable presence in the practice sessions to be very separate from our experience of daily life—more like something weird but helpful. And for a long time there was certainly doubt, especially on my part, about how to take the whole experience. Gradually, however, the sense of Rinpoche's presence in the practice became more and more blended and integrated with our every moment. As this happened we began to have a genuine sense of understanding the inseparability of guru and the phenomenal world, and thus have been led to a deeper understanding of the inseparability of the guru and one's own mind.

HOW ARE WE TO UNDERSTAND THESE EXPERIENCES?

What, then, are we to make of these events? Were they simply wish-fulfilling inventions of our own minds, products of our grief and longing to communicate with him again? If they were, they certainly offered a deeper wisdom than any we could have come up with from our mundane minds, and they were in a language and with a humor more akin to that of Rinpoche than of Karen, myself, Pat, or others.

Certainly, however, the guidance and instructions should not be taken as coming from a disembodied version of that same eleventh Trungpa Rinpoche, the plump little man with a limp and a wry smile, whom we had known and loved so well on earth. That would be precisely the kind of naïve theism and spiritual materialism that Rinpoche so decried. But still, the question remained: what to make of them?

On the one hand, of course, according to Western psychiatry, "hearing voices" is regarded as a symptom of schizophrenia. On the other hand, such phenomena are well-known in virtually all societies, including Tibet, that are not based on the philosophy of scientific materialism. We knew that Rinpoche had communicated with the Rigdens and strongly urged us to do so as well.

For example, one of his sangyums told us of a time when Rinpoche said to her, "I am going to visit the Rigdens tonight, and you should come too." When she asked how to get there, he replied, "Just project your mind." She said that she had tried to do this, but just fell asleep. When they awoke the following morning, Rinpoche said, "Where were you? They were all waiting for you to come and be introduced." And, at the end of his farewell address for the Seminary, in 1984, after expressing his tremendous appreciation to his gathered vajrayana students, Rinpoche said, "I will be with you all the time, to oversee your practice. And the lineage will be with you to protect you. Try to come and visit us, if you can, in either the ethereal level or the physical level. I love you all."

Rinpoche once told Sam Bercholz, in a conversation about the Rigdens instigated by Rinpoche himself, that it was very important to know that the relationship the Rigdens have with individuals is real and personal; it is as if you can feel the Rigdens' breath at your neck. According to Sam, Rinpoche strongly insisted that it was not just he who could contact the Rigdens, but that they were accessible to anyone who was moved to do so. And too, he had said that Paul's receiving of messages would be experienced by others. So there were such clues that these things should not be simply dismissed.

On the ultimate level—the level of nonduality, of unconditioned mind free from concept—there is no separate guru; the guru's mind and one's own mind are inseparable, as the tradition emphasizes again and again. And one has to begin from that point of view: whatever, or whoever, this "CT" is, who or which is producing these messages, at that level it is not ultimately separate from one's own mind, nor the same as one's own mind. However, we are in the world that, relatively speaking, is a world of duality. Mahayana / vajrayana Buddhists as well as Shambhala warriors acknowledge duality, work with duality. While at the ultimate, nondual level there is no one or many, same or different, at the relative level of duality there *are* seemingly separate beings: all of us believe ourselves to be separate from each other, and there is the guru who appears to be separate from myself.

Perhaps, then, it is an open question. Bearing in mind that there will always be a mix of egoistic, wishful thinking, do the messages come entirely from the receiver's ordinary, small mind? From some aspect of the guru's mind? From the space of wisdom in which the two are not separate? From some aspect of Rinpoche's being, still resting in the inner realm of the dralas and not yet completely dissolved back into the dharmakaya? Rinpoche had encouraged us, exhorted us, to "meet these ladies and gentlemen of the drala principle." And Rinpoche was recognized as *kami* or, in Shambhala terms, drala by the Zen master, Eido Shimano Roshi, at the time of Rinpoche's cremation. The story, as David Schneider tells it is this:

Eido Roshi came to Karme Chöling after Rinpoche's death in 1987, where Trungpa Rinpoche was to be cremated. Unable to stay for the ceremony because of prior commitments, Roshi meditated with

Rinpoche's body, met with his wife and eldest son (the present Sakyong Mipham Rinpoche), and performed private rituals. He also left as a gift a box of priceless incense that was subsequently used at the cremation. Roshi felt so touched at Karme Chöling that he stayed until the last minute before his flight, soaking up the atmosphere of devotion, and of the mindful, cheerful, indefatigable preparation that had been going on for weeks. As his car finally raced at illegal speeds toward the airport, he proclaimed to his attendant over and again that he'd at last seen the greatness of Trungpa Rinpoche; he'd seen Rinpoche's greatness in the environment of Karme Chöling and in the comportment of his students. Roshi announced to his stressed driver that Trungpa Rinpoche is in fact kami.[93]

While being careful not to turn this into a personality cult and start to worship a dead person, could we say that an aspect of Rinpoche's presence now abides in some fashion as a transcendent drala—our primary ancestral drala—just as King Gesar does? We are left with questions, and with some wise advice and pragmatically helpful instructions.

Others, too, have experienced the presence and availability of Rinpoche's mind (even if they've never met him), each in their own unique way, just as Rinpoche had predicted they would in response to questions about Paul's original messages. I should emphasize that "hearing" Rinpoche in the way we and others have done is, I believe, not necessarily a sign of any significant practice accomplishment and, likewise, *not* hearing him in this way is not a sign of any *lack* of accomplishment. And it is certainly not the only way of communicating with that mind. Rinpoche often said, "Practice is the only way you can know my heart." And in at least one situation, while celebrating a feast practice with a group of Vajrayogini practitioners, he commented, "Sometimes when you have doubt, you might want to have a private word with me. But you are having a private word already, so probably you don't need too many private words." Many practitioners do feel Rinpoche's presence during practice sessions and also that they can communicate with him then. While we must always be wary of ego's wishful thinking, I believe that is a correct view.

I believe that these kinds of experience are much more ordinary than we are willing to accept in our modern nihilistic society, and my intention in writing about them is to raise the possibility that there may well be much more to death, life, and the cosmos than is given to us in our narrow modern education. When I have talked about dralas in public or restricted programs, there has often been at least one person (usually a woman) who has come up to me afterward saying, "Thank you so much for talking about these things. I used to experience them as a child but I was told not to be stupid." The definition of what is "normal" in Western culture may well be one of the narrowest such definitions of all times and places—perhaps that accounts for the vast numbers of people locked up either in mental asylums or prisons, or wandering the streets homeless and jobless.

Many who have these kinds of experiences with Rinpoche or with other gurus may be afraid to acknowledge the experiences. This fear is likely a direct result of the persecution by the medieval Christians of "heretics"—people who claimed to have contact with divine energies outside of the Church (mostly women healers who were burned in the tens of thousands)—and the scourge of scientific materialism and nihilism that took over from Christianity and dominates our society today. I feel that these people who feel they are communicating with the guru, either verbally or in other images, should be encouraged to trust their hearts in this regard, and I hope my stories will help them do that. Trusting such blessing energy is in accord with what I have heard from other great Tibetan teachers.

Such experiences are commonplace and accepted in most societies not dominated by scientific materialism, including Japan (a generation ago) and Tibet.[94] Certainly in those societies such communications are made in the proper environment and with the appropriate ritual, and people with that talent are trained to do so. So in those situations there is little risk of the possibility of contacting negative forces. This can be an issue in a culture where there is little open discussion and study of these experiences, especially if people merely dabble in such things without properly understanding what they are doing, and why they are doing it. As I mentioned in relation to Karen's experience at Bedford Springs in 1982, Rinpoche generally discouraged such dabbling.

It seems that Rinpoche's death left not an answer, then, but a continuing opportunity to contemplate these things deeply. The teachings provide us with a clear mirror in which to see, to whatever depths we are capable, our own individual and societal conditioning that are obscurations to our wisdom. After all, it is said that the awake state of mind is always already there—all we have to do is to remove the obscurations that prevent us from realizing it. And so I report these experiences in the hope that they can awaken further questioning regarding the nature of the mundane reality in which we normally believe ourselves to exist.

DOES SCIENCE HAVE ANYTHING TO SAY
ABOUT CONTINUITY OF MIND AFTER DEATH?

All of us are deeply influenced by scientific materialism, in spite of our apparent rejection of it. Feeling Rinpoche's mind to be so present and communicable after his death, I realized that as a trained scientist I needed to try to understand the possibility of continuity after physical death in Western terms, that I had to try to put this together with my scientific background. I examined a considerable amount of Western research concerning continuity of some kind of awareness after physical death, and eventually I came to the conclusion that the more rational and plausible assumption was that indeed there is *some* kind of continuity.[95] Still, I wondered, "Hasn't science *proved* that there is no continuity of anything at all after death?" And yet, upon examination, the answer to this question must certainly be that science has nothing to say about this. Scientists actually don't have evidence that there is not continuity, or that there are not other realms of being—but nonetheless scientists simply deny the evidence that there might be, basically as an article of faith—because such evidence does not fit into the materialistic philosophy at the basis of the modern scientific world-view. Most mainstream scientists cling tenaciously to the view that mind is nothing other than the workings of the brain.

There is continually growing evidence in support of phenomena such as pre-cognition, distance viewing, healing by group intention, and psychokinesis, all of which depend on a view of mind that is not entirely localized in the brain. And some of this evidence is gathered in experimental situations that are well-controlled by all normal scientific criteria. The best account of these phenomena yet available is *Extraordinary Knowing*[96] by Elizabeth Lloyd Mayer.

Elizabeth Mayer was a psychoanalyst who set out on a fifteen-year quest to understand these experiences when her daughter's antique wooden harp was recovered with the help of a dowser, two months after the police had given up and all other possibilities had come to naught. The great value of Ms. Mayer's work is that, all through her pursuit, she is respectful of both the skeptical view and the view of those who do have such experiences or who conduct genuine well-controlled scientific experiments in the phenomena. As a psychoanalyst she inquires into the widespread fear in the conventional scientific community (as well as the general culture) of accepting the data even when it is so strong. She develops a view of two kinds of knowing—intuitive knowing, or direct perception, and the rational knowing of logic—and discusses the conflict we all feel between these two and how we might resolve it. This seems to pinpoint for me the conflict I felt all the way through my journey with Rinpoche, including this phase of receiving "messages," namely the conflict between the rationality of the brain and the direct perception of the heart.

We must certainly take into account what science has definitely proven to be true, or not to be true; however, as the Dalai Lama so succinctly put it, "A clear distinction should be made between what is *not found* by science and what is found to be *non-existent* by science. What science finds to be non-existent we must accept as non-existent, but what science merely does not find is a completely different matter."[97] Conventional scientists have found the fundamental nature of mind neither in the brain, as they have so long sought and hoped for, nor in all of phenomena, nor in space, either. They have, as yet, little helpful to say on the matter.[98]

A MIDDLE WAY

If there is a middle way, even in regard to death, what might it be? To try to understand this, let us look at some ideas that Rinpoche himself conveyed to us about death. First, and in a sense foremost for all of us, is the fact that we are continually dying at every moment. As we saw in the discussion of the skandhas, our personality, our sense of *me*, as well as the world of appearances created by and for this *me*, is born and dies every fraction of a second. When we are afraid of death, or sorrowful about death, what is it that we fear or grieve for? Is it not largely our personality—*me*, my relationships, my life—that we fear to lose? From this point of view, then, death is happening all the time.

As Rinpoche taught, following the Buddha himself, death is in life, and whatever is born must die; impermanence is the nature of all created things. We know superficially, conceptually, that every one of us, including *me*, will die. But, at a deeper level, I don't believe it of *my* self. The only epitaph on French painter Marcel Duchamp's gravestone is: "It always happens to others." And *that* is what we believe deeply, and what is the basis of almost all our actions… that I, the precious *me myself*, will last forever. Yet, the Buddha said, in the *Sutra of Buddha Teaching the Seven Daughters,* "If one knows that what is born will end in death, then there will be love."[99] The delusion of permanence—believing that we and others will go on forever, so that there is always time later for communication and forgiveness—hardens our heart and encourages selfishness, while the continual remembering of impermanence brings a sense of sadness, tenderness, and love. And Gurdjieff too, when asked if there is any hope for humanity, gripped in the insanity of wars and mutual destruction, commented that only one thing could now save mankind from the madness out of which we destroy each other and our world. The only thing that could save us from this sleep is if a new organ could be planted in each of us that would cause each one of us, always and everywhere, to remember the certainty of our own death.

With this as the basis of our understanding, Rinpoche also gave clues that, in another sense also, death is no different from life. He was no more a nihilist than he was an eternalist, and clearly it was not his view that everything ends at death. What happens to us after death, he taught, is a continuation in a different form of the habitual patterns of our life. Death is happening at every moment, thereby bringing continual discontinuity to our lives. The big Death is simply another instance of this... the "great discontinuity," or "the continuity of discontinuity," as Rinpoche himself called it.

He had said to me, as the plane landed in Denver back in 1974, "If we crash, I'll see you in the bardo"; and in response to my question of how I would find him he had said "Don't worry, I'll find you." I now believe that he meant this actually, not only for myself but for all his students who have sincere and deep devotion to him, whether they met him in his body or not; he can be there, if we remember him, to guide us through the journey of mind through the bardo. Likewise, in his final few years he had started the strange practice of singing the Shambhala Anthem in a high screeching falsetto, usually accompanied by one or two ladies. It was both weird, hilarious, and somehow moving to see his enjoyment. When asked on one occasion why he did it, he replied, "So that my students can find me in the bardo."

THE JOY CONTINUES

In 1982, Rinpoche had given a public talk on "Creating an Enlightened Society," which took place in front of hundreds of people in a grand old church in Boston.[100] During the question-and-answer period, this exchange occurred between Rinpoche and a newcomer:

Questioner: Is there a way to understand better what it means to love someone and have that person die and to know that a lot of

"THE JOY, WHICH IS A SMILE, ALWAYS HAPPENS."
Photograph by Susanna Janowitz.

people are going to die throughout one's life? Is there a way to understand that?

R: Well, I think the basic point here is that death means another sense of a living situation. It's kind of life in a different planet, a different realization. Reality of death shouldn't be cultivated, and the realities of life shouldn't be cultivated… saying that once your life is out then you are off altogether. So one should maintain some sense of loyalty in a situation of death. I think some sense of joy is always…. Joy doesn't depend on life or death… never… never… never. Joy is always joy. Joy doesn't depend on a smile alone. Joy depends on the brilliantness of light [luminosity], always, whether you live or die. So I think you could let people who are dying [know that] that kind of joy of living brilliantness, which is a smile… always happens. And that brings a sense of cheerfulness. In the Shambhalian language we talk about seeing the Great Eastern Sun eternally…. So joy always comes.

Q: So are you saying that joy remains regardless of the fact that there is death.

R: That's right, not joy of this and that. But just purely joy without the "of." Just joy. Joy and space, as Great Eastern Sun shines.

In speaking of the continuity as a "kind of life in a different planet," Rinpoche is, perhaps, referring to the view that the karmic patterns, which we have created through our ego-centered actions in this life, do continue; that is, our actions in this life in some way sow seeds in the cosmic realm which come to fruition in future lives. Cause and effect go on. And in speaking of the joy that remains, "which is a smile," he seems to be once again referring to that luminosity and humor which has been one of the themes of this story.

Rinpoche wrote in his will, "I take my joy along with me," telling us, in other words, that he too would continue with joy. He also gave us many clues regarding the living continuity of our connection with him, beyond merely dwelling on memory alone. For example, at the 1976 Seminary, this exchange occurred between him and a vajrayana student:

Q: What happens if the guru dies before the students finish [the path]?

R: Well, the students should continue. There is no choice. When your schoolmaster dies, you don't therefore just run around the world…. You go back to school.

Q: Oh, so you wouldn't work with another teacher?

R: Not necessarily. There is also glowing warmth somewhere in the neighborhood.[101]

In the Farewell Address at the end of the 1979 Seminary, he said about his own long-deceased guru, Jamgön Kongtrül:

I am planning to let his Holiness Karmapa know what we are doing, so that his life will be prolonged. I am planning to tell Khyentse Rinpoche too, as well as my teacher, Jamgön Kongtrül, who is always here—and I am sure he will be very pleased. My only regret is that I wish he could be here in his physical body so that I could introduce all of you to him. That has somewhat taken place, but somewhat it is uncertain.[102]

At the inner level, Rinpoche emphasized again and again that the dralas exist as much as we do. He said, as I quoted previously, "Why on earth do you have to create a barrier to exclude the dralas from your life? They are longing to meet you." Rinpoche concluded the draft of his will, written during his Mill Village retreat: *Altogether we are happy to die. We take our joy along with us. It is unusually romantic to die.*

Born a monk
Died a king—
Such thunderstorm does not stop.
We will be haunting you along with the dralas.
Jolly good luck![103]

And another poem, "Death or Life," written in July 1985, expresses a similar commitment:

Death or life:
I still grind the sun and moon.
Whether your kingdom is established or not,
I will be the ghost that will manifest Tiger and Garuda
Whether it is a joke or serious business
I will hang around as a ghost or anger
Until you succeed in accomplishing the Kingdom of Shambhala.
Joy for you.
Nonetheless, powerful haunting cloud should hover in your
    household and on your head:
The Dorje Dradul as misty clouds or brilliant sun.
I will be with you until you establish your kingdom.[104]

It seems, then, that he left many clues that he believed he would continue to be present for us, after his physical death, "along with the dralas." He spoke of King Gesar, the progenitor of the Mukpo clan and king of medieval Tibet who unified warring tribes and brought peace throughout Tibet, as an "ancestral drala." And Rinpoche implied that a human being can become a drala when he wrote:

> *Finally, the wisdom of the ultimate and inner drala can be trans-*
> *mitted to a living human being. In other words, by realizing*
> *completely the cosmic mirror principle of unconditionality and*
> *by invoking that principle utterly in the brilliant perception of*
> *reality, a human being can become a living drala—living magic.*
> *That is how one joins the lineage of Shambhala warriors and*
> *becomes a master warrior—not just by invoking but by*
> embodying *drala.*[105]

CHANGE CONTINUES

As we contemplate these things, it may begin to seem clear that Rinpoche was letting us know that he would, indeed, somehow "hang around" as the closest ancestral drala of the Shambhala lineage, and the main link with the drala realm for anyone who cared to open to that lineage.

Rinpoche's death, then, seems far from the end of the voyage, either for those who knew him in his dear, lame body, or for those who did not have that fortune, good or bad. Rather, it looks more like an invitation to a fresh direction, as he so often invited us in his life on earth. The sense that the mind of Rinpoche is in some way still available to those who are open to it is very strong. Many people who never met Rinpoche have been brought to the dharma through vivid dreams of him, or through feeling a deep and immediate connection with him on reading his books, and this has continued after his death. Rinpoche's presence is felt, especially, in Shambhala Centers in which the environment is so much a reflection of his mind. He put tremendous energy and care into creating environments during his life, environments that are created by an awake mind and are able to transmit that wakefulness to present and future generations.

The tremendous force of his seventeen-year presence in the West continues, perhaps even more strongly, as the years go by. Seeds that he sowed are still sprouting and growing; some, such as Naropa University, are shining in the full bloom of youth; others are kept alive, but barely, by their stalwart guardians, such as the Mudra Theater group, the Upaya Council for dispute mediation, the Ashoka Credit Union, conceived to be eventually an independent banking system, and many other projects which I have not had the space to mention.

Thirty years after Rinpoche's first proclamation of the vision of Shambhala, it is most extraordinary to realize how much has been done in Nova Scotia to join the vision of Shambhala with the goodness of the local culture. Many Shambhalians, local Nova Scotians as well as many "from away," have established families in Nova Scotia, set up businesses, consulting services, and organic farms, founded a Shambhala-based school, organized environmental agencies, and generally entered into the life, culture, and business of the province. The Shambhala Buddhists are well known in the province and there is a great deal of mutual respect and interchange between the two cultures to the benefit of both. In 1998, the Premier of Nova Scotia was invited to speak at the annual meeting of the Board of Directors of Shambhala. He was unable to attend as a Conference of Canadian Premiers had been scheduled at the same time. However the letter he sent to the Chair of the Board included the following paragraph:

> I want to express my appreciation for the contribution the Shambhala/Buddhist community has made to Nova Scotia. The community has brought much to the province over the past decade. Nova Scotians appreciate both the innovative contributions of many individuals in the fields of health, education, the arts, business, and the social services, as well as the confidence the Shambhala group displays in Nova Scotia as a place where a dynamic future founded on basic human goodness can be created.[106]

SOME SEEDS HAVE BEGUN TO BLOSSOM

It took many years for the seeds that Rinpoche had sown in us to blossom, or at least to show tender shoots in myself and others. Yet, to try to put into words the outcome of this voyage of practice and devotion is like trying to see a comet in the night sky. I recall one occasion when a famous comet had been around for a few days and my father came to me excitedly one evening saying, "Let's go and see the comet." We drove out to a hill and looked up—the comet was supposed to be near Cassiopeia—but we found that the only way we could see it was to not look directly at it. Try to grasp one's experience in words and it slips away, try to say what one has discovered and one wonders…

And the idea of getting something out of the practice of meditation is not the point, of course, as Rinpoche emphasized over and over again. It comes back to hopelessness, not in the sense of depression or despair, but in the sense of genuinely giving up the hope of getting anything out of meditation or out of anything else. The point is that we already have all we need—and I believe I am beginning to realize this at last. And so, as the years have gone by, I have begun to give up hope—at least a little. The hard shell of arrogantly feeling I am or should be, or should at least pretend to be, someone special has begun to drop away (if my friends would permit me to say so!) and I can, quite joyfully, feel a little more humble. I know, more genuinely now, that I am *really* just a beginner. But when you enjoy the path, as the Dalai Lama says, "It's good to know you are just beginning, because then you have a lot more of the path to enjoy!"

Perhaps this conclusion of the quote from Lodro Sangmo (who I quoted on Rinpoche's goal for more male/female balance on the Board, in chapter 10) can give some idea of the kind of change that came about in myself, as well as in many others:

> *My hope for anyone who does not have the experience of being seen completely, heard completely, and loved completely, is that you have that even for a moment in this lifetime. For if you do, you will understand better how deep this need is in us. Is it the powerful brilliance of our own nature longing to break out? You will understand better the heart-bursting appreciation many of us still feel for this long-dead Tibetan with the warm smile. And the quite remarkable transformation of even the once-stuffy, always brilliant Jeremy, that I have witnessed, would make sense to you. Somehow being on this path for all these years, and the utter love Jeremy feels for his teacher, has softened his edges, taken the prickles off the rose, so he has not become different but who he always was inside—now visible and out in the open for all of us to enjoy.*

I too saw such softening and opening among many of my friends and colleagues; and, as well, I saw a growing strength and joy. I have seen many of Rinpoche's students change in this way almost miraculously. Yet, as Lodro Sangmo says, they are not different from who they always were. It is as if at last we are able simply to *be* who we always were, without constantly wanting to be something else—better or greater or whatever it may be.

There have been fellow students who for many years I could barely stand to be with for ten minutes. Even though I knew they were good people and struggling on the path just as I was, their rough edges, whether of angry self-righteousness or seductive "come-hither," were just too unpleasant to be around, at least in my perception. Then, years later, suddenly I would see them again—just the same people, yet those same characteristics that had seemed so unpleasant to me had subtly changed, as no doubt had I. The inner core of "look at me" seemed to have dissolved a little and there was genuine communication and even affection between us. As dear friend Jerry Grannelli once said at a recent occasion when many of us were together again for the first time in many many years, "The definition of Buddhist Alzheimer's is that you can't remember why you hated someone!"

Through the voyage of being with Rinpoche and following the path of practice and understanding he laid out, I have been shown a previously unrecognized capacity for love and friendliness toward both myself and others. Along with this is the power of windhorse—to be able to rouse a sense of cheerfulness, presence, and humor whenever I begin to feel myself slipping and sliding once more into that black hole. Raising my own life energy of windhorse enables me to feel less separate from the energy and vividness of the world around me, and this in turn brings appreciation and the aspiration to make whatever small effort I can to help others. To gradually learn to appreciate and feel the reality of dralas—the personal drala of windhorse, the dralas of the elemental and subtle energies of the world, and potency and humor of the ancestral dralas of Shambhala—has been a continuous adventure.

And, as perhaps the source of all of this, I was gradually able to overcome the nihilism of my scientific upbringing. I learned to trust, at a level far deeper than mere conceptual understanding, that the cosmos is so much vaster, richer, and more multilayered than is dreamed of in the minds of materialists and so-called "realists." I have seen through the mistaken philosophy—though truly *religion* might be a better term—of scientific materialism and the deep conditioning that I, along with all others brought up in the modern educational system, were subjected to as children when we were too young to question. This has brought the possibility of opening, however briefly, to luminosity beyond thought; sensing/feeling, as if through a glass darkly, the light that is neither inner nor outer but is the natural radiance of all that appears.

These gentle, but vivid hints of "what is left" perhaps are made possible also from the intense contemplation during all those years of what I gradually came to see as the essential message of both the Buddhist and Shambhala teachings: that in our normal ways of living there is a disparity between appearance and reality; and it is this that brings our deep anxiety and fear. Through practice and study, appearance and reality can gradually be brought together, and when they coincide, even for a moment, *that* is the realization of emptiness and joy. As it is said of the great bodhisattvas, in the *Heart Sutra*, "Since there is no obscuration of mind, there is no fear. They transcend falsity and attain complete nirvana [realization of emptiness/luminosity]."

In this contemplation, the question then becomes: what are appearances and what is reality? What is the process of perception that gives rise to appearances, and what is the reality from which those appearances arise? And here we are back to the old issue of the view of perception in Buddhism and cognitive science, which I have already discussed. Over the years, I contemplated these things, especially the extraordinary agreement between Buddhism and cognitive science that what we think we are experiencing as an outside "real" world is in fact 99.99% the creation of our brain/heart/mind. And at the same time I was examining directly the nature of perception through the meditative practices that Rinpoche had given us. Then gradually I began to feel at a deeper level than mere thought that there truly may be nothing substantial *behind* the appearances. Touching this discovery brings a sense of relief and freshness, and the ironical humor that was Rinpoche's hallmark until his last breath. At those moments the world really does appear like a mad dream, yet that dream-like appearance seems closer to the truth of how things are than when I take my world to be real.

In the end, the sitting practice of mindfulness and awareness seems to be the foundation of all of this—simply sitting, letting go. Of what? Of everything. The joy of sitting practice, which I felt at the very beginning of my voyage, has been the thread (sometimes a very thin thread) through all of this. Even now, it is far easier said than done. Nevertheless, by just sitting without expectation, the natural stability and clarity of my mind gradually strengthens, little by little. Then I am able to turn that mind upon itself and inquire, "Who? What? Where is that mind?" Not finding anything brings further giving up and a little bit of relaxation in genuineness. With this comes a small further step in understanding the truths of basic goodness, the cocoon by which I cover that, and the way out of the cocoon to realize that basic goodness, our inherent nature of wisdom.

It can be tremendously inspiring and uplifting to look back over our lives and to realize that we have, after all, gained some understanding of these precious and noble truths. And the most important thing seems to be to try to remember to bring that stable, clear, and inquiring mind into daily activity, at the same time as being in the activity— to continue that openness expressed in my very first question, "What?" The most important practice of all seems to be to remember, remember, remember... at each moment of the day.

My greatest longing is that I might be able to pass on to others even a small spark of the love and insight that I received through the years with Rinpoche. The vision of an enlightened society, putting my energy toward helping the world in whatever small way I can, is what makes it all worthwhile. It is important to try to help alleviate the tremendous physical and psychological suffering in our world. But, sadly, much of this work is reactive—putting patches, absolutely necessary patches, no doubt—on the situation while not fundamentally changing anything.

I believe that Rinpoche's primary teaching was that the only way to genuinely help the world is to help others to see the cause of that suffering—belief in personal or national ego—and the possibility of being liberated from that suffering through realization of egolessness, basic goodness. As James George writes in his book, *Asking for the*

Photograph by Bob Morehouse.

Earth,[107] "To solve the ecological crisis, we must resolve the spiritual crisis too; and I think there can be no doubt that it is the spiritual crisis that will have to be solved first, for only when we have begun the inner transformation toward which the spiritual crisis is leading us will we be able to change our outer behavior on a scale that will permit the earth to recover." This view can be extended beyond the ecological crisis to all the man-made crises of famine, the appearance of diseases previously unknown, and warfare with weapons that could destroy most of life on earth.

As the years have gone by, my relationship to Rinpoche has constantly changed. Love for Rinpoche, and the joy that goes with that, has grown clearer and deeper, less obstructed by all the remorse about what I did or didn't do or say, all the clever questions I didn't ask. At the same time, the longing and heart-rending sadness at being separate from him also only deepens. So the journey with Rinpoche seems to go on and on... Perhaps it will go on until I finally realize my own inseparability from that wisdom. Once, in the early days of tantra group meetings, there were many of us crowded into Rinpoche's room, asking him about the meaning of the vajrayana transmission on the nature of mind—"Is it like this, Rinpoche?" "Is it like that, Rinpoche?" This went on for some time while Rinpoche sat in a corner, rather darkly just saying, "No." After a while I said, "Rinpoche, you seem to be disappointed in us." To which he replied, "I will be disappointed in you until you attain enlightenment." That was good news—he would actually stick with us until we attained enlightenment, which might be a very long time!

My aspiration for readers and author alike is that the conviction may grow in us in the truth of this verse from the *Mahayanasutralankara* by Asanga, which seems to summarize the whole inconceivable voyage:

> *After the awareness that there is nothing other than mind,*
> *Comes the understanding that mind, too, is nothing itself.*
> *The intelligent know that these two understandings are not*
> *   things,*
> *And, not even holding on to this knowledge, they come to rest*
> *   in the realm of totality.*

"THE ENERGY BEHIND THAT INSPIRATION COMES FROM A
LINEAGE OF TWO THOUSAND FIVE HUNDRED YEARS OF
EFFORT, ENERGY, AND SPIRITUAL POWER. NOBODY IN THAT
LINEAGE JUST TOOK ADVANTAGE OF THAT POWER, BUT THEY
RECEIVED INSPIRATION FROM IT, AND EVERYBODY WORKED,
PRACTICED, AND ACHIEVED. AND THEIR INSPIRATION HAS
BEEN HANDED DOWN GENERATION BY GENERATION."

CHÖGYAM TRUNGPA RINPOCHE,
FROM *TRANSCENDING MADNESS*

EPILOGUE:
The Living Lineage Continues

INPOCHE strongly emphasized over and over again, in
many different circumstances and many different ways,
that he was simply the spokesman for a lineage of
enlightened humans that went all the way back to the
Buddha, and would continue into the future. When I asked him a question at Tail of the Tiger in 1971 referring to "your teachings," before answering the question he smiled and said, "My teachings? You mean the Buddha's teachings." He spoke frequently of his own teacher, Jamgön Kongtrül, and of the Kagyu lineage of great teachers, particularly Naropa, Marpa, Milarepa, and Gampopa. He also showed tremendous respect and love for the sixteenth Karmapa, head of the Kagyu lineage. Furthermore, Rinpoche not only looked back to the past, to where the teachings came from, but also to how they would continue as living teachings after his death.

Rinpoche had emphatically made the point, until close to the end of his life, that he had empowered only one lineage holder in the Buddhist tradition, namely the Vajra Regent, and only one in the Shambhala tradition, namely the Sawang. And his investiture *as* Sawang, in 1979, was perhaps of greater significance than lineage holder or even the regency, as it was the empowerment of the crown prince to become the future monarch of Shambhala. As we have seen, however, Rinpoche also empowered the Sawang as vajra master, to "go out and gather students," in the Vajrayogini abhisheka in Germany in 1986. Thus it was now clear and definite that the Sawang was to be considered a second practice lineage holder. Rinpoche empowered no one else as lineage holder, though sadly a few of his students are beginning to claim that he did. Perhaps this was because he knew that after the death of such a powerful figure as himself schisms can so easily arise if there is not a clear successor; and probably also there was simply no one else ready at the time. Thus, he had laid careful plans for the continuity of his lineage after his death.

THE REGENT TAKES THE REIGNS

The summer following the cremation was a quiet one for the Regent. We all knew that he would be Rinpoche's immediate successor, not only as the Buddhist lineage holder, but also as president of the entire system of organizations, Vajradhatu, the Dharmadhatus, and Nalanda Foundation and its divisions of Shambhala Training and Naropa Institute, as well as all the smaller organizations set up under Rinpoche's guidance and inspiration.

The first Board gathering since the cremation took place in a large and beautiful house on a hillside overlooking St. Margaret's Bay. As the others departed, the Regent asked me to stay for a while to speak with him. Seeming quiet and soft, he said, "Now we must work together." I recalled to him the six or seven years of growing differences between us, to which he replied, simply, "That was then, this is now. Now we must go on together." It seemed very genuine, as if that period of dissonance could finally be left behind and now we could be friends again as we had in the beginning. In September, the Regent stepped into this role with his usual energy, humor, and bravery sometimes amounting to outrageousness.

I continued in my role on the Board as Director of Education overseeing Shambhala Training in particular, its main office having now moved from Boulder to Halifax. The Regent asked us to re-design the curriculum of the entire Shambhala Training Graduate Program, which follows Level Five. Unlike the first five Levels, the Graduate Program had become rather complex and confusing over the years. This we did and, during the summer of 1988, a large gathering of Shambhala Training teachers was held in Boulder to present this new curriculum. The Regent was teaching Seminary at RMDC—the first and last Seminary he was to teach as vajra master—and when he came down from RMDC to give a talk to the conference he was walking with a stick, very shakily, and he didn't look at all well. There was speculation that he might have AIDS.

WE LEARN OF HIS ILLNESS

In September, on his way to take a retreat in California, the Regent called a Board meeting in Boston. He met with each Board member individually and told everyone that he did, indeed, have AIDS. When he met with me, he was very simple, did not express fear or regret, but just said, "this body is just a shell; it doesn't really matter what happens to it." He asked us not to tell the sangha, saying that we should keep going, and "I need your support." We listened with respect, and agreed to continue.

It took only a few weeks for news of the Regent's AIDS to spread in the sangha and beyond. It also became rumored that the Regent had continued to sleep with people, men and women, knowing that he was HIV positive. When one of these partners did contract AIDS, there was an uproar both within the sangha and more widely in the press and among other Buddhist organizations in North America.

The sangha became utterly divided; there were some people who stuck by the Regent and avowed that he could do no wrong since, they claimed, he was an enlightened being. There were people who were simply completely overwhelmed by their personal anger toward the Regent, perhaps some of it a surfacing of resentment, jealousy, and anger that had built up toward him during those many years of his

regency. At the same time some of the anger came from intelligent criticism and genuine outrage at his hurtful behavior toward fellow students, which many had harbored and even tried to express to him for
many years. Perhaps most people, like myself, were deeply split within
themselves; they loved and deeply appreciated him, and at the same
time felt that he had betrayed them and betrayed his position as Regent
and Rinpoche's lineage successor. Though he did publicly apologize
for his mistakes, a battle raged in the sangha for several years, a battle
that could have destroyed Rinpoche's life work entirely, and in fact
almost did. The Regent moved to Ojai, California, with a group of
devoted students and never returned to Halifax.

PAINFUL SCHISM IN THE SANGHA

There was a wide range of views among the Board members, though
only Carl Springer joined the Regent in Ojai. The remainder of the
Board, including the Dapöns, took on the responsibility to hold the
sangha together from Halifax. In spite of the differing views, the Board
as a group took a hard-line position of opposition to the Regent, asking him to withdraw from teaching and stay in retreat. The Regent
gathered his forces in California and held his seat from there. Advice
was sought from His Holiness Khyentse Rinpoche and the four Kagyu
princes with no resolution. A Seminary was set for the summer of 1990,
which the Regent was to teach.

However, by the spring, his health was deteriorating, along with the
health of the sangha and, for the sake of both, Khyentse Rinpoche
advised him to stay in retreat and not to teach the Seminary. It was led,
principally, by the Lodro Dorje Holm, who continued in the role of
head of Practice and Study that Rinpoche had entrusted him with so
long ago. On the last day of Seminary, we heard that the Regent had
died. It is said that his body remained warm for a few days after his
death—a sign that he was able to hold his mind in samadhi and thus
that he had accomplished some level of meditative attainment in this

lifetime. His body was brought to RMDC and cremated in a traditional ceremony presided over by the Sawang.

The split in the sangha continued in full force after the Regent's death. It perhaps reflected a deep split in the Regent's person: on the one hand was his tremendous generosity of spirit, buoyant humor, and brilliance as a teacher as well as his bravery and outspoken contempt for hypocrisy. On the other hand there was his intense separation of people around him into those who were "for me" and those who were "against me," along with his disregard for conventional norms. And there was his sometimes abusive behavior toward people which might have been unskillful attempts to break through their self-centeredness, or possibly simply an expression of his own arrogance.

Even at relatively high levels of realization there can be obstacles such as "a vivid clinging to love for friends and hatred of enemies"[108] or "getting so conceited, arrogant and disdainful that he might consider himself to be no longer in need of his guru,"[109] both of which were apparent in the Regent's behavior. I myself do not doubt that the Regent had some realization of the true nature of mind. But he was clearly a student on the path, the number one student, and as such was a powerful and generous example to all of us. It is only tragic that he died before he was able to work through some of these obstacles and become the true lineage holder that Rinpoche trusted he could be.

However we may ultimately understand this, the split and subsequent battle in the sangha was painful beyond belief, dividing families and friends. This period brought to the surface so much of our latent jealousies, antagonisms, and basic aggression that it became a tremendous catharsis for many of us, individually as well as for the sangha as a whole. Rinpoche had so often told us that the guru's job is to squeeze our egoic pimples until they burst, and it seemed that this might be the final squeeze of the guru, this time applied to the entire sangha. Whether the sangha would be burst asunder completely, or just our ego-pimples would be popped, was by now quite uncertain.

THE SAWANG TAKES HIS SEAT

The day the Regent died, the Sawang Ösel Mukpo was with Jamgön Kongtrül Rinpoche, the one who, among the Kagyu princes, we had most turned to for advice during the previous two tormenting years. Our other source of refuge and counsel had been Khyentse Rinpoche, to whom both "sides" of the divided sangha had sent delegations and been in frequent phone contact. In 1986, the Sawang had been studying for two years at a school in Oxford, England, in preparation for entering the University—one of Rinpoche's dearest wishes for him throughout his difficult school years. However, at that time, Rinpoche had told the Sawang that he should go to study with Khyentse Rinpoche in Nepal after his death. At the time of the cremation, Khyentse Rinpoche had asked the Sawang to return to Nepal with him, telling him that he would "have to take responsibility for continuing his father's teachings." The Sawang remained in Bhutan for three years, under Khyentse Rinpoche's close dharma tutelage and grandfatherly friendship, and with his increasing trust as the future lineage holder.

During the conflict, the Sawang had taken no part in it, but had stayed in Nepal continuing his studies with Khyentse Rinpoche who, toward the end, had again told him, "You will have to go back and take over your father's work." Kongtrül Rinpoche and Khyentse Rinpoche had met with some members of the Board in the summer, when it was clear that the Regent would soon die. They had jointly stated that the Sawang was to carry on as the lineage holder and leader of the organization after the Regent's death.

Thus the Sawang was, at the moment of the Regent's death, in Karme Chöling where Kongtrül Rinpoche was conducting the Vajrayogini abhisheka; the Regent had requested Kongtrül Rinpoche to give this abhisheka when he realized that his own health would not allow him to conduct it as planned. When he heard of the Regent's death, Kongtrül Rinpoche again conferred by phone with Khyentse Rinpoche in France. The following day, the Sawang was, there and then, proclaimed Rinpoche's lineage successor in both the Kagyu and Nyingma lineages. He was now in the perhaps unenviable position of being the only holder of all three lineages of a great mahasiddha—Kagyu, Nyingma, and Shambhala—and the inheritor of a sangha tearing each other apart.

THE SAWANG RELUCTANTLY TAKES OVER

When I first heard the news of the Sawang's being empowered to carry on his father's work, I was both delighted and concerned. I had watched him through ten years, growing from a painfully shy young boy to a still shy young man, and I felt utterly confident that he was pure. That is to say, I felt sure that he would not get lost in puffing up his own ego and misusing his position. At the same time, I was not at all sure that he had the power to really continue his father's work, and to take it forward to another level. On the second point I was to be dramatically and gloriously proven wrong. However, his remarkable and almost miraculous transformation was to take a few years.

The Sawang had no place he could rest in, no place to call home, and for the next four years he lived out of a suitcase. He traveled throughout North America and Europe, visiting over fifty of the Dharmadhatus that had by then been established. He listened endlessly to all the pain of the sangha, never taking sides, just listening, and urged us to be kind to each other. When people complained that no new members were joining their Centers, he rejoined, "How do you expect other people to like you when you can't stand each other?"

I was reminded of an occasion when Rinpoche asked a group of students what they would do if they were suddenly placed in charge of a nation. After everyone had gone around and said what they would do, all suggesting some way in which they would change things for the better, they asked Rinpoche what he would do, to which he replied, "I would tell people to carry on as they were, and I would travel the country seeing what they were doing and how they lived." This was precisely how the Sawang acted in those first few years.

The Sawang asked all the Directors to resign, appointed a new governing Board, and took on the role of president of the organizations. In

1992, in a further effort to bind the sangha and the organizations into one, he placed Vajradhatu and Shambhala Training under one administrative umbrella and renamed the whole unified organization Shambhala. Altogether, especially considering his youth and utter inexperience in handling such a situation, he carried out his duties admirably and effectively, and gradually the sangha settled down. It became clear that the organizations his father had set up were going to survive, thanks to his ceaseless energy, his care and his openness, as well as the loyalty of everyone to his father's vision. Nonetheless, the Sawang remained painfully hesitant, almost as if he did not know quite who he was.

People criticized him from all angles, their favorite refrain being, "your father would have done this," or "your father wouldn't have done it that way." It is a classical psychological burden, and extremely hard for the son to step into the shoes of a great father, without losing his own confidence and genuineness, his own way of going on in his life. Anyone of a lesser inner strength than the Sawang would certainly have crumbled in those first few years.

And the tragic misfortunes continued: in 1991, the great Dilgo Khyentse Rinpoche, beloved teacher and friend to Rinpoche, grandfather-teacher to the Sawang, head of the Nyingma lineage, and guru even to the Dalai Lama, died at the age of 81. In 1992 Jamgön Kongtrül Rinpoche, who had accompanied His Holiness the Karmapa on all his travels to America, who had endeared himself so much to the sangha, and who had been such a strong and gentle guide through our troubles, was killed in a car accident. He was just 39 years old. In 1996, there followed the death of Tulku Urgyen, another Nyingma master and yogi with whom the Sawang had been continuing his studies. It was a painful and lonely period.

From the time of his first taking his seat, in 1990, people had been supplicating the Sawang to take on the mantle of the Sakyong King of Shambhala, as his father had intended. As I have already related, Khyentse Rinpoche performed the enthronement of Rinpoche as Sakyong in 1982, in a ceremony identical to the ceremony, known as *The*

Blazing Jewel of Sovereignty, that is traditional for the enthronement of kings. When Khyentse Rinpoche had died, his successor as head of the Nyingma lineage was His Holiness Penor Rinpoche, with whom Khyentse Rinpoche had instructed the Sawang to study after his death. Accordingly it was natural that it would be to Penor Rinpoche that the Sawang would go to request the Sakyong enthronement. This he did in the autumn of 1994, traveling to Namdroling Monastery in Southern India, the seat of Penor Rinpoche.

MIPHAM DISCOVERED

It was at Namdroling Monastery, a few days after his arrival, that another seemingly miraculous event occurred. Penor Rinpoche had a visionary dream in which he recognized the Sawang as the *tulku* of Mipham the Great, possibly one of the greatest teachers in the history of Tibetan Buddhism, certainly of recent centuries.

During his lifetime, Rinpoche had not wanted the Sawang to be recognized as a tulku. He knew that if such a recognition took place he would be under very great pressure, from the more traditional Tibetan teachers, to send the Sawang back to Nepal or Bhutan to receive the training traditional for a tulku, and he, of course, had very different plans. His Holiness the sixteenth Karmapa was one of the principal Tibetan leaders whose job it was to find, through visions, the tulkus of previous teachers.

When the Karmapa had visited America for the first time, in 1974, Rinpoche had asked him explicitly not to recognize the Sawang. Needless to say, though, Rinpoche was aware of the Sawang's special qualities. The Sawang tells the story of the first time he drove over to the house in which His Holiness was staying, to visit him with his father. After the visit, Rinpoche told him to go and wait in the car, which the Sawang did quite nervously since he believed that Rinpoche was going to discuss his possible tulku-ship with His Holiness. When Rinpoche joined him, he turned to the Sawang with a smile and said, "It's alright, you're one of us." Rinpoche had implored His

Holiness not to publically recognize the Sawang as a tulku since, he told him, he had other plans for the Sawang.

MIPHAM THE GREAT

Mipham the Great was born in 1846, in Kham in Eastern Tibet. Kham also included the Surmang region of which Rinpoche had been both civil governor and abbot until forced to escape from Tibet. It is said that he could understand all of the subjects of dharma and worldly knowledge with little study and he was regarded as completely possessing all the qualities of Manjushri, the bodhisattva of wisdom and transcendent knowledge. He was asked to compose the definitive view of the Nyingma lineage, so he embarked on writing clear and authoritative works on the hinayana and mahayana as well as the vajrayana. Mipham's works have subsequently become the foundation of study, not just for the Nyingma lineage, but also for the Kagyu lineage. And his life and work are revered by all schools of Tibetan Buddhism.

As well his vast writings and teachings on the buddhadharma, Mipham Rinpoche gathered together the extensive oral tradition of stories and songs of King Gesar of Ling, progenitor of the Mukpo family, the family lineage of Rinpoche and the Sawang. He himself wrote commentaries, praises, songs, and poetry about Gesar and Shambhalian themes. He designed many of the Tibetan prayer flags and inspired the practice of windhorse; many of the group chants and practices for raising windhorse contained in the Shambhala teachings given to us by Rinpoche were originally written by Mipham.

As an old man, Mipham wrote the seed syllable of Manjushri, *dhih*, on the tongue of Dilgo Khyentse Rinpoche when he was just a few months old, thus passing on the blessings of his lineage to Khyentse Rinpoche, who then passed them on to Rinpoche and the Sawang. Before Mipham died, in 1912, he said to his students that now he was going to Shambhala. So at the very moment that the Sawang felt ready to assume the mantle of Sakyong, King of Shambhala, he was recognized as the tulku of this great and renowned teacher, Mipham Gyatso, who himself had brought together the teachings of Nyingma with Shambhalian practices related to Gesar.

GOODBYE SAWANG, HELLO SAKYONG

The formal enthronement ceremony, in May 1995, establishing the Sawang as Sakyong, was one of those grand affairs that the sangha had so relished putting on during Rinpoche's time. Over 3000 students were attracted from all over North and South America and Europe. It truly marked a transformation from Sawang Ösel Mukpo to the Sakyong Mipham Jampal Thrinley Dradul Rinpoche. During the ceremony, the obviously delighted new Sakyong gave a short speech in which he invited all the senior students of his father to jump in and join him in spreading the dharma. In the course of the speech he mentioned the Sawang and, with a gentle wry smile, asked, "Remember him?" From the time of the enthronement, the Sawang's blossoming as the Sakyong was rapid and dramatic. After the enthronement he spent a month in Namdroling, the monastery of Penor Rinpoche, to begin his formal study of the teachings of Mipham. For several subsequent years, he returned to Namdroling to continue this study for several months at a time.

I began to realize that a dramatic change was happening before our eyes during a delightful moment after he returned from his second visit to Namdroling, in 1996. He met with the Executive Committee of Shambhala, which was the group of people actually managing Shambhala at that point, although there was a new and very large volunteer Board of Directors that was rather ineffectual. The Executive Committee consisted of David Brown, the Sakyong's chief secretary, and John Rockwell, the executive director of Shambhala, together with the heads of departments of Finance, Publicity, Buddhist Study and Practice, and myself—I had rejoined the staff to head up Shambhala Training International.

When we first sat down with him, the Sakyong gave us a broad and mischievous smile, and confidently proclaimed, "I want you to know

THE SAWANG ÖSEL MUKPO IS ENTHRONED AS SAKYONG,
KING OF SHAMBHALA.

that I am not my father, I am not like my father, and will not necessarily
do things the way my father would have done it." There was so much
joy and energy in the room that everyone clapped and burst out into
cheers. I felt that *this* would be just what his father would have wanted,
and that even now the space of Rinpoche's mind was lit up with a
smile. He went on to point out how, likewise, the forefathers of the
Kagyu lineage were each unique: from Tilopa the wild forest yogi,

through Naropa the ex-University professor, to Marpa the rough farmer, Milarepa the yogi-poet, and Gampopa the monk.

At a Kalapa Assembly that year, I was about to give a talk on the Sakyong's life, and had asked him what he would like me to say. As he reached the point in his story when he was recognized as Mipham, he breathed a small sigh and said, "it is so good to finally be able to be who you are." And this felt completely genuine, and to myself, true. During that Assembly he told the gathered group of several hundred senior students that his father used to say to him, "We come from the same place, and we have the same job to do," and, "I built the gate, but you must lead them through it."

THE SAKYONG SHAKES THINGS UP

As the years have gone on, the Sakyong's presence and radiance have expanded more than I could ever have imagined. Remembering my doubts in 1990 that he would ever have the power to really expand and continue the direction his father had set, I now have them no more. Even people who had previously never met him began to comment that it was almost as if he were enveloped in golden radiation.

The Sakyong also began to shake things up. He introduced approaches to meditation different from the "standard" approach that people had settled into; he brought new directions to study and practice, introducing the teachings of Mipham and the Nyingma lineage; and he changed the forms of the shrines and structures of government and the kasung.

The Sakyong taught vajrayana seminaries almost every year, since 1999, with increasing clarity, strength, and confidence. Just like Rinpoche, he is continually experimenting to try to find how best to introduce the vajrayana dharma and the Shambhala teachings to the West, in which conditions are so different from those in Tibet; in which the life-style is rapidly speeding up; and in which, at the same time, people are losing their life-force, their dignity, and their confidence.

He has gradually brought together the apparently separate streams that Rinpoche had brought to us, vajrayana Buddhism and the Shambhala teaching. Rinpoche had emphasized again and again that these two profound teachings complement each other. However, over the years the two streams had grown separate as different students had concentrated on one or the other of the two, and become strong spokespersons for their favorite. Now the Sakyong was bringing us back to the original view, that they cannot be accomplished separately. In the year 2004, he proclaimed that from then on the teachings that his father had brought to the West and that he was continuing to develop and propagate would, altogether, be known as Shambhala Buddhism; this would be the path that his students would follow.

Like the action of a master of shiatsu—the Japanese form of healing which consists of pressing on the sore spots gently, but with steadily increasing pressure to a painful point, until something relaxes and there is a large release of energy—the Sakyong was pressing the sore spots of the entire community of Shambhala. And, though his moves were painful for some people, a lot of energy was released. Not all of Rinpoche's students were pleased with this new manifestation, some of them continuing to be very critical of the changes that he introduced. Yet it seemed to me that constant change and shaking up was precisely one of the most profound and powerful of Rinpoche's teachings.

The sometimes precipitous changes that Rinpoche made would often, too, produce groans and resistance among some sectors of the sangha. The Sakyong took all of this with openness, confidence, and a sense of humor—one thing, certainly, in which he was no different from his father. And new students, younger and older, began to flock to hear the Sakyong teach, to read his books, and to begin to practice the path of Shambhala Buddhism. The glorious banner of good windhorse was flying high over Shambhala again!

HE VISITS TIBET

In the year 2001, the Sakyong made his first visit to Tibet, where he was offered deep respect and joyful praise, sometimes almost amounting to adulation. The simple delight of seeing the son and heir of Trungpa Rinpoche, and the tulku of Mipham Gyatso the Great, in one radiant youthful body was overwhelming. Everywhere he went, he was met with huge crowds asking for his teaching and blessings, with feasting and celebration. He visited Surmang, the region in which Rinpoche's monasteries were situated, and many of the retreat places of his father in the Surmang region, as well as places where Rinpoche had studied with his own teachers as a young man, all of them now, of course, in ruins.

He visited Golok, the area in Eastern Tibet where Mipham Gyatso had lived and taught, and where the great King Gesar had ruled. Finally the Sakyong visited the family of Mipham Gyatso. He met twice with the ex-Governor of Golok, Ju Kunde, the grand-nephew of Mipham Gyatso, and his closest living relative. Ju Kunde, the main holder of Mipham's family lineage, received the Sakyong and his party in his home. After serving tea and snacks, he rose and, with great emotion and dignity, offered the Sakyong three of Mipham's personal effects. The most significant was Mipham's jade seal. He also offered a text written in Mipham's own hand on the subject of Shambhala and a cup that Mipham used until the age of seventeen. These items had been handed down from generation to generation within his family, and now he felt it was appropriate to give them to their rightful owner.

TWO GREAT FAMILIES COME TOGETHER

In the year 2005, the Sakyong was married to the Tibetan Princess, Semo Tseyang. This marriage was profoundly auspicious—among Tibetans it was said to be the most significant such marriage in hundreds of years. Princess Tseyang is the youngest of four daughters of Namkha Trimed Rinpoche, who is regarded as a primary holder of the lineage and tradition of King Gesar. Namkha Rinpoche, who belongs to the Nyingma school, is himself a *terton*, a discoverer of terma, and has received many terma of profound vajrayana practices relating to King Gesar. He and Trungpa Rinpoche had met when they were both

THE SAKYONG MIPHAM RINPOCHE AND THE SAKYONG WANGMO
KHANDRO TSEYANG. *Photograph by James Hoagland.*

young, at which time Trungpa Rinpoche had passed on to Namkha Rinpoche a complete cycle of teachings from the Nyingma tradition and had written a short sadhana on Gesar for Namkha Rinpoche at his request. Thus, this marriage brought together two great families holding the Nyingma teachings of Buddhism and the Gesar/Shambhala tradition of enlightened society.

The Sakyong in his whole being bridges East and West in so many ways: born in India to Tibetan parents, and spending his first seven years there in a Tibetan refugee camp; in his formative years, being educated in American schools, as well as trained in the highest Buddhist and Shambhala teachings by his father the great mahasiddha; and then taking the vision of Shambhala back to Tibet. And, at the time of writing this, he is only in his forties; what wonders are still to come?

The Sakyong is, I believe, magnificently leading his and Rinpoche's students through the gate his father built.

Photograph by George Holmes.

Colophon

Oh Rinpoche, father guru, noble Vidyadhara Sakyong,
May your gentle mischievous smile that cheers the darkest mood
continue to be seen in each small green bud of spring.
May your limitless love that melts and nourishes the coldest heart
continue to be felt in the brilliant heat of the summer sun.
May your raging great roar that cuts aggression
continue to be heard in the autumn thunder.
May your clear sharp mind that clarifies confusion
continue to be known in the crisp winter morning.
And may your profound wisdom that is not separate from our own
continue to be realized in the peaceful white light of dawn.
May your presence within the space of mind, in the environment
of the world, and in the embodiment of the living lineage, continue
to benefit all beings for many generations to come.
May the Great Eastern Sun be Victorious!

Glossary

(Note: in preparing this glossary I have made valuable use of the glossary in *The Life of Marpa the Translator*[110] and *The Encyclopedia of Eastern Philosophy and Religion*.[111] Any errors of definition or interpretation are my own.)

abhidharma The earliest compilation of Buddhist philosophy and psychology. The teachings and analyses concerning psychological and spiritual phenomena contained in the discourses of the Buddha and his principal disciples are presented in a systematic order. As the various schools of Buddhism developed over the centuries, each added their own interpretations and insights. In Tibetan schools, the abhidharma is the main course of study for several years.

abhisheka (Sanskrit; anointment or empowerment) The abhisheka is a ceremony, that could take one or many days, in which the student is fully introduced, or entered in, to the mandala of a particular deity by the vajra master. In this way, the student is empowered to practice the corresponding *sadhana*. The abhisheka is usually accompanied by a *lung*, that is, a complete reading of the text, and a *tri*, an explanation of the practice by the vajra master.

Ashe (Tibetan; primordial or first stroke. Pronounced *ah-shai*) In the Shambhala teachings, *A-*, primordial or first, is the open space of mind before the first thought, or first gesture; that first thought or gesture is *-she*. Ashe is the power to express basic goodness and is also known as "the essence of life." Ashe symbolizes primordial confidence and compassion. The execution of the stroke of Ashe is the practice that expresses and nourishes those qualities. There is no connection between this and the traditional use of the term *ashe* that is related to inner yogic practices.

bardo (Tibetan; in-between state) Popularly, the bardo is known as the state between death and re-birth. However, in the Tibetan tradition there are six bardo states, three referring to the various states we go through in this life and three referring to the stages of transition from death to re-birth. The correct Tibetan title of the text well-known as *The Tibetan Book of the Dead* is *Bardo Thödol,* literally *Liberation through Hearing in the In-between State.* The Bardo Thödol is a manual to be read to those who are dying or recently dead to guide them through the bardos between one life and the next, and to help them attain enlightenment in the bardo, or at least obtain a good re-birth.

basic goodness The fundamental nature of human beings, equivalent to buddha nature or primordial purity in the Buddhist teachings. The fundamental nature of basic goodness is unconditioned and beyond all concepts of "good" or "bad."

blessings The spiritual atmosphere or energy of the lineage gurus that can be felt as coming toward or descending on the student when there is devotion and openness.

blind faith Belief that in its very nature cannot be proved or disproved in human experience. Examples would be the belief in a separate, all-powerful creator God or the belief that everything in the universe is reducible to nothing but lifeless, mindless stuff.

bodhisattva vow This vow signifies our entry into a mahayana level of practice, in which we make the commitment to work to attain enlightenment for the sake of others.

compassion Warmth that arises within clarity. This warmth and clarity come from seeing the suffering of oneself and others that is caused by clinging to belief in ego. It gives rise to action that benefits others, free from self-interest. It is the ultimate generosity—giving without expecting anything in return. In contrast, Rinpoche spoke of "idiot compassion" as trying to make someone feel good in a way that only increases delusion and therefore, ultimately, suffering.

Chakrasamvara The main male deity of the Kagyu lineage. The Surmang monastery, of which Rinpoche was the Abbot, was a principle center for the Chakrasamvara practice, including very elaborate masked "lama dances" in which all the teachings related to the deity are evoked symbolically. Chögyam Trungpa Rinpoche was said to have achieved his enlightenment through the practice of Chakrasamvara. The sadhana of Chakrasamvara is the second practiced on the Kagyu path, the first being that of Varjayogini.

cocoon Equivalent to the Buddhist "ego," the cocoon is made up of all the emotional and conceptual hang-ups that cover our basic goodness and obstruct ourselves and others from seeing it.

coemergence The vajrayana view that samsara and nirvana, confusion and wisdom, arise together at every moment of our experience. Thus coemergent wisdom can be found right within apparent confusion.

confidence The quality of strength, upliftedness, and gentle radiance that comes from being genuine.

crazy wisdom (Tibetan: *yeshe tsolwa*; literally, "primordial wisdom run wild") The highest manifestation of enlightened mind usually taking a wrathful form. The actions of a master of crazy wisdom naturally create chaos in the environment that breaks through the conventional logic and limited, fixed reference points of others.

consort The term "consort" is used in vajrayana Buddhism to refer to special sexual partners whose relationship is based primarily on inner spiritual practice. In English the term "consort" is usually reserved for a marriage partner (for example, Prince Consort).

dakini (Tibetan: *khandroma*; a female figure who moves in celestial space, i.e. at the highest level of reality; colloquially, "sky-dancer") A wrathful or semi-wrathful female deity, of which Vajrayogini is an example, the dakini symbolizes compassion and emptiness. The term can also refer to a female messenger or protector.

Dapön The heads of the two main branches of the Dorje Kasung—the kasung branch which is the general service branch and the kusung which is the branch dedicated to personal service to the Sakyong.

dathün A full month (Tibetan: *da*) of meditation sessions (Tibetan: *thün*).

deity The vajrayana deity that a practitioner invokes during sadhana practice symbolizes a particular wisdom energy. By identifying with that deity the practitioner awakens the corresponding wisdom in him or herself. The deity is usually visualized surrounded by a retinue, symbolizing the various aspects of wisdom, and residing in a glorious palace, the parts of which symbolize aspects of the path. During an abhisheka, the vajra master identifies with the deity and directly communicates the wisdom of that deity to the students. Thus in practicing the sadhana the practitioner also identifies with the wisdom mind of the teacher.

devotion (Tibetan: *mögü*) A combination of *möpa*, longing, and *güpa*, humbleness. Devotion is genuine love for the teacher and teachings that is a combination of longing for the teachings and the humbleness of knowing how far one has to go. Devotion is an important aspect of the vajrayana path in which longing, or admiration, comes from seeing the vast vision of the vajra master and longing to join that, longing to become one with the mind of the guru; and humbleness, or absence of arrogance, is being willing to give up clinging to our own petty little version of reality so that we may join that vision.

Dharmadhatu (Sanskrit; space of dharma) Less primordial than the vajradhatu, this is the space of mind that is full of all possibilities of manifestation, awake or confused. Also the name given by Rinpoche to the local meditation centers in cities.

dharmakaya See **kaya**.

dignities The four stages of the path of the Shambhala warrior. Termed *meek, perky, outrageous,* and *inscrutable,* they are symbolized by the mythological animals tiger, lion, garuda, and dragon. The term *dignity* is used here in the manner described by the Oxford English Dictionary as: "The quality of being worthy or honorable; worth, excellence"; also "An honorable office, rank or title."

Director A member of the Vajradhatu/Nalanda Board of Directors. From 1977, there were two Directors of the First Class, Rinpoche and the Regent; and Directors of the Second Class, Sam Bercholz, Charles Lief, Ken Green, Jeremy Hayward, John Roper, Carl Springer, and Ron Stubbert. David Rome and the Lodro Dorje Holm were also full members of the Board of Directors but not in the capacity of Directors. The Directors were also known as Ministers (and the Board as the Cabinet) in the context of the Kingdom of Shambhala. In the text, merely to make this distinction clear, I have capitalized Directors in this sense; directors of other aspects of the organization, such as practice centers, are not capitalized.

dorje (Sanskrit: *vajra*; literally "diamond" or "king of stones") As an adjective it means diamond-like, indestructible, invincible. Also a ritual implement used in vajrayana sadhana practices and symbolizing *upaya*, or skillful means. The dorje is held in the right hand, while a bell, or *ghanta*, symbolizing wisdom, is held in the left. Together, the crossed bell and dorje suggest the union of wisdom and skillful means, the state of enlightenment.

Dorje Kasung (Tibetan; indestructible protector of the command or word) The Dorje Kasung, first known as the Vajra Guards, is a division within Shambhala set up to provide service and protection to the teacher and the teachings. The Dorje Kasung were later divided into two: the Dorje Kasung, who provide general service to the sangha and protection for visiting dignitaries and teaching environments; and the Dorje Kusung (Tibetan: *kusung*; protector of the body), who provide personal service for the Sakyong.

drala (Tibetan; above the enemy) In the Shambhala view, the enemy is aggression. The dralas are energies within ourselves and in the environment that, when we open to them, can increase our strength and confidence to overcome aggression in ourselves and in the world.

duhkha (Sanskrit; suffering) The deep anxiety and fear at the very basis of the ordinary confused mind, *duhkha* is caused by the grasping of ego onto anything that helps it to solidify its own existence; this causes suffering because it goes against the truth of the impermanence of all composite things, and the non-existence of any substantial ego. Genuine and complete realization of this non-substantiality of ego, through the meditative practices of the path, brings liberation from *duhkha*.

ego Refers to the deep-rooted belief that the terms "me," "myself," or "I" refer to an actually existing permanent, single, independent entity. Being an attempt to fixate something permanent in a constantly changing flow of experience, the belief in a truly existent ego is the cause of suffering. This belief causes us to try to hold on to what we believe to support and protect the "I" and to push away what we believe to be harmful to the "I"—the result is passion and aggression.

egolessness The realization that the self has no solid permanent basis but is a continually changing flow. When we closely examine the inner world of our mind as well as the outer world of appearances, we find that there is only change. Nothing is permanent except space itself. Our thoughts, feelings, emotions, and perceptions are never the same from one brief moment to the next. Some things in the outer world appear to be relatively permanent, such as the sun, but even that is an illusion—even the sun is changing and will die. If we look within for anything permanent that we can truly call a "me," it cannot be found. Constant searching for this ego leads eventually to the deep realization, beyond merely thinking about it, that what I call "me" does not really exist. This is egolessness.

enlightened society A society guided by the vision of basic goodness and founded on the sanity of sitting meditation.

enlightenment (Tibetan: *chang-chub*. Sanskrit: *bodhi*) Preferably translated as awakening. A person awakens to nowness, which is emptiness and luminosity or cognizance, and is the true nature of all reality including him or herself. In this state of awakening, emptiness is seen to be no different from phenomena. There are gradual stages of enlightenment: the awakening could be very brief or the realization of emptiness could be permanent and extend through the entire body, speech, and mind of the person. In the latter case he or she has become a buddha.

fire puja (puja, Sanskrit; ceremony) Having accomplished the requisite number of repetitions of the deity mantra, students then purify and seal that practice by performing the fire puja.

four karmas (karma, Sanskrit; action) The four enlightened actions that transcend ego: pacifying, enriching, magnetizing and destroying.

four maras The ego-centered actions which are the confused aspects of the four karmas. The four maras are: an artificially generated peacefulness, greed and acquisitiveness, seductiveness, and hatred.

garuda The mythological bird that symbolizes the Shambhala dignity known as "outrageous." The garuda is said to arise from its egg fully grown and to be able to fly in space without needing to land. It has a fearsome expression and holds in its beak a snake that symbolizes the root kleshas, passion, aggression, and ignorance.

Great Eastern Sun The guiding vision of an enlightened life or society. "Great" symbolizes that this vision is available to all and is at the heart of all good human societies. Our life is guided by this vision when we wake up to our basic goodness and that of others. Enlightened societies have arisen throughout history, in all geographical locations and all cultures. "Eastern" symbolizes the direction of dawn, or waking up, and going forward. The ground of enlightened society is waking up to our basic goodness. From this point of view we need never look back. It is also an expression of a sense of richness and wholesomeness. "Sun" symbolizes an unceasing source of energy.

When we connect with this vision it empowers us and connects us into a timeless reservoir of awake energy.

guru (Sanskrit; literally, "heavy, weighty one." Tibetan: *lama*; "high one") Colloquially the term has come to mean any teacher but as it is used in the vajrayana tradition it is equivalent to vajra master and refers to a realized teacher.

habitual patterns Patterns of thought, speech, and action that are determined karmically and that repeat themselves mechanically unless we can step out of them through insight and discipline.

hinayana See **yana.**

ikebana Or *kado,* the "way of the flower." The placing of flowers as a contemplative art form, in contrast to "flower arranging" for decorative purposes alone.

Kagyu (Tibetan; Command Lineage) One of the four major schools of Tibetan Buddhism. The Karma Kagyu was the sub-sect of the Kagyu school within which Chögyam Trungpa Rinpoche was trained.

Kagyu princes A term used for the four main students of His Holiness the sixteenth Karmapa, each a major tulku of the Kagyu school— Jamgön Kongtrül Rinpoche, Tai Situ Rinpoche, Shamar Rinpoche, and Gyalstap Rinpoche.

Karma Dzong (Tibetan; fortress of the Karma Kagyu) The local meditation communities in Boulder, Colorado, and Halifax, Nova Scotia. Dorje Dzong (indestructible fortress) is the building housing Karma Dzong and the administration of Vajradhatu.

karma (Sanskrit; action) The universal law of cause and effect, or action and reaction. According to the Buddhist understanding of karma, one's present experience is a product of previous actions and intentions, and likewise our future conditions depend on our present intentional acts. The origin of karma is the false belief in ego, which seeks to maintain itself and thereby produces a chain reaction of repetitive thoughts and acts. There is "group karma" of families and nations as well as individual karma. However, the law of karma is not the same as determinism: previous actions create karmically only the conditions within which a present action is constrained; the action itself is up to us. It is analogous to a chess game in which the position of all the pieces on the board is completely determined by previous moves, but the next move is up to us.

kaya (Sanskrit; body) The *trikaya* is the three bodies: *dharmakaya*, *sambhogakaya*, and *nirmanakaya*. These are the three modes of being of a buddha, or enlightened one, that correspond to mind, speech, and body in the ordinary being. Dharmakaya is enlightened mind itself, clearly knowing, unchanging, empty of all concept, the true nature of reality. Sambhogakaya (literally, body of enjoyment) corresponds to the speech of a buddha; it is the buddha's environment of communication and compassion. Nirmanakaya is the physical form of a buddha who takes birth as a human being for the sake of continuing his or her compassionate action in this earth realm. From the point of view of the ordinary, dualistic state of mind, in which we experience ourselves as separate from our environment, the three kayas also correspond to three realms of being. Dharmakaya corresponds to the vast, unconditioned realm of mind beyond all forms and conceptual boundaries. The sambhogakaya corresponds to a realm of subtle energies. This is the dwelling place of the deities, the yidams and dralas; it is also the realm in which the Pure Lands are said to exist. The nirmanakaya corresponds to the physical realm.

King Gesar Gesar assumed the throne of the Kingdom of Ling in Eastern Tibet at the age of fifteen at a time when the region was broken up into warring tribes. Believed to have lived during the eleventh century, King Gesar unified and expanded the Kingdom bringing peace and establishing the dharma throughout the greater region. He is considered to have been an emanation (or re-birth) of Padmasambhava and, like Padmasambhava, to have conquered negative, ego-oriented forces and demons through his miraculous powers. The exploits of the enlightened King Gesar and his warriors became the subject of the greatest epic of Tibet, passed on from generation to generation by poets and bards and containing much of the wisdom of the warrior culture.

Kingdom of Shambhala A mythological Buddhist kingdom, known as an enlightened society throughout Asia and as far north as Siberia. There are a variety of beliefs regarding the historical reality of the Kingdom of Shambhala: that it actually existed on earth; that it has only mythological significance; that it is visible only to those who have sufficiently purified and awakened their own hearts and minds through the practice of meditation; and that the Kingdom existed on earth for a period during and after the time of the Buddha and eventually disappeared into a more subtle realm.

klesha Conflicting, or negative, emotions that are based on ego-clinging and are the primary obstacles to awakening to our Buddha nature. The root kleshas are passion or clinging, aggression or hatred, and ignorance or confusion. These are the root causes of further kleshas such as jealousy, pride, envy, doubt, false views, and so on. When the energy of the kleshas is seen clearly, free from ego-clinging, that energy itself is wisdom. Thus the five kleshas of passion, aggression, ignorance, pride, and jealousy become the five buddha wisdoms of the five buddha families.

kusung See **Dorje Kasung.**

kyudo The "way of the bow," the Japanese art of archery. Shibata Sensei taught kyudo as a meditative practice, which he referred to as "standing meditation," and contrasted true kyudo with "sports-style kyudo."

lhasang (Tibetan; calling the highest principle) A ceremony to invoke or bring down the dralas in order to purify the space and magnetize positive energy. Juniper is burnt on lighted charcoal. As the smoke rises up, it is said to purify the space of outer and inner aggression and obstacles, while at the same time drala energy is attracted into the space by the rising juniper smoke.

lineage holder See **lineage.**

lineage A line of realized masters, men or women, who pass on the core teachings through direct transmission from teacher to student. There are four main schools, or lineages, in Tibet—Nyingma, Kagyu, Sakya, and Gelug—each of which has many sub-lineages. Each lineage begins when a teacher attains a high level of realization, acknowledged by others, and is sent forth by his own vajra master to gather disciples. The realized master then chooses and empowers one or more of his or her own students as lineage holders to pass on the teachings to the next generation of students, thus creating a lineage.

luminosity (Tibetan: *ösel*) Ösel, luminosity, can also be translated as clarity or cognizance, reflecting the fact that the mind, through its clear transparent nature, clearly illuminates or knows whatever it turns to as its object. Appearances are nothing other than expressions of mind's luminosity.

lungta (Tibetan: *lung*, wind; *ta*, horse) See **windhorse.**

mahamudra (Sanskrit; great seal, symbol, or gesture) The state of being in which the emptiness of all phenomena, including ego, is directly realized. In this state all experiences are transformed into the wisdom to see reality and the great compassion to work tirelessly for the sake of others.

mahasiddha (Sanskrit; one of great accomplishment) A rare being whose realization goes far beyond that of even many renowned Tibetan teachers.

mahayana See **yana.**

mandala (Sanskrit; group, society, organization. Tibetan: *kyil-khor*; "center and periphery") In a mandala the numerous elements of a complex and chaotic situation are unified into an ordered whole through meditative practice. In sadhana practice, this ordered whole is represented visually as a palace with four gates in the four cardinal directions in the center of which the yidam resides as a personification of wisdom. In the meditative state, the totality of one's environment, body, and mind are seen as mandala.

Minister See **Director**.

Nalanda Foundation The non-religious organization founded by Rinpoche in 1974 to incorporate Naropa Institute and later Shambhala Training, Alaya preschool, and Vidya elementary school. Nalanda Foundation was named after the great Buddhist university, founded in the second century and flourishing until it was destroyed by Muslim invaders in the twelfth or thirteenth century. A center of learning bearing the same name was established in Tibet in 1351.

ngöndro (Tibetan; preliminary practices) The preliminary practices to be accomplished before receiving the empowerment to practice the sadhana of a particular deity. There are four preliminary practices: prostrations, mantra, mandala, and guru yoga.

nirmanakaya See **kaya.**

non-theism Belief that all phenomena exist only relatively to the observing subject, including any and all deities. From the point of view of non-theism there is no external savior; one achieves awakening through one's own effort. Non-theism should be distinguished from atheism, which positively asserts the non-existence of all deities.

Nyingma (Tibetan; "Ancient Ones") One of the four major schools of Tibetan Buddhism. The Nyingmas follow the original, or "old," teachings and practices of vajrayana brought to Tibet by Padmasambhava. Rinpoche's root guru, Jamgön Kongtrül of Shechen, belonged to this lineage. Thus Rinpoche brought together the teachings of both Kagyu and Nyingma lineages.

nyams (Tibetan; temporary experiences) Temporary experiences of bliss, luminosity, and non-thought that may or may not occur on the path of meditation. They are considered side-tracks to the main goal of practice, the realization of emptiness.

Padmasambhava Renowned Indian scholar and master of meditation who brought Buddhism to Tibet in the eighth century. Padmasambhava is revered and considered to be a second Buddha by many Tibetans.

regent The regent is traditionally one of the vajra master's closest students whom he empowers to hold all his teachings and transmissions intact and uncorrupted after his death and to pass them on to the next generation of students. There is only one regent, though the vajra master may also empower other students as lineage holders—those who are authorized to pass on the vajrayana teachings to others.

Rigden (Tibetan; holder of awareness, or holder of the family, hence "holder of the awareness family") The Rigden principle, or primordial Rigden, is the equivalent of the awakened mind of the Buddha, dharmakaya. At this level the Rigden transcends existence or nonexistence. On a relative level, a Rigden is the secular equivalent of a buddha, that is, an enlightened leader of a secular society. Rigden is also the title of the monarchs of the ancient Kingdom of Shambhala.

Rinpoche (Tibetan; Precious One) A term bestowed in Tibet on highly realized teachers.

sacredness The natural purity, immaculateness, and goodness of the world and everything in it. It is the conceptual mind that projects the dichotomies of *good* and *bad*, *for* and *against* on the simplicity and purity of the world as it is. The world is inherently sacred; it is not made sacred by blessings from outside, but is sacred in its own genuine nature.

sadhana A vajrayana ritual practice in which a particular form of wisdom is aroused in one's own being through evocation of the qualities of the particular deity that embodies that wisdom.

samadhi A state of meditative absorption in which the meditator's mind is one with the content of the meditation. This might refer to an artificially created trance-like state in which the senses are blocked, or to an unconditioned experience in which the mind rests in its natural state of bliss-emptiness.

sambhogakaya See **kaya.**

sangyum (Tibetan; secret mother or consort). An honorific term, commonly used to denote the wife of a lama. Secret here does not mean hidden from the public, or secret*ive*. Rather, it refers to the innermost aspect of mind. Thus the sangyum is consort at all levels: outer, inner, and secret; body, speech, and mind.

scientific materialism Also known as scientific reductionism. The view that all phenomena in the universe, including life, mind, and consciousness, can be reduced to the organization of particles of matter. The nature of these particles is essentially unknown, but is assumed by most scientific materialists to be inherently without life or mind, which are considered to be merely an outcome of complicated arrangements of particles. Scientific materialism is a metaphysical system that, in its very nature, cannot be proved or disproved by the methods of science.

setting sun The vision of a life or a society driven by the three types of materialism: material, psychological, and spiritual. This is contrasted with the vision of the Great Eastern Sun.

Shambhala An enlightened society based on the belief that all beings have inherent wisdom and compassion. A society in which people are encouraged to follow the basic teaching and practice of meditation in order to reveal that wisdom in themselves and each other, and in which the structures of the society are organized according to this principle of basic goodness. The vision of Shambhala is based on the Tibetan tradition of the Kingdom of Shambhala.

Shambhala Buddhism The form of Buddhism taught within Shambhala International (see below). The three lineages brought to the West by Chögyam Trungpa Rinpoche—Kagyu, Nyingma, and Shambhala—were unified into one stream, Shambhala Buddhism, by his son and heir, Sakyong Mipham Rinpoche. The Buddhist teachings show us how to clarify our minds and open our hearts while the Shambhala teachings give us methods to rouse our life force and connect with the natural power and energy of the phenomenal world. The Shambhala teachings provide a cultural container and vehicle to put our Buddhist aspirations into practice in the world.

Shambhala Center The name now given to the city meditation centers, previously known as Dharmadhatus.

Shambhala International The international organization of city meditation centers and residential retreat centers that offer programs of practice and study in a community of practitioners. The organization was founded by Chögyam Trungpa Rinpoche as two separate organizations—the Buddhist religious organization, Vajradhatu, and the non-religious organization, Nalanda, which included Shambhala Training, Naropa Institute, the schools and other non-religious activities. These two organizations were unified by his son and heir, Sakyong Mipham Rinpoche, under the umbrella Shambhala International.

Shambhala Training A non-religious, non-sectarian program of training in mindfulness and awareness in daily life, as well as other Shambhala practices to develop confidence, such as the practice of windhorse and the stroke of Ashe.

shunyata (Sanskrit; emptiness or openness) The view that the true nature of reality is not conditioned by any conceptual ideas or forms whatsoever, even ideas of existence or non-existence. Whatever we perceive, experience, or think is empty of substantial reality, like reflections in a mirror.

siddhi (Sanskrit; ability or power) Relative siddhis are special abilities attained through meditative practices, e.g. clairvoyance, pre-cognition, or the power of healing. Ultimate siddhi is the realization of emptiness. One who fully attains such powers is known as a siddha.

sitting meditation The practice of mindfulness and awareness (Sanskrit: *shamatha* and *vipashyana*. Tibetan: *shi-ne* and *lhagthong*). Through mindfulness we bring our minds back to the present, as it wanders off over and over again. Doing this our minds develop stability, strength, and clarity and become a useful tool, rather than a constant distraction. Awareness is the recognition of the openness of mind, the space around our thoughts and emotions. The development of awareness brings insight into the fundamental nature of the mind.

skandha (Sanskrit; heap) The five skandhas are the constantly changing components that make up what we call our "self." Traditionally, these five skandhas, though impermanent, are relatively long-lasting elements—the body, feelings, impulses, state of mind, and mental contents. Rinpoche taught, based on teachings from the mahamudra tradition, that the five skandhas are the almost instantaneous components of each brief moment of experience.

spiritual materialism One of three forms of materialism: physical, psychological, and spiritual. All describe aspects of ego's tendency to seek ways to strengthen and puff itself up. Physical materialism is the accumulating of physical comfort, objects and wealth out of selfish, ego-oriented concerns. Psychological materialism is the accumulation of ideas—political systems, philosophies, psychologies, and so on—for the purpose of strengthening and expanding ego. Spiritual materialism, the most subtle form, is the perversion of spiritual teachings in the service of bloating one's sense of self.

tantra (Sanskrit; thread, continuity) A general term referring to the practices and texts of vajrayana. There is a thread of continuity on the path of meditation from the beginning that is grounded on the understanding that we already possess the wisdom of buddha nature, basic goodness; the path is then clearing the obstacles to realizing this nature; and the fruition of the path is fully awakening into that inherent wisdom, i.e. becoming a buddha.

terma (Tibetan; hidden teachings) Teachings that were hidden by great beings of the past, especially Padmasambhava, to be re-discovered by great teachers of a later generation at the time they are needed. The teachings could be hidden in rocks, lakes, or other geographical formations; they could also be hidden in the realm of vast mind. One who is able, through special ability and training, to discover terma is known as a *terton*.

theism Dualistic belief in a separate, eternal, creator deity. Belief that fulfilling the required obligations to that deity will ultimately save one from suffering. Theism tends to be accompanied by belief in an eternal self or soul, which, if one behaves properly in this life, will dwell in the realm of the deity after death. The *principle* of theism is distinguished from the religions, such as Christianity, Judaism, and Islam, that doctrinally proclaim a creator god or gods and a savior principle. Both these religions as well as other spiritual traditions (such as Buddhism and Taoism) that do not speak of external gods can be taken theistically or non-theistically. The inner contemplative understanding of Christianity, for example, is non-theistic, whereas a simplistic belief in Buddhism—taking the tenets of Buddhism on blind faith, and Buddha or the guru to be some kind of savior—is theistic. This is the theism in our attitude to Buddhism that Rinpoche so strongly warned against.

transmission Direct communication, or pointing out, of the vajrayana teachings beyond words, through gesture or symbol. During a transmission, there is a meeting of minds of guru and student and a sense of empowerment or blessings.

tulku The "rebirth" or "reincarnation" of a previous enlightened teacher.

Vajra See **dorje**.

vajra master One who is accomplished in the vajrayana teachings, is capable of transmitting them to others, and is empowered to do so.

Vajradhatu (Sanskrit; indestructible space) The primordial, immutable vastness of mind. Also the name given to the umbrella organization started by Chögyam Trungpa Rinpoche, to encompass all the activities of the Dharmadhatus, or local meditation centers, the residential practice centers, and the central administrative offices.

vajrayana See **yana.**

Vajrayogini The main female yidam of the Kagyu lineage. The sadhana of Varjayogini is the first practiced in the Kagyu system, followed by that of Chakrasamvara.

warrior In the vision of Shambhala, the warrior is a man or woman who acts in the world with gentleness, fearlessness, and precision in order to overcome aggression and help others.

windhorse (Tibetan: *lungta*) The energy of our life force. Our life-force energy is called "windhorse" because it is powerful like the wind yet, like a horse, we can learn to ride it even when that energy is as strong and potentially overwhelming as a tornado. Windhorse is aroused when mind, heart, and body are synchronized and acting together in harmony, particularly through the **practice of raising windhorse** (could also be "raising our, your, or my windhorse; also raising *lungta,* etc.). This brings fundamental confidence and strength.

yana (Sanskrit; vehicle) The vehicle that carries the student along the path to enlightenment. The three *yanas—hinayana, mahayana,* and *vajrayana*—are the three major stages of a student's journey, according to the view of Tibetan Buddhism. Hinayana, the first stage, involves working with one's own confusion and negativity, the recognition of ego as the cause of one's suffering, and the practice of mindfulness and awareness to see through the process of ego. This opens into mahayana, the second stage, in which one sees that others too suffer in a similar way to oneself and involves the intention to develop the wisdom and compassion to help others. Vajrayana, the final stage, involves working directly with the energies of the world to transform confusion into wisdom. Although these stages are described sequentially, they are practiced simultaneously; that is, when one reaches the vajrayana stage one does not leave behind the hinayana and mahayana but builds on them, just as one does not remove the foundation and walls of a house when one adds the roof.

Notes

PREFACE

1. Fabrice Midal. *Chögyam Trungpa: His Life and Vision*. Boston: Shambhala, 2004.

CHAPTER ONE, 1970

2. Chögyam Trungpa. *Born in Tibet*. Boulder: Shambhala, 1977.
3. Chögyam Trungpa. *Crazy Wisdom*. Boston: Shambhala, 1991. pp. 3–13.
4. Quoted in Chögyam Trungpa. *Shambhala: The Sacred Path of the Warrior*. Boston: Shambhala, 1998. p. 14.
5. Sherab Chödzin Kohn. "The Delegpa and the King." *Kalapa Journal*, Number 2, p. 70. Halifax, 1999. (Available to authorized students.)
6. *Born in Tibet*. p. 254.

CHAPTER TWO, 1970

7. Chögyam Trungpa. *Meditation in Action*. Boston: Shambhala, 1996. Chapter 2. 1970
8. James Jeans. *The Mysterious Universe*. Cambridge: Cambridge University Press, 1931.
9. Ludwig Wittgenstein. *Tractatus Logico-Philosophicus*. London: Routledge and Kegan Paul, 1961.
10. For an excellent introduction to Gurdjieff's teachings, see John Shirley. *GURDJIEFF: An Introduction to His Life and Ideas*. New York: Tarcher/Penguin, 2004.
11. The talks on "Work" and "Sex" were published as "Work" and "Love" in Chögyam Trungpa. *The Myth of Freedom*. Berkeley: Shambhala, 1976. pp. 83–90.

CHAPTER THREE, 1971

12. Chögyam Trungpa. *Glimpses of Abhidharma*. Boulder: Prajna Press, 1978. For a simpler explanation of this process, see Chögyam Trungpa. *Cutting Through Spiritual Materialism*. Boulder: Shambhala, 1973. pp. 121–128.
13. *Glimpses of Abhidharma*. p. 9.
14. Jamgön Kongtrul Lodrö Thaye. *Myriad Worlds*. Ithaca, NY: Snow Lion Publications, 1995. p. 199.
15. *Glimpses of Abhidharma*. p. 16.
16. Ibid. p. 31.
17. Ibid. p. 9.

18. Joseph Ledoux. Quoted in Tor Norretranders. *The User Illusion: Cutting Conscious-ness Down to Size*. New York: Viking, 1998. p. 283.
19. Jeremy Hayward. *Shifting Worlds, Changing Minds: Where the Sciences and Buddhism Meet*. Boston: Shambhala, 1987.
20. Vernon Mountcastle. Quoted in John Eccles and Karl Popper. *The Self and Its Brain*. New York: Springer Verlag, 1981.
21. Richard Gregory. Quoted in Jonathan Miller, ed. *States of Mind*. New York: Pantheon, 1983.
22. Arthur Zajonc. *Catching the Light: The Entwined History of Light and Mind*. New York: Bantam, 1993.
23. Chögyam Trungpa. *The Heart of the Buddha*. Boston: Shambhala, 1991. p. 185.
24. *The Heart of the Buddha*. Chapter 5, p. 85. A compilation of talks given by Rinpoche at refuge vow ceremonies from 1973 to 1978.
25. Tulku Thondup Rinpoche. Introduction to Douglas Penick. *The Warrior Song of King Gesar*. Boston: Wisdom Publications, 1996.
26. *Crazy Wisdom*. p. 63.
27. Chögyam Trungpa. *Journey Without Goal: The Tantric Wisdom of the Buddha*. Boston: Shambhala, 2000. pp. 25–30.

CHAPTER FOUR, 1972

28. *Myth of Freedom*. pp. 73–80.
29. Chögyam Trungpa. *Glimpses of Shunyata*. Halifax: Vajradhatu Publications, 1993.
30. *The Heart of the Buddha*. Chapter 6, p. 108. A compilation of talks given by Rinpoche at Bodhisattva Vow ceremonies from 1973 to 1978.
31. Herbert Guenther. *Life and Teaching of Naropa*. Boston: Shambhala, 1995.

CHAPTER FIVE, 1973

32. *Cutting Through Spiritual Materialism*. p. 219.
33. Ibid. p. 220.
34. *The Heart of the Buddha*. p. 59.
35. *Journey Without Goal*. pp. 55–63.
36. Chögyam Trungpa. *Illusion's Game*. Boston: Shambhala, 1994.
37. *Journey Without Goal*. pp. 117–123.
38. Ibid. pp. 125–130.
39. Ibid. pp. 133–142.

CHAPTER SIX, 1974–75

40. Thrangu Rinpoche. *Journey of the Mind: Putting the Teachings of the Bardo into Effective Practice*. Vancouver: Karme Thekchen Chöling, 1997.
41. *Journey Without Goal*. pp. 47–54.
42. Jamgön Kongtrül. *The Torch of Certainty*. Boulder: Shambhala, 1977.
43. Chögyam Trungpa. *Glimpses of Realization*. Halifax: Vajradhatu Publications, 2003.

CHAPTER SEVEN, 1975–76

44. Chögyam Trungpa. "Three Lineages," in *Collected Vajra Assemblies, Volume One*. Halifax: Vajradhatu Publications, 1990. (Available to authorized vajrayana students.)
45. Tulku Thondup. *Hidden Teachings of Tibet*. London: Watkins, 1986.

Chapter Eight, 1977

46. *The Heart of the Buddha.* p. 132.
47. Karma Chagme. Translated by the Nalanda Translation Committee.
48. *Shambhala: The Sacred Path of the Warrior.* p. 117.

Chapter Nine, 1978

49. Many of these talks are included in *Shambhala: The Sacred Path of the Warrior,* Part One. For other descriptions of the Shambhala path of warriorship, see: Sakyong Mipham. *Ruling Your World: Ancient Strategies for Modern Life.* New York: Morgan Road Books, 2005. Jeremy Hayward. *Sacred World.* Boston: Shambhala, 1998.
50. *Shambhala: The Sacred Path of the Warrior.* Chapter 20.
51. Ibid. pp. 84–85.
52. Diana J. Mukpo. *Dragon Thunder: My Life with Chögyam Trungpa.* Boston: Shambhala, 2006.
53. Chögyam Trungpa (Dorje Dradul of Mukpo). *Collected Kalapa Assemblies, 1978–1984.* Halifax: Vajradhatu Publications, 2006. (Available to authorized students.)
54. *Shambhala: The Sacred Path of the Warrior.* pp. 99–115. Also: *Sacred World.* Chapters 14–16.
55. Huston Smith. *Forgotten Truth.* New York: HarperCollins, 1976.
56. *Ruling Your World.*

Chapter Ten, 1979

57. Chögyam Trungpa. *Great Eastern Sun: The Wisdom of Shambhala.* Ed. Carolyn Gimian. Boston: Shambhala, 2001. p. 140.
58. Susan Blackmore. *Consciousness: An Introduction.* London: Hodder and Stoughton, 2003.
59. Jeremy Hayward and Francisco Varela, eds. *Gentle Bridges: Conversations with the Dalai Lama on the Sciences of Mind.* Boston: Shambhala, 1992.
60. Daniel Goleman, editor and narrator. *Destructive Emotions, How Can We Overcome Them: A Scientific Dialogue with the Dalai Lama.* New York: Bantam, 2003.
61. Chögyam Trungpa. *Training the Mind and Cultivating Loving-Kindness.* Boston: Shambhala, 1993.

Chapter Eleven, 1980

62. Jeremy and Karen Hayward. *Sacred World: The Shambhala Way to Gentleness, Bravery, and Power* (2nd Edition). Boston: Shambhala, 1998.
63. Chögyam Trungpa. *Dharma Art.* Boston: Shambhala, 1996. p. 1.
64. Chögyam Trungpa. *Secret Beyond Thought: The Five Chakras and the Four Karmas.* Halifax: Vajradhatu Publications, 1991.

Chapter Twelve, 1981

65. *Collected Kalapa Assemblies.* p. 360. (Available to authorized students.)
66. Thrangu Rinpoche. *Vajradhatu Sun,* December 1990/January 1991.
67. Chögyam Trungpa. *Supplication to Padmasambhava.* Translated by the Nalanda Translation Committee, 1991.

68. Chögyam Trungpa. "He Raised the Dharma Victory Banner in All Directions. " *Best of Vajradhatu Sun,* December 1981/January 1982. Halifax: Shambhala, 2001.

CHAPTER THIRTEEN, 1982

69. *Shambhala: The Sacred Path of the Warrior.* p 84.
70. Ibid. p 69.
71. Chögyam Trungpa. "Creating an Enlightened Society," a video. Halifax: Kalapa Recordings, 1995.
72. Jeremy Hayward. *Perceiving Ordinary Magic: Science and Intuitive Wisdom.* Boston: Shambhala, 1984.
73. Jeremy and Karen Hayward. *Sacred World: The Shambhala Way to Gentleness, Bravery, and Power* (2nd Edition). Boston: Shambhala, 1998.

CHAPTER FOURTEEN, 1983

74. Jeremy Hayward. *Perceiving Ordinary Magic: Science and Intuitive Wisdom.* Boston: Shambhala, 1984.
75. Jeremy and Karen Hayward. *Sacred World: The Shambhala Way to Gentleness, Bravery, and Power* (2nd Edition). Boston: Shambhala, 1998.
76. Chögyam Trungpa. *The Memoirs of Sir Nyima Zangpo, W.O.D.S.* Boulder: Vajradhatu Publications, 1984. (Available to authorized students.)
77. Sakyong Mipham. *Ruling Your World: Ancient Strategies for Modern Life.*

CHAPTER FIFTEEN, 1984

78. Chögyam Trungpa. *Vajrayana Seminary Transcripts, 1984.* p. 40. (Available to authorized vajrayana students.)
79. Fleet Maull. *Dharma in Hell: The Prison Writings of Fleet Maull.* Boulder: Prison Dharma Network, 2005.
80. Walter Fordham. "Lord Mukpo's Research Expedition to Prince Edward Island." *Kalapa Journal,* Number 2. Halifax, 1999. p. 26. (Available to authorized students.)
81. Chögyam Trungpa. *First Thought Best Thought.* Boulder: Shambhala, 1983. p 124.

CHAPTER SIXTEEN, 1985

82. *Dragon Thunder.* p. 366.
83. *Journey Without Goal,* p. 139.
84. Reginald Ray. "Gone Beyond Lhasa," *Shambhala Sun,* September 1994.
85. *Chögyam Trungpa.* p. 450.
86. *Secret Beyond Thought: The Five Chakras and the Four Karmas.*
87. "Vidyadhara Visits Europe." *Best of Vajradhatu Sun,* February/March 1986.

CHAPTER SEVENTEEN, 1986–87

88. "500 Haligonians Attend Opening of Dorje Dzong Halifax." *Best of Vajradhatu Sun,* February/March 1986.
89. Chögyam Trungpa. *Collected Works, Vol. 8.* Boston: Shambhala, 2004.
90. "Vidyadhara Recovering." *Best of Vajradhatu Sun,* January 1987.
91. "Vidyadhara Recovering."
92. Unpublished transcript.

Chapter Eighteen

93. David Schneider. Introduction to *The Teacup and the Skullcup: Chögyam Trungpa on Zen and Tantra*. Halifax: Vajradhatu Publications, 2007.
94. See references in Jeremy Hayward. *Sacred World*.
95. Carl B. Becker. *Paranormal Experience and the Survival of Death*. New York: SUNY Press, 1993.
96. Elizabeth Lloyd Mayer. *Extraordinary Knowing: Science, Skepticism and the Inexplicable Powers of the Human Mind*. New York: Bantam, 2007.
    See also: Dean Radin. *Entangled Minds*. New York: Paraview Pocket Books, 2006. Richard S. Broughton. *Parapsychology: The Controversial Science*. New York: Ballantine Books, 1991.
97. Dalai Lama. *365 Dalai Lama: Daily Advice from the Heart*. San Francisco: Harper Collins, 2004.
98. Susan Blackmore. *Consciousness: An Introduction*.
99. Quoted in Judith L. Lief. *Making Friends with Death*. Boston: Shambhala, 2001.
100. "Creating an Enlightened Society," a video.
101. *Vajrayana Seminary Transcripts*, 1976. p. 61–62. (Available to authorized vajrayana students.)
102. *Vajrayana Seminary Transcripts*, 1979. p. 64. (Available to authorized vajrayana students.)
103. Quoted in *Dragon Thunder: My Life with Chögyam Trungpa*. p. 394.
104. Chögyam Trungpa. *Royal Songs*. Halifax: Trident Publications, 1995.
105. *Shambhala: The Sacred Path of the Warrior*. p. 176.
106. *Kalapa Journal*, Number 2, May 1999. (Available to authorized students.)
107. James George. *Asking for the Earth: Waking up to the Spiritual/Ecological Crisis*. Rockport, MA: Element Books, 1995.

Epilogue

108. Dakpo Tashi Namgyal. *Mahamudra: The Quintessence of Mind and Meditation*. Boston: Wisdom Publications, 2006. p. 390.
109. *Mahamudra: The Quintessence of Mind and Meditation*. p. 391.

Glossary

110. *The Life of Marpa The Translator: Seeing Accomplishes all*. Translated by the Nalanda Translation Committee under the Direction of Chögyam Trungpa. Boulder: Prajna Press, 1982.
111. *The Encyclopedia of Eastern Philosophy and Religion*. Boston: Shambhala, 1989.

Resources

For information regarding meditation instruction or inquiries about a practice center near you, please contact one of the following:

Shambhala International
1084, Tower Road,
Halifax, NS
B3H 2Y5 Canada
Telephone: (902) 425-4275, ext 10
Fax (902) 423-2750
Web site: www.shambhala.org (This site contains information about the more than 100 meditation centers affiliated with Shambhala.)

Shambhala Europe
Annonstrasse 27
50678 Cologne, Germany
Telephone: 49-0-700-108-000-00
E-mail: europe@shambhala.org
Web site: www.shambhala-europe.org

Dorje Denma Ling
2280 Balmoral Road
Tatamagouche, NS
B0K 1V0 Canada
Telephone: (902) 657-9085

Fax (902) 657-0462
E-mail: info@dorjedenmaling.com
Web site: www.dorjedenmaling.com

Karme Chöling
369 Patneaude Lane
Barnet, VT 05821
Telephone: (802) 633-2384
Fax: (802) 633-3012
E-mail: karmecholing@shambhala.org

Shambhala Mountain Center
4921 Country Road 68C
Red Feather Lakes, CO 80545
Telephone: (970) 881-2184
Fax: (970) 881-2909
E-mail: shambhalamountain@shambhala.org

Dechen Chöling
Mas Marvent
87700 St Yrieix sous Aixe
France
Telephone 33 (0) 5-55-03-55-52
Fax: 33 (0) 5-55-03-91-74
E-mail: dechencholing@dechencholing.org

Audio and videotape recordings of talks and seminars by
Chögyam Trungpa and Sakyong Mipham are available from:

Kalapa Recordings
3008 Oxford St, suite 201
Halifax, NS B3L 2W5
Canada
Telephone: (902) 421-1550

Fax: (902) 423-2750
E-mail: shop@shambhala.org
Web site: www.shambhalashop.com

For publications from Shambhala International, please
    contact:
Vajradhatu Publications
3008 Oxford St, suite 201
Halifax, NS B3L 2W5
Canada
Telephone: (902) 421-1550
E-mail: shop@shambhala.org
Web site: www.shambhalashop.com

Naropa University is the only accredited, Buddhist-inspired
    university in North America. For more information,
    contact:
Naropa University
2130 Arapahoe Avenue
Boulder, CO 80302
Telephone: (303) 444-0202
Web site: www.naropa.edu

Index

Appreciations

DAVID SCHNEIDER invited me to give the talk that started this project, at Sutrayana Seminary in Dechen Chöling in 2004, and then organized the petition of students and faculty supplicating me to "write these stories down." Thank you David and all those who signed the supplication.

My appreciation goes to the many people who read and commented on the manuscript at various stages: Christie Cashman, Carolyn Gimian, Ari Goldfield, Ed Halliwell, Karen Hayward, Vanessa Hayward, Andrew Holecek, Lodro Dorje Holm, Melissa Howell, Sherab and Judi Kohn, Janine Kotre, Mitchell Levy, Grant Maclean, Larry Mermelstein, Fabrice Midal, Diana Mukpo, John Rockwell, David Sable, Laura Sackville, David Schneider, Emily Sell, Ann Weil, Anna Weinstein. All your comments, critical and encouraging without exception, were invaluable in helping to mold the story into a form that might be genuinely helpful to others. Any errors in historical fact or in the statement or interpretation of dharma are, of course, entirely my responsibility. Appreciation to those who kindly offered their accounts of meeting Rinpoche: Patricia Hayward, Vanessa Hayward, Karen Hayward, Sherab Kohn, Lodro Sangmo, Dr. Mitchell Levy, and Madeline Bruser.

Special thanks to Emily Sell, a longtime editor and friend, who read the manuscript and offered detailed comments at a crucial stage, when we doubted that it would be publishable. Her comments encouraged me to continue and guided a fresh start. Also to Carolyn Gimian, Ellen Kearney, and Fabrice Midal for their help in searching for photographs. Thanks to all the photographers, known and unknown, whose photos appear in these pages. We have made every effort to trace all of you. If you recognize as yours any that are not attributed, please let us know and we will rectify the error in subsequent editions.

The calligraphies on pages 164, 226, and 237, and the excerpt from the poem "Death or Life" are used with kind permission of Lady Diana Mukpo.

The quote from the poem "Meetings with Remarkable People," on page 353, from *First Thought, Best Thought*, by Chögyam Trungpa © 1983, and all quotes from *Shambhala: The Sacred Path of the Warrior*, by Chögyam Trungpa © 1984 are reprinted by arrangement with Shambhala Publications Inc., Boston, MA. www.shambhala.com

Many thanks to Wisdom Publications for their enthusiasm for the manuscript and especially to my editor Josh Bartok for his encouragement and for his careful and valuable suggestions to improve the manuscript, and to Tony Lulek and the production team for their patient and creative work. Thanks also to Helen Berliner for her able work on the index.

I am deeply grateful to my dear wife Patricia whose help was a precious thread from the very beginning as we began the task of transcribing the tapes. Her constant interest, loving encouragement, and detailed editorial suggestions brought warmth and clarity to the whole journey of writing the book.

There are no words adequate to express my gratitude to my own teachers, first and foremost the Vidyadhara Chögyam Trungpa Rinpoche, and the other great Tibetan meditation masters with whom I have had the good fortune to study and practice, especially Khenpo Tsultrim Gyatso Rinpoche. Without their miraculous presence shining spiritual light on this earth so many of us would simply have become lost in the "thick black fog of materialism" and "sunk into the slime and muck of the dark age," as our plight was so graphically described by Rinpoche.

And finally deep gratitude goes to the Sakyong Mipham Rinpoche, who leads the Shambhala sangha forward, fulfilling and expanding on his father's vision of creating an enlightened society, with wisdom, humor, and patience.

About Wisdom

Wisdom Publications, a nonprofit publisher, is dedicated to making available authentic works relating to Buddhism for the benefit of all. We publish books by ancient and modern masters in all traditions of Buddhism, translations of important texts, and original scholarship. Additionally, we offer books that explore East-West themes unfolding as traditional Buddhism encounters our modern culture in all its aspects. Our titles are published with the appreciation of Buddhism as a living philosophy, and with the special commitment to preserve and transmit important works from Buddhism's many traditions.

To learn more about Wisdom, or to browse books online, visit our website at www.wisdompubs.org.

You may request a copy of our catalog online or by writing to this address:

Wisdom Publications
199 Elm Street
Somerville, Massachusetts 02144 USA
Telephone: 617-776-7416 • Fax: 617-776-7841
Email: info@wisdompubs.org • www.wisdompubs.org

THE WISDOM TRUST

As a nonprofit publisher, Wisdom is dedicated to the publication of Dharma books for the benefit of all sentient beings and dependent upon the kindness and generosity of sponsors in order to do so. If you would like to make a donation to Wisdom, you may do so through our website or our Somerville office. If you would like to help sponsor the publication of a book, please write or email us at the address above.

Thank you.

Wisdom is a nonprofit, charitable 501(c)(3) organization affiliated with the Foundation for the Preservation of the Mahayana Tradition (FPMT).

ALSO AVAILABLE FROM WISDOM PUBLICATIONS

Never Turn Away
The Buddhist Path Beyond Hope and Fear
Rigdzin Shikpo
192 pages, ISBN 0-86171-488-1, $14.95

A meditator's meditator, Rigdzin Shikpo began the practice in the mid-1950s and eventually became a prominent student of several renowned Tibetan Buddhist teachers, including Chögyam Trungpa and Dilgo Khyentse Rinpoche. Over the years, he has developed his own utterly unique style made of straight talk and sparkling, inspiring insights.

"One of the finest, most compelling books on Buddhism I have ever read."—Reginald A. Ray, author of *Indestructible Truth*

A Saint in Seattle
The Life of the Tibetan Mystic Dezhung Rinpoche
David P. Jackson
768 pages, ISBN 0-086171-396-6, $34.95

In 1960, the Tibetan lama Dezhung Rinpoche (1906–87) arrived in Seattle after being forced into exile from his native land by the Communist Chinese. Already a revered master of the teachings of all Tibetan Buddhist schools, he would eventually become a teacher of some of Western Buddhism's most notable scholars. This is the inspiring and unlikely biography of a modern buddha.

"A fine addition to the library of anyone who wants to understand the modern history of Tibet and of Buddhism in the West."—*Buddhadharma*

One City
A Declaration of Interdependence
Ethan Nichtern
224 pages, ISBN 0-86171-516-0, $15.95

"Nichtern, a twenty-nine-year-old teacher in the Shambhala tradition, grew up in a generation coveted by advertisers, and knows well the effects of relentless consumerism: the rootless desire it creates, the feeling of constant inadequacy. [...] *One City* crackles with his humor and fresh insight."—*Tricycle*

"Buddhism 3.0 meets the global consciousness movement."—Daniel Goleman, author of *Social Intelligence*

Mindful Politics
A Buddhist Guide to Making the World a Better Place
Edited by Melvin McLeod
304 pages, ISBN 0-86171-298-6, $16.95

Mindful Politics offers the perspectives of 34 important authors and thinkers on how each of us, right now, can make the world a better place. Included are Thich Nhat Hanh | Sam Harris (author of *The End of Faith*) | The Dalai Lama | Jerry Brown | Pema Chodron | Trungpa Rinpoche | bell hooks | Ezra Bayda | Meg Wheatley ...and many more

"Marvelous!"—John Kabat-Zinn, author of *Coming to Our Senses*

Mind Training
The Great Collection
Translated and edited by Geshe Thupten Jinpa
720 pages, cloth, ISBN 0-86171-440-7, $49.95

"The practice of mind training (*lojong*) is based on the essential Mahayana
teachings of impermanence, compassion, and the exchange of self and
other that the eleventh-century master Atisha brought to Tibet from India.
The lojong teachings are a source of inspiration and guidance shared by
masters of all Tibetan traditions. For the first time, this early collection of
the instructions of the great Kadampa masters has been translated in its
entirety. The clarity and raw power of these thousand-year-old teachings
are astonishingly fresh, whether studied as a complete anthology or
opened at random for inspiring verses on the heart of Buddhist practice."—*Buddhadharma*

The Nyingma School of Tibetan Buddhism
Its Fundamentals and History
Dudjom Rinpoche
Translated, edited and annotated by Matthew Kapstein
    and Gyurme Dorje
1584 pages, ISBN 0-86171-199-8, $90.00

The Nyingma School of Tibetan Buddhism covers in detail and depth both the
fundamental teachings and the history of Tibetan Buddhism's oldest
school. This, the first English translation of His Holiness's masterwork,
constitutes the most complete work of its type in the West. The book
includes fascinating biographies, chronologies, and glossaries that eluci-
date Buddhist doctrine and provide fascinating insights into the Buddhist
history of Tibet.

Beautifully presented, this single-volume edition represents a truly wonderful gift, and features illustrations in black and white and in color, plus
maps, bibliographic information, and useful annotations.

Wisdom Anthology of North American Buddhist Poetry
Edited by Andrew Schelling
304 pages, ISBN 0-86171-392-3, $22.00

Playful, thoughtful, and important, the 28 poets found in *The Wisdom Anthology of North American Buddhist Poetry* offer innovations on traditional and time-honored Buddhist poetic forms. Contributors include Diane di Prima I Lawrence Ferlinghetti I Norman Fischer I Sam Hamill I Jane Hirshfield I Mike O'Connor I Gary Snyder I Eliot Weinberger I Philip Whalen I Michael McClure I Leslie Scalapino I and more...

"There is so much that one could say about this compendium. Nothing else even comes close."—*Pacific Rim Review of Books*

Pure Heart, Enlightened Mind
The Life and Letters of an Irish Zen Saint
Maura O'Halloran
352 pages, ISBN 0-86171-283-8, $17.95

One of the most beloved Buddhist books of all time—having inspired popular musicians, artists, a documentary film, and countless readers—is now in an expanded edition loaded with extras. Absolutely absorbing from start to finish, this is a true story you might truly fall in love with.

"A fascinating portrait of an apprentice sage. The book unfolds as a grand adventure."—*New York Times Book Review*